DATE DUE	
JAN 1 9 1988 5116	
OCT 2 1 1988	
OCT 2 8 1988	
MAR 2 1989	
APR 1 3 1989	
OCT 1 0 1989	
MAR 1 9 1990	
APR 2 0 1990	
NOV 1 8 1990	
DEC 3 1990	
APR 1 0 1991	
OCT 1 5 1992	
NOV 2 1 1992	
APR 2 1 1997	
BRODART, INC.	Cat. No. 23-221

The POSTER

A Worldwide
Survey and History

To François Mathey

This book was
printed in
June 1985
on the presses of
Printer Industria Grafica S.A.,
Barcelona, Spain.

Photogravure: GINSA, Barcelona

Pictorial Research: Marie Christine Gauthier

Design: Jean-Louis Germain

ALAIN WEILL

The POSTER

A Worldwide Survey and History

G.K.HALL&CO.

BOSTON

Library of Congress Cataloging-in-Publication Data

Weill, Alain.
  The Poster: A Worldwide Survey and History.

  Translation of: L'Affiche dans le monde.
  Includes index.
  1. Posters—History.   I. Title
NC1806.45.W4313   1985   741.67′4′09   85-5846
ISBN 0-8161-8746-0

Original title: *L'Affiche dans le monde*
published in Paris by Editions Aimery Somogy.
© 1984 Editions Aimery Somogy, Paris.

English-language edition arranged by
Posters Please, Inc., New York City
English-language text © 1985 Posters Please, Inc.

Translated from the French by Marilyn Myatt.

Published in the United States and Canada by
G.K. Hall & Co.
70 Lincoln Street
Boston, Massachusetts 02111

Printed in Spain.

Photo credits

The numbers are page numbers where posters are reproduced.

Table of Contents

Acknowledgments

Putting aside the very many heads of institutions to whom we went for documents and information, I want particularly to thank the following:

In Paris: Claudie Roger, curator of the Iconographic Collections of the Bibliothèque Forney; Réjane Bargiel and Harry and Christophe Zagrodski at the Musée de la Publicité (the latter was particularly helpful for the chapters concerning Poland and Scandinavia); Cécile Coutin, curator of the Musée des Deux Guerres Mondiales; Jacques Bacquier and Jacques Fivel of the Galerie Serpente, and Jean-Louis Capitaine of the Galerie Ciné-images.

In New York, my friend Jack Rennert arranged the English-language edition of this book, and also generously shared his photographic archive wih me. Another long-time friend, George Theofiles of Shrewsberry, Pennsylvania, provided research help. Merrill Berman, exemplary collector of the avant-gardes, has also come to my aid with enthusiasm and diligence.

I have had the good luck to be helped in my work by two collaborators who have been as efficient as they were indulgent: Corinne Massiot and Nathalie Mei. To them should be added Bernadette Courtiade who, during the long months of this work's gestation, was always ready to provide help and support.

To all of them, again, my gratitude and affection.

—Alain Weill

Foreword

Undertaking a history of the poster throughout the world is a little foolhardy but, I think, necessary. This is because the quantity of documents is enormous—tens of thousands of images, very haphazardly inventoried: here, you have to sift and choose, there, search out an unlikely document. But this gigantic effort seemed necessary, because no work of this type exists in French and most works on the poster have been in English or German and have almost always given a preponderant place to the country of their author's origin.

In this work, I have tried to treat all countries where advertising graphics have attained importance, in proportion to their place in world production. The place I have given France, then, depends upon its creativity at a given period.

This said, to summarize the history of the poster in one volume demands that the larger currents be winnowed and organized, sometimes at the expense of necessary nuances, and also requires that the great masters be mentioned without allowing room for all those who, in one fashion or another, added their building stones to the structure.

I think that in any case, with these few reservations, this work gives an idea of the poster's evolution in the principal countries where it developed from its beginnings up to the Second World War. For the post-war period, where documents are overabundant and temporal perspective lacking, I have tried to bring out the general tendencies and then, in some specialized chapters, to focus on the trends that seemed best to reveal contemporary creativity. In this period, France is an important example of commercial advertising in the western world.

I think that, with abundant pictorial support, this book should fill the role we have envisioned for it: to allow for an overview of a very unequally studied and documented subject. The bibliography provided at the end will allow the reader, if he wishes, to go more deeply into the areas that particularly interest him. I hope, for my part, to inspire that wish.

—Alain Weill

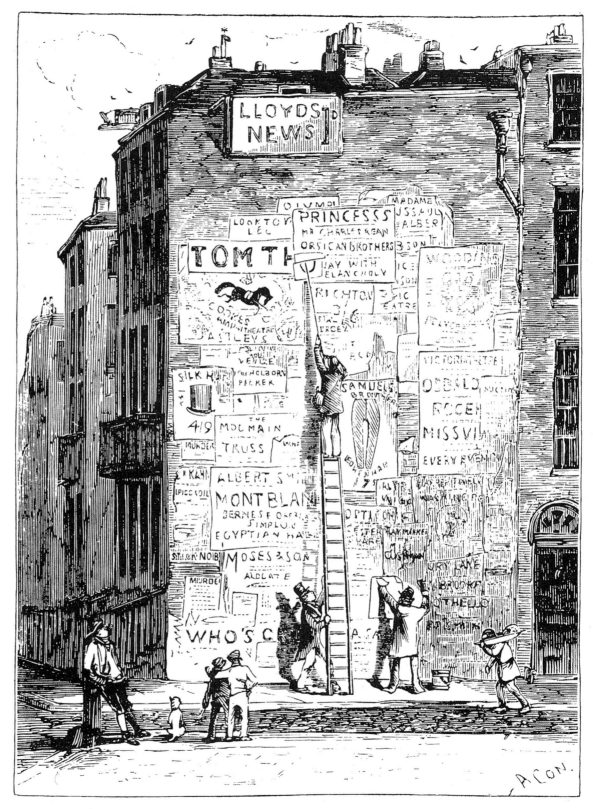

1. An English engraving
from the 19th century.

Predecessors of the Poster

Life in society implies publicity; to be applicable to everyone, the rules of the organization of life must be known by everyone; to be indisputable, they must be inscribed, be it onto stone, onto animal skin, or onto some other prop. Though it may be undemonstrable, it is reasonable to think that the most distant ancestors of the poster can be found in cave paintings.

In all primitive societies, traces of writing or signs belonging to the realm of communication are to be found: we can cite, from Datz[1], "the sticks of the Scythians and the Tartars which we rediscover today among Australian natives, along with the old wampum of the Iroquois, the painted skins of other American Indians, the talking wood of Easter Island and the pebbles of Yucatan." To this list could be added "the quipus, knotted cords of different colors, used by the Peruvians to conserve the memory of great events and to make known to the people the deeds of their sovereigns." Datz finds the first example of publicity in an inscription placed on Mount Heng Chan by Yu the Great in 2278 B.C. Better known and more important is the code of Hammurabi, King of Babylon, which can be dated at around 2050 B.C. All the civilizations of the Mediterranean basin inscribed, in the same manner, the fundamental rules of organization of their society. Moses, in transcribing onto stone the ten commandments which he had just received from God, was doing precisely that.

All sorts of inscriptions abound in the Mediterranean basin, especially in Egypt, which shows that writing was very widespread there. Maindron[2] mentions for example an inscription in Greek discovered in 1872 by M. Clermont-Gannereau on the temple at Jerusalem, dating from Herod's time, forbidding entry into the temple to foreigners on pain of death. He also quotes—and now we are approaching the poster proper—an Egyptian papyrus from Alexandria now in the Louvre, dating from 164 B.C., offering a reward to whoever would bring back two escaped slaves. We know that in Greece, official publicity was mounted on swinging wood panels called axones. But it is to the Roman Empire, which has left rich and complete evidence, that we can trace the organization of a system of outdoor publicity comparable to our own.

In the forum of all the Roman cities was erected an *album*, a wall whitened with lime (which gave it its name), and often richly ornamented. This wall carried all legal notices or inscriptions, painted in red or in black. Any alteration or defacement of these displays brought severe punishment. Similarly, as the walls of Pompeii attest, private advertisement flourished on the more frequented streets. Maindron, citing Edouard

1. P. Datz: *Histoire de la Publicité*. Paris: J. Rothschild, 1894.
2. E. Maindron: *Les Affiches Illustrées*. Paris: G. Boudet, 1896.

2. Johannes Mentel's handbill advertising his own printing. c. 1469.

Fournier, mentions theater advertising in which not only is the name of the actress shown in gigantic letters, but, painted in glaring colors, she is pictured in her most noted scene—not very different from our present-day posters! A certain Callades excelled in this type of picture to such a degree that Pliny cites his *tabellae comicae* among the most interesting examples of painting. Along with the theater and circus games, for which the impressario did not fail to mention that there were tents for protection from the sun—*Vela erunt*—can be mentioned the advertisements of booksellers, and the numerous political inscriptions promoting candidates for the city's many elective offices.

The barbarian invasion overturned all of these structures: after the Merovingian influx, it was Charlemagne who, in creating the chancellery, reconstituted the issuing of the texts of law. The Chancellor recorded them on scrolls which were sent to the counts, who were charged with disseminating them. As all Europe had fallen into illiteracy it was the town criers, throughout the whole Middle Ages, who disseminated publicity. These were government functionaries, whose duty included the announcing of official deeds of property, of lost objects and other matters of public interest. They were to be found everywhere: in England, where, according to Hiatt[1], in 1299 a certain "Edmund the criour" plied his trade; and in France, where Philip Augustus ceded his rights to this profitable activity to the city of Paris for 200 pounds. To this official town-crying were added the cries of street merchants, making the medieval town a joyous cacophony.

The invention of printing by Gutenberg around 1450 furnished the necessary technique for reproduction—of books or posters—which until then could only have been transcribed by hand. Since the populace remained largely illiterate, the first placards which have come down to us are tied to the activities of booksellers and editors.

This type of advertisement, a simple printed sheet indicating the pub-

3. William Caxton's placard for his own *Pyes of Salisbury*. 1477.

¶Een schoene ghenuechlicke eñ seer vreede hys
tone van eenre vrouwe gheheeten Meluzyne/
eñ van harer afcoemste eñ gheslachte vā haer
voert ghecomen synde.eñ van harer alre won
derlike eñ vrome wercke eñ seyten die sy gedaē
eñ bedieuen hebben Ende es nu nyewelyc wt
den walsche ghetransateert in duptsche /ende
met schoonē personagen ende figueren na den
epsch der materien verciert Ende mē salse met
vele meer andere niewe boecken vinden te coo
pe ter plaetzen hier onder gheschieuen

4. Gerhard Leeu used a woodcut to advertise his
publication of *Meluzyne,* a book of legends, in 1491.

lications and the place where they could be found, was quickly diffused throughout the Rhineland, the cradle of the new industry.

Walter von zur Westen[2] counts more than twenty specimens from this era, naming among them one by Johannes Mentel dated around 1469, and those by Peter Schäffer of Mainz and by Gesenschmidt of Nuremberg as examples. In England, where printing developed very rapidly, there remains one of the incunabula of the pioneer printer William Caxton, dated 1477, for the "Pyes of Salisbury", a collection of ecclesiastical rules he edited and printed. Like all the bills of this period, it is very small (5x7 inches), but the inscription "supplico stet cedula" (please do not remove) leaves no doubt as to its intended use. Pictures appeared for the first time in 1491 when Gerhard Leeu at Antwerp decorated his placard with a woodcut from the Legend of Melusine.

Starting in the sixteenth century, the poster began to be used for diverse purposes. Eberhardt Altdorfer, an artist of quality, engraved a remarkable

1. Charles Hiatt: *Picture Posters*. London: Bell & Sons, 1895.
2. Walter von zur Westen: *Reklamekunst*. Bielefeld and Leipzig, 1914.

Vnd vnd zuwiffen fey jedermänniglich/ daß von heut Dienftags an/ wie auch folgende zwen tag/ Mitwochs vnd Donnerftag/ der Orientalifche Elefant in dem neuen Comödienhauß auff der Schüt/ wirdt zufehen feyn/ da Er dann mehr als zuvor gefchehn/ fich mit wunderlichen Künften wirdt fehen laffen/ foll ein Alte Perfon geben 4 kreutzer/ ein kleine perfon 2 kreutzer: mag fo lang zufehen als jhn beliebt/ dann man wirdt den gantzen Tag/ morgens von 7 biß zu 11 vnd nach Mittag von 1. biß 6 vhren/ folchen fehen laffen.

5. Anonymous: 17th century
German fair poster.

Efsieurs & Dames,

Il eft arriué en cefte Ville, vn tres-honnefte Homme lequel à amené deux Animaux defquelz voyez la vraye Figure cy deffus, lefquelz Animaux ont efté prefenté au Roy, dans le Ieu de Paulme du Louure à Paris, à la veuë de plufieurs grands Princes & Seigneurs, lefquels n'ont iamais veu leurs femblables, lefdicts animaux ont efté pris en Affrique, les noms defquels ne font pas bien cogneus, quelque-vns les appellent Mago, les autres Tartarins, les Holandois qui les amenent des Indes, les appellent Bleuf-nez, lefdicts Animaux font plufieurs belles exercices, comme fauter, dancer, tenant efpée & verre en main, &c. fi bien que celuy qui les conduict defire & promet renuoyer tous ceux qui luy auront faict l'honneur de les veoir auec vn tres-parfaict contentement, lefdicts Animaux fe montrent en la rüe *de S.t Gervais, au logis de l'Aigle d'or. à Geneve* à l'Enfeigne *de l'Aigle d'or. ce 4. d'Auril 162~*

6. Anonymous: Poster for performing monkey. Geneva, 1625.

plate in 1518 for a lottery at Rostock: at the top of the picture he illustrates the drawing of the lots, which he shows at the bottom. Von zur Westen also cites a poster for the singing school of a certain Hans Sachs, decorated with his portrait, dating from the end of the sixteenth century.

As the poster gained importance, those in power tried to control it. In France, Francis I, in an edict of November 13, 1539, reserved to himself, aside from signboards and the verbal solicitations of merchants, all publicity. He ordered "that the laws be attached to a tablet, written on parchment in large letters in the sixteen quarters of Paris and in the suburbs in the most prominent places, in order that everyone know and comprehend them. It is forbidden to remove them upon pain of corporal punishment and it is commanded that the neighborhood commissaries guard and watch over them."

It was in effect the reinstatement of the Roman *album*.

The history of France is very turbulent in this respect, judging from the draconian edicts of February 15, 1652 and January 15, 1653, which totally limit the freedom of publicity and thus of creativity. Their virulence is itself a proof of significant clandestine poster activity. It also explains why the most remarkable posters to be found in France at this period are,

7. Anonymous: Poster for a religious brotherhood. France, 1602.

8. Anonymous: German recruitment poster from the 18th century.

9. Anonymous: French recruitment poster, 18th century.

according to Maindron, illustrated placards for religious meetings to attract the faithful; the oldest goes back to 1602.

Outside of France, the absence of such severity seems to have permitted the dissemination of the poster: from the beginning of the seventeenth century, traveling performers began to use illustrated posters. One of the oldest is a poster for a performing monkey, dating from 1625. As usual, there is a space left for adding by hand the place where this prodigy may be seen: on April 7, 1625, it was at Geneva, at the Golden Eagle, in the sample reproduced here.

The placards were as numerous and diverse as the proposed attractions: "there are acrobats, riders, rhinoceroses, elephants, trained seals, giants, dwarfs, children without hands, singers without arms, eskimos, Lapps, fireeaters, a waterswallower named Manfredi, magicians . . .", enumerates von zur Westen. The wider their distribution, especially in Germany, Holland, and Italy, the more these engravings declined in quality, either because they were entrusted to clumsy artists, or because, copied repeatedly in quantities, they tended to retain less of their artistic value.

At the end of the seventeenth century and in the eighteenth century, copper engraving was placed at the service of advertising art in a very specific domain: trading cards, which became widespread in England, and were often signed by eminent artists like Hogarth, or the Italian emigré Francesco Bartolozzi, who set up a veritable studio. In France, one sees the same phenomenon with visiting cards signed by Cochin or Moreau the Younger. Major artists also illustrated various proclamations, some attaining a size of up to 3 feet, exceptional for the period, and coming from the hand of Mignard or Phillipe de Champaigne. In Germany the artistic quality is much inferior, be it Nilson in Nuremberg or Bolte in Berlin.

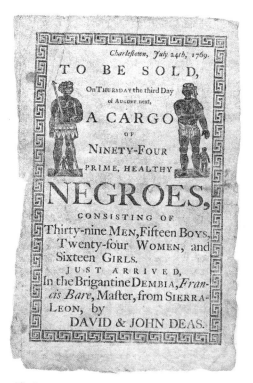

10. Anonymous: An American broadside advertising a slave auction. 1769.

11. Anonymous: French umbrella maker's poster from the 18th century.

12. Edme Bouchardon: *The bill poster*. 1742.

Wood engravings, whose authors are unknown, remained by far the most widespread process in Europe as a whole: one finds schedules for mail-coaches in England, a poster for the *Hotel of the Three Kings* in Basel, recruitment posters everywhere, and in France one from an umbrella-maker. In the United States, where the first broadside—an archaic term for a printed public proclamation—titled "The Oath of Man," was published by Stephan Day in 1639, there appeared posters for publications, plays, and businesses.

Aside from these few illustrated documents, the greater part of the production, announcements, legal notices, sales, etc. remained purely typographical. Engraving was in fact very expensive and printers used all-purpose stock illustrated formats, fitting the text into them. French theater posters of the 18th century are good examples of this usage of stock allegorical borders.

For easier identification, the various royal theater companies used another method: colored paper. The Hotel de Bourgogne chose red, the Hotel de la Mazarine green, the Opera yellow.

In Paris, things must have gotten out of hand with indiscriminate plastering of every available space with posters by the beginning of the 18th century, because we suddenly find a stringent regulation issued by the City Council in 1722. Among other things, it specified that bill posters had to be literate; their names had to be submitted to the chief of police by the union of booksellers and printers; they had to hang a sign at the door of their lodgings; and they were required to wear a badge and an escutcheon. Their number was fixed at forty. They had to verify that every poster given them bore the authorization of the chief of police, and submit a copy to the guild of booksellers and printers.

Mercier, in his history of Paris, describes the royal bill posters thus: "There are forty of them, just like the French Academy, and for an even greater likeness, no one can be counted a bill poster if he doesn't know how to read and write. The bill posters are distinguished from all other talent once they have joined that illustrious company. They have a copper badge in the buttonhole; they carry a little ladder, an apron, a glue-pot and a brush. They put up advertisements, but they don't advertise themselves. The forty immortals are not always so wisely modest.

"A bill poster is the epitome of indifference. He sticks up with an impassive face the profane, the sacred, the judicial, the death-sentence; the lost dog; he never reads anything of what he plasters against the walls except the magistrate's permit. Once he sees that official stamp, he would stick up even a notice of his own death sentence.

"They who advertise the Comedie and the Opera have never set foot in them. When they've put the writing perpendicular to the street and it's quite straight, they contemplate it with an air of satisfaction and go.

"They are forbidden to put on the doors and walls of churches and monasteries posters of comedies, novels, and profane books; but the subject is sometimes ambiguous, and the columns of temples are tolerant; they peacefully receive what the bill poster applies to them."

Despite this rigorous regulation, clandestine billposting continued to thrive in Paris. Mercier, always ironic, explains how it was done: "A man, burdened with a huge basket, apparently became fatigued and stopped at a milestone, against which he leaned to rest, with the basket still on his back. During this time a little boy crouched down in the basket had only to pass his hands over a poster spread with glue along both edges to stick it to the wall. He quickly burrowed back in, covering his head, and the man walked off with slow steps, leaving the announcement to the view of the curious."

Clandestine or not, posters covered Paris—as they did the other cities of Europe. Daniel Defoe confirms it in his description of London, plastered over with placards. The French Revolution in the late 18th century only increased the number of these placards, but the poster underwent at the same time another revolution: the invention of lithography.

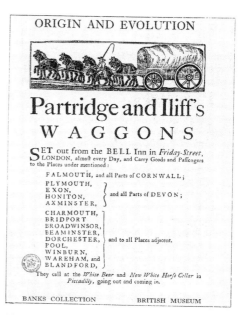

14. Anonymous: An English livery service poster from the 18th century.

13. Anonymous: A theatrical poster. France, 1768.

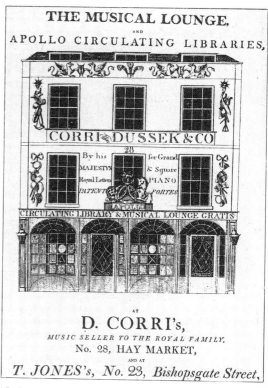

15. Anonymous: Poster of an 18th century English music store.

16. Senefelder at the age of 60. From a drawing by Conguy. 1831.

The Poster in the Age of Lithography

Wood engraving and, even more, copper engraving were very expensive procedures whose use was necessarily limited. This explains why, setting aside theatrical announcements which used stock ornamental borders and previously engraved blocks which the printers kept on hand, there are few illustrated posters among the mass of documents from the 18th century. Another obstacle to the development of the art of advertising is that the engraved plaques of wood were small in size, considerably limiting the size of posters.

The invention of lithography around 1796 by Aloys Senefelder brought the solution to these problems. Aloys Senefelder was born in Prague on November 6, 1771. Highly talented, he entered the university but was forced to break off his studies after the death of his father in 1791, in order to support his mother and his eight brothers and sisters. He began a career in acting without great success, and wrote for the theater with no better outcome. He decided that the best way to publish his own words was to print them himself, and attempted to find out how he could obtain the costly typographical materials. Since he lacked the money to buy metal, he decided to use stone. In this tight financial bind, he received his first support from Franz Geissler, director of music at the Royal Court, who, seeing one of his attempts, proposed to provide a studio for him. From there emerged, in 1796, the first lithographic plates: scores of the works of Geissler. Their quality was far from perfect and Senefelder himself stated that "various scores were printed with unequal success." However, they attracted the attention of a rich music publisher from Munich, Falger, who made available his advice and his purse. Senefelder could pursue his researches and improve his technique even further with the support of a third protector, Steiner, the Director of Public Instruction in Bavaria. The perfection of autography (a drawing with a grease crayon on damp paper applied on the stone by the press leaves its imprint) led in 1798 to the invention of lithography.

If the procedure is of great complexity in the different stages of its execution, it is in principle quite simple: a drawing is made with a greasy substance on a very fine-grained stone (lithographic limestone) which is then washed with acidulated water so as not to retain the ink of an ink-filled roller except on the greasy parts. All that is then necessary is to press a sheet of paper firmly against the stone to obtain a reproduction of the design.

At last Senefelder had succeeded, and associated himself with Anton André, a music publisher in Offenbach, Germany. In a few years, a handful of enterprising men proceeded to spread the technique of lithography throughout Europe. As in most such cases, the inventor was a deplorable businessman and failed in practical matters where others, often

17. Anonymous: An early 19th century French beer poster.

his one-time collaborators, succeeded: Akerman in London, Dal-Ancri in Rome, the Society of Amateur Lithographers in Vienna, Arnz and Company in Düsseldorf, Mannheim, Heidelberg and Frankfurt. In Paris, Senefelder was beaten to the punch by the Comte de Lastérie, who had been working on a patent for several years, and by Godefroi Engelmann. However, Senefelder moved to Paris anyway, with his nephew Knecht, occupying himself primarily with the writing of his treatise on lithography. Returning to Munich in 1824, he was plagued by ill fortunes and died, blind, in 1834.

Godefroi Engelmann (1788-1839) played a considerable role in perfecting Senefelder's invention. It is he who first solved the problem of lithography in color—chromolithography—which had baffled his predecessors. J.C. Leblond, in the *Encyclopedie,* had clearly defined the principles of color engraving: "It is in seeking the rules of coloring that I found the way of printing objects in the primary colors, that is red, yellow, and blue. The different mixtures of these three colors produce every imaginable nuance, as many tints as can be made from the most skillful painter's palette. But they could not be blended, by printing one on top of another, the way the brush blends them on canvas: so the colors must be used in such a way that the first appears through the second, and the second through the third, so that transparency creates the effect of the brush. Each of these colors is distributed by the medium of its own particular plate: so three plates are necessary for the stamping of a print in imitation of painting."

Exactly the same process, with a separate stone supplying each color, is used for chromolithography. But Senefelder, unable to make the necessary adjustments, due to insufficient mechanical means and to the fragility of the paper, never fully succeeded. Good results were obtained for works in flat tints like the frescoes of Pompeii (Berlin 1832) or the mosaics of the Alhambra (London 1834) but it was not until 1837 that Engelmann entirely mastered the procedure. He also has the merit of being the first, from the start, to employ first-rank artists like Regnault, Carle Vernet, Géricault, Isabey, Bonington, Deveria, etc. . . . In the rest of Europe, lithography was served only by minor artists, most notably painters of animals.

By 1830, when Louis Philippe came to the throne in France, black-and-white lithography was a well-established procedure, thanks to Friedrich König who created the first steam-operated presses, and in association with Friedrich Andreas Bauer invented numerous improvements which allowed the presses to stamp more than 1000 plates, of the type perfected by Brisset, per hour.

As for the poster, no interesting developments had occurred since the middle of the 18th century. Maindron[1] notes that "these years, so important for the country's history, are barren from the point of view we are concerned with here." Apart from the posters for *Bonne bière de Mars,* colored by stencilling, nothing new had appeared.

It is the extraordinary development of illustrated books, under the new monarchy, that brought the art of advertising to another decisive stage. To promote these books, publishers brought out posters lithographed by the artists who had illustrated them, in folio formats, which were distributed to booksellers who provided subscriptions for the books. This was a major revolution for the poster which, for the first time, was being created by artists of recognized talent who brought to it at once effectiveness and prestige.

The first of these posters is for *Faust,* lithographed in black and white by Deveria in 1828, which had a second run in 1832 for *Beaucoup de tabac, toujours de tabac.* In the same year Lalance set his hand to *Une Vie de Courtisane.* There followed, from 1835 to 1838, a series of anonym-

1. E. Maindron: *Les Affiches Illustrées.* Paris: G. Boudet, 1896.

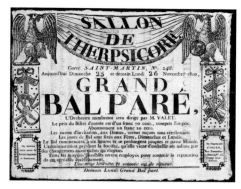

19. Anonymous: A French ball poster from 1810 using stock borders.

20. Anonymous: *Arlequin Afficheur* (1830) was an enlarged classified advertisement pasted on the walls of Paris.

18. From a drawing by Honoré Daumier: *The bill poster.* France, mid-19th century.

21. Gavarni (Sulpice-Guillaume Chevalier):
Poster for E. Sue's book, *Le juif errant* (The
Wandering Jew) illustrated by Gavarni himself.
1845.

22. Gérard Grandville: *Vie des animaux* (Scenes
of the Private and Public Life of Animals).
c. 1840.

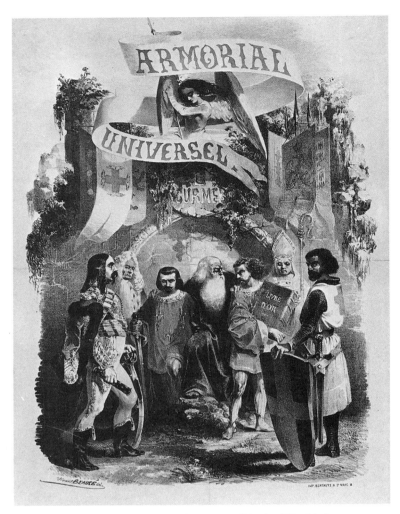

23. Vivant Beaucé: *Armorial universel*. (Universal Book of Heraldry).

ous posters whose success definitively imposed the use of the medium
on all the large publishing houses. The publishers made use of the cream
of Parisian talent: Beaucé, de Beaumont, Bertall, Calame, Cham, Gavarni,
Tony Johannot, Henri Monnier, Nanteuil, Raffet, and many others.

Spurred by this example, tradesmen also began using lithographed
posters, but well-known artists, seemingly scorning advertising, did not
work for them. There were drawings, often mediocre, for clothing stores,
tricycles, and the most diverse and often preposterous inventions. From
1845, the popularity of almanachs gave rise once again to posters by the
likes of Cham, Charles Vernier or Edouard Moine. The colors are still
timid and maladroit: the poster has yet to triumph over this final obstacle.

Images on wood or zinc (notably the process of Firmin Gillot, the
ancestor of phototypography), colored by stencils and more economical,
were still used by theater entrepreneurs who glued them onto printed
backgrounds. Bright colors in large formats finally appeared triumphant
on the walls of Paris around 1840—but it was not thanks to lithography!

Jean Alexis Rouchon, about whom little is known, began around this

24. Bertall (Albert d'Arnoult): Poster for a gastronomical series. 1845.

time to cover walls with gigantic multicolored sheets, engraved on wood by a process like that used in making wallpaper. The patent he registered on November 18, 1844 is quite clear on the matter: it specifies "the application of the printing of wallpaper to the printing of colors on posters."

But these posters, essentially for Parisian businesses and theaters, were after all perhaps most revolutionary by virtue of their size, the largest of them reaching dimensions never before seen: *Au prince Eugène,* 280 cm x 138 cm, *La Belle Jardinière,* 270 cm x 220 cm, *Au Bon Pasteur,* 263 cm x 143 cm. In England, American circuses also brought the first large color placards to London: lithographs made by firms such as Currier and Ives, somewhat crude and vulgar. The lack of subtlety, the glaring colors, are reproaches also made against chromolithographs printed on the continent. "This isn't art, it's illumination", was the reaction. The artistic color poster had yet to find its father—who was to be Jules Chéret.

25. Anonymous: Poster of a French pipe manufacturer. (Lithographed by Van Geleyn). 1866.

26. Jean-Alexis Rouchon: The revolutionary paper *La République*. 1848.

Jules Chéret

27. Jules Chéret: *Princesse de Trebizonde*. 1869.

In the middle of the 19th century, the industrial revolution turned the world upside down. The steam engine and its most spectacular application, the railway, marked the beginning of modern times. Urbanization and mass production were the consequences. Towns developed rapidly, and their walls were propitious for publicity. With the increasing production of manufactured goods, and, for the first time, supply exceeding demand, publicity became a necessity—and the advertisment, in the form of posters or through the press, invaded the world.

All the evidence that has been gathered indicates that towns were covered with posters having one point in common: an absolute lack of artistic value. The poster existed but the art of advertising had not yet been born.

In order for it to develop, in order for it to be recognized, the intervention of an artist of talent was necessary. Furthermore, this artist had to be an accomplished lithographer in order to arrive at a total mastery of color.

It is Jules Chéret who is recognized, rightly, as the father of poster art. From 1860, he gave the poster the final impetus which allowed it to establish itself in France and the world over.

Jules Chéret was born in Paris on May 31, 1836, into a family of artisans. Apprenticed to a lithographer, he familiarized himself with the tiresome labor of designing lettering for prospectuses, all the while taking drawing classes in the evenings. On Sundays he went to the Louvre to admire the works of Watteau and Fragonard, his models. Seeing no future in his work, he made two trips to London. Upon his return from the first of these trips, he created his first poster, for Offenbach's *Orphée aux Enfers*. It was a success, but without a future, and he resolved to cross the Channel once more. In London he discovered the American circus posters in loud colors, but, most important, met the man who would become his patron: the perfumer Rimmel.

Rimmel brought him along on his travels (for instance to Venice, where he discovered Tiepolo, "his god") and advanced him the money to open a studio in Paris in 1866. There he installed English machines which allowed the use of stones of large sizes, and produced in quick succession two posters, for *La Biche au Bois* and *Le bal Valentino,* which opened the way to success.

The first designs still made timid use of color but Chéret was already working with a stunning economy of means: one stone for black which traced the design, one for red, and one for a graduated background with blues and greens at the top of the picture and yellows and oranges at the bottom. His first clients were mainly the great entrepreneurs of Parisian theater (notably the *Folies-Bergère*) but also manufacturers and tradesmen, who, in view of his success, began to call upon his services. In

1881 he sold his studio to Chaix, while keeping charge of its artistic direction. In 1889 he received official consecration when his work was displayed at the Exposition Universelle, and he received the légion d'honneur. Manet hailed him as the "Watteau of the streets"—the critics, led by Felicien Champseaur, Gustave Kahn, and J.K. Huysmans, were unanimous in their praise.

In 1890 (by which time he had already produced more than a thousand posters), his most beautiful designs began to appear: he abandoned black outlines for blue and worked with primary colors. Achille Segard described perfectly his method of working:

28. At the Concert des Ambassadeurs, the curtain was made up of Chéret's posters. Circa 1895.

29. Jules Chéret: Poster for a skating rink. 1894.

"A sketch on paper is transferred by the artist to each of the lithographic stones. He does not use a grid. He uses the lithographic crayon to indicate half-tones; the ink makes for solidity, lets him define the essential features of the drawing. As many stones as primary colors: red, yellow, blue! The three impressions are sometimes completed with a fourth, to enrich the grays: from the apposition or superimposition of primary tones every possible variety of coloring is obtained. When the artist distributed his reds, he thinks of what both will result when the blues extinguish them or exalt them. There is no technique or teaching that can be relied on here: it's a question of conjecture or feeling. One can feel very well how

30. Jules Chéret: *Vin Mariani*, English text version. 1894.

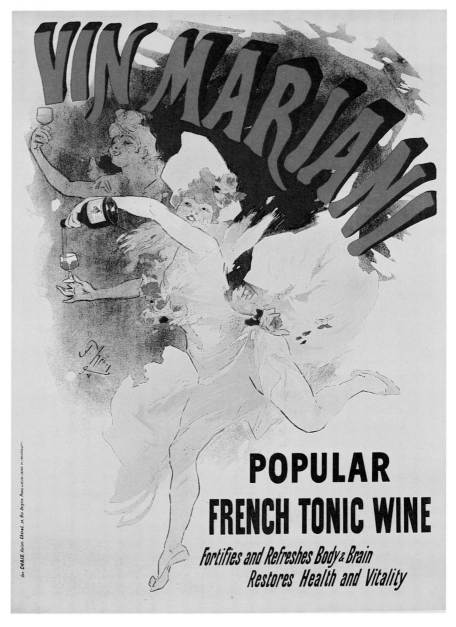

31. Jules Chéret: The poster for the opening of the *Moulin Rouge.* 1889.

32. Jules Chéret: *Folies-Bergère,
La Loïe Fuller.* 1893

the artist distributes first of all the most brilliant touch of color—pure
yellow or vermillion—and how it is around this touch that he seeks his
gradations, his contrasts, all the nuances or delicacies which contribute
to the perfect harmony of the whole."

Speaking of Chéret's best output of the 1890's, Crauzat was moved to
rave about "a hooray of reds, a hallelujah of yellows and a primal scream
of blues."

The year 1888 yields, among the plentiful examples of Chéret at his
best, *L'Amant des danseuses;* 1889, *Le Moulin Rouge;* 1890, *Le Jardin
de Paris, La Diaphane, Le Théâtrophone;* 1891, *Yvette Guilbert, La*

33. Jules Chéret: *Théâtrophone*, an early coin-operated jukebox. 1890.

34. Georges Meunier: *Trianon-Concert*. 1895.

Librairie Sagot, Le Savon Cosmydor; Les Pastilles Geraudel; 1892, *L'Olympia, Les Pantomines lumineuses au Musée Grevin, Le Bal a l'Opéra, Emilienne d'Alencon;* 1893, *L'Arc-en-ciel, Le Carnaval a l'Opéra, Loie Fuller;* 1894, *L'Eldorado* and *Le Vin Miriani;* 1895, *Lidia* and *Papier Job;* 1896, *Les Grands Magasins du Louvre;* 1897, *La danse du feu (Loie Fuller);* 1898, *Le Bal masqué à l'Opéra;* and 1901, *Cleveland Cycles.* He executed a successful series for *Saxoleine* (1891-1894); another one for *Palais de Glace* (1893–1896), and for *Halle aux chapeaux* (1891–1892).

Maindron, in his *Affiches Illustrées* of 1896, establishes the list of Chéret's works based on Beraldi's *Graveur du XIXeme siècle:* he counts 882 posters. From this time forward, his eyesight weakening, Chéret in effect abandoned the poster to devote himself to frescoes. Lucy Broido, in her recent study of Chéret, arrived finally at a total of 1,069 posters, the last, dated 1921, for the *Casino de Nice.* The patriarch of posters died in 1932 at the age of 96.

If the "chérette", the central figure of most of his posters, his drawing or his composition seems classic today, if his colors no longer astonish, we must for a just appreciation return Chéret to the years in which they were produced, when the mere use of an alluring woman to sell a product was revolutionary.

It is undeniably Chéret who pointed the way for all Europe. A look at the dates will show that the major works of those who followed his example come twenty years after his first designs.

Chéret's style was furthermore so strong and original that he inspired disciples, mainly his colleagues at the Chaix printing house, who could never free themselves from his influence. We can cite Georges Meunier, certainly the most talented, author of some fifty posters, of which *Bullier, Lox, L'Excellent,* and *Etrennes à la place Chichy* are the best; René Péan, who specialized in travel posters; Lucien Lefevre and Lucien Baylac, so much like Chéret that they are confused with him; and Gaston Noury.

Fortunately he also served as an example to artists of perfectly individualistic talents, who made the years 1880–1900 the golden age of the poster in France.

35. Jules Chéret: *Job* cigarette paper. 1895.

36. Edouard Manet: Bookstore placard for *Champfleury—Les Chats*. 1868.

The Golden Age of the Poster in France

37. An early 20th century postcard.

The movement starting with Chéret's first posters was much slower taking off than is often imagined: more than twenty years separate the *Bal Valentino* from the first years of the Nineties when the artistic poster truly began to flourish. If two brilliant accidents are excluded—one by Manet, for Champfleury's novel *Les chats* (1868), the other by Daumier, for the *Entrepots d'Ivry* (1872)—no first-rank artist involved himself in advertising in the years 1860–80. And it is to be noted that these two posters are simply black-and-white lithographs—prints in fact—glued to a printed background.

Working alongside Chéret were the Choubrac brothers: Leon (who often signs himself Hope) who died in 1885, and Alfred, who during this time signed hundreds of show posters, mostly mediocre designs. The other purveyors of images for the public's pleasures are the printers Emile Levy who identified his shop's product as "French Posters", and Charles Levy—doubtless a relative, who, to distinguish himself and to be modern, baptized his enterprise "American Posters". All these designs are, however, still the work of anonymous lithographers in which can be found only the charm of a naive and popular art.

But the need for posters was felt more and more, and, since laws reflect the philosophy of those in power—in this case the industrial magnates—poster publicity was at last liberated.

A French law of July 29, 1881 abrogated all previous statutes, deprived the municipalities of any rights to regulation and proclaimed absolute liberty of bill-posting. Instantly, the walls of the larger cities were assaulted and postable spaces commanded high prices: in 1884, the City of Paris made its gable walls available for an annual rent of 15,000 francs—all 14,703 square meters of them. (Gable walls are the walls on the sides of buildings, without windows, which overlap over neighboring structures.)

The public relief administration and the railway companies did the same. The bill-posting companies which made use of these spaces were quickly set up and expanded, employing hundreds of workers who could in a day cover the city with freehanging posters (on walls and fences) or posters hung on their own billboards with guarantees of maintenance and permanence. Such organization brought with it a necessary standardization of formats: multiples of the *colombier* (61 x 82 cm) and the *aigle* (110 x 70 cm) were used.

Soon the cities were overrun with posters: Maindron, in 1886, complains that "without regard for police ordinances, poster hangers use every unoccupied space, without restraint and without respect, and overrun us to the point of robbing us, poor Parisians, of the sight of our monuments."

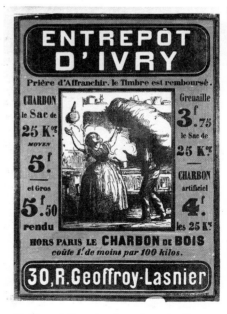

38. Honoré Daumier: A coal merchant's poster. 1872.

The first major artist to come to Chéret's rescue was Eugène Grasset. A Swiss who had come from Lausanne in 1871, he brought Art Nouveau to the aid of the poster: it was to become a worldwide vehicle of the art of advertising. In France, Grasset was the pioneer of an attempt, like that of William Morris of England, to reconcile art and industry. Breaking away from the realism inherited from the Renaissance, Art Nouveau attempts to symbolize, to stylize, taking as its model the work of the artisans of the Middle Ages, and as the inspiration for its themes the flora and fauna of France. It is however no servile copy and, in an interview with Henry Nocq, Grasset insisted that "copying and introducing medieval art into modern life is odious. Like the artisans of the Gothic period, we follow our imaginations and not books of archeology. The maker must follow his own inclination. His fantasy is limited only by the necessary utility of the object he invents." Even if in his illustrations to *Les 4 Fils Aymon* he was led by his subject into the Middle Ages, in his classes and lectures, in his *Méthode de composition ornamentale* and *La plante et ses applications décoratives,* he sets the example of true nature studies.

Interested as he was in all the applied arts, he came naturally to the poster. In 1885 it was the *Fêtes de Paris* with a herald on the back of a horse with an exaggerated mane. The composition and the pure colors make plain the influence of the Japanese Ukiyo-E school of engraving, as do the thick outlines, similar to the lead of stained glass. Two more classic plates followed, with composition daring for the period: the *Lib-*

39. Eugène Grasset: *Salon des Cent* Exhibition (before letters). 1894.

40. Eugène Grasset: *L. Marquet* inks. 1892.

41. Eugène Grasset: *Georges Richard Cycles & Automobiles.* 1897.

rairie *Romantique* and *L'Odéon* (1890). With his two posters for Sarah Bernhardt in *Jeanne d'Arc* (1889–90) and *L'Encre Marquet* (1892) Grasset was the first to adorn walls with a pensive woman with long hair, dressed in materials in stylized patterns. The colors are applied in flat tints. With the *Grafton Galleries* and the *Salon des Cent,* the style of the woman surrounded with a luxuriant and stylized flora became definitively fixed: it will become an archetype.

We can also cite among his many creations the *Madrid Exposition* (1893); *The Life of Napoleon* for the *Century* magazine which, along with his wooly horse, revealed the artistic poster to Americans; the exhuberant *Suzy Deguez* (1895) and the very sober *Cycles Richard;* the *Je sème a tous vents* which he designed for Larousse; the sculptor *Falguière* (1898); and, for the exposition of 1900, *L' Andalousie au temps des Maures.*

42. Pierre Bonnard: *France-Champagne.* 1891.

43. Edouard Vuillard: *Bécane Liqueur.* 1891.

At the beginning of the Nineties, the influence of the arts of Japan on a whole generation of young artists brought life to the poster. Saturated with the Ukiyo-E engravings which the Goncourt brothers and some great collectors had made fashionable, these young talents found in prints— more exactly in lithography— a mode of expression adapted to their interests. As André Mellerio notes, "what is immediately striking in the color lithography movement is the number and also the diversity of the artists who occupied themselves with it." From the print to the poster is but a step which all these artists happily took: they found in it the possibility of expressing themselves in large formats, of making themselves known to the public, and, not negligibly, of making some money. The Nabis, who brought together in 1889 Bonnard, Vuillard, Sérusier, Ibels, Valotton and Roussel, by their love for the arts of Japan, all belonged to the movement.

Bonnard got things moving in 1891 with *France—Champagne:* flat against a yellow background, a vividly outlined young woman in the middle of the foam overflowing from a champagne glass; one can see the influence of Utamaro, and of Gauguin, who had just exhibited at the Café Volpini. There follow *La Revue Blanche,* a mysterious portrait of Missia, the wife of Thadée Natanson, the magazine's guiding spirit; two posters for the *Figaro* and the *Salon des Cent.* Vuillard tried only a bizarre composition for the apéritif Bécane; Vallotton made three, for *L'Art nouveau,* the *Plan Commode de Paris* and *La Pépinière,* where, as usual with him, he plays with the outline and the contrast of black and white. Maurice Denis tried his hand, the best known outcome being the *Dépêche de Toulouse.* Ibels was the most prolific. Infatuated with cabarets, like his friend Lautrec (they would both put their names to the album of lithographs, *Café Concert)* he made posters for Hélène Henry and Jane Debary; the great profile of *Mévisto; Les grandes luttes au Casino de Paris;* as well as, on the theme of the circus, a parade for *Pierrefort* and, for the *Salon des Cent,* a Harlequin, a Pierrot, and a Colombine.

According to Claude Roger-Marx, it was upon finding Bonnard's *France-Champagne* on a wall that Lautrec, enthused, paid a call on the artist, who had him presented to Ancourt, his lithographer. From then on, Lautrec was impassioned with this art which he brought to its summit: in less than ten years, he produced more then 400 lithographs, of which 31 were posters. Immediately after Lautrec's initiation, still in 1891, Zidler, the director of the Moulin Rouge which he frequented, proposed to him the formidable honor of making a poster to replace the one executed two years before by Chéret. His trial effort was a masterpiece: a dark silhouette of Valentin *"Le Désossé,"* ("Boneless") in a cinematic close-up, and the black mass of spectators who fill the background of the image make la Goulue and her startling petticoat (the paper has been left white) stand out radiantly beneath the yellow lanterns. Beginning with this first design, Lautrec showed his genius. For the neutral, exterior vision of Chéret he substituted an interior, immediate vision: where Chéret had drawn his usual little woman, a graceful allegory encircled by pierrots under the windmill's blades, Lautrec shows us what really happens, painting the people as they are, without concessions.

"In his posters Chéret suppressed black—it's admirable. We put it back—it's not too bad."

44. Henri-Gabriel Ibels: *L'Escarmouche,* (a weekly journal). 1893.

45. Maxime Dethomas: Poster for the book *Montmartre.* 1897.

This remark made by Lautrec to his friend Henry Nocq is perfectly illustrated in his poster for the Moulin Rouge. Enchanted with Japanese engravings, like the Nabis, Lautrec loved the flat patches of vivid color, the powerful outlines and bold compositions: he made a riot of colors which can shout as they will. He used yellow, blue and red for *Bruant à l'Eldorado,* yellow and blue for the *Chaîne Simpson.* His layouts are bold and dynamic: a few strokes set the stage for *Madame Eglantine's* troupe, for *May Milton* or for *Caudieux.* He plays ravishingly with the diagonal, which gives movement, and which one finds ascending in *Babylone d'Allemagne* and descending in the *Vache Enragée;* it constructs the supper table of the *Reine de Joie* and the bar of the *Chap Book.* He did not hesitate to cut off Yvette Guilbert's head in the *Divan Japonais,* and placed a gigantic bass fiddle in the foreground of *Jane Avril au Jardin de Paris.* For the *Mirliton,* Bruant was shown from the back, a supreme defiance of convention. If his outline is thick and powerful for spectacles, sports and dramatic scenes like *Le Pendu,* he can become tender, like his palette, for *Confetti,* the *Salon des Cent,* or the *Revue Blanche.* Finally, certain posters are treated like prints, with judicious dabs of soft color, even monochrome *(L'Aube, La Chatelaine).*

After almost a century, Lautrec's posters have retained all their force, all their modernity, and their popularity has not ceased to grow.

A unique talent, Lautrec has furthermore had no disciple and no direct influence on the French poster, which is fundamentally opposed to his expressionism. One can only cite Jacques Villon in *Le Grillon* and the *Guingette Fleurie;* Lobel (of whom nothing is known) for the *Salon des Cent* and *Pierrefort;* and Maxime Dethomas *(Montmartre).*

46. Henri de Toulouse-Lautrec: *Moulin Rouge*. 1891.

47. Henri de Toulouse-Lautrec: *Divan Japonais*. 1893.

48. Henri de Toulouse-Lautrec: *Confetti*. 1896.

49. Jacques Villon: *Le Grillon*. 1899.

50. Henri de Toulouse-Lautrec: *May Milton*. 1895.

51. Manuel Orazi: Poster for the *La Maison Moderne* shop of Meier-Graefe. 1900.

At the same time, still at the beginning of the Nineties, Art Nouveau—Grasset and his disciples—brought vitality to the art of advertising: it is in the nature of things that these creators who had in common an interest in all of the decorative arts should acquire an enthusiasm for the emerging advertising art. Paul Berthon, Grasset's pupil, took up and elaborated his master's thesis: "You see, our new art is not and cannot be anything other than a development of our French art, stifled by the Renaissance. We want to create an original art, with no other model than nature, with no other rule than imagination and logic, while using for its details the flora and fauna of France and following very closely the principles which made the arts of the Middle Ages so decorative. . . . I seek only to copy nature in its very essence. If I consider a plant as a decorative motif, I don't reproduce all the veins of its leaves nor the exact tint of its flowers. Perhaps I would have to give its stem a more harmonious, more geometrical line or its flowers original colors which the plant I have before my eyes never had. I would not hesitate to paint the hair of my figures in yellow, red, or green if the composition as a whole required those colors."

In practice, Berthon had trouble freeing himself of Grasset's influence:

52. Georges de Feure: For the poster and print dealer *Pierrefort*. 1898.

53. Paul Berthon: *Salon des Cent*. 1895.

54. Carlos Schwabe: *Salon Rose Croix*. 1892.

his *Salon des Cent* is a mark-down of Grasset's, as are *L'Araignée d'Or* or *L'Almanach d'Alsace-Lorraine.* However, he finds an original palette, of warm pastel tones, made up of ochres, yellows, browns and red: he uses it for *L'Ermitage* (1897), *Sainte Marie des Fleurs, Le livre de Magda* and *Les Leçons de Violon* (1898), *La Source des Roches* (1899), *L'Extincteur Harden* and *Les Arts Libéraux* (1900). Maurice Pilliard Verneuil, another pupil of Grasset's, made a poster for Docteur Pierre's toothpaste, several for *Le Monde Moderne,* and *Le Laurenol No. 2* (1899), applying the same rules and principles.

In 1884 Manuel Orazi made two posters for Sarah Bernhardt in *Théodora,* using a mosaic background which would later be popularized by Mucha, and a curious poster for *Thais* in the form of a fragment of manuscript. He achieved his masterpieces much later, after the *Rêve de Noel* for Lyane de Pougy: the *Loie Fuller* poster for the Exposition of 1900, all in half-tones, printed in several gradations of color, whose decorative motifs go well beyond the standard style. For the *Maison Moderne,* Meier-Graefe's department-store, Orazi produced a veritable inventory of Art Nouveau creations. If his *Ligue Vinicole de France* is less inspired, he created for *Contrexeville* a poster where the raw reds, yellows and blues startle, are composed with a boldness reminiscent of Hohenstein.

Georges de Feure (Georges Van Sluijters), a Dutchman settled in Paris, approached all the disciplines of the decorative arts with great variety and equal success. His posters for the *Salon des Cent* (1893), *Paris Almanach* (1894), *Loie Fuller* (1895), *Jeanne d'Arc, Pierrefort* (1896), and *Le Journal des Ventes* (1899) use the feminine type and the symbolist atmosphere. For his Café-Concert posters the style is rawer, more in a caricature style *(Isita, Naya, Fonty, Edmée Lescot, Jane Derval,* etc.)

It was not until 1895 that there came an artist who so incarnated this style of poster that it is often given his name: Alphonse Mucha.

Coming from a Czech background, Mucha settled in 1887 in Paris where he worked as an obscure lithographer until Christmas Day of 1894,

55. Manuel Orazi: *Loie Fuller*. 1900.

56. Alphonse Mucha: Sarah Bernhardt in *La Dame aux Camélias*, 1896.

57. Alphonse Mucha: *Cycles Perfecta*. 1897.

58. Alphonse Mucha: *Job* cigarette paper. 1896.

when Sarah Bernhardt, discontent with her posters, demanded new ones on the spot. Mucha, the only available artist at the printer Lemercier, was given the job. His poster for *Gismonda* enthused the divine Sarah, who gave him a six-year contract, during which he made his posters along the same design: an elongated format (about 215 x 76 cm), with the text arranged on the top and bottom of the sheet allowing the actress to be represented life size, standing, in bedizened costumes and the jewels she liked to wear in her roles. Gold, silver and bronze enriched the composition even further. After *Gismonda* came *La Dame aux Camélias*, bedazzled with silver (1896); succeeded by *Lorenzaccio* the same year, then *La Samaritaine* (1897), *Médée* (1898), *Hamlet* and *La Tosca* (1899). Discovered overnight, Mucha became the artist of the day, the Art Nouveau poster-maker without peer. For Grasset's style, which remained a bit cold and rigid, he substituted a sensual woman whose hair spreads to infinity, in the midst of exuberant vegetation. If *Gismonda,* with its mosaic decor, reveals his byzantine influences, he is above all a virtuoso draftsman, a decorator of genius, who is able, as for example in his great poster for *Job,* to integrate the initials of the trademark with the background and even into the figure's jewelry. The charm and the allure of his drawing did not escape the publisher Champenois who, having signed a draconian contract with him, obliged him to produce at a relentless pace: cigaret

59. Alphone Mucha: Second design for *Job*.
1898.

paper *Job* (two posters, 1896 and 1898), *Nestlé* (1897 and 1898), *Lefèvre-Utile* (1896). Mucha also provided for all these trademarks a whole line of minor advertising material. We can also mention *Bénédictine* (1898), *Trappistine* (1899), the *Vin des Incas* (1897), the *Bières de la Meuse* (1897), *Cycles Waverley* and *Perfecta* (1897), and the printer *Cassan Fils* (1897). Mucha made two posters for the *Salon des Cent* (1896-1897), and for *La Plume*, a frontispiece of Sarah Bernhardt. He also lent his talent to *Monaco-Monte Carlo* (1897), to the Austria-Hungary pavilion at the *Paris 1900* Exposition, and to the *St. Louis Exposition of 1904*. The same year he left to conquer America, after which he returned to establish himself in his native land where he consecrated himself to the great project of *The Slav Epic*, a series of mammoth historic tableaux of his people.

Other minor masters have left some remarkable images and so deserve to be quickly mentioned. We know nothing of the life of Henry Thiriet but some of the most vigorous Art Nouveau compositions belong to him, such as the winged angel of *Cycles Omega* (1895) or the white cyclist of *Cycles Griffiths*. If his *L'Affiche française* and *Pierrefort* are more classically static in Grasset's manner, he regains all his verve in the two richly animated scenes of *Absinthe Berthelot* (1895) and of *Blanc à la Place Clichy* (1898). Marcel Lenoir was a mystic fond of mysterious women heavily outlined and colored in flat tints (*Arnould*), while Maurice Realier-Dumas preferred pastel shades and slender women (*Incandescence par le gaz*, 1892; *Paris—Mode*, 1893; *Champagne Mumm*, 1895).

The poster's great center of propagation was Montmartre. At that time it was at once the bohemian neighborhood, where many painters and poets lived and worked, and also the quarter for nightlife where the high

60. Alphonse Mucha: One of several designs for *Lefèvre-Utile*, a calendar for 1897. 1896.

61. Henri Thiriet: *Griffiths* Cycles. 1898.

society of pleasure seekers gathered. It was fashionable for aristocrats and the wealthy middle class to come to the cabarets to be regaled by entertainers, among which Rodolphe Salis and Bruant have remained the most famous, or to mix with the rougher elements at the dance halls. The proprietors of these establishments naturally called upon local talent to prepare their publicity, since the artists were also often their friends.

Adolphe Willette was one of the quarter's liveliest spirits: he decorated numerous cabarets with frescoes (*Le Chat Noir, La Cigale, Tabarin*), participated in the leading satirical journals, and was one of the first to interest himself in the poster. Like Chéret's, his style is that of the French painters of the eighteenth century, from whom he derived his ubiquitous figure: Pierrot. Unlike Chéret, however, he was no colorist, and usually contented himself with a monochrome drawing (*L'Enfant prodigue*, 1890; *La Revue déshabillée*, 1894; *Salon des Cent*). He also made a poster for the elections of 1889 presenting himself as an antisemitic candidate (for which some critics have never forgiven him). Color appeared in some few plates, very tender for *Fer Bavarais*, bright for *L'Elysée Montmartre* and for *Cacao Van Houten*, his bizarre concession to Art Nouveau.

Another key figure in Montmartre was Steinlen. Born in Lausanne, he arrived in Paris—or more exactly Montmartre—in 1881, and quickly made himself well known at the Chat Noir (for which he made a lantern and a fresco titled *Apotheosis of the Cats*), and at the Mirliton, the one-time Chat Noir taken over by Bruant for whom he illustrated brochures, books (*Dans la rue*), and his newspaper (*Le Mirliton*).

Steinlen was generous, a dedicated socialist, and a great friend of animals. His famous cat, lording it wide-eyed over the environs of the *Chat Noir* (1896), was introduced in a poster for *Lait Sterilisé de la Vingeanne* (1894), and *Compagnie française des chocolats et des thés* (1895), beside the artist's daughter. There are also cats in the poster for the *Exposition à la Bodinière* (1894), and they are together with dogs for *Clinique Chéron* (1903). For *Motocycles Comiot*, it is a flock of geese that surrounds the pretty motorcyclist (1899), and for *Cocorico*, of course, the proud profile of a rooster. Steinlen is a marvelous observer of the life that surrounds him. He sets it forth in *La Rue*, for the publisher *Charles Verneau* (1895), *Mothu et Doria* (1893) or *La Traite des Blanches*. The tensions between rich and poor, exploiters and exploited, are always present—they break out in *La Feuille de Zo d'Axa* (1899), *Le Petit Sou* (1900), *Paris* (1898), and *L'Assommoir* (1900). Steinlen's posters can be charming pictures, delicately outlined with warm reds for milk or chocolates, but when politics are involved his colors become somber, his line thickens and hardens, to represent struggling workmen, the downtrodden or, during the first World War, soldiers or war victims (*Journal de Poilu*, 1915; *Journée serbe*, 1916).

Paul Balluriau (1860–1917), his co-worker on *Gil Blas*, worked in a similar style on *Pauvre Femme* and *Margot la jolie* (1897), and above all on the only French trade-union posters of any graphic interest, caricatures for the railway-workers srike in 1910. Roedel was influenced by Steinlen in the *Moulin de la Galette* (1896), the *Moulin Rouge* (1897), and the *Exposition des Chats;* as was Hélène Dufau (*La Fronde*, 1898; *L'enfant à travers les âges*, 1901). Lucien Métivet also worked in the same spirit (*Eugénie Buffet*).

Montmartre was also the domicile of one of the most original talents of this time: Jules Alexandre Grün. If in his posters he had not treated

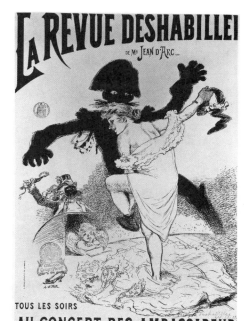

62. Adolphe Willette: *La Revue Déshabillée*. 1894.

63. Théophile-Alexandre Steinlen: Poster for the dairy *Quillot Frères*. 1894.

64. Théophile-Alexandre Steinlen: Poster for the printer *Charles Verneau*, titled *La Rue* (The Street). 1896.

mainly carousers and coquettes, with facility but without genius, he would be one of the greatest poster artists of the period: in fact he is the only one to use flat tints without outlines, allowing the paper itself to function as a design element, to compose scenes that are often of great graphic audacity.

He used few colors: a black background which also served as the men's clothing, a vivid red, and the paper kept white to play with: some white dots on a black background often make the buttons of the uniforms of merry gendarmes emerging from the night *(Au violon, Quelle machine acheter, Pneus ferrés Gallus)*. The figures are radiant, coquettes and merry revellers *(Tréteau de Tabarin)*, voluptuous long women *(Revue à Poivre, Les Petits Croisés)*, or women surrounded by ribald males *(La Pépinière, Chauffons, chauffons, Pour qui votait-on*, etc.). He also gladly

65. Jules-Alexandre Grün: *Concert de la Pépinière*. 1902.

66. Auguste Roubille: *Le Smart Carman*. (A costume jewelry shop). 1899.

67. Adrien Barrère: Music-hall performer *Dranem*. c. 1905.

turned to caricature, representing the celebrities of the Almanach du Gotha crowding the nightclub at Fursey or the songsters of Montmartre in full dress at the Trianon. Of a radically different make is his series of posters for Monte-Carlo, rich in colors and of great variety in composition *(Tir au Pigeon, Concours d'Aviation, Concours de Chiens, Course de Canot Automobiles,* etc.).

Abel Faivre *(Le Logis de la Lune Rousse)* and Charles Léandre *(Les Cantomines de Xavier Privas,* 1899, *Les Vieux Marcheurs, La Lune Rousse, Fête Henri Monnier)* also lent their pens to the Montmartre gaiety.

All the artists we have just listed collaborated on satirical or artistic reviews of the period, of which there was an enormous number, the principal ones being *Le Rire, L'Assiette au beurre, Courrier français, Cocorico, Gil Blas, Le Chat noir, Le Mirliton.* Working with the staffs of these satirical journals, the poster artists found themselves often divided by political issues; thus, when France's most notorious scandal broke out in 1894, Willette, Forain and Caran-d'Ache sided with the anti-Dreyfus right, while Steinlen and his group were on the pro-Dreyfus left.

Gustave Jossot merits a place apart: virulently anticlerical, he was also a gadfly of the *bourgeois,* and in his art he employed a thick outline and glaring colors which made his posters "howl on the walls". He makes the wealthy *(Sales gueles,* 1895) and the Academy *(Salon des Cent,* 1894) ridiculous, but he can be powerful and effective for *Sardiens Amieux,* with their bizarre ragpicker, *Guignolet Cointreau* (1898), or in his poster for the tailor Lejeune. He is the only French poster artist who can be called expressionistic. Roubille, with his lively drawing and powerful outline, left the classic *Smart Carman* and *Spratt's Patent Foods.*

With the illustrators can be included the caricaturists: Sem, Barrère, de Losques and the young Cappiello. They have in common having worked almost exclusively for show business, making caricatures of the stars enlarged to poster size, the outline clean, the colors in flat tints.

Sem (Serge Goursat) noted for the acidity of his wit and the cruelty of his caricatures (his albums of the Deauville races, for which he also made a poster, spare none of the personalities of the moment), made some well-composed posters *(Scala, A fleur de peau, Revue du Casino de Paris).* His poster for *Footitt* at the Folies Bergere is a masterpiece of composition where, without an outline, by flat tints of raw colors and blank paper, he constructed the head of the famous clown.

Adrien Barrère left a very complete gallery of the fabled performers of the café-concert: *(Mayol, Dranem, Fragson, Eugénie Fougère, Jeanne d'Alma,* etc.); all these posters represent faithful portraits of their subjects, well laid out, outlined and colored. Starting in 1905, he also publicized the early Pathé films in many posters where one recognizes the first silent film stars (Max Linder, Charles Prince, André Deed, etc.).

The young De Losques, dead at the front in 1915, had in his short career, with an incomparable style and a line that captured his models' expression, worked for the revues of the Folies-Bergère where he represented Chevalier, Jeanne Derval, Jeanne Bloch, etc. He also made posters for Pathé.

Arriving in Paris where he began his career as a caricaturist, Leonetto Cappiello, before revolutionizing commercial art, made some placards in this light spirit for *Hélène Chauvin,* for the magazine *Frou-Frou,* and for several shows at the Folies-Bergère.

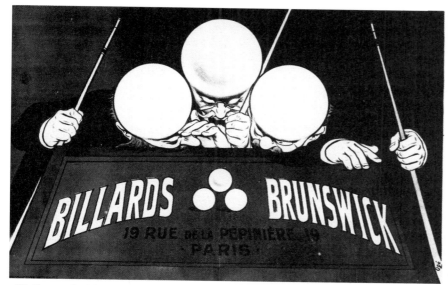

68. Eugene Ogé: Poster for billiard balls. c. 1900.

69. Albert Guillaume: *Armour & Co.* meat extract. c. 1895.

70. Henri-Gustave Jossot: Poster for a tailor. 1903.

Paris sheltered hundreds of painters at this period. A great many of them brought what talent they had to the great adventure of the poster, for which demand continued to grow as it became the vogue. They contributed to the formation of a gigantic mass of posters which, sometimes for its quality, but above all for its quantity, made Paris from 1895 to 1900 the world capital of advertising art.

To the disciples of Chéret already listed can be added Pal (Jean de Paléologue) who utilizes in a majority of his posters women of succulent forms, notably for cycles *(La Francaise, Gladiator, Falcon)* and products *(Rayon d'or, Orbec Mousseux),* but also shows *(Folies Bergère),* newspapers, and everything else! Henry Gray (Henri Boulanger) also had an enormous production, very unequal, with a woman omnipresent. Misti (Fernand Mifliez), working in the Chéret vein, is a specialist in bicycles which he glamorizes by inserting pretty cyclists *(Clément, Griffon, Gladiator, Rouxel,* et *Dubois).* He also dealt in most diverse subjects, from the *Fête de Neuilly* to *Menthe Pastille.* Albert Guillaume, caricaturist, is one of the most prolific poster artists for beverages and various products for whom he makes use of a whole gallery of figures: carnival athletes *(Bouillon Armour),* officers *(Grog Dupit),* brawny laborers *(Vin d'or),* dandies *(Hannapier),* etc. Firmin Bouisset was the specialist in children, immortal creator of the little girl of *Chocolat Menier* (1892), but also the little chimney-sweep of *Job* Cigarette Papers, and the schoolboys of *Lombard* and *Suchard* chocolates. Ogé specialized in caricatures of the great: Queen Victoria and Kruger for *Dum Dum* pills, the heads of state at the Hague tribunal for the *Menthe-Pastille;* he created a minor masterpiece in the three bald heads for *Brunswick* billiard balls.

Let us also mention Fernel, Gerbault, Tichon, Redon, and Auzolle; Fraipont and Hugo d'Alesi, specialists in tourist posters; Eugène Vavasseur, originator of the three brothers for Ripolin Paints; and O'Galop (Marius Rossillon), creator of the Michelin tire man. With all this talent massed behind it, the poster was in its glory.

71. Pal (Jean de Paléologue): *Rayon d'Or* oil lamps. c. 1895.

72. Eugène Vavasseur: *Ripolin* paints. 1898.

73. O'Galop (Marius Rossillon): *Michelin* tires. c. 1910.

74. Firmin Bouisset: *Chocolat Menier*. 1893.

76. Louis Anquetin: *Marguerite Dufay.* 1894.

75. Manuel Robbe: *Plasson Cycles.* 1897.

Even the deans of academicism, led by Puvis de Chavannes, president of the Société des Beaux-Arts, bowed to the inevitable. De Chavannes himself designed propaganda for the *Union pour l'Action Morale:* "The Childhood of Saint Geneviève", a reproduction of his fresco in the Pantheon! Rochegrosse did posters for the Opéra *(Walkyrie, Louise, Don Quixote)* and the *Automobile Club de France.* Clairin represented, in 1895, his friend Sarah Bernhardt in *Théodora,* and the orientalist Dinet tried his hand, for the 1900 World's Fair, at *L'Andalusie au temps des Maures.* Other fine art painters jumped on the bandwagon, too: Bottini *(Cycles Médinger,* 1897), Helleu *(Sagot);* Boutet de Monvel *(La Petite Poucette,* 1891; *Dentifrice du Dr. Pierre,* 1894); Manuel-Robbe *(L'Eclatante,* 1895); *Cycles Plasson,* 1897), and the ceramics painter Moreau-Nélaton *(Les Arts de la Femme, Bec Auer* 1895). Louis Anquetin *(Le Rire, Marguerite Dufay,* 1894) and Eugene Carrière *(L'Aurore,* 1897; *Exposition Rodin,* 1900), also made incursions into advertising art. Forain designed posters for the *Salon du Cycle* and *La Vie de Bohème* (1895).

It must be said that, surpassing its original function of advertising, the posters, dethroning the Japanese print, became the fashion of the times as an art form. In the wake of pioneers like Ernest Maindron who began writing *Les Affiches Illustrées* in 1886 (and completed it with a second volume in 1896), France became populated with poster-maniacs. "Today it's the poster that delights the amateur of prints . . . and posters must be catalogued like engravings and etchings—and why not!" (Henri Beraldi in *Le graveur du XIXème siecle).* If they sometimes attempted bribing printers and billposters, collectors also now could obtain prints from the specialist poster dealers' galleries that had opened: Arnould, Pierrefort and especially Sagot: "It's on the left bank, in a narrow shop frequented for a long time by iconophiles crazy about modern prints, at 18 Rue Génégaud, run by a bustling and active man of keen intelligence and rare sureness of taste, Monsieur Edmond Sagot, where the passion for illus-

77. F.-A. Cazals: *Salon des Cent* poster showing Paul Verlaine and Jean Moréas at the exhibition. 1894.

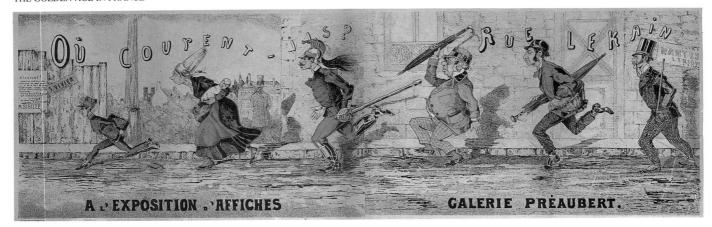

78. Anonymous design for the poster show in Nantes. 1889.

79. Pierre Roche: Poster for the gallery *Salon de la Plume*, printed on laminated paper by Charpentier.

80. James Ensor: *Salon des Cent* exhibition. 1898.

81. Jean Peské: For the monthly periodical
L'Estampe et L'Affiche. 1898.

trated placards has found its headquarters, or rather its central focus."
(Octave Uzanne). They had their journals: *L'Estampe et l'Affiche* of
Clémend Janin and André Mellerio, from 1897 to 1899; *Les Maitres de
l'Affiche,* sold by subscription between 1895 and 1900; or *La Plume,* an
artistic and literary review which published several special numbers on
the poster, and was distributed by mail. It was *La Plume* which organized
the *Salon des Cent* on its premises on the Rue Bonaparte, and whose
posters are signed with the greatest names (Ibels in 1893, Jossot and De
Feure in 1894, Lautrec in 1895, Berthon, Rassenfosse, Mucha, Bonnard
in 1896, Willette and Mucha in 1897, Bouisset in 1898) but also by many
other artists who tried their hand at the new genre (Ranft, Cazals, Henri
Detouche, Rops, André des Gachons or Pierre Roche; and Henri Bouillon,
who made experiments with translucent paper). The critical review directed by George Bans had its own collection of posters by the likes of
Jossot, Mondier, Couturier and Lebègue. Exhibitions followed upon one
another by the dozens, starting at the 1889 World's Fair. The most
important of these, organized in 1896 by A. Henriot at Reims, brought
togeher 1,671 entries from every country. In fact, the movement had
rapidly spread throughout the world.

82. Maxfield Parrish: *Poster Show*. 1896.

The Poster Conquers the World

In the middle of the Nineties, the movement which had been developing for several years in France spread, little by little, over the whole world. In every country the scenario is about the same, and the artistic poster, during its introduction, profited from three types of support: from collectors, from magazines and from all the dissidents of academicism who can be grouped together under the label of Art Nouveau.

Collectors, like Bella of London (who commissioned Lautrec's poster *Confetti),* discovering this new fashion in Paris, hurried to import it into their own countries. Exhibitions with French posters predominating multiplied rapidly: in 1894 in London, at the Royal Aquarium, and in Leeds; in 1895 in the United States at the Pratt Institute in Brooklyn, as well as in Boston, New York, and Chicago; in 1896 in Dresden, Vienna, Barcelona, Brussels and Liège; in 1897 in Düsseldorf, Moscow, Saint Petersburg, and Oslo; in 1898 in Berlin and Cracow. If we mention only the principal reviews and works purveying this new fashion, they can be counted in the dozens. They revealed to the public the beauty of French billboard art in its maturity, and exercised a profound influence on artists and potential advertisers. The message was disseminated in journals like *The Poster* in London, *The Poster* and *Poster Lore* in New York, or *L'Affiche artistique* in Belgium, as well as in books—Hiatt's *The Poster* in London and Sponsel's *Das Moderne Plakat* in Germany.

Magazine publishers played a special role: in America, it was *Scribner's, Lippincott's,* and *The Century;* in Germany, *Pan, Jugend, Simplicissimus:* they were the first to call on young artists to illustrate their covers, and soon also to create their posters.

All these young creators were in conflict with academicism, and were strongly impressed by Japanese art and the pronouncements of William Morris and of the Arts and Crafts movement in England. In a few years Art Nouveau washed like a great wave over Europe, sweeping away classic precepts and opening the way for modern art.

In Belgium, the vortex of these currents, there was the *Libre esthétique, Le Sillon* and *Pour l'Art* to defend the avant-garde ideas; in Germany there were the secessionists, championed by *Pan, Jugend, Simplicissimus;* and in Austria, it was *Ver Sacrum.* The Italian "Liberty" style found its mouthpiece in *Emporium;* in Barcelona *Luz, Pel* and *Ploma* defended modernism. All these movements found the poster the most spectacular way to promote their ideas about art; and these publications testify most eloquently on their enthusiasm, from Vienna to Glasgow.

Not much is left of this fantastic flurry: after a few years, the movement sank back, as for example in Spain; but come what may, the artistic poster and the first foundations of graphic art existed henceforth in the principal countries of the western world.

83. Mosnar Yednis (Sidney Ransom): *The Poster* magazine, published in London. 1898.

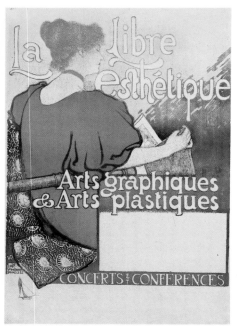

84. Théodore Van Rysselberghe: Poster for the artists group *La Libre Esthétique*. 1896.

Belgium

It was in Belgium, immediately after France, that the artistic poster found its second adopted country. Despite its small size, Belgium, thanks to the conquest of the Congo, to coal-mining and technology, had very rapidly become one of the richest and most advanced countries in the world. At the same time, in this period of colonial expansion and of growing nationalism, a remarkable intellectual elite developed which, profiting from a privileged geographic situation, made Belgium the crossroads of European cultural currents.

Before 1890, the illustrated poster was almost nonexistent. Only posters of American circuses, the same which had struck Chéret's eye in London, put an occasional touch of color on the walls. The first efforts by Duyck and Crespin in 1886 were monochromes. "The printing was absolutely inadequate: no printers were properly equipped to print a color poster," noted Maurice Bauwens in *Les Affiches étrangères*. After his baptism at the World's Fair of 1889, Chéret was revealed to Brussels the following year at a poster exhibition, and then honored in 1891 by an invitation from "The Twenty" group.

86. Henri Ottevaere: Exhibition of the group *Pour l'Art*. 1894.

The cultural circles in Brussels were as numerous as they were remarkable, and one of the most influential ones was The Twenty (Les XX), a group founded under the impetus of the lawyers Octave Maus and Edmond Picard. In 1893, they renamed themselves the Libre Esthétique, which gathered together, until World War I, much of the European avant-garde. They published a magazine under their name, as did several other similar organizations.

Among these other torch bearers of the new art form were *Pour l'Art*, founded in 1892; *Le Sillon*, begun in 1893; and *L'Art Idéaliste*, to name only the most important. All these publications were the pretext for poster-making by first-rank artists: K. Knopff made one for The Twenty in 1891, Van Rysselberghe two for the *Libre Esthétique* in 1896 and 1897, followed by a series by Combaz, who was succeeded by Lemmon.

85. Gisbert Combaz: *La Libre Esthétique*. 1899.

87. Fernand Toussaint: *Le Sillon* (A Belgian artistic society's publication). 1895.

88. Adolphe Crespin: For the architect *Paul Hankar*. 1894.

89. Victor Mignot: A bicycle exhibition held at the skating rink *Pole Nord*. 1897.

Le Sillon called upon Toussaint in 1895, Stevens in 1896 and in 1899, and in 1900 on Smeers. Delville in 1892, Ottevaere in 1894, and Fabryen in 1895 designed the placards for *Pour l'Art*.

All these painters only produced posters for these cultural endeavors, thereby earning Demeure de Beaumont's appraisal of "sometime poster artists".[1] When Combaz designed a poster for Toison d'Or, the shop for decorative art opened by Edmond Picard's sons, or Van Rysselberghe for the Maison Lembrée, a print-seller, or for Marie Mockel, concert impresario, they remained in that specialized domain.

If Brussels became in the Nineties one of the capitals of the poster, it is in part thanks to printers like Mertens, Veuve, Monnom, Gouveloos, Goosens or DeRycker, as well as to a constellation of talented young artists. But much credit goes also to the Belgian manufacturers and merchants, dynamic and prosperous, who demanded, like their Parisian counterparts, beautiful images for advertising.

Duyck and Crespin, who from 1886 had been pioneers, produced an important body of work, always a little stiff and sometimes a little heavy *(Vélodrome d'Hiver, Ville de Bruxelles, Nieuport Bains)*. The few posters made by Crespin alone, whether for himself, for the architect Hankar or the chemist Goldschmidt, are very much superior. He demonstrates there his talents for ornamentation and composition. Léon Dardenne, an artist at the newspaper *Diable au corps,* was also one of the first to take interest in the poster. For *Le petit Bleu* and *L'afficheur Bulens,* he created scenes that are almost naive, full of popular humor.

Victor Mignot was a real advertising man who worked only part-time for the newspaper *Libre Critique,* but concentrated his efforts chiefly on poster work for clients who included cycle-makers *(The Record, Leon Mans),* manufacturers *(Champagne Berton)* and owners of the skating-rink *Le Pole Nord.* His posters are schematized: the principal figures (most often a woman) in front, elongated as if stretched; behind them, blending into a background in halftints or detached like shadow-puppets, the supernumeraries who enrich the composition. The lettering, always vividly drawn and never straight, is slapped haphazardly but efficaciously on the picture.

If Paris had Mucha, Brussels had Privat-Livemont. The same meticulous drawing, the same feminine type, the same taste for ornamentation. Despite what some French critics tried to insinuate at the time, Livemont was no plagiarist, much less a disciple (his first poster dates from 1890, 5 years before Mucha's *Gismonda);* but like Mucha, he was a master of the eye-arresting line. In some ways his experiments were even more graphic. His palette, in opposition to the bronze-greens and golds of Mucha, is rich in vivid colors: the acid green of *Absinthe Robette,* the superb blue of *Bec Auer,* or the violet of *Café Rajah.* Livemont also often doubled the outline drawn around his figures with a narrow halo which made them stand out from a background of tangled lines and patterns: the steam from Van Houten Cocoa or from Rajah Coffee which come to blend into the lettering, roses from the Cologne Boldoot, and in the case of the artistic commune at Schaerbeck, the cherries and donkeys which were its emblems. For the serial stories of the newspaper *La Reforme* ("The Peddler's Daughter," "A Mother's Pride," "The Anarchist Mask")

1. Alexander Demeure de Beaumont: *L'Affiche Illustrée—L'Affiche Belge.* Toulouse, 1897.

90. Privat-Livemont:
Bec Auer lamps. 1896.

91. Henri Cassiers: *Red Star Line*. 1898.

92. Privat-Livemont: Poster for a brand of bitters. 1897.

he plays with his virtuoso drawings to make grand-guignol pictures which are really high camp.

At the opposite pole from Art Nouveau exuberance, Henri Meunier was an artist of exceptional purity. He took his colors in flat tints and his thick outlines from Japanese prints to construct strong and clear images: "With two or three pure colors, he fixes an impression that penetrates and imposes itself like the very truth," justly notes Demeure de Beaumont. Whether for a concert *(Quatuor Ysaye)* or for a product *(Savon Starlight)* he can find the synthetic image, like a moment in suspension, which creates an atmosphere focusing one's attention. The broadly applied colors contribute to it: the flamboyant yellow which floods the *Casino de Blankenberghe,* piercing the blue night, the sky and sea; the blood red of the sun for *The Testament of Baron Jean.* After that, whether he makes concessions to the volutes of Art Nouveau *(Café Rajah)* or adopts a more Japanese composition *(Cartes postales Dietrich),* the force of his posters remains compelling.

Henri Cassiers was the painter of Flanders. Both in travel posters, as in the one for the beach resort of *Coq sur Mer,* or in product advertising, as in *Carriages Germain,* he always represented, in a strongly outlined and richly colored composition, scenes peopled with Zeeland peasants in their traditional costume. But Cassiers is above all the great specialist in maritime posters. His series for the Red Star Line and the American Line, where he confronts fishermen with transatlantic liners, are classics in the genre. Another specialist, Georges Gaudy, devoted himself to the bicycle and the automobile. Although occasionally he fell into symbolist allegories *(Courses Bruxelles-Spa),* he generally preferred to represent charming cyclists on their machines.

Unlike France, where almost all artistic activity was concentrated in the capital, Belgium had a secondary creative center of exceptional quality: the city of Liège.

"And now, we must speak of the triumphant triumvirate of Liège, the three musketeers of the poster, but there are in fact four of them: Berchmans, Donnay, Rassenfosse and the printer Besnard," exclaimed Demeure de Beaumont. We share his enthusiasm, so true is it that Liège was at the turn of the century a capital of advertising art thanks to the meeting of these three great artists and the unbeatable printer.

Of the three, it was Rassenfosse, disciple and friend of Rops, who was the first to interest himself in the poster. With ease and refinement, he represents women in every manner—bare-headed or hatted, bust or full-length—for cycles *(Belgium Legia),* shoe-polish *(Huile Russe),* beverages *(Distillerie Constant Denis, Brasserie Van Velsen,* or *Bock Champagne Felix Moussoux),* light fixtures *(Le Soleil),* or numerous artistic events. What is most surprising about him is the great variety of his talent: one finds, design after design, a new experiment, a change of approach. If he is most often a realist, painting with his assured line a slovenly woman polishing her shoes, but dynamically colored, or two women arm-in-arm for the *Casino Grétry,* some of his images are almost Nabi: in *Savon Sunlight,* he gives us a green background against which he contrasts the maid's black dress, the white tablecloth and the bathtowel (blank paper), and the pink flesh of the bathing lady. In his poster for the gas-burner *Soleil,* a flame outlines in yellow the profile of a woman clothed in purple flat-tints. The poster for wrestling matches at Liège also uses outlines and flat tints, with spectators depicted in the style of Vuillard. Then again, all subtlety and finesse, he drew, for the brasserie Van Velsen, with an ulfaltering line, a woman emptying a stein of beer. The same engraving finesse can be seen in his poster for Rops: there, he participates in one of the experiments of Besnard, letting him print it on orange paper. He does the same for *L'Art Indépendant,* this time on green paper. This enrichment, upheld by a sure technique, was developed after the first World War.

Berchmans, for his part, astonishes with his power and vigor, and his output of posters was considerable. Even in his least-known plates *(Orange Bitter Netermans, F.N., Lampe Belge, Distillerie de l'Hélice, Lempereur et Bernard, Serrurier Bovy,* etc.) we can be sure to find solid draftsmanship with strong outlines, good sense of composition and accented colors. His most famous successes are of an astounding modernism: such as his poster for *The Fine Art and General Insurance Co.* where the pure red of the menacing blaze in the background cuts through the graceful profile of the woman who is taking off her bracelet. Others include *L'Art Indépendent,* all outlines and black paper which has the force of a line engraving; *Le Bock de Koekelberg* with its impeccable design, finely outlined in

93. Georges Gaudy: *Legia* bicycles and cars. 1898.

94. Emile Berchmans: Poster for an insurance company. 1896.

95. Henri Meunier: *Rajah* coffee. 1897.

96. Emile Berchmans: *Koekelberg* beer. 1896.

black on the face, the woman's hair and the glass, and in white on her hat and dress. The outline swells and thickens for the *Salon de la ville de Liège* of 1896. The colors remain few, warm, poured into flat tints. Berchmans succeeds with simple elements—a perfect mastery of blacks and greys, seconded by one or two vivid colors—red or oranges—and vigorous, strongly outlined drawing in a sober and clear composition. He left us a legacy of strong and vivid images that have survived the passage of time without a wrinkle.

Their friend Donnay is more grave and meditative: the atmosphere his posters release has nothing to do with the life poured forth by Berchmans and Rassenfosse. His women neither laugh nor drink: they are thoughtful, whether they represent a photographic exhibition (*Exposition Universelle de Liège*), or play the harp (music for the publisher Leopold Muraille). His body of work, full of contained emotion, is of great pictorial purity. It does not however shun a richness of color, such as striking yellows and blues—the play of sun on water for the *Société du Sport nautique de la Meuse*. Emotion bursts out and becomes dramatic for the *Fine Art and General Insurance Co.* (which had also commissioned posters from Berchmans and Rassenfosse), his strongest creation. As with Berchmans, red dominates, but fire—twisting flames raging in full force—is not the only menace, as we also see two hands of a thief clutching the jewelbox, ready to remove it from the embers about it. With only three colors, red, green, and black, and playing with the white of the paper, Donnay thus constructed a poster of exceptional power. Other less important artists like Emile Jaspar, Ubaghs and Dupuis also worked with Besnard.

Liège was not a city with only one printer: there was Gordinne, who put out the works of Armand Henrion and local artists like Koister and Faniel. Outside Brussels and Liège, the rest of Belgian production seems slight: in Mons, there was Marius Renard, in whom we detect a kinship with the artist of Liège. In Gand, Montald, the symbolist painter, made some posters, bizarre incursions of symbolist dreams and pre-Raphaelite reminiscences into advertising art. In Antwerp, we can mention Nys (*Anvers-Brussels Exposition,* a poster for Turkey), a good colorist with a fine line, and Van Neste, who worked in a very Art Nouveau style.

To complete this listing, we must evoke types of posters which were less prestigious but which also played their role in the evolution of publicity: like Charles Levy in Paris, or Strobridge in Cincinnati, it was the Marci printing house which supplied the posters for popular entertainment. Posters by artists like Léon Belloguet, though far from artistic subtlety, covered the walls with effective and colorful designs for beers (*La Vignette*) or the carnival of Bintje.

The political poster was also full of interest: the confrontation of Catholics and Socialists produced a series of powerful enlarged caricatures, most often in black and white. Color is generally reserved for events like the opening of the *Maison de Peuple* which Van Biesbroeck announced in the purest Art Nouveau style.

The beginning of the century saw, in Belgium as elsewhere, an exhaustion of creativity as well as of Art Nouveau. With his poster for *Tropon* (1898), Van de Velde had already envisaged the things to come. In stylizing the three sparrows of the German food manufacturer, used in posters, vignettes, and packaging, he created a logo in the modern sense of the term, abandoning all realism and the whole classic arsenal of advertising (the woman, the child, etc.) of the period. The transition to the decorative style which triumphed in the Twenties came about in a less revolutionary manner, by an evolution pioneered by the architect Creten: his posters of 1907 (*Belgische Tentoonstelling Amsterdam*) and 1910 (*Exposition Universelle de Bruxelles*) announce the abandonment of Art Nouveau arabesques for the stylizations of Art Deco.

England

Like Belgium, England saw the birth and development of the artistic poster at the beginning of the Nineties. As poster-hanging had not been strictly limited as it had been in France before the law of 1881, the city walls were crowded with placards, carelessly put up, mainly typographical and, when illustrated, vying with one another in ugliness. The standardization of formats around the "Double Crown", and two laws, the "Advertisement Rating Bill" of 1888 and the "Advertisement Stations Rating Bill" of 1889, attempted to organize this vast chaos. The quality of the posters, however, remained to be improved.

The path toward that goal was opened as far back as 1871, by Fred Walker, member of the very honorable Royal Academy of Painting, who,

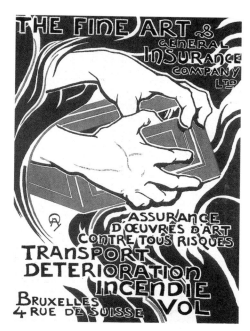

97. Auguste Donnay: Poster for an insurance company specializing in fine art. c. 1895.

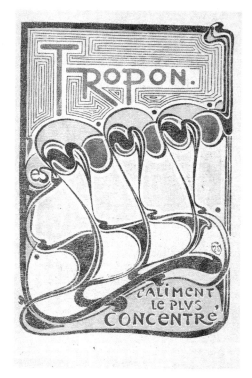

98. Henry Van de Velde: *Tropon* food products. 1898.

63

99. Fred Walker: Poster for the
dramatization of Wilkie Collins' classic
mystery. 1871.

to announce the play *The Woman in White,* had made a drawing from which W.H. Hooper made a woodcut. Perfectly graphic and adapted to the needs of the poster, it could serve as an example. Walker was convinced of it: "I am impressed on doing all I can with a first attempt at what I consider might develop into a most important branch of art," he wrote.

Alas! His example was not followed by English manufacturers, mired in Victorian prudery and conformity, who in contrast to their French counterparts thought to obtain quality advertising by contenting themselves with the reproduction of Royal Academy pictures. It was thus that Henry Stacy Marks gained the nickname Trade Marks, Sir Edward Poynter left monumental propaganda for insurance companies, and the seascapes of William L. Wylie served the shipping companies. Let us also mention Sir James Linton, Sir Herbert Herkomer and Sir John Millais, whose famous picture *Bubbles,* sold to Pears' Soap, had a great success. McKnight-Kauffer condemns them without mercy: "Bad painters design bad posters: Herkomer, Leighton and Millais are good examples."

Among the constellation of Academicians, only two merit particular mention. One was Walter Crane, whose numerous forays into the domain of advertising met with setbacks, but who crusaded against vulgarity: "I fear there is something essentially vulgar about the idea of the poster, unless it is limited to a simple announcement or directions or becomes a species of heraldry or sign painting . . . the very fact of the necessity of shouting loud, and the association with the vulgar commercial puffing, are against the artist and are so much dead weight."

Although clearly having failed to understand the true problems of advertising communication, Walter Crane exercised a beneficial influence as a theoretician, as Price[1] notes, on disciples like R. Anning Bell, who must be credited with a beautiful poster for the *Liverpool Art School.*

The second Academician of consequence, Maurice Greiffenhagen, was able to free himself from all the academic inanity: his *Pall Mall Budget* is a true poster.

On the whole, though, one can only regret with Hiatt[2] that "English artists of established reputation were so anxious to infuse their posters with esthetic qualities, that for the most part they overlooked the obvious fact that their work was in vain unless it really fulfilled its primary purpose of advertising."

But then suddenly a man by the name of Aubrey Beardsley dropped a bombshell in the form of his poster for the Avenue Theatre, landing like a rock in the pool of conformity. It had been scarcely pasted on a few walls before it unleashed a fierce controversy: his defenders saw in it for the first time the appearance of a modern image, very Japanese; his detractors called it a horror, a scandal (" 'ave a nue poster," railed *Punch*). Even if the poster work of Beardsley, who died at 25, was limited (*The Yellow Book, Keynotes series, The Pseudonym,* and *Autumn Libraries*), his style impressed a whole generation. H. Spielmann[3] described him as "a draughtsman of weird and singular power who, after importing into his art elements so suggesively opposite as his distorted echoes of Chinese and Annamite execution and Rossetian feelings (seen with a squinting

1. Charles Matlack Price: *Posters.* New York: George W. Bricka, 1913.
2. Charles Hiatt: *Picture Posters.* London: Bell & Sons, 1895.
3. Arsène Alexander et al.: *The Modern Poster.* New York: Scribner's, 1895.

100. Henry Stacy Marks: A soap poster from about 1880.

101. Herbert Herkomer: Bookstore poster for a magazine. 1890.

102. Aubrey Beardsley: *Avenue Theatre*. 1894.

103. Aubrey Beardsley: Poster for a popular library series. 1896.

eye, imagined with a Mephistophelian brain and executed with a vampire hand), showed a deep natural instinct for the beauty of line, for the balance of the chiaroscuro, and the decorative effect." The undeniable bizarre style apart, Beardsley had an unerring instinct for composition, and above all for exploiting the contrast between black and white which were a preponderant influence on many artists: to note the most celebrated, the American Will Bradley.

The breach once opened, the poster designed along truly graphic criteria could develop, thanks mostly to young artists who had traveled abroad.

First, Dudley Hardy put on the walls of London for the magazine *To-Day,* a yellow girl "with sober contours, even a little angular, the effect achieved and on the white paper the figure standing out radiantly, to the detriment of chromos overloaded with colors in half-tones" (Joseph Pennel).[1]

The yellow girl, like the *Gaiety Girl* which succeeded her, was directly inspired by Chéret: "She is too light-hearted, too irresponsible to be a

1. M. Bauwens et al: *Les Affiches Etrangères Ilustrées.* Paris: G. Boudet, 1897.

104. Dudley Hardy: For the play
A Gaiety Girl. 1894.

105. John Hassall: For a children's book. 1898.

106. Dudley Hardy: Theatrical poster. c. 1897.

girl of this gray-skied rainy country." But she adapted very well, with rawer colors and less subtle outline than used by French artists. Dudley Hardy soon became the fashionable poster maker, working principally at first for the Savoy Theatre *(The Chieftain, Oh! Susannah, The Yeoman of the Guard, Cinderella, J.P.,* etc.). His popular humor perfectly suited the Gilbert and Sullivan repertory. Let us add with Hiatt[1] that "the lettering of Mr. Hardy's posters is admirable. It is invented by the artist and forms an essential part of the design."

John Hassal was another of the early makers of true posters, with a personality even more original than that of his friend Hardy. Although his ambition was to be a painter, he answered an ad from the printer David Allen in order to make a living, and this attracted him to advertising art. A seven-year contract followed, and hundreds of posters, ranging from shows *(Poppy and Her Trainer, Little Bopeep, Cinderella, Wild Rabbit, The Mummy,* etc. . . . .) to ads for the British Vacuum Cleaner Co. His 1909 poster *Skegness is So Bracing,* a model of visual communication, remains a classic of the English poster, a perfect application of its maker's principles: "ideas, ideas, ideas."

Hardy and Hassel, even if they gleaned their understanding of what a poster should be by taking inspiration from French models, created nevertheless a style of image typically English: the drawing, strongly outlined, the blaring colors, the lettering have nothing in common with the subtleties of Chéret or Mucha. Perhaps the gray and fog of London necessitated more vivid colors; but the quality of English printers was also a factor. In any case, that is what can be read between the lines in Rogers'[2] description of the other makers of posters for the entertainment industry: Mosnar Yendis (Sidney Ransom), Albert Morrow, Will True, Stewart Browne, Alec Ritchie: "That there is much in common in their posters is possibly the result of the fact that they have nearly all devoted themselves to the theatrical playbill and that the bulk of their work has been done for a single firm of lithographers." The firm in this case is David Allen & Sons.

It is true that the theater and the press provided most of the work for these artists, since English manufacturers remained very timid. Let us add some satirical illustrators who also tried their hand at the poster, such as Phil May, Raven Hill, as well as Forrest, Beeton, and Solon.

However, some true creators in advertising arose in the wake of Hassal's pioneer efforts at the beginning of the 20th century. Will Owen, so like Hassal that he is sometimes confused with him; Cecil Aldin, who made the dog taken from Hassal's work his mascot and who worked for *Colman's Blue, Cadbury's Cocoa* and *Ellis Davies Tea;* and Lewis Baumer, who put his restrained graphics to the service of *West-end, Midland Railways* and *O.K. Sauce.*

Among others, H. Ryland, in a very colorful style, specialized in food and beverage products *(Hall's Wine, Suchard).* Tom Browne worked for various products *(Cerebos, Whiskey Rodrick Dhu),* often composing humorous scenes for them.

W.S. Rogers, author of the excellent *Book of the Poster,* propounded some concepts which revealed his qualities as a theoretician. He also applied them in practice in posters he designed for the *Article Club*

1. Charles Hiatt: Op. cit.
2. W.S. Rogers: *A Book of the Poster.* London: Greening & Co., 1901.

108. Phil May: To advertise
his own book. 1898.

107. Mosnar Yendis (Sidney Ransom): Theatrical poster. 1898.

109. W. S. Rogers:
A bicycle exhibition. 1899.

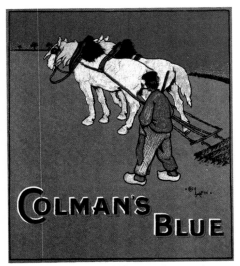

110. Cecil Aldin: An 1899 poster for a wash product.

111. Herbert McNair, Margaret and Frances Macdonald: Exhibition in Scotland. c. 1895.

112. Beggarstaff Brothers: Theatrical poster. 1895.

Exhibition (very Art Nouveau), the *London Letter, Stanley Show Cycles,* and the *Automobile Club Show.*

Despite this list of fine graphic artists, Great Britain—with a few brilliant exceptions, like the posters of the School of Glasgow—would be singularly lacking in genius if it were not for the providential appearance, in 1894, of the Beggarstaff Brothers, whose conceptions were to revitalize the art of the poster the world over. From the meeting of James Pryde and William Nicholson was born this tandem of genius, with its purely invented name (they were in fact only brothers-in-law).

For a poster show at the Westminster Aquarium, they decided on four projects, using imaginary trade names: Nobody's Candles, Nobody's Washing Blue, Nobody's Pianos and Nobody's Nigger Minstrels. Pryde revealed how they worked: "We decided that a silhouette treatment was the best, and it had this advantage, that it had not been done before. Moreover, it was a very economical way of producing a poster for reproduction, for the tones were all flat. To get this flat effect, we cut out the designs in colored paper and pasted them on flat boards or paper." (quoted by Bevis Hillier[1]).

The process might seem simple, but: "Our designs may not look as if much time was spent upon them, but I can assure you that it has taken all the artistic knowledge we possess to bring them to the simple state in which you see them." In fact, in carrying the experiment of Lautrec, their idol, even further, the Beggarstaffs arrived at absolute stylization, their economy of means being the outcome of perfect mastery of drawing and composition.

Charles Hiatt made no mistake: "If each 'Nobody' is not rapidly converted into "Somebody," the various manufacturers and proprietors of the articles mentioned above must be very stupid people."

Alas, the turn of events proved that English manufacturers were in fact stupid—or that it was still too early for them to assimilate this radically new conception of the poster. And so the printed works of the Beggarstaffs are ridiculously few: *Hamlet,* printed by themselves in stencil in 1894; in October of the same year *Kassama Corn Flour;* then, *A Trip to Chinatown, Beefeater* (actually brought out by Harper's), *Rowntree's Cocoa, Don Quixote, Cinderella, Black and White Gallery,* and *The Hour Illustrated.*

Their colors in flat tones, avoiding an outline where possible, and the power and simplicity of their composition, were certainly a direct influence on artists like J.W. Simpson *(The Book of Book-plates)* or Gordon Craig *(The Masque of Love),* but their conceptions went much further, to be taken up by the Germans and by a whole generation of poster artists everywhere.

In the years preceding the First World War, an institutional backer of major importance took an interest for the first time in producing quality posters. Under the direction of Frank Pick, London Transport's advertising became exemplary thanks to graphic artists of the first order like Frank Brangwyn, Spencer Pryse, Hatrick, and the Gill brothers. It marked the beginning of the British travel poster which was to flourish after the War.

1. Bevis Hillier: *Posters.* London: Spring Books, 1969.

113. Beggarstaff Brothers: Poster for the London presentation of the play, *A Trip to Chinatown*. 1895.

America to 1914

In the middle of the nineteenth century, the United States was most certainly the country where the poster had developed the furthest. Enterprising showmen like Barnum were no doubt responsible for this. In any case, it was for them that large formats in woodcut were regularly used for the first time. As Rogers[1] wittily noted, "It's the country of big things."

La Forgue in his *Affiches Etrangères*[2] confirmed this: "The mammoth poster is really the ancestor of the modern poster." He also described the method of production of these gigantic displays, which could reach the size of 28 sheets: "The whole poster is composed of a certain number of stones or blocks of wood which are assembled so that its contours can be traced, after which the frame is broken so that the pieces can be distributed to the draftsmen. Execution on stone is by far the more expensive, so that very large posters are still made on wood."

Pioneers of the large poster, the Americans also developed the lithog-

114. Anonymous: Poster for a wagon maker, printed by G. H. Dunston of Buffalo, N.Y., around 1885.

raphed color poster, and the big printing houses like Strobridge in Cincinnati, Forbes in Boston or Courier in Buffalo were the first to bring out large-format posters. The United States would occupy an eminent place in the beginnings of the color poster were it not for the execrable artistic quality of these plates. The English impresario Charles Cochran, writing in *The Poster* in 1898, has left a description of his first trip to New York: "Seven years ago, when I first visited America, I was struck with the horrors that looked down upon me from the hoardings. The huge theatrical

1. W. S. Rogers: *A Book of the Poster*. London: Greening & Co., 1901.
2. M. Bauwens et al: *Les Affiches Etrangères Illustrées*. Paris: G. Boudet, 1897.

posters, although beautifully printed, were entirely lacking in taste as regards design and color."

Charles Price, in his book *Posters*,[1] published in New York, confirms on all points Cochran's judgment: "Not only were the most fundamental principles of poster design as such ignored, but the principles of the design of any kind seem to have formed no part of these first essays in a new field. Interest in the art was entirely sacrificed to the interest in mechanical process."

American writers (Price, Bunner) give this phenomenon two sorts of explanation. The first is the very uncultivated level of the populace, which, although it readily marveled at images, had no sort of cultural or artistic tradition: the poster artists consequently went for crudity, using vulgar designs which enchanted their public, whether for shows or for products like medicines where the grossest trick—the "Before and After" ploy—was repeatedly used: Before taking the product the figure is old, sick, and dejected, while after taking it, he is youthful and dapper.

The second explanation, also very important, is that most American lithographers were German or of German ancestry, and their sole aim was to give a true likeness: to obtain a result that would be quasi-photographic.

La Forgue describes the treatment given to the designs of one of the first American artists to have been tempted to make a good graphic image. The lithographer would have none of it, because "He had brought back from Germany, his country of origin, preconceived notions according to which he set about subduing the values, effacing the contours, and finally giving the composition that flat and insignificant quality which, for him, was the supreme expression of art."

In the Eighties, the reaction came from the press, and it is they who instigated the development of quality posters in the United States. The periodicals which proliferated in this era acquired the habit of having their covers designed by artists, and then, logically, printing at the same time a poster, usually basically just a placard to be put in store windows at the point of sale to attract attention.

The first posters of this type date from 1889 when *St. Nicholas* and *The Century* commissioned the Englishman, Louis Rhead, to make their posters. *Harper's*, through its Paris correspondent, Mr. Child, addressed itself to Grasset, considered the artist least likely to shock the very puritanic American society. Chéret would have been too "risqué" (he did not appear on the walls of New York except accidentally in 1894 for the revival of *The Black Crook)*. Grasset made a number of posters and magazine covers for America. His "wooly horse" for the life of Napoleon in *The Century* was a major success and exerted a real influence on what was then, from the graphic point of view, virtually virgin territory.

The real trigger was given by *Harper's* which, starting from 1893, decided to bring out a poster every month, consigning this work to Edward Penfield.

Born in 1866, having studied at the Art Student's League of New York, Penfield was the first great American poster artist and the one whose talent is most original. Price reports that his inspiration did not come from French masters but that he took as his first models the Egyptian sarcophagi at the Metropolitan Museum: their colors in flat tones, with

115. Eugène Grasset: Bookstore poster for the 1897 Christmas issue of *Harper's*.

116. Edward Penfield: *The Northampton* bicycle. c. 1900.

1. Charles Matlack Price: *Posters*. New York: George W. Bricka. 1913.

117. Edward Penfield: *Harper's* for June, 1896.

118. Edward Penfield: *Harper's* for February, 1896.

strongly marked outlined, served as his point of departure. For six years Penfield, varying his images with the seasons, composed posters of a high graphic quality for *Harper's.* The often vivid colors are harmoniously distributed in flat tints, the figures, strongly outlined, are grouped in the foreground, the lettering is well integrated. His little scenes of high East Coast society, chic and athletic, are models of composition, at first glance a little stiff and emotionless but, in fact, full of little touches of humor. In the preface to *Posters in Miniature*[1] Penfield himself said: "We are a bit tired of the very serious nowadays, and a little frivolity is refreshing."

In his lithographic treatment, Penfield is close to Steinlen: in his sketches, the technique of the illustrator of *Gil Blas* reappears—but the analogy between the two artists, excepting their common love of cats, stops there. Aside from his production for *Harper's,* Penfield made some commercial posters, such as *Stearn's Bicycles* (1896), *Orient Cycles* (1895), and the *Northampton* (1900), of a power which has nothing to envy Lautrec, and several calendars *(Poster Calendar* 1897, *Golf Calendar* 1899, *Stencil Calendar* 1904, *Automobile Calendar* 1907). Penfield also later made trips where he took along his sketchbooks (Holland 1907, Spain 1911), subsequently publishing his impressions in book form. His style became that of an illustrator: softer colors, fewer flat tints, lighter outline.

The other major personality of the American poster of the Nineties was

1. Percival Pollard: *Posters in Miniature.* New York: R.H. Russell, 1897.

119. Edward Penfield: *Harper's* for June, 1897.

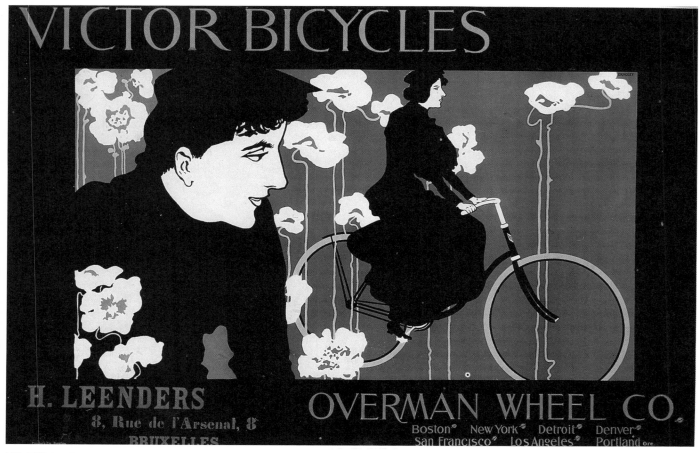

120. Will Bradley: *Victor Bicycles*. c. 1895.

Will Bradley, whom the *Saturday Evening Post* saluted as "the dean of American designers". Bradley was one of those artists who arouse controversy. He was often called "the American Beardsley," and it is true that the deformation of his figures and the use of black-and-white were probably discovered by him in the *Yellow Book* and the works of Beardsley. Yet La Forgue's[1] opinion still seems correct: "They have tried to reproach him with emulating Mr. Beardsley. We don't think this accusation is well founded. . . . where these two artists resemble one another is in having daringly broken with routine."

Born in Boston in 1868, having learned the printing trade, Bradley was from the age of 17 a designer at one of the biggest Chicago printers. Turning freelance, he received his decisive commissions in 1894: the covers of the *Inland Printer* and the seven posters for the *Chap Book* from 1894 to 1895. In this series he allowed free rein to his astonishing graphic compositions, playing with only three colors and, as a good disciple of William Morris, treating the lettering with exceptional care and talent. His work for *Ault and Wiborg* (for whom Lautrec would make a poster) and especially for *Victor Cycles* place him among the greatest

1. M. Bauwens et al: *Les Affiches Etrangères Illustrées*. Paris: G. Boudet, 1897.

poster artists of his time. Octave Uzanne in 1897 saluted him as "the most surprising and perhaps the best of the young American poster artists." After a brief fling at running his own magazine *(Bradley, His Book)* and a publishing house (Wayside Press), Bradley continued on a long career as writer, designer, art director and even filmmaker. He died in 1962 at 94.

Louis Rhead, who arrived in America in 1883 and was one of the pioneers of the illustrated magazine cover and the poster from 1889 to 1891, worked for *St. Nicholas, The Century,* and *Harper's.* His meeting with Grasset at his exhibition at the Salon des Cent in Paris in 1894 affected him profoundly, and upon his return to the United States, his numerous posters, notably for *The Sun* and *The Century,* show this influence.

Starting in 1894, the artistic poster—that is, the magazine poster—became the rage in America: "It seems that editions of posters surpass in number and in demand editions of the reviews themselves."

Poster collecting spread, competitions multiplied. That of the *Century* in 1895, opened in France for its special issue on *The Life of Napoleon,* has remained famous: the jury preferred Metivet's project to Lautrec's, who then had a hundred copies, very rare today, printed at his expense.

121. Will Bradley: Poster for the literary "little magazine," *The Chap Book.* 1895.

122. Louis Rhead: *Prang's Easter Publications.* 1896.

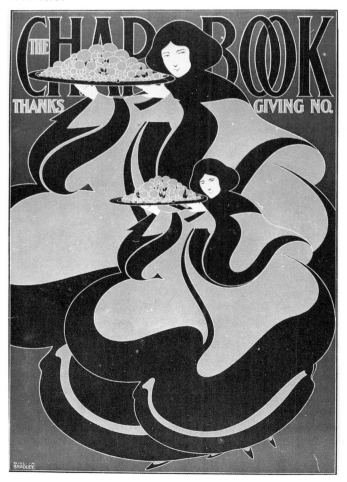

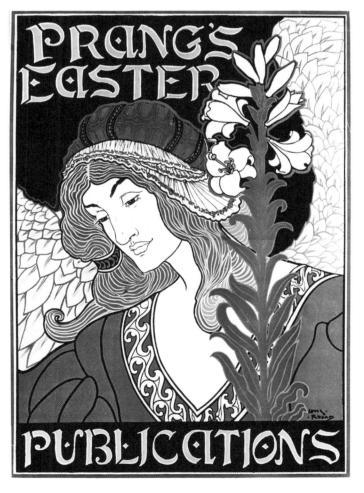

123. Will Bradley: Poster for his own magazine. 1896.

124. Ethel Reed: Book poster for Copeland & Day. 1896.

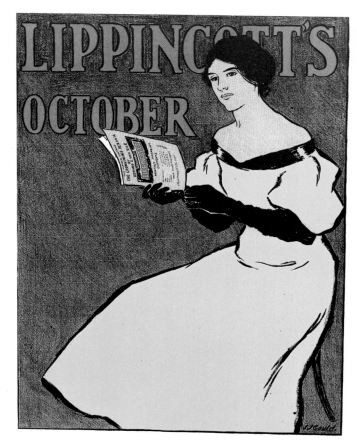

125. J. J. Gould: *Lippincott's* of October, 1896.

To the poster competition for Columbia Bicycles in 1896, 600 artists contributed designs. The winner was Maxfield Parrish.

Born in 1870, the son of a painter from Philadelphia, Parrish was in the Nineties a prolific illustrator for *Harper's* and *Scribner's*. We think however, with Price, that "one of his many characteristics is a love of detail (at the expense of the poster's efficiency) with quaintly elaborate, almost over-studied technique . . . it might be said that his work lacks strength through too much finesse and none of his posters could attract attention across the street." But certainly with one exception: his beautiful design for the Poster Show of 1896.

From then on poster artists were legion: Will Carqueville, who designed *Lippincott's* posters, is a less talented Penfield, like J.J. Gould; E.B. Bird, a great lover of clowns, is a lesser Bradley.

Frank Hazenplug used vividly outlined drawing and well organized space *(Chap Book)*. We can also mention Claude Fayette Bragdon and J.C. Leyendecker, and Brill who worked for the *Philadelphia Sunday Press*.

America can also flatter itself with having had women poster artists, who were not to be found at all in Europe at the time. Ethel Reed depicted woman, child, and flower admirably: well outlined, well composed, tastefully colored, painstakingly lettered, all these designs are of the highest level (*Penny Magazine, Copeland and Day, Miss Träumerei, Folly or Saintliness*). Blanche McManus had as well a talent of great originality. On the West Coast, *The Lark* of San Francisco attracted the somewhat more conventional talent of Florence Lundborg.

After 1900, when the fashion of artistic posters had passed, advertising art consolidated itself and new names appeared—the influence of Bradley disappeared to make way for that of the German school and notably of Ludwig Hohlwein.

There were the Leyendecker brothers, whose chic young people wear Arrow shirts and drive Pierce-Arrow automobiles; and R.J. Wildhack, who, according to Price, "eliminates detail but suggests its existence; he keeps his action at the front of the stage and grandly ignores the background."

Louis Fancher was very close to Hohlwein, and Adrian Gilspear was a disciple of Penfield. Let us also cite M.C. Perley, George Brehm and Adolf Treidler. By 1910, it could be said that a school of commercial graphic art existed in the United States. Only the theatrical poster, which had remained in the hands of specialist lithographic printers, was confined to total oblivion.

126. Maxfield Parrish: *The Century* magazine. 1897.

127. Elisha Brown Bird: *The Red Letter*. c. 1896.

Spain and Italy

The artistic poster did not arrive in Spain and Italy until the second half of the Nineties, in the baggage of Art Nouveau—"modernismo" in Spain, "Liberty" in Italy. Until then these two countries were distinguished only for posters for their characteristic public entertainments: the corrida in Spain, the opera in Italy. But if in Spain—or more precisely in Catalonia—advertising art was at the turn of the century only a brushfire, in Italy, on the contrary, thanks to shrewd backers like the department store Mele or Campari liquors, a brilliant school of graphics had been able to develop.

Spain

The first Spanish posters are posters for corridas, the oldest of which goes back to 1761 at Seville. At first they were typographical, then, according to an article in *The Poster*, illustrated with woodcuts after

129. Alexander De Riquer: Poster for a furniture and drapery store. 1899.

128. Miguel Utrillo: *Oracions*. c. 1899.

130. Joaquin Xaudaro: *Los Artistas Album*. c. 1897.

131. Anonymous: For a corrida in San Sebastian. 1887.

132. Alexandro De Riquer: Exhibition of the artists group *Circol de Sant Lluch*. 1899.

1785. In the nineteenth century Daniel Urrabieta Vierge achieved the best results from this technique. Lithography was used starting in 1830. It allowed specialists in the genre (Calandin, Canals, Cebrian, Esteban, Gandela, Narbona, Pastor, Perea, and the most talented of all, because he is the least garish, Unceta) to produce designs in large formats which, at the turn of the century, were vividly colored. The other posters for shows were nothing remarkable. After 1827 the posters of the Barcelona school saw, thanks to Joaquin Verdu, their formats enlarged and their lettering improved; but everything remained typographic. For the feast of Merced in 1877, the first chromolithographed poster was brought out. Nothing decisive, however, occurred before 1896-1897.

In 1896 the first large exhibition of posters, mainly French, was held in Barcelona. For the Fourth Exposition of Industrial Art, Pellicer, maker of official posters since 1888, and de Riquer were commissioned.

The next year, the cabaret *Les Quatre Gats,* Barcelona's version of the *Chat Noir,* opened its doors: the whole avant-garde, including Picasso, gathered there. De Riquer, Utrillo and Rusinol wrote about the poster for the review *Luz;* the first poster competition was launched. From then on for a dozen years competitions and exhibitions followed upon one another.

The "modernist" poster was essentially of French inspiration: its principal protagonists (Casas, de Riquer, Rusinol) had lived in Paris and had each found their models there.

Alexandro de Riquer was very much inspired by Grasset in his first posters: for the *Fabrica de Salchichon Juan Torres* or the *Granja avicola de San Luis,* the woman is in the foreground with free flowing hair, the outline is thick. Starting in 1897, his drawing became more refined, very likely in imitation of Mucha whose ornamental style and mosaic backgrounds he adopted (*Galletas Grau, Mosaicas de Escofet-Tejerat).* His few colors are harmonious and delicate.

Adria Gual (*Libra d'Ores, Teatro Lutrin),* like Santiago Rusinol, who designed only three posters, joined the influence of French Art Nouveau with that of the Americans.

Ramon Casas, the other great Catalan poster artist, found his influence largely in the artists of Montmartre on whose fringes he had lived. His synthetic approach often gets him compared to Steinlen or Lautrec, but we are of the opinion of Leon Deschamps who, in an article for *La Plume,* finds similarities with Ibels. His *Anis del Mono* or *Fuster* are good examples of them. His friend Miguel Utrillo, in his few posters, reflects his influence; his brother, Antonio Utrillo, the most prolific of Catalan artists, is of the same bent, like Joan Llaverias and Francesco de Cidon.

As in the rest of Europe, one also finds posters signed by caricaturists (Cornet, Xaudaro) and, for official expositions, the usual compositions, full of historical reminiscences and allegories, authored by Joan Llimona and Josep Friado.

Leon Deschamps notes in the Spanish poster "the accentuation of raw colors and too-pronounced gold." We see there an interesting phenomenon which leads the poster artists in Mediterranean countries, where the light is strong, to exaggerate colors. The same characteristic is found in Italian Liberty posters, beside which Grasset, Mucha, or Berthon seem pale.

133. Antonio Utrillo: Poster for the sales outlet of the *L'Art* printing shop.

134. Ramon Casas: Liqueur *Anis del Mono*. 1897.

135. Giovanni Mataloni: *Brevetto Auer* gaslight fixtures. 1895.

136. Adolfo Hohenstein: *Tosca.* 1899.

Italy

As Vittorio Picca notes in *The Modern Poster:*[1] "In Italy in the last century operas were the beneficiaries of poster advertising. They were usually ornamented with rococo decoration and sometimes engravings representing the principal characters."

Furthermore it is by means of the opera poster that we can follow the evolution of the beginnings of advertising art in Italy. The first lithographed poster was prepared by Rossetti for Gounod's *Faust* in 1863, but it is for Puccini's *Edgar* in 1889 that Hohenstein designed the first poster having true graphic qualities, although in a small format. His publisher Ricordi, known the world over for his opera scores, was the prime mover of the Liberty poster. Hohenstein turned up again in 1895 for *La Bohème* by Puccini: the image, much influenced by Chéret, occupied from then on the greater part of the design. In the same year the first commercial design worthy of the name was brought out by Mataloni for *Brevetto Auer:* "a beautiful nymph whose bare body is draped in a thin veil gives us a voluptuous smile wreathed by a radiant corona from the gas flame," as Picca describes it. And it was in 1895 that the first Venice Biennale took place and the review *Emporium,* mouthpiece of the Liberty movement, was founded. However it was not until three years later that the movement truly took off, with the first great posters by Hohenstein, the likes of which could soon be seen coming from Ricordi: Mataloni, Metlicovitz, Laskoff, Villa and Dudovich. While the artistic poster was dying in France, in Italy new talents, "like strong children who have suckled good milk and then overpowered their nurses" (as Crauzat exclaims a little emphatically in *L'Estampe et L'Affiche),* surpassed their Parisian masters.

Adolpho Hohenstein can stand as father to the Italian poster. Although he certainly had an eye on Mucha and, like him, loved large elongated formats, the similarity stops there. His figures were treated with impeccable photographic realism, and colored with a palette of dazzling richness which plays with the effects of light and shade. From the beginning, the boldness of his compositions left the French poster artists far behind. For the *Corriera della Sera,* in 1898, he depicted Hermes perched on a street lamp. His poster for the jeweler *A. Calderoni* showed the same inventiveness, with a woman examining a stunning decorative case. In the same year, his poster for the opera *Iris* was a pastel-toned vision, while in a poster for *Tosca,* in 1899, Hohenstein produced a masterpiece of composition, light and shade on a red background. With all the flamboyance and excess of the Italian temperament, he played with forms and colors: we can see it in the poster for *Monowatt* bulbs, an allegory with Apollo's chariot team in vivid blue, and in a poster for *Cintura Calliano,* a belt supposedly curing seasickness, in which Hohenstein showed a belted muscleman defying the sea. The virtuosity with which he makes his figures emerge from an overloaded frame reached its height in the posters for *Monaco,* whether publicizing trapshooting or motorboat races. The light – and the shade – of warm climates emerged from his rich yellows in posters for *Bitter Campari.* Hohenstein made so many posters that only a fraction can be mentioned, but they all have the same freedom, the same richness of invention in layout and in ingenuity of the lettering. Under his artistic direction at Ricordi, other major talents developed.

1. Arsène Alexandre et al.: *The Modern Poster.* New York: Scribner's, 1895.

137. Adolfo Hohenstein: Poster for safety matches. c. 1900.

138. Adolfo Hohenstein: The opera *Iris*. 1898.

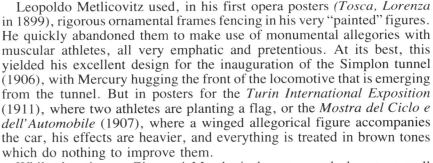

140. Leopoldo Metlicovitz: Poster for a Milan newspaper. c. 1900.

139. Leopoldo Metlicovitz: *Tosca*. 1899.

Leopoldo Metlicovitz used, in his first opera posters *(Tosca, Lorenza* in 1899), rigorous ornamental frames fencing in his very "painted" figures. He quickly abandoned them to make use of monumental allegories with muscular athletes, all very emphatic and pretentious. At its best, this yielded his excellent design for the inauguration of the Simplon tunnel (1906), with Mercury hugging the front of the locomotive that is emerging from the tunnel. But in posters for the *Turin International Exposition* (1911), where two athletes are planting a flag, or the *Mostra del Ciclo e dell'Automobile* (1907), where a winged allegorical figure accompanies the car, his effects are heavier, and everything is treated in brown tones which do nothing to improve them.

While the pioneer Giovanni Mataloni always stayed close to a well balanced Art Nouveau style *(La Tribuna,* 1897; *Festa di Cervara,* 1904), Franz Laskoff provided much more interest. He went to Beardsley and the Beggarstaffs for inspiration. His powerfully symbolic images are irreproachably laid out, with flat tones of color ignoring the outlines, like cutouts *(Saint-Petrus,* 1900; *Costina's Coffee* and *Suchard,* 1901). He plays like a virtuoso with black and white *(Musica e Musicisti,* 1902, *Caffaro),* and gives a wink to the Beggarstaffs in his *Noel de Pierrot,* where he puts their Hamlet back on stage!

Marcello Dudovich, a most prolific artist whose career was to be very long, began under several influences: Penfield *(Italia Ride),* Hohenstein *(Festi di Maggio),* Mucha *(Onoranze e Volta).* He rapidly found his own style, very graphic, with rich colors. *La Liquore Strega,* where a voluptuous woman leans over a glass, and *Zenit,* vehement object lessons in poster art, are two masterpieces. He specialized in mannered scenes where elegant men and women, treated in harmonious flat tones, drank Campari *(Cordial Campari,* 1913) or attended car races *(Corse di Brescia,* 1907). He naturally became the quasi-official poster-artist for Mele, the great fashion department store, where he could exercise his talent audaciously without fear.

Though he settled in France, Leonetto Cappiello honored some commissions in his native land. The most successful are *Livorno* and *Portofino-Kulm,* both of them travel posters.

The poster artists who worked beside these masters are legion: Villa, who also worked for Ricordi, very prolific but unable to reach their heights; Ballerio, very Art Nouveau; Beltrami; Bistolfi; Bompard; Mazza; and Terzi, who brings in animals (the monkey of *Dentol,* 1914), to mention the most important.

If the Italian artist Cappiello went to try his luck in Paris, the French-born Achille Mauzan, just out of the Lyons Beaux-Arts school, left for Italy. He settled in Turin, capital of the emerging Italian cinema, where, according to professor Menegazzi's research, he completed, between 1909 and 1913, the incredible number of 1500 posters printed in four or five identical colors in order to speed the work along. The whole panorama of passions and sentiments associated with silent movies are there to titillate. From 1912 on, he worked for Ricordi, and with one of their representatives started a business venture named "Clamor." This led to commercial advertising, such as posters for the Mele store, until the First World War broke out.

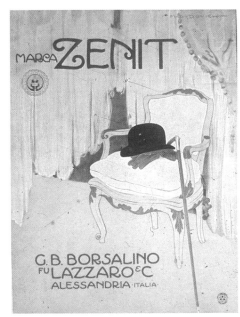

141. Leopoldo Metlicovitz: Opening of the Simplon Tunnel. 1906.

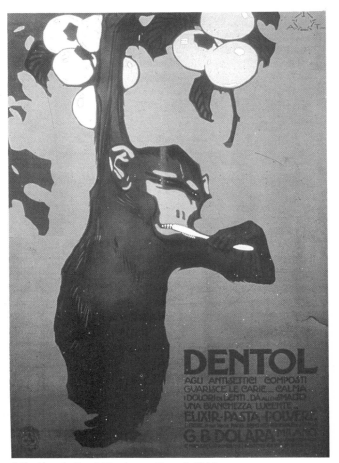

142. Aleardo Terzi: Toothpaste *Dentol.* 1914.

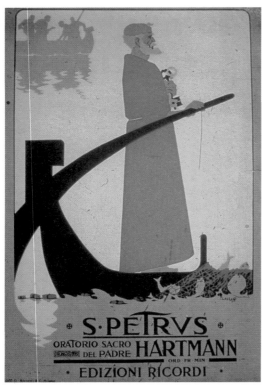

144. Franz Laskoff: For the *St. Peter* Oratorio. 1900.

145. Leonetto Cappiello: For the summer resort of *Livorno*. 1901.

146. Marcello Dudovich: *Strega*. 1905.

147. Marcello Dudovich: *Mele & Ci*. department store. c.1910.

148. Johan G. Van Caspel: Poster for a Dutch bicycle. 1896.

The Netherlands

The Dutch did not take up poster art until late, and then very gradually. According to the explanation of Dick Dooijes and Pieter Brattinga[1], quoted in *A History of the Dutch Poster,* this had to do with the configuration of Amsterdam and other Dutch cities: unlike Paris, London or Brussels, they had narrow streets, with their canals creating an urban design without grand boulevards. There was little space for the display of posters. They existed nevertheless, but until the 1890s they had no artistic merit whatever.

In 1890, an Amsterdam tea merchant, E. Brandsma, decided to hold a contest for the best poster, offering a number of attractive prizes. The winning entry was that of E.S. Witkamp and N. van der Waay. It was

1. Dooijes, D. & Brattinga, P. *A History of the Dutch Poster.* Amsterdam: Scheltema & Holkema, 1968.

149. Jan Toorop: *Delftsche Slaolie*
salad oil. 1895.

probably the first poster in that country to have combined artistic criteria with commercial ones. Not until three years later would the architect Nieuwenhuis design for the table oil *Delftshe Slaolie* a true poster, in which the bottles are depicted with care. The same year, another architect, Berlage, made a bizarre poster in the form of a stained-glass window, for *Tramwegmy.* Still, it wasn't until 1895 when another *Delftshe Slaolie* poster, by Toorop, finally let Dutch advertising art enter the international scene.

Born in Java, Jan Toorop was a part of the Art Nouveau movement from its beginning. He had been a member since 1885 of the Libre Esthétique in Brussels, where he showed his work. His style is a strange mixture where one finds the symbolist woman treated with the most fantastic exaggerations of style, with reminiscences of Indonesian marionettes in the figures. His two women preparing a salad lost in a tangle of crackling lines are a strange image to use to sell an oil. His design for *Het Hoogeland* was in the same vein. His style simplified with the years: *L'Assurance Arnhem* was much less encumbered; with the fisherman of *Katwijk am Zee* (1900), brilliant colors appeared, and in 1912, for the play *Pandorra,* there were geometric lines. In the year 1895, Braakensiek made the *Exposition Universelle* poster, which is only imitation Chéret (or even imitation Choubrac, to judge by the *Maandaghouders Review* of 1896).

Holland was still waiting for a real commercial poster artist, who was not long to appear, in the person of Jan Van Caspel. His style is very unadorned, and only the composition and the discreet outline evoke Art Nouveau *(Hinde Rywielen,* 1896; then the *Hollandsche Revue,* and the lithographer *Amand).* He is occasionally much more ornamental, and then he recalls the Belgian Crespin *(Cacao Caspar Flick)* or Grasset (in *Delicatesse Thee, Ivens Photo Artikelen).* His images remain well constructed. George Rueter worked in the same spirit.

As strange as that of Toorop is the poster of Johan Thorn Prikker for the semi-annual review *L'Art appliqué* (1896). Close to The Twenty of Brussels, and a great admirer of Flemish primitives, Prikker had an appreciation of line and robust ornament, which was best revealed in his poster for the Dutch Art Exhibition at Krefeld (1903). Another Dutch artist, Antoon Molkenboer, designed the very sober *Teekenschool Hendrick de Keijzer* in 1896, followed in 1897 with a poster for the bookbinder *Élias van Bommel.* In both cases the image is monochrome, and the text, in capitals, is grouped at the top and bottom, giving the impression of a woodcut. Still another master, Lion-Cachet, demonstrated a similar economy of means, using cut-outs and a rectangular layout in which he played with the smoke, in his design for *Boele* cigars.

Besides these original talents were naturally many lesser Chérets and lesser Muchas like Zon *(Delftsche Slaolie, Spiritus Gloelicht, Assurance Hollande).* Though original, van Konijnenburg's designs are more enlarged illustrations than real posters.

As in most countries at the turn of the century, business, which in following a fashion had been able to concern itself with producing images of an artistic quality, fell back into banal mediocrity. From then on only public events and exhibitions permitted artists to express themselves.

Roland-Holst, a mystic much involved in the symbolist and Rosicrucian movements, produced exceptional posters for the theater: "Roland-Holst has done more than produce artistic and effective posters, he has tried to

150. Theodorus M. A. A. Molkenboer.
Teekenschool Hendrick Keijzer. 1896

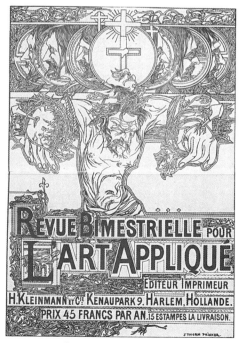

151. Johan Thorn-Prikker: The semi-annual magazine *L'Art Appliqué.* 1896.

152. Richard N. Roland Holst: Poster for the allegorical play *Lucifer*. 1910.

convert the poster into an authentic work of art; and in this enterprise he has come very close to the limits of the possible." He always used a fairly large format (about 80 x 120 cm). His lettering is well arranged above and below the image. He constructs his figures and decorative elements around the central axis of the page, making perfectly structured images (*Marsyas, Lucifer*, 1910).

A. Hahn was an artist of the same quality, but with a suppler, less rigorous approach *(Koloniale Tentoonstelling*, 1914; *Hamlet*, 1912; *N.V. Tooneelvereenigin*, 1912). His political involvement caused him to use his brush in the service of the socialists *(Stemt Rood)*. Immediately before and during the War, one finds images authored by C. Pol *(Entos)*, Diedenhoven, and Lebeau who will be mentioned further on. Quite unusual are Raemaekers and Van der Hem, working for the music halls, and, for commerce, J.W. Sluiter with his strongly outlined drawing.

Scandinavia

Sponsel and von zur Westen devote a chapter to Scandinavia: though nothing astonishing happened there, we will summarize the main lines of development.

In Sweden, the first posters which attracted the attention of art lovers appeared on the occasion of two exhibitions: in Malmö in 1896 and in Stockholm in 1897.

Most production was for the promotion of alcoholic beverages and showed a paradox: though at the time the most common beverage was punch, it was beer that had the most commercial backers and furnished artists with most of their subjects. The reason is very simple: beer had yet to take a place in Swedish gastronomy, so it was the object of especially dogged campaigns. Thus there was a whole guild of artists specializing

153. Koren Wiborg: Fishing industry exposition at Bergen. 1898.

154. Johann Vincenz Cissarz: *Germundsons* coffee. 1894.

155. Albert Engstrom: Poster for a Swedish students' choir performance at the Paris World's Fair of 1900.

156. N. Hansen: Tourist poster for *Vortland*. 1898.

in beer posters: E. Westman, Albert Engström, Gjögren, Ostberg. The posters show all sorts of figures sitting with relish before a mug of beer. The artists did not shy away from any association, however grotesque; from the coquette to the Buddha, every human category was represented.

Besides these posters with very commercial purposes, there were many designs for books which were very close to their French equivalents.

Above all, a little book called *Jul*, published specially for Christmas, gave artists the opportunity to prove their talents. Engström remains the best known of them.

Though the decline of poster art set in quite rapidly in Sweden, the Danish poster had a more lasting success. The initial conditions were far from favoring it: traditional painting was marked by a rational, sober style, and a tendency to depict simple scenes. The poster, at least at the beginning, had purely and simply followed this route: dull colors, bleak ambiance, total lack of affective or emotional connotation. The Danish poster failed in its advertising mission; one might say it even went contrary to it.

Another generation of artists had to arrive before this stylistic ponderousness was forgotten. These young people generally came from sectors that were close to pictorial art: ceramics and printing. They made their debuts by way of printing, by designing book covers. Their principal representatives were Gerhard Heilmann and Hans Tegner.

Even if these illustrations were especially successful, they were nonetheless Danish in the choice of motifs: nature, plants, and animals were the favorite subjects.

In Denmark as elsewhere, the necessity of following the French masters was felt. The artist who played the role of intermediary and launched the poster in his own country was Paul Fischer. The French example did not really influence the style of illustrations any more than the subjects that were treated: the Danish poster always lacked originality and piquancy, and generally the faculty of abstraction.

Unlike other European countries, Denmark produced no humorous posters, the feeling for caricature being stolidly absent. A single artist who makes an exception to the seriousness of his compatriots is Alfred Schmidt. His poster on Mark Twain is a good example of his comic vein. The most versatile of poster designers was Baldemar Undersen, who mastered the whole panoply of artistic effects without ever repeating himself.

No posters came from Norway, where evolution had stopped at the level of the illustrated magazine cover. The only poster known abroad was that of Koren Wiborg for the International Fishing Exposition in Bergen in 1898.

The rest of the Norwegian production is of inferior quality. Among book designs, there were certainly some works that are not without charm, but in a style that is traditional, scrupulous of detail. The Norwegians did not favor the production of commercial posters. Nonetheless, some names are preserved: Erik Mernskiold, Otto Sinding and Gerhard Munth. Edward Munch, the only Norwegian artist of international stature, illustrated programs for the Théatre Libre in Paris; most of his production in the graphic domain took place outside Norway.

Germany

Julius Meier-Graefe, in *Les Affiches Etrangères,* published in 1896, declared: "It is difficult to speak of the German poster because properly speaking, the poster as conceived in France does not exist . . . advertising in big cities makes use almost exclusively of newspapers." If advertising art in France was on the verge of decline, in Germany it was almost nonexistent. Writers of the time give several reasons for this: Jean-Louis Sponsel[1] blames it on the restrictions on poster-hanging and the few exterior spaces, notably the Litfass columns, which were reserved for exhibitions, tourism, and theatrical announcements. Commercial advertising had to be satisfied with small interior posters.

He also cites the redoubtable role of overconscientious German lithographers, which Dr. Hans Sachs[2] confirms, explaining very well why relations between art and industry were impossible at that time: "Here the old prejudices of the bourgeois against art and artists still reign. For the bourgeois manufacturer would no more think of having his products promoted by a 'flighty' artist (for a lithographer would certainly produce his message in a finer and more serious way) than an artist of this time would degrade his brush for such profane ends."

While the poster flourished in France, Germany was still ignorant of its elementary rules: advertisements were only dreary enlargements of art-school productions, resolutely historical, in the purest style of the Bavarian renaissance.

Speaking of the posters of the young Dopler, Meier-Graefe[3] judges them perfectly: "instead of simple decorative lines, a hodgepodge of trifles; instead of simple colors, tones like brown gravy." If Berlin at the time had no artistic past, Munich, a city with an old cultural tradition, was living through its Greek period: all its posters are neo-classic pastiches, like those of Nikolaus Gysis.

For these reasons, the artists who condescended to make a poster were careful to show that they knew how to paint, without taking the lithographic execution of their model into account at all, and never intervening in it. The only ones to do their work soundly from the point of view of the poster were the lithographers at the Friedlander printing firm in Hamburg. From 1872, like Strobridge in America, this house would provide admirable posters to the circus and music-halls for several generations.

The first poster worthy of the name did not appear until 1896 for an exposition in Dresden: *Die Alte Stadt* by Otto Fischer. For the first time the design is graphic, the colors vivid, the lettering skillfully distributed.

This vision of a woman in regional costume in the foreground, with the old town in the background, broke completely with the usual allegories. The same year, for the Berlin Industrial Exposition, Sutterlin drew a muscular hand brandishing a hammer. Although the art critic Meier-Graefe, who did not have much sympathy for the Berliners, carped that "in that brutal execution, of coloring as well as of line, the Berlin coarseness finds it expression," still there had been definite progress.

This poster served as a pretext to the young Edmund Edel for a pastiche where his representation of the Barrison Sisters created an uproar: things were beginning to move!

1. Jean Louis Sponsel: *Das Moderne Plakat.* Dresden: Gerhard Kühtmann, 1897.
2. In *Gebrauchsgrafik.*
3. M. Bauwens et al.: *op. cit.*

157. Nikolaus Gysis: Art exhibition in Munich. 1888.

158. L. Sutterlin: Industrial fair at Berlin. 1896.

159. Otto Fischer: An arts and crafts show at Dresden. 1896.

160. Johann Vincenz Cissarz: Poster for a laundry powder. 1898.

161. Franz von Stuck: *Secession* art exhibit at Munich. 1893.

München
Ausstellung im Alten National
Museum · Maximilianstr. 36 Juni Oktob.
Kunst im Handwerk

162. Bruno Paul:
Exhibition *Art in Crafts* in
Munich. 1901.

164. Thomas Theodor Heine: Humor magazine *Simplicissimus.* 1897.

163. Thomas Theodor Heine: Poster for a Berlin ink manufacturer. 1896.

The best posters of this period were made by Johann Vincenz Cissarz in Stuttgart, Franz von Stuck in Munich ("Despite his pronounced hellenistic tendencies, his poster *Kunstausstellung Secession,* is the best one produced so far—it is impressive," wrote Julius Meier-Graefe[1]), and Hans Unger in Dresden.

In 1896, Fritz Rehm won the competition of Kenner cigarettes with a project that was resolutely modern. The same year, also in Munich, the publisher Albert Langen, who regularly used avant-garde designers for his book covers, founded *Simplicissimus. Jugend* (which gave its name to *Jugendstil)* also appeared, following Berlin's *Pan* by a year. These reviews, like their later counterparts, the *Berliner Tageblatt* (Lilien) and *Die Insel* (Weiss), employed a constellation of artists, and it is from their covers that the posters of Joseph Sattler for *Pan,* Fritz Dannenberg and Zumbusch for *Jugend* and Heine for *Simplicissimus* came. From this prestigious team, which also includes Bruno Paul, Albert Weisgerber, Christiansen, Angelo Jank, F. Von Reznicek, Olaf Gulbransson, and Edward Thony, one artist—Thomas Theodore Heine—emerged as the "German Lautrec."

Son of a Leipzig chemist, Heine started from Düsseldorf on the artistic studies he eventually consummated in Munich. He was a caricaturist of genius, one of the offspring of Daumier, but his talent was protean: he was also painting at the time in the purest impressionist style. In his first two posters for *Simplicissimus* (the bulldog, the woman with Devil) he came up with absolutely new images, inspired by the French poster and its Japanese sources: colors in flat tones, vigorous outlines, bold composition. In 1896, in Berlin, he tried the Beggarstaff Brothers' ploy, offering various nameless products to manufacturers. He was more successful than they—one of his designs, a devil dipping his pen in an overturned inkwell,

1. M. Bauwens et al.: *op. cit.*

165. Ernst Neumann: Motor boat show in Berlin. 1910.

was bought by Zeiss & Co. For the rest, his production is feeble, but each of his designs has its importance: his posters for *Simplicissimus* are of shocking boldness in a country where all political posters were forbidden. His poster for *Die 11 Scharfrichter (Eleven Henchmen)* cabaret launched the Munich equivalent of the *Chat Noir.* His poster for the Berlin Secession of 1901 was reissued for years.

In 1905, for the Berlin Art Exposition, he overtly mocked the Kaiser who had fulminated against "gutter art:" he pictured a lady whose flowers were wilting while a poor woman gathered fresh ones in the gutter. It was worth a few censorship problems for him. And, finally, for *Zust Automobiles,* he again used the bulldog.

Heine's role as artistic director of *Simplicissimus* and his insolence in jarring the established order made him a key figure. He was surrounded, in Munich, by other remarkable talents: Bruno Paul *(Kunst im Handwerk,* 1901, and *Die 11 Scharfrichter),* Albert Weisgerber *(Der Bunte Vogel, Garlachs Jungendbücherei)* and Ernst Neumann, whose few posters are very boldly composed: *Die 11 Scharfrichter* and especially *Sosa Tennis Balls* (1908), or the *Motorboot und Motoren Ausstellung* (1910). The caricaturists Olaf Gulbransson *(Conrad Dreher)* and Emil Preetorius *(Licht und Schatten)* were also good occasional poster artists.

However, these artists lacked the support of merchants and manufacturers. Without their commissions, the poster, after six or seven years, withered to a marginal outlet, with the artists depending on special events or expositions in order to express themselves.

As Von zur Westen[1] notes, the poster in Munich retained an essentially artistic character and had no intrinsic advertising value.

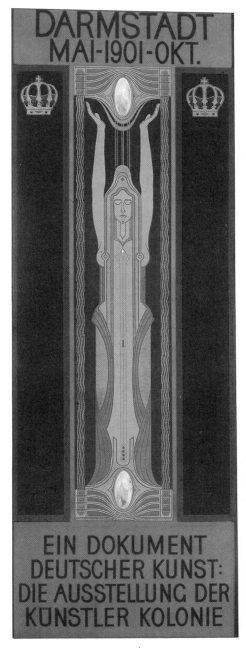

166. Peter Behrens: An art exhibition at Darmstadt. 1901.

1. Walter von zur Westen: *op. cit.*

167. Olaf Gulbransson: *Conrad Dreher*. 1912.

168. Albert Weisberger: *Der bunte Vogel*, a Munich bohemian cafe. 1911.

It was in Berlin, the city of commerce, that posters first appeared as vehicles with a concrete advertising aim. The movement developed out of the Hollerbaum and Schmidt printing house, under the remarkable direction of Ernest Growald, who finally put artists and merchants in direct contact while maintaining a high artistic quality. He brought together Edmund Edel, Lucian Bernhard, Julius Klinger, Paul Scheurich, Julius Gipkens, Ernst Deutsch and Hans Rudi Erdt. The Steglitz Studio, created in 1900 by Ehmcke and Kleukens, also worked toward this same end.

Edmund Edel, who had been through the Academie Julian in Paris, adapted the French style to his posters, adding that grain of insolence so dear to Berliners. Painter of the common life, Edel, who called himself "Berlin's jester," drew his typical characters in the service of brandy and bouillon-cube makers. Every year on New Year's Eve, the city watched for his poster for the *Morgenpost*. His production for the theater was also considerable.

But Lucian Bernhard was the first to break with Chéret and open new paths for the advertising poster, with *Priester* matches (1906) and *Stiller* shoes (1908). For the object on display, presented most often by a supercilious young woman, he substituted a simple picture of the object on sale with a text, also reduced to its simplest expression: usually just the trade name. His "Sach Plakat" (Object Poster) brought a true revolution to advertising and overturned established ideas. This new approach required an absolute mastery of drawing, of stylization, and of composition. Bernhard added to this the science of color and an unusual talent as a typographer (some of his designs are exclusively typographical). For *Manoli* cigarettes, *Hag* coffee, or *Adler* typewriters, he made sober and powerful images that stop the eye, yielding a strong and direct message.

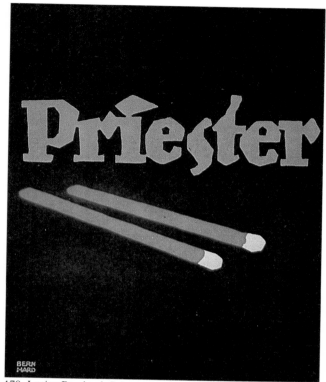

169. Edmund Edel: Travel magazine *Die weite Welt*.
1900.

170. Lucian Bernhard: *Priester* matches. 1906.

171. Lucian Bernhard:
Stiller Shoes. c. 1904.

Bernhard's system suffered, as Ervine Metzl[1] notes, from the small format of German posters (especially when his love of typography led him to overload them). Hellmut Rademacher[2] found another defect in the style in that, once generalized, it led to repetition and monotony and, eventually, the indifference of the passer-by.

The "Sach Plakat" was in fact quickly adopted by a constellation of less talented followers, such as Joelo and Ludke. It also influenced great poster artists like Hans Rudi Erdt and Julius Gipkens.

Hans Rudi Erdt, transplanted from Munich where he had studied, had a vigorous graphic style. He played with flat tints of color and had a profound sense for stylization. For Hollerbaum and Schmidt, he made several object posters *(Manoli, Nivea, Die Woche)*. Happily, his talent did not stop there: a painter of modern life, he was particularly at ease with *Opel* automobiles or sporting posters. For *Problem* cigarettes, where he plays with smoke rings, he is equally excellent.

Julius Gipkens, a self-taught artist from Hanover, also deeply felt the influence of Bernhard. His drawing is less emphatic, more sensitive, his colors more delicate, and his compositions are generally weaker: the

1. Ervine Metzl: *The Poster: Its History and Its Art*. New York: Watson-Guptill, 1963.
2. Hellmut Rademacher: *Das Deutsche Plakat von den Anfangen bis zur Gegenwart*. Dresden: VEB Verlag der Kunst, 1965.

172. Lucian Bernhard: *Steinway & Sons*. 1910.

173. Hans Rudi Erdt: A fair to promote tourism. 1911.

Kaiser briquets, *Pneumatik Continental,* and *The Chat Noir* are brilliant exceptions.

With Julius Klinger, who came from Vienna to setttle in Berlin, we approach a true genius of the poster, whose every placard is delectable in containing a new discovery, a trick of art that enraptures the eye. Never vulgar, always amusing, with the elegance of the Viennese, he is inimitable and unimitated: his line seems facile, it flows so naturally, but it is absolutely precise. His colors and layouts are in perfect balance: The *Lustige Blätter,* the *Palm Cigarren,* the *Turkishes Fest* and the *Hollerbaum & Schmidt* posters are delectable. He could also come up with stunning modernistic designs for *Admiral Palast* and the *Berliner Theater Taitun.*

Paul Scheurich also had an original talent. He presents his figures artfully, playing with the small detail that, in the midst of his broadly distributed flat tints, creates atmosphere. He may humorously jam together

174. Julius Gipkens: *Kaiser* briquettes. 1913.

fat revelers to sell beer, or, for *Doyen* cigarettes, come up with a slender aristocrat. His poster for the printer *Hollerbaum & Schmidt* is a model of economy of means.

From 1905 until the war, Berlin poster artists were legion.

Ernst Deutsch (who later changed his name to Dryden and worked as a set designer in Hollywood) came from Vienna; he was the painter of the elegant life. His series for *Richard's Grill* was a kaleidoscope of chic Berlin. He could find audacious compositions *(Tanz Turnier)* and, sometimes, play with color *(Salamander Shoes).* Fritz Rumpf favored the same subjects.

Knut Hansen, of Danish origin, was an elegant poster artist. He was the only one in Berlin not to break away from a very marked French influence. Hans Lindenstaedt, like Louis Oppenheim, can be compared to Erdt and to Gipkens.

Let us finally mention two typically Berliner poster artists: Haase, with his popular humor, and Jo Steiner (though of Viennese origin) who started a veritable portrait gallery of stars of the Berlin cabarets *(Bier Cabaret, Linden Cabaret),* which he continued after the war. His caricatures are

175. Julius Klinger: A gala at the Admiralspalast dancehall. 1913.

176. Julius Klinger:
Palm Cigarren. 1906.

177. Paul Scheurich: *Broyhan* beer. 1911.

178. Ernst Deutsch: Poster for a dance contest. 1914.

179. Knut Hansen: Variety show at the *Jungbrunnen* cabaret. c. 1900.

not lacking in boldness: he did not hesitate to use the primary colors of expressionism.

While Bernhard triumphed in Berlin, Munich produced the greatest and most prolific German poster artist: Ludwig Hohlwein. Born in Wiesbaden in 1874, Hohlwein attended Munich Technical School, where he became an architect. He quickly abandoned this discipline to devote himself to posters. He was athletic, an excellent horseman, fond of nature and hunting—it is only natural that he should have designed the poster for the *Ausstellung für Jagd und Schiesswesen* (Hunting and Shooting Exhibition) in 1906. It was followed by an order from the sporting-goods store *Hermann Scherrer* which set him on his poster career. Beginning with his first efforts, Hohlwein found his style with disconcerting facility; it would vary little for the next forty years. The drawing was perfect from the start: if he was particularly at ease with animals, horsemen, or hunters, still nothing seemed alien to him, and in any case, nothing posed a problem for him.

His composition was simple and rigorous: one, two figures at the most, placed in the foreground against a uniform background to make them

180. Ludwig Hohlwein: *Hermann Scherrer*. 1907.

181. Ludwig Hohlwein: *Wilhelm Mozer*. 1909.

stand out. Hohlwein, who had no doubt seen the experiments of the Beggarstaff Brothers, used colors in flat tones, seldom outlined. But, unlike the Englishmen, he paints images that are not flat.

His figures are full of touches of color and a play of light and shade that brings them out of their background and gives them substance. If he amused himself at the beginning with a technique of decoupage (*P.K.Z., Gebrüder Wollweber*), he was above all interested in movement and mass: his use of shadows for the horse of the *Hermann Scherrer* riding lady is exemplary. His sense of color and composition is as perfect as it appears obvious. If his still-life with a lobster for the *Wilhelm Mozer* delicatessen is compared to similar efforts by Gipkens or Paul Leni or even the Swiss Otto Baumberger, his superiority leaps from the design. He treated every subject proposed him with the same ease: be it for a show (*Kitty Starling*), coffee *(Hag)*, or tea *(Marco-Polo)*; he used Chinese, Japanese or African images he retained from his memories of travel. He amuses himself for *Stiller Schuhe*, making an object poster that by its composition, colors,

182. Ludwig Hohlwein: An object poster for *Carl Stiller Jr.* shoes. 1910.

183. Ludwig Hohlwein: *Marco Polo* tea. 1913.

184. Ludwig Hohlwein: *Panther* shoes. c. 1913.

and the flowers he adds, softens the cold ruggedness of Lucian Bernhard's masterpiece on the same theme. If he cannot be connected to any school and left no disciple himself, Hohlwein still left his mark on a whole generation in Germany, of course, but also abroad, especially in England.

McKnight-Kauffer reports in Austin Cooper's[1] book: "The liveliest memory I have of a visit to Munich in 1908 is of one of Hohlwein's first posters on the walls, a silhouette in grey on white."

Next to this giant, and perhaps to counterbalance his omnipotence, six artists formed, before 1914, a group calling itself simply Die Sechs (The Six): Franz-Paul Glass, F. Heubner, Carl Moos, Emil Preetorius, M. Schwarzer and Walentin Zietara. For a fixed price they all prepared a design for the client, leaving the choice up to him.

Carl Moos was the specialist in sports and fashion. Like Hohlwein, he plays with light and shade, and uses flat colors without outlines with mastery. Glass, Schwarzer, and Heubner were young artists who foreshadowed the mannerism of the Twenties. Zietara was the humorist of the group.

Walter Schnackenberg made his debut both with sophisticated images and scenes of a decadent morbidity *(Odéon Casino)*. Pirchan exemplifies great modernity in his compositions and his flat tints *(Ruby Betteley)*.

Talents appeared everywhere: Erich Grüner in Leipzig, Mayer in Col-

1. Austin Cooper: *Making a Poster*. London: The Studio, 1938.

Innenplakat   Odeon-Casino

185. Walter Schnackenberg: *Odeon Casino*. 1912.

186. Seché (Joseph Sechehaye): *Wiener Cafe*. c. 1920.

ogne, Sigrist in Stuttgart, Hellmuth Eichrodt in Karlsruhe, to name only
a few. The movement found itself greatly encouraged by the creation, in
1907, of Deutsches Werkbund (German Work Guild) by the architect
Muthesuis, theoretician of "objectivity". On the pedagogic level as well
as in relations with industry, it was of great service to advertising art.

Peter Behrens, who was given charge of architecture and design at the
big industrial giant A.E.G., was one of the first to put into practice these
principles which the Bauhaus later systematized after World War I.

At the threshold of the war, when France had only Cappiello, Germany
swarmed with graphic artists who asked only to express themselves.

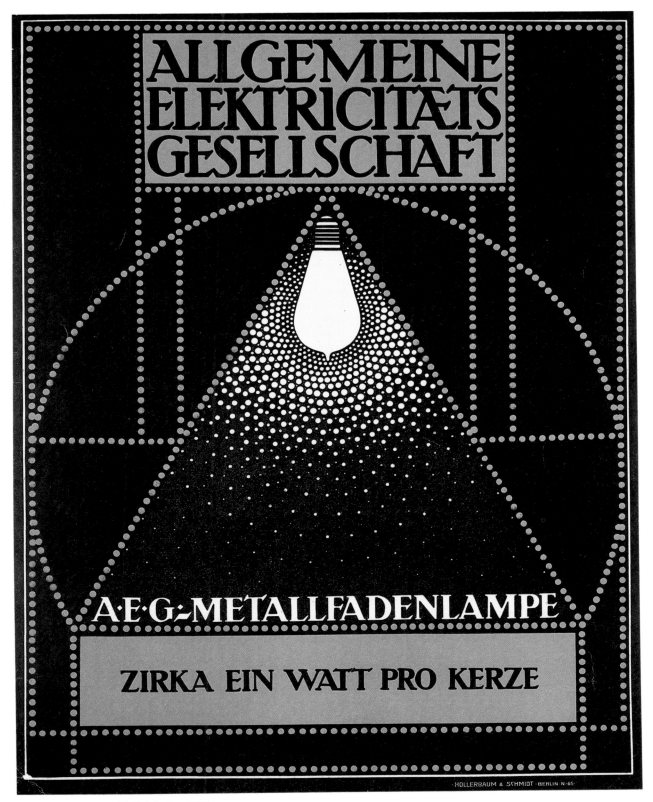

187. Peter Behrens: *AEG* lightbulbs. 1907.

189. Heinrich Lefler: *Auer Licht*. c. 1895.

Austria

The artistic poster was even slower to develop in Austria-Hungary than in Germany, since most of its best talents were exiled (Klinger, Deutsch, Orlik, Jo Steiner). The situation in Vienna in the 1890's was particularly depressing[1]: the Weiner printing house, a gigantic lithographic firm, had literally monopolized the market for outdoor advertising, usually using its own designers. The results, such as *Die Türken vor Wien,* in 1883, for example, are uninteresting: composition crowded with detail, maladroit drawing. They are even worse with Johann Hoff's *Malzextract,* a tawdry affair without any suspicion of artistic merit. The few artists who signed their work were also quite mediocre: Hans Schliessmann, a caricaturist on the *Fliegende Blätter,* generally ignores any rules of composition. The others provided fairly coarse imitations of French posters: Emil Ranzenhofer copied Chéret *(Apollo)* or Art Nouveau *(Lurion* Coffee). Copying comes close to plagiarism when Docker, in 1899, remade a Privat-Livemont for the bulb manufacturer *Ideal Glühlampen-Unternehmung.*

The first artist who deserves to be called a poster artist was Heinrich Lefler. Taking his inspiration from the pre-Raphaelites, from Grasset and from Boutet de Monvel, he made a poster for *Auer Licht* lamps in 1895. The same graphic qualities, in a soberer style, can be found in J.M. Auchentaller *(Styria Fahrräder* Cycles, 1899, *Ansichtskarten Loterie,* 1910). The accidental participation of expatriated talents aside (Klinger: *III. Automobile Ausstellung, Frühlingsschau,* 1914; Orlik: *Parfumerie Gottlieb-Taussig),* commercial advertising remained poor.

Quite the opposite was the movement of an elite which, from 1898 to the war, created a collection of stunning experiments for its own exhibitions and some theatrical shows.

1. As seen in the exhibition "The Diary of the Street" at the Wiener Rathaus, Vienna, 1981.

188. Gustav Klimt: The first art show of the *Secession* group. 1901.

Calling itself The Secession, this group came into being in 1898, composed of the circle of the architect Otto Wagner, the Group of Seven (the architects Hoffmann, Olbrich, and Pilz, and the painters Kainradl, Karpellus, Kurzweil and Koloman Moser), and of dissidents of the Fine Arts Academy (Künstlerhaus) grouped around Gustav Klimt. The Secession had for its mouthpiece the review *Ver Sacrum*.

This hotbed of artists, taking up the ideas of William Morris and the Arts and Crafts movement, took over the renewal of the decorative arts by defying the traditional hierarchy of fine art. Under the direction of Josef Hoffmann and Koloman Moser, the group opened its so-called Viennese Workshop ("Wiener Werkstätte"). In these years of wild creative intensity, where exhibitions followed one upon another, making the world's avant-garde flock to Vienna, architects and painters found every pretext to try their hand at posters.

Klimt took the first Secession Exhibition poster upon himself: Athena watching the combat of Theseus with the Minotaur, symbol of the struggle between classic and modern; Joseph Maria Olbrich, for the next, made an architect's drawing of the Secession premises, which he had also designed. The works of Koloman Moser followed: in 1899, it was another winged pre-Raphaelite divinity, treated in only three colors with exhuberant virtuosity; but in 1902, his stylization of three women's faces was as complete as it was characteristic, with lettering ornamented to the limit of legibility. This rigor, this elaboration of the decorative motif were pushed to an extreme by Josef Hoffmann in his two posters for the Wiener Werkstatte in 1902 and 1905; and they turned up again in works by Ferdinand Andri, Mangold and Alfred Roller.

It appears that the artists wanted to vie with each other in virtuosity; the poster *Kunst im Hause* of 1905, by Leopold Forstner, is almost illegible. On the other hand, the poster for the 1908 *Kunstschau* (Exhibition) by

192. Koloman Moser: Exhibition No. 13 for the *Secession*. 1902.

190. Ferdinand Andri: The 26th art show of the *Secession*. 1904.

191. Alfred Roller: The 16th *Secession* exhibition. 1903.

193. Viktor Schufinsky: *Cabaret Lucifer*. c 1904.

194. Alfred Roller: *Secession* show No. 14. 1902.

195. Oskar Kokoschka: Poster for a Viennese art show. 1908.

196. Koloman Moser:
Frommes Kalender. 1899.

197. Egon Schiele: *Secession* exhibition No. 49. 1918.

198. Arpad Basch: Agricultural machinery factory *Kühne E.* 1900.

199. Václav Oliva: Art gallery *Topičuv Salon.*

Löffler, a flat profile in vivid colors, richly outlined, is of stunning modernism. At this exhibition, Löffler presented a poster section that included works by Delavilla, Forstner, Kalvach, Klinger, Kokoshka, Lange, Moser, Schufinsky and Wimmer. He scored again in 1909 with, this time, an image that was almost abstract.

Viktor Schufinsky's poster for the cabaret *Lucifer* is of a rare force and economy of means: the devil, a red mass compressed at the bottom of the poster, carries on his shoulders a radiant young Grace whose body is entirely formed from the blank white paper. Oskar Kokoshka, for the *Kunstschau* of 1908, showed a young girl in a garden: colors in flat tones, partially outlined, on a vegetal background already on the verge of abstraction. And finally, in 1918, just before his death, Egon Schiele made the famous *Secession Ausstellung* poster.

It is obviously impossible to list all these posters which, due to their originality of conception and richness of execution, all have a special interest: from the early very pre-Raphaelite designs to those just before the war which bordered on abstration—the Viennese artists tried all styles.

However, these perfectly elitist posters remain documents more precious for the history of art than for that of advertising. As remarkable as the graphic feats were, they often made the lettering barely legible and had no perceptible impact on commerce or industry.

Vienna did not produce all the graphic creation in the old Empire. Hungary also had a solid school of poster artists, influenced by Paris: Arpad Basch and Geza Faragoy had both encountered Mucha and moved in his wake. Behind them arrived Michael Biro, Robert Bereny and Marcel Vertes who would find their expression on the political scene.

In Prague the first poster worthy of the name was that of Hynais for the *Ethnographic Exposition of 1895*. It was from this city that Emil Orlik set out to conquer Vienna and Munich. The avant-garde, united in the "Manes" union of artists, produced some good posters: for his own exhibit at the art gallery Topičuv Salon, for example, Vaclav Oliva created a fine composition praised by Von zur Westen, which was reproduced with another of his works, *Zlatá Praha*, in *Les Maîtres de l'Affiche*.

200. Arnošt Hofbauer: Another poster for *Topičuv Salon.* 1898.

119

201. Emile Cardinaux:
Zermatt. 1908.

Switzerland

Until the very end of the century it was Paris where all young Swiss artists came looking for success, often making a substantial contribution to the development of the poster. Grasset, who came from Lausanne to settle in Paris in 1871, was one of the founding fathers and the main theoretician of Art Nouveau. Steinlen joined him 10 years later, in 1881, and became, with Lautrec, the greatest Montmartre poster artist. Vallotton, who was only an occasional poster maker, produced his best woodcuts in Paris.

During this time nothing notable happened in Switzerland: the poster for the Swiss National Exposition of 1883 was chosen in a competition that was won by Albert Lüthi—a design with a pastiche of a sixteenth-century stained-glass window. Here, as almost everywhere, art had not yet emerged from classicism. The first attempts of Hans Sandreuter, disciple of Böcklin, in Basel, starting in 1889, remained paintings reproduced by a lithographer.

202. Robert Hardmeyer: Laundry firm *Waschanstalt Zürich A.G.* 1905.

203. Emile Cardinaux: Agricultural fair at Bern. 1914.

204. Burkhard Mangold: *Winter in Davos.* 1914.

It was Ferdinand Hodler who, starting in 1891, overturned traditional ideas with the posters for his exhibitions and some commercial works *(Olli oil)*. His stylized rigor, his monumental figures, the pure colors he uses – these are all new elements in the Swiss posters. His subsequent consecration in Vienna *(Secession;* Exhibition of 1904) gave him a prestige that allowed him to open a breach in Helvetic conformism.

Poster displays being still totally anarchic, the first productions worthy of interest are to be found in advertising cards, called "monocards," invented by Karl Bührer. They introduced the public to the designs of Cardinaux, Hardmeyer (his famous rooster), Hohlwein, Mangold, Moos, Schupp and Streffel. After the failure of monocards, Bührer interested himself in posters. The result was a single format, definitively instituted in 1914, which takes as its base of calculation the diagonal of the centimeter: for a standard poster, the "world format" became 90.5 x 128 centimeters. Despite its name it never passed the frontiers of the Swiss Confederation where, scrupulously applied, it remains the model of neat and well organized poster display.

Hodler's artistic principles were taken up by one of his disciples, Emile Cardinaux, who designed his famous *Zermatt* (Matterhorn) for a 1906 monocard that was made into a poster in 1908. For the first time a graphic approach was taken to the problem posed by the poster. Cardinaux, who had learned lithography in Munich, produced functional designs in keeping with the limits of the technique he was utilizing: the colors are simplified, the layout and composition firm, the lettering arranged at the bottom. The Swiss poster can be said to have been born with the creation of the *Zermatt.*

Cardinaux had the luck to find a peerless printer, Wolfensberger, to render his compositions. Wolfensberger, who all his life brought together talents of the first order, was to play an essential role in the spread of the Swiss poster throughout the world.

When the first visual shock of *Zermatt* had passed, Cardinaux provoked a veritable uproar for the Swiss Exposition of 1914: his design, which had been awarded a prize by a jury that included Hodler, represented a horseman—yellow like the flag he brandished—mounted on a green horse. The public—Swiss or foreign—jarred in its habits, selected another poster, more tame and touristic, to be printed.

The other poster artists working in Switzerland at the time had only a mediocre, local talent: there was Sandreuter in Basel; Eduard Stiefel in Zurich; and in Geneva, there were Marguerite Burnas-Provins, Band and Forestier, gathered in the "Swiss Society For Artistic Posters", which despite its name accomplished nothing remarkable.

Starting in 1910, new talents appeared. In Basel, it was Burkhard Mangold, who in his beginnings was still close to the painting of his fellow townsman Sandreuter, and who had a sense for layout that made him a good poster maker: his figures are in the foreground against a background that makes them stand out *(4 Jahreszeiten,* 1912). With *Winter in Davos* in 1914, his audacious and dynamic composition, his flat colors and subtle outlines, Mangold became a thorough graphic artist. Like him, the young Otto Baumberger, who made his first posters in 1911, opted for a resolutely graphic and modern style.

On the verge of the War, Switzerland, with its standardized public posting, its fine lithographers and a promising younger generation, stood ready to occupy a place of first importance in the world.

Japan

Japanese engraving having influenced all European poster making, it was to be expected, inevitably, that works like *Les Affiches Etrangères* and *Das Moderne Plakat* should devote chapters to Japanese advertising art. As both of them reproduce designs of Kabuki actors – which are more prints than posters – they tell us nothing specific. The information that T. Hayashi gives us in *Les Affiches Etrangères* is in the realm of legend: "One day, centuries ago, a Buddhist priest, on the pretext of saving the people from the contagion of an epidemic disease, glued to all the houses the image of a patron saint on which he had written the name of his temple. He invited the population to visit the sanctuary, the better to protect itself. At the same time, the pediment of the entrance accorded the holy image the honor of its hospitality. The good example given by the compassionate priest was quickly followed by other people on the pretext of showing their gratitude and making vows to the savior. Profiting from the fact that in temples inscriptions in the way of supplication were tolerated, a manufacturer posted cards bearing his name and commercial qualifications. This ingenious system of making oneself known found its imitators, and little by little they replaced the equivocal practice with a frank and attractive one."

In fact the poster appeared in the eighteenth century in the Edo period (the old name for Tokyo). Residence of the Shogun, Edo was populated with Samurai (knights without any other cause to defend) and with Shonins (energetic merchants and artisans).

At the time, this city had the largest population in the world, and changes of residence were rigorously regulated. Information reached people by newspapers printed from woodblocks *(Yomiuri),* posted on walls like posters. The two most popular spectacles, the Kabuki theater and Sumo matches, were the first to really use exterior advertising.

For the Kabuki, polychrome wood-engravings were printed—these were the images that overturned the canons of occidental art when they were imported to Europe. These engravings, picturing the principal actors, were sold as art but, accompanied by a text, also used as posters. For Sumo matches, their promoters posted the "banzuke," which gave the hierarchic list of wrestlers and their portraits. This system, uniting text and image, was used for all sorts of purposes. Beginning at this time, one finds artists specializing in the genre, like Tokokuni Utagawa, from whom came a poster for the large store *Echigo-Ya* (which later became Mitsukoshi) dated 1818, and many Sumo posters from around 1830. After 1860, the principal artist was Yoshiki Ikkesai.

These posters were hung at the crossroads *(tsuji),* and later, in the public squares *(hirokoji).* Above all, they were found at the meeting-places favored by the Japanese where they could be hung without censorship: in the public baths and at the hairdressers.

In 1868 the Shogun was deposed, and, entering the Meiji era, Japan opened itself to the West. Industry and commerce developed, and posters proliferated – for tobacco, beer, and the most diverse medicines. The posters *(nishiki-e)* were still polychrome wood-engravings, the results of a joint effort by designers, engravers, and printers. Other advertising objects were distributed, such as the *Uziwa,* advertising fans, or saki bowls given away by restaurants.

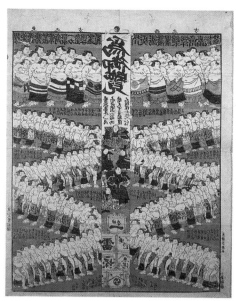

205. Yoshiki Ikkeisai: A "banzuke" for a sumo event. 1859.

207. Anonymous: Poster for a clothing store.

206. Anonymous: For *White Snow* toothpaste. 1890.

At the end of the 1870's, lithography was introduced into Japan, allowing the first poster to be printed, at the beginning of the 80's, by the tobacco-merchant Fuchigami-Ya. This type of poster was still sporadic, and parsimonious with color. The real leap forward of industry and commerce, and so of advertising, followed the victory in the Russo-Japanese War of 1904-1905.

In 1904, the Mitsukoshi department store ordered a woman's portrait from the painter Kiyushu Habakabe. It was an enormous success, and this type of poster spread. Mitsukoshi, which relied heavily on posters for its advertising campaigns, held a poster competition in 1911.

All these posters, certainly influenced by the Germans who supplied equipment to the Japanese, were gaudy kaleidoscopes which required up to 35 applications of colors. They were very meticulous reproductions of pictures, but had nothing to do with graphic art. Paradoxically, the country which, by its layouts and by its graphic abridgements, had inspired Europe, became infatuated in turn with the most conventional art that the Occident could export – no doubt it had for the Japanese the same novelty, the same strangeness!

In 1914, offset printing was introduced into Japan, together with color phototypography. The first posters produced were for the Meiji-Ya grocery and the Osaka Shosen shipping company. Osaka Shosen brought out, under the authorship of Ryuyo Machida, the first poster which, in the force of its composition, can be said to have been derived from Western style advertisement: a gigantic Sumo wrestler with his feet planted on the terrestrial globe.

The French poster from 1900 to 1914

While the German poster was undergoing a formidable development, advancing in every domain the conception of a true advertising art, France lay dormant, emptied of all talent. Lautrec died in 1901; Mucha had left France in 1904; the Nabis and most other artists devoted themselves only to painting. Furthermore, the poster could no longer content itself with being a decorative print, a beautiful image with lettering added. The need for perhaps less artistic but in any case more effective advertising was felt.

208. Leonetto Cappiello: *Chocolat Klaus*. 1903.

209. Leonetto Cappiello: *Cachou Lajaunie* breath freshener. 1900.

From this creative desert emerged only one man who, pursuing his experiments in the same direction as the Germans, found his own solution to the problem of advertising communication: Leonetto Cappiello.

Born in 1875 in Livorno, Italy, Leonetto Cappiello arrived in Paris in 1898. He established himself at first as a caricaturist in numerous publications with his portraits of prominent personalities in strong outlines and flat colors. Furthermore, it was for a satirical periodical, the *Frou Frou,* in 1899, that he made his first poster, which brought him many commissions: the *Folies-Bergère,* the *Petit Coquin, Hélène Chauvin,* the *Le Furet* corsets and the *Amandines de Provence,* in the year 1900 alone. These posters are actually enlarged caricatures in which Cappiello already shows his mastery of composition and applies one of his fundamental principles: unified backgrounds against which the figure readily stands out. This concern for legibility differentiated him from most of his fellow artists who were more concerned with detail than with effect. In 1903, with the green lady astride a red horse for *Chocolat Klaus,* he definitively broke with realism to investigate graphic expression. In 1905, with the devils advertising the liqueur *Anis Infernal,* he began to associate a figure with a trade-name. After the fire-breathing clown for the medicinal plaster *Thermogène* (1909), and the *Cinzano* zebra (1910), his style was settled and the modern poster was born. With a brilliant intuition, Cappiello had found the answer to the two fundamental problems of the poster: legibility and mental association.

To be legible the poster must be simplified: a light figure on a somber background, or vice-versa; he called it "the science of the blot": "The poster was created to be placed in full light and viewed at a distance. It should never be in harmony with its surroundings, on the contrary, it must be in complete opposition. . . . my first preoccupation is the science of the blot."

It should also create an effect of surprise, "an indispensable condition of all advertising." The colors used should be those which most strike the retina. But what above all makes a good poster is line, what he called "the arabesque," synthesizing the idea: "It is the line that should be sought, and secondary importance given to color and to detail which should only strengthen it, embellish it, and enrich it."

To be effective, the poster should also be immediately associated by the passer-by with a trademark: so a figure must be invented—animal, cartoon, or whatever—which by repetition will be inseparable from the product.

Very differently from the Germans, Cappiello found a system that could be applied in France where taste and a certain tradition made the application of the object poster and other typically Germanic solutions difficult at the time.

The influence of Cappiello was enormous, and the walls were covered with images drawn in his style, mostly servile and mediocre imitations. Only after the War, with the arrival of a new generation, would France find its true creative wealth.

210. Leonetto Cappiello:
Thermogène. 1909.

"Fate tutti il vostro dovere!"

LE SOTTOSCRIZIONI AL PRESTITO SI RICEVONO PRESSO IL
CREDITO ITALIANO

211. Achille Mauzan:
Poster for World War I
defense bonds. 1917.

The First World War

213. Alfred Leete: *Join Your Country's Army.*
1914-15.

Until 1914, the state had made no use of the illustrated poster: there were only official posters that, by their strict typographic sobriety, were clearly differentiated from the large body of advertising. They contented themselves with proclaiming the law from their specially reserved places. Since the government played virtually no role in commerce and industry, its duty stopped there. The conflicts which broke out between 1870 and 1914 only appeared on the walls when exploited by manufacturers: Ogé's *Dum-Dum* pills, for instance, made light of Queen Victoria at the time England was fighting the Boers.

212. Saville Lumley: *Daddy, what did YOU do?*

214. Jules Abel Faivre: *On les aura!* A defense
bond drive. 1916.

215. Lucian Bernhard: German war loan poster. 1917.

216. Howard Chandler Christy: Navy recruitment. 1917.

When the war broke out in 1914, the major powers, trained in the Napoleonic school, counted on a tactical exercise which would not last long. They had forgotten technical advances like the machine-gun. The result was that after the halt of the German offensive on the Marne and a few weeks of naval hide-and-seek, they found themselves face to face on a few hundred miles of ground, entrenched and unable to pierce the enemy lines. No one had foreseen this, and no one foresaw that it would go on for four years. All the nations which had been thrown into the conflict quickly realized that they did not have the means to endure this drain on their resources: men, money, everything began to give out and after a few months morale gave out as well.

In a few weeks the illustrated poster was enlisted in the war effort. While some countries on the Continent with a draft system had little trouble mobilizing millions of men, England, which had only a professional army, had to produce recruitment posters. Frank Brangwyn and George Spencer Pryse, who designed their posters directly at the front, were the first, at the time of the invasion of Belgium, to call on the English to enlist. Many posters followed: the famous *Your Country Needs You* – Lord Kitchener's face, the pointed finger, the brief slogan; its succinct style made it a model of the genre, notably for James Montgomery Flagg in the United States with his Uncle Sam in the same pose, *I Want You for U.S. Army*.

To this clear and dignified call to arms were soon added more mundane images, whose archetype is *Daddy, what did YOU do during the Great War?* by Saville Lumley: a little girl poses the terrible question to her father, petrified in his armchair. Women also had their role to play: *For the glory of Ireland, will you go or must I?* says the Irishwoman to her husband; and even stronger is Charles Dana Gibson's mother bringing her son to Uncle Sam: *Here he is.* More poignant for the Americans was a poster of terrible symbolism, made by Frank Spear after the torpedoing of the Lusitania which killed 128 American women and children: a mother and child sinking to the ocean floor, with the single word *Enlist*.

What was soon most needed was money to keep the infernal machine going: every nation had to borrow. Abel Faivre with *Money Fights for Victory* where the Gallic rooster comes out of a gold-piece to floor a German soldier, followed by his famous *On les aura!* ("We'll beat them!"), made what were no doubt the best posters in their field. There were also allegories of Saint George and the dragon, soldiers mounting assaults (such as Mauzan's *Fate tutti il vostro dovere!* (Do Your Duty) whose soldier also points at the viewer), bombarding cannons, warships, planes and other visible proofs of the exorbitant cost of operations. Giving money because a duty and any means were legitimate to convince the citizen to do so. But he could not be frightened into giving, which is why, to arouse patriotic spirit, the horrors of war were scrupulously avoided. The enemy was symbolic: the German eagle, the Gallic rooster, the British lion, a pointed helmet or a flag – hardly more; certainly never scenes of butchery.

As the war continued and millions of soldiers and civilians were killed or maimed, money was needed to dress the wounds which it was now becoming more difficult to conceal: the wounded, prisoners, orphans, refugees needed charity. They were the motive for exercises on the theme

217. Fritz Erler:
Another *Kriegsanleihe*
(war loan) poster. 1917.

218. W. Kühn:
The seventh Austrian
war loan drive. 1917.

219. Théophile-
Alexandre Steinlen:
Journée du Poilu. 1915.

220. Frank Brangwyn:
British wartime promotion poster.

221. Joyce Dennys: Recruitment poster for the *Women's Royal Naval Service*.

ZEICHNET
KRIEGS-ANLEIHE
FÜR U-BOOTE GEGEN
ENGLAND

Souscrivez à l'emprunt de guerre pour la construction de sous-marins contre l'Angleterre

222. F.W.K.: German war loan
drive to build submarines
against England. c. 1917.

223. Joseph C. Leyendecker: American war bonds drive. 1917.

224. John Norton: *Liberty Bonds* drive. 1917.

of desolation in which Steinlen and Fouqueray, helped by their natural style, were particularly at ease. Poulbot, for *Les Journées du Poilu* ("Soldier's Day") posters, used poor ragamuffins. The best posters of this type were those of Hohlwein. With great restraint and sincere emotion, with his usual sobriety—a few flat tones used to make a figure—he designed a few remarkable posters: *Volksspende für die deutschen Kriegs- und Zivilgefangene, Ludendorff Spende für Kriegsbeschädigte*.

To insure provisions for the war effort, posters were needed to urge that food be economized. In Germany, Gipkens made a whole series suggesting gathering acorns and nuts and planting sunflowers. Bernhard produced a typographic placard to the glory of the potato. In France, the National Committee on Provisions and Economy ran a contest for schoolchildren, whose winning posters were published; in the United States, it

225. Julius Gipkens: German wartime campaign in which children are asked to collect fruit pits. c. 1918.

was art school students who called for restraint. Everything had to be salvaged, from used bottles to hair!

With these hundreds of messages which both sides had untiringly kept conveying to the populace, the poster became more and more conspicuous. George Theophiles[1] estimates the American production alone, in twenty months of conflict, at 2500 different designs! This gigantic production was well organized, with specific orders alternating with competitions. In Germany, the Verein der Plakatfreunde played the role of coordinator: the greatest poster artists worked for it. In the United States, there was a committee organized by Charles Dana Gibson which brought together the major American illustrators who, at a weekly luncheon, divided orders

1. George Theophiles: *American Posters of World War I.*
   New York: Dafran House, 1973.

226. French school kids drew this poster asking people to grow their own vegetables. 1917.

227. Ludwig Hohlwein: Campaign for funds for handicapped soldiers.

that they fulfilled without pay. Art schools and universities also produced a windfall of designs, most of them of mediocre quality. In England the Royal Academicians, above all Frank Brangwyn, were most called upon. In France, aside from a few competitions, the genre was entrusted to specialists like Abel Faivre, Fouqueray and Poulbot.

228. Walter Schnackenberg: Charity drive to help Germans returning from abroad.

Russia

In 1912, in Moscow, a group comprising Bulyuk, Mayakovsky, Krutchonik and Khlebnikov issued a startling artistic creed titled *The Insult to Universal Taste*. The delirious verbal violence of the manifesto was close to that of the Italian futurists. The link between futurist poetry and cubist art, here as in Europe, laid the foundations for a new graphic art and a new typography. Cubo-futurism, to use Malevich's term, grew up on the ruins of modernism and neoclassicism. In 1917, the Revolution broke out, a gigantic historical earthquake that, for around 10 years, was to liberate the creative energies of the Russian avant-garde.

The ebb and flow of a populace of millions of workers and illiterate peasants, carried along by the whirlwind of events, evade any dogmatic analysis. On March 15, 1917, the Czar abdicated. Power was divided among Kerensky's provisional government, the Duma, and a soviet of soldiers and workers. Lenin was in Zurich: "If the Revolution does not change into a victorious Paris Commune, it will be stifled by the Reaction and the war."

The memory of 1870 was in the hearts and crayons of poster artists.

To the glory of *The Dead of the Paris Commune, revived under the red flag of the Soviets,* Kozlinsky depicted his commune with Notre-Dame in the background and the red of the flag above the city in arms. In pictures and in posters, the revolutionary, in seven-league boots, was shown striding determinedly over cities and their teeming crowds.

On April 3, Lenin returned and announced the formation of the communist state before bewildered millions. In July, a reaction was organized; but it collapsed in August. At the beginning of October, Lenin secretly returned. There were twelve on the Central Committee. Lenin quelled the insurrection. Of the ten days that shook the world, he later said: "That was easier than lifting a pen."

The Bolshevik minority, assembled in twenty years of clandestine struggle, faced 150 million subjects of the Czar, exploited for centuries. Lunacharsky, a cultured esthete and a friend of Lenin, was named People's Commissar of Education. He would play a great role as mediator between politicians, mainly preoccupied with the message, and the artistic and intellectual avant-garde drunk with visions of total liberty.

The Futurists founded the association KOMFUT (The Futurist Communists). Malevich published virulent articles against the artists who did not encourage the revolutionary effort. Mayakovsky gave speeches. "Up with Futurism," he wrote from Moscow to Lili Brik in December 1917.

In April, 1918, Lenin launched the program for propaganda by means of monumental art and art in the streets. The artists who had become poster propagandists were concerned with the immediacy of the message

229. Dimitri Moor: *Death to World Imperialism.* 1919.

they were to deliver. The ideas were simple: peace without annexation—the people's right to self-determination—the lard to the peasants—the factory to the workers. The streets were decorated, painted with all the anger, the humiliation, the enthusiasm of the crowds who assembled, listened, marveled there: "The traditional book should be flung in all

230. Vladimir Kozlinsky: *The dead of the Paris Commune Revive under the Red Flag of the Soviets.* 1921.

231. El Lissitsky: *Beat the Whites with a Red Wedge.* c. 1920.

directions, multipled by a hundred, high-colored and in the form of posters displayed in the streets," said Lissitsky.

The poster for propaganda and agitation was the most dramatic expression of the art of the Revolution. Its expressionist grandiloquence touched hearts and caused tears to flow: Dimitri Moor's poster declaring *Death to World Imperialism* shows graphically the plight of an immense phantom of the emaciated peasant. Naturalism tended the flame of revolt and rekindled fraternity: Deni's capitalist, an obese monster, swims up to his neck in a river of gold coins. Moor's is a greenish hideous sea serpent, coiled around a factory and dying from the blows of workers and soldiers. The posters of Aspit, Nikolaiev, Radakov, Kocherguin, Kogut or those of the painters Kupreinanov and Kustodiev are in the same vein. The futurists go further. The futurist poetry and image are belligerent. The image is violent and ephemeral. It provokes rather than demonstrating or analyzing. The posters created by Mayakovsky, Malyutin, Cheremnyk, Lebedev and Kozlinsky for the Russian Telegraphic Agency (ROSTA), posted on the front of empty shops (from which they get their name, "ROSTA windows"), have this extraordinary sense of speed, a vocation of immediacy. The present is instantaneously memory. Nothing takes root. The peasant, the soldier, woman, the worker, the capitalist, the Czar, the enemy at the front, limned in a few heavy pencil-strokes and vividly colored, recall to mind, most often through laughter, that a new world was being born. The ROSTA poster is a montage of subtitled images that, often by way of a story, offers a quick lesson on the meaning of the revolution.

The peasant carrying loaves who was evidently slow in bowing to revolutionary demands, gets a rhyming but direct message: "Give up your

232. Michail Cheremnyk & Vladimir Mayakovsky: Rosta Window #241, ridiculing peasants who refuse to give up their bread. 1920.

233. Vladimir Lebedev: Rosta Window exhorting people to work. 1921.

234. Alexander Rodchenko: Cover of the magazine *LEF*. 1923.

bread without a grudge! Or else to Siberia you'll trudge!" So says a "Rosta window" by Mikhail Cheremnyk and Vladimir Mayakovsky, justifying the Red Army's confiscations of food.

Trains, painted with allegoric scenes to the glory of the new forces, traveled the countryside, from Turkestan to the Caucasus, along the banks of the Don. Old boats, veritable floating frescos, carried the message on their sides. This populist art, close to the traditional Russian poster marked by the icon, product of the peasant imagination, permitted language barriers to be overcome in a country of multiple nationalities.

During 1919 and 1920, a revolution raged within the vast land. Bolshevik Russia was assailed from all sides. The Americans were in Siberia, the English in the Gulf of Finland, the French in Odessa; in the east the Czechs, in the West the Poles. The Red Army, the proletariat and a portion of the peasantry waged total war. The Army also faced its own countrymen, the more conservative White Russians, in a bitter confrontation. Lissitsky's poster can be considered a major event: *We will drive a Red wedge into the Whites,* it proclaims in the service of the Red Army. A ROSTA poster from Smolensk, *What have you done for the Front?,* attributed to Malevich, already gave an example of a stunning combination of abstract motifs. Would art without figures at last become a popular language?

In 1919 Lunacharsky made Chagall the official art commissar of the city of Vitebsk. The painter was however soon replaced by his guest Malevich and the suprematist artists of the UNOVIS group; the walls of the city, for two years, reverberated with squares, triangles, circles of all colors. In Moscow, the Cubo-futurists took charge of these newly created trends. The association of young artists OBMOKHOU, who came from the Stroganoff school which had been reorganized after the October coup, became in 1920 the celbrated VKUTEMAS whose theories foretold those of the German Bauhaus. In the old Fabergé firm, a cadre of artists, day and night, constructed theater backdrops, made projects for monumental architecture, printed newspapers (it would be interesting to know what became of the unique lithographic newspaper, *October in the Cube),* and designed posters proclaiming the death of bourgeois art. The schools flourished. Joy, disarray, wild creativity, carried away heads and hearts with them. Theories confronted one another. Malevich wrote: "To all those who invoke the construction of utilitarian objects and who wish to subjugate art, I maintain that practical and constructed things do not exist." Chuzbach replied: "If there is a proletarian art, we consider art as something temporary, until it loses itself in life, and takes the form of activity which takes hold of the emotions in such a way as to communicate to humanity the value of its needs."

Fed by the same naive idealism and by the pathetic desire to lose nothing of the extraordinary liberty that had been won, men proceeded to deliver themselves up to a war without mercy.

In March of 1921, the soviet of Kronstadt, avant-garde of the Revolution, revolted against the Central Bolshevik power. It fell to Trotsky and to Tukhatchevsky to subdue the city. The revolution devoured itself. It was necessary to find a compromise between the utopias which had enabled men to live through four years of revolts and civil and international war, and the urgent necessity of feeding, organizing and equipping a vast and devastated country.

The Tenth Congress adopted a policy of détente, the New Economic

Policy (N.E.P.). Commercial relations abroad were renewed. Transport companies developed. Private publishing houses reopened. Mayakovsky created the MAF, a company that had books and reviews printed abroad, then had them imported under special permit to be distributed in Russia. He became editor of the magazine *LEF* (abbreviation of LEft Front) which gathered together people like Babel, Eisenstein, Vertov, Meyerbold, Rodchenko, Brik, the Stenberg brothers, and Klutsis. In November of 1921, the powerful Institute of Artistic Culture, INKHOUK, rejected Malevich's candidacy, expelled Kandinsky, and proclaimed "Productivism" the official doctrine in reaction against "the idealist and theoretical tendency of the years 15-19". Artists were urged to open their eyes and plunge into the constructivist era; Lissitsky was its theoretician. In "The Typography of Typography", an article published in 1923, he gives rules for a new typography which effects, according to him, a revolution as important as that of Gutenberg's invention of printing. Author of the doctrine of functionalism, he defended the standardization of utilitarian objects as the introduction of an esthetic of the industrial era. Rodchenko followed him on this path. With Rozanova, he founded the Plastic Arts division of the Moscow Vkhutemas: "We have a vision of a new world served by industry, technology and science."

Reality is a dynamic system subject to infinite transformations. The artist is in the position of observer: "Constructivism is a window onto the contemporary world — an eternal art does not exist. Everything is subject to change; the constructivist way is the art of the future."

The Vkhutemas courses trained designers. The Agitreklama (Action Poster) Society of Stepanova, Levin, Lavinsky and Rodchenko, with the seriousness and effectiveness of constructivist graphics, defended the products of Soviet factories.

The poster in which Mayakovsky made a gift of his imagination and

235. Alexander Rodchenko & Vladimir Mayakovsky: Poster for the nationalized rubber industry, *Rezinotrest*.

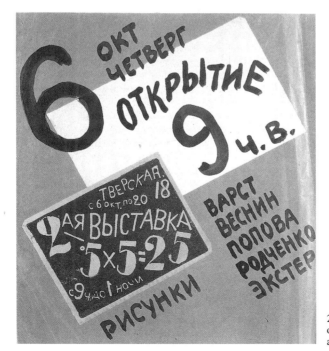

236. Alexander Rodchenko: Design for an exhibition of five painters (Varst, Vesnin, Popova, Rodchenko and Exter).

237. Alexander Rodchenko & Vladimir
Mayakovsky: Another poster for *Rezinotrest,*
suggesting it should produce galoshes for
export. 1923.

238. Gustav Klutsis: *We Will Fulfill the Plan of Great Works.* 1930.

tenderness to his country in the midst of revolution, is great, clear and
droll: *There never was nor will be a better nipple, ready to be sucked
for a hundred years,* declares the crisp, ecstatic design, showing the lips
of the baby clown, drawn by Rodchenko, to which every sort of mouthpiece is offered. *Nothing remains of the old world but IRA cigarettes,* is
how incorrigible Russian smokers consoled or congratulated themselves!
Mayakovsky made a book of all his country's advertising slogans, *The
Russian Poster,* which has unfortunately never been translated. "All Moscow was decorated by our group, we designed all the signs for Mosselprom
(cigarettes) and the Gosizdat shops. Black, red and gold. We made the
advertisements for Ogonyok, Chaieupravlenye (tea trust), Rezinotrest
(rubber trust). We've made fifty posters, about a hundred signs, commercial notices, packaging, newspaper and magazine illustrations," recounted
Rodchenko. And it was by passing himself off as an advertising agent
for the rubber trust Rezinotrest that Mayakovsky obtained his visa for a
visit to the United States!

Books and newspapers again became the best media for education and
information. Their adveritsing usually fell to traditionalist painters, who
became poster artists of necessity. Akimov, Deneika, Kustodiev,
Favorsky, Moor gave a finicky, infantile – though not entirely without
artistic merit – tone to book advertising. After Lenin's death in 1924,
Lunacharsky had more and more trouble protecting the avant-garde in

239. Stenberg Brothers:
Poster for the film
A Man With a Movie Camera. 1928.

240. Anton Lavinsky: Poster for the film *The Battleship Potemkin*. 1925.

the face of the growing hostility of a generation of populist artists who were preparing the way for Stalinist ugliness.

Book advertising did not remain the preserve of the defenders of a mediocre mass culture. Rodchenko, Lissitsky, Telingater, Popova and Stepanova, with photomontage and daring typography, continued to defend their innovative ideas, accessible to all: in the book poster, the lettering, large and tall, became a simple yet major geometric element, juxtaposed and integrated at the same time with the drawing of the book itself; the reader, the book, the lettering were equalized. Klutsis developed, with photomontage, the forms of a mass culture intimately tied to technological and industrial progress: the photo was a documentary eye upon the realities of the worker's life; the slogan — eulogy or production, defense of work, fight against illiteracy — raises itself, glorious, above the images of a mythical world. Its effectiveness comes from the interplay of two different spaces, that of the photo and that of the lettering, and of two antagonistic visions of the world, the real and the slogan.

The film poster came later. Lenin had defended film as art serving propaganda, but it was after his death, between 1925 and 1929, that Soviet cinematography surprised the world. Sergei Eisenstein made *Strike, Battleship Potemkin, October;* Vertov produced *A Sixth of the World, The Eleventh Year, Kino-Eye, The Man with a Movie Camera;* Pudovkin filmed *Mother* and *The End of St. Petersburg;* Dovzhenko directed *Arsenal* and *Earth,* to name only the greatest.

On the graphic front, the Stenberg brothers, graphic artists, were up to the level of the cinematic image. The theater was their first school. They worked on stage sets with Medunetzky at the Constructivist Laboratory in 1919 and 1920. Decorators at the Kamenny Theater, they designed the posters for tours abroad. Their first cinema poster, signed STEN, was prepared in 1924. They worked together until the accidental death of Georgi in 1933. (The first Soviet film poster was probably Mayakovsky's for his film *Creation Can't Be Bought,* in 1918, which he wrote and in which he played the leading role.) Vladimir and Georgi Stenberg had a builder's mentality and a highly developed sense of space. Their image is a montage of different planes which turn and slide on top of one another. Bodies, faces incline, fly off, perpendicular or parallel to diagonals that evoke another place or another time. Space is suggested more by vertigo than by perspective.

Rodchenko's poster, of great symmetry and geometric precision, close to a perfect balance of blacks and whites, evokes the victory of light over shadow: the image of *A Sixth of the World* doubles back, coils over itself, projecting a raw light on the face of a woman appearing out of the blackness. Gerasimov and Prusakov play with the lettering, a geometric debris made of colorful patchwork. With Ruklevsky and Semyonov, the

241. Stenberg Brothers: Film *Velikosvetskoye Pari (High Society).* 1927.

242. Boris Prusakov: Film *Zakon Gor (The Eagle of the Caucasus).* 1927.

243. Boris Prusakov: Poster for one of the earliest Armenian films, *Khaz-Push*. 1927.

graphic image tries to vie with the cinematic image's 18 frames per second. For Dubrovsky's documentary against alcoholism, Semyonov throws a body from the top of a building, tosses the livid face of a hopeless man into the void, leaves a lifeless hand in the foreground, abandons a helpless woman. Without pathos and even with humor, Prusakov also had this fascination with speed, which he admirably communicated with photomontage: the principal element is the motor: the automobile, the locomotive, the plane. He dismembers the human body. Heads, arms, hands continue or forestall the movement of the machine. We can also mention the posters of Yukov, Naomov and Lavinsky, which also largely use photomontage, a favored procedure of the poster artists of the 30's.

In 1927, famine and misery menaced the country, which had been boycotted by the West. In power since 1924, Stalin, little by little, eliminated all the leading actors of the Politburo. In 1929, at the Sixteenth Congress, he decreed the collectivization of agriculture and high-level industrialization, which became the cause of the forced displacement of millions of people. There was civil unrest, subdued by the machine-gun and by mass deportations.

In these times of murderous folly, nothing beautiful remains of the Revolution and its images but the red: beautiful and red, two meanings which are covered by the same word in the Russian language.

Until his death in 1953, Stalin reigned alone. "Father of the People, Savior of the Revolution," he relied on discipline, fanaticism and the mysticism of a new bureaucratic system subjugated to a liturgy and an iconography at the service of a cult: the cult of the language and thought of a single man which became the language and thought of a whole country. Art and science bowed before the dictator who was shown caressing the head of a blond child shining amidst the wheatfields, while the immortal worker, his hoe on his shoulder, left to join his comrades.

244. Gustav Klutsis:
*The Development of
Transportation Under the
Five-Year Plan.* 1929.

245. Kurt Schwitters: Dada magazine *Merz*. 1923.

The Avant-Gardes

The Soviet Revolution allowed the constructivists and suprematists to put their ideas into practice. The hundreds of posters they produced made for a most favorable moment in the history of world graphic art and justify a chapter devoted to them. The same currents of ideas were to be found in western Europe, new formal conceptions of the poster, new typography, use of the photo and of photomontage. They remained however the perquisites of an avant-garde which, while revolutionizing established notions, produced posters for its own needs and very rarely for the advertising world, properly speaking. With their abandonment of ornamentation, characteristic of Art Nouveau, and with a concern about the poster's function, Bauhaus and De Stijl laid the foundations for modern visual communication, and their influence can still be seen today the world over.

Cubism, which at the beginning of the century had revolutionized fine arts, concerned itself mainly with painting and sculpture: it had only a minor influence on the poster.

The Futurist Manifesto that Marinetti published in the *Figaro* in 1909, exalting speed, the machine, and war, was the modern world's first consciousness of itself. About typography, he wrote: "I am hostile to what is called a harmonious composition; if necessary we will use three or four colors per page and twenty different sorts of characters. We will represent rapid perceptions in italics and we will express a cry in boldface: a new artistic typography is born." Marinetti's poems, like Apollinaire's ideograms, without having any direct influence, were typographically the first intuitions of the future. "They have doubtless served less as models than as breakers of traditions" (Moholy-Nagy).

McKnight Kauffer[1] defined perfectly in 1924 what the artists of his generation had been able to draw from them: "A common error of judgment is often made in the unintelligent use of the terms 'cubistic' and 'futuristic' generally applied to any poster design that does not look like all other posters. Some contemporary designs have shown both these tendencies individually, but few have been designed either with cubistic or futuristic finality."

In Zurich, in 1916, at the cabaret Voltaire, two Germans (Ball and Huelsenbeck), two Rumanians (Tzara and Janko) and an Alsatian (Arp) created dada.

The reverse of futurism's credo, dada was a nihilistic and desperate reaction to the horrors of the war. In the third number of their review, all typographical rules were overturned: the lettering no longer serves the text but is composed in all liberty, making images which formed a sense of their own. Dada, which spread over all Europe, brought together the

1. E.McKnight-Kauffer: *The Art of the Poster*. London: Cecil Palmer, 1924.

246. Mart Stamm: Architecture Exhibition in Rotterdam. 1928.

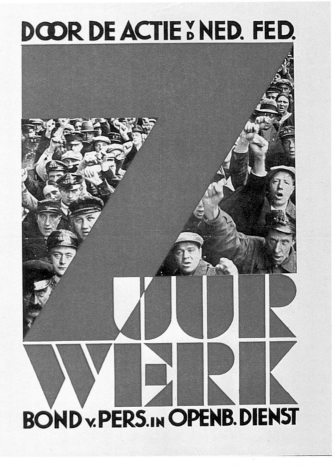

247. Paul Schuitema: A Labor union poster, *7-hour Workday*. c. 1930.

major personalities of the avant garde, from Schwitters to Heartfield, from Duchamp to Ernst.

In 1917, Van Doesburg, the painters Huszar and Mondrian, the architect Oud and the poet Kok founded the magazine *De Stijl* in Holland. Even if Van Doesburg had dadaist sympathies, the movement was radically contrary to dada, with its "neo-plasticism", strongly marked by Calvinist asceticism, seeing itself as a purifying force.

Mondrian wrote in the first number of *De Stijl:* "This new plastic idea will ignore the particulars of appearance, that is to say, the natural form and color. On the contrary, it should find its expression in the abstraction of form and color, that is to say, in the straight line and the clearly defined primary color."

Carried over into the poster, the conceptions of *De Stijl*—horizontal and vertical lines, the use of rectangles and color and of a purified typography arranged in masses—are those of Zwart, Schuitema, Huszar, Mart Stamm and Van Ravesteijn. Stripped of all unnecessary decorative elements, of any will to beautify, the poster was brought back to its original function: communication. Piet Zwart very well expressed this intention in 1931 on the subject of stamps—it is equally valid for the

248. Piet Zwart: Film
Exposition in The Hague.
1928.

250. Walter Dexel: Poster promoting the use of gas in the home. 1924.

249. Walter Dexel: Exhibition *Photography of Today*. 1929.

251. Herbert Bayer: *Kandinsky* exhibition. 1926.

poster: "I think that in determining the elements which played a role in the conception of the stamp, I have clearly shown that the original aim was not to design what is called a pretty stamp: the aim was to conceive a stamp that would utilize the technical possibilities of our times, a reasonable composition with functional elements, and its utilization at the post office."

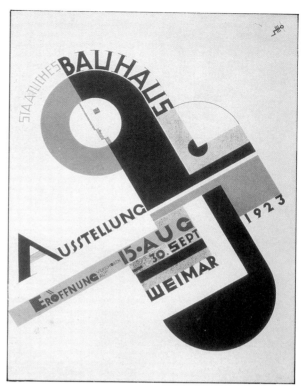

252. Burger, Hötzel & Schlemmer: *Das Triadische Ballett*. 1924.

253. Joost Schmidt: *Bauhaus* exposition at Weimar. 1923.

In the middle of the Twenties, Zwart was one of the first to add photography to these elements; while Werkman, using letters engraved on wood, followed typographic possibilities to their limit.

Created in 1919 in Weimar by the architect Gropius, the Bauhaus, after a short mystic period under the influence of Itten, where its chosen model was the artisan of the middle ages, moved closer to the conceptions of Lissitsky and of the Vkhutemas as well as of Van Doesburg and de Stijl. Moholy-Nagy's arrival, in 1923, was catalytic.

At the beginning, Laszlo Moholy-Nagy worked in the movement's metal workshop, but also at the printing press where he had as students Herbert Bayer, Joost Schmidt and Joseph Albers, who became teachers in their turn. In Dessau, where the Bauhaus was forced to emigrate, commissions began to arrive regularly (thanks to the Werkbund): for the paper money of the state of Thuringia (designed by Bayer), or the type-writer-ribbon cases by Schmidt.

Joost Schmidt replaced Bayer in 1928 in the printing shop, which was renamed "Commercial Art." It specialized in three-dimensional advertising and stands for expositions.

When the Bauhaus, having taken refuge in Berlin, had to shut its doors in the face of Nazi pressure in 1933, the workshop was called "Advertising", and its head, Walter Peterhans, directed the photography studio at the same time.

These transformations, even within its teachings, very much charac-terized the evolution of the Bauhaus under Moholy-Nagy, who gave

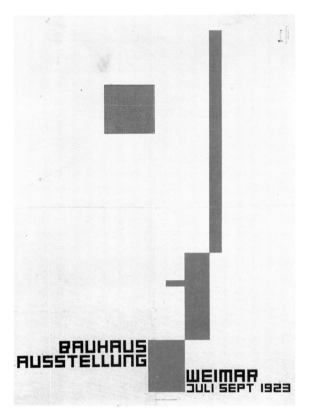

254. Fritz Schleifer: Original poster for the *Bauhaus* exposition at Weimar, before it was postponed. 1923.

256. Kurt Schwitters: Exhibition of modern living design by Bauhaus architects at Karlsruhe. 1929.

255. Herbert Bayer. *Section allemande . . .*

preferential place to typography and then to photography in the logic of his own work.

"We began to realize that the form, the size, the color and the arrangement of the typographic material (letters and signs) had a strong visual impact. With the possibilities for organizing these messages, this means that in what is printed the content is also pictorially defined.

"Typography is a medium of communication: it should be a clear and convincing message."

These two texts by Moholy-Nagy, written in 1923 and 1924, spell the end of Dadaist ravings, as can be seen in the series *Merz* by Schwitters, and in the work of De Stijl.

The Bauhaus posters of this period, by Bayer, Walter Dexel, or Schmidt, are essentially typographical (existing side by side with the very different images of Itten or Schlemmer). Asymmetry is used fluently, the lettering crosses itself at a 45° or a right angle, and is dynamically composed, taking on the function previously filled by the image. This new typography brought into use clear and legible characters, of the sans-serif type made for the London Underground in 1916 by Johnson, with Herbert Bayer and Joseph Albers making the posters.

Bayer, taking up one of Moholy-Nagy's ideas, suggested abandoning capital letters: "Why two characters, A and a, for a single sound, a. One

257. Max Buchartz: Schubert Festival in Essen. 1928.

258. Max Buchartz: Applied Art Exhibit in Essen. 1931.

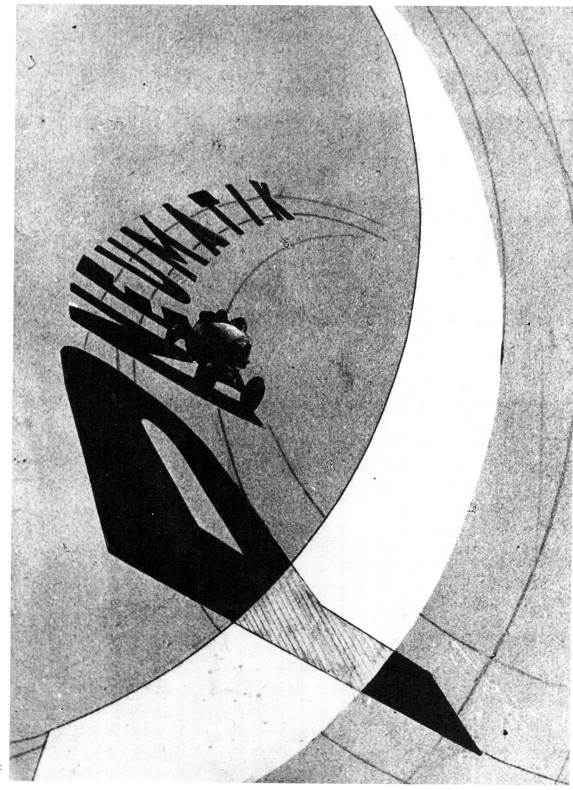

259. Laszlo Moholy-Nagy:
Pneumatik. 1926.

260. El Lissitsky: Russian Exposition at Zurich. 1929.

261. Jan Tschichold: Poster for the film *Laster der Menschheit (Lusts of Mankind).* 1926.

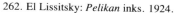

262. El Lissitsky: *Pelikan* inks. 1924.

character for one sound. Why two alphabets for one word, why two systems of characters when a single one gives the same result?"

From 1920, Moholy-Nagy took an interest in the photogram—the use of photographic film to make images of objects—along with Man Ray, who in Paris baptized it the "rayogram".

Lissitsky, who traveled often to the West in that decade, used the first processed photo for a poster for Pelikan inks in 1924. With *Pneumatik* (1926), Moholy-Nagy opened the way to montage and special photographic effects. At the end of the 20s, all forms of photography became one of the avant-garde's favorite modes of expression: the Soviets, Bauhaus, De Stijl used it fluently, including the dadaist John Heartfield in his anti-Nazi montages, or Max Buchartz and Jan Tschichold, other major personalities of the period.

Born in 1902 in Leipzig, Tschichold had carried out in solitude some of the same experiments as the Bauhaus. At first he was a typographer, who in his theoretical works *(The New Typography, Asymmetrical Typography)* laid down the principles of a new order.

"The relation between abstract painting and the new typography does not lie in the use of abstract forms but in similarity of method; in both cases, the artist must first scientifically study his materials, then by exploiting contrasts, transform them into one entity. . . . works of abstract art are subtle and well-ordered creations made from dissimilar elements.

263. Jan Tschichold: Film *Die Hose* (released in English-speaking countries as *Royal Scandal*). 1927.

264. Jan Tschichold: Poster for *Die Kameliendame* (German release of the American film *Camille*). 1927.

Because that is exactly what typography tries to do, it can find instruction and encouragement in the study of painters who express the forms of the modern world and are the best teachers of the visual order."

Tschichold added photography to these principles, which, joined with an asymmetrical typography, make up his posters. His series for the Phoebus Palast cinema, where the rapid change of programs made great economy of means necessary, was exemplary, as were Müller's linogravures.

The Nazi seizure of power put an end to such experiments. The principal figures of the avant-garde fled, mainly to America (Bayer, then Moholy-Nagy) and Switzerland (Tschichold), taking with them their experience and their bent for teaching.

Of these fifteen rich and eventful years, the only material remains are a few dozen designs signed by a handful of innovators. But they were the foundations of a new graphic universe which, once laid—in part because of the forced emigration of some of its founders—spread over the world.

The foundations of this new approach are found, without any doubt, in architecture. Frank Lloyd Wright wrote: "We need sciences now where intuition used to guide us." The urge to "construct" that can be seen in the graphic art of this period conforms undeniably to the architects' procedure. It is not coincidental that Gropius was an architect, as were Bayer, Lissitsky and many others. The role of architecture as keystone in these new conceptions was recognized everywhere:

"Architecture, the art I prefer to all others, has inspired in me a horror of deforming details and a love of vast surfaces whose impersonal nudity predestines them for great advertising frescoes", wrote Cassandre.

This architectural world is that of the purists Le Corbusier and Ozenfant, who sought the principle of forms, of modernism, and of the machine in which Léger believed. They saw the poster as an element of progress: "Iconographic culture no longer comes from the museum. It comes from the picture-gallery of our modern streets—from the riotous and exaggerated colors of lithographed posters." (Lissitsky, 1922).

With typography revolutionized, photography and photomontage appeared in the wake of the pioneers in commercial advertising of the Thirties. And so with Cassandre in France, McKnight Kauffer in England, and Herbert Matter in Switzerland, the application of some of the theories of the Bauhaus and De Stijl were realized.

265. C. O. Muller: Poster for the film *Manege (Circus Ring)*. 1927.

266. Ernst L. Kirchner:
*KG Brucke in Galerie
Arnold.* 1910.

Germany

Barely out of the war, Germany, ruined and famished, entered, with the dissolution of the monarchy, into revolution, and then into an unprecedented economic depression.

The struggle between communists and socialists and the parties of the right, the formation of militia – all of this was a pretext for posters where, in view of the state of finances, graphic force had to supplant richness of colors.

Well before 1914, the expressionsts who gathered around *Die Brücke* and the review *Der Sturm* had created an art that broke away from bourgeois expectations. "Expressionism is characterized by deformations, heightened in the intensity of expression and the treatment of reactions to psychic acts by an ecstatic pathos and a dramatic accentuation of literary allusions, by the graphics of a sensitized humanity."[1] Using wood engraving or lithography with a very few violent colors, the expressionists designed posters for their exhibitions before, during and after the great war: Pechstein: *KG Brücke* (1909), Kirchner: *KG Brücke in Galerie Arnold* (1910), Kokoshka: *Der Sturm 19;* then, among many others, Pechstein: *Freie Secession 1917,* and Heckel: *Ausstellung Neuzeitlicher Deutscher Kunst.*

With the revolution, all these artists put their brushes in the service of a cause which corresponded to their deepest aspirations. They were encouraged in this by Dr. Adolph Behne, who founded in 1918 the Arbeitsrat für Kunst (Labor Office for Art), and who saw the new poster artists in this way: "They do not advertise for a firm but for an idea. They do not address themselves to a special public but to every sort of public – to the masses. That is why they need to use new forms – and search for new men to do it."

These new men were the "November Group" which included Pechstein, Klein, Richter, Jaeckel, Dix and Gross among its members. The ardor of political contest animates their posters where one sees all the characteristics of expressionism, broken lines and nervous drawing. Whether they truly touched the masses is another story: one can reasonably think that Käthe Kollwitz' simply drawn posters, with their transparency, authenticity and immediacy of sentiment, were more understandable. It is more interesting to note that the expressionist style defended the revolution under Pechstein's crayon *(The New Liberty Will Not Set with the Dawn),* made calls to work and to strike-breaking under that of Fuchs, or even to combat bolshevism *(Stop Bolshevism at Home!* by Fritz Heubner).

The revolution crushed, political struggle remained violent throughout the Twenties. The political parties called on Hohlwein, Scheurich,

267. Käthe Kollwitz: *Berliner Winterhilfe* charity drive. 1924.

---

1. Hellmut Rademacher: *op. cit.*

268. Hans Poelzig: Poster for film
*Der Golem: wie er in die Welt kam
(The Golem)*. 1920.

269. Max Pechstein: *An die Laterne (To the Lamppost)*. 1919.

270. Heinz Fuchs: An attempt to quell civil unrest by poster: *Workers! Starvation is near; strikes destroy, work enriches; do your duty—work*. 1918-19.

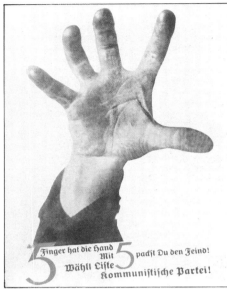

271. John Hartfield: Election poster of the
Communist Party, No. 5 on the ballot: *5
Fingers hat die Hand* (The Hand Has 5 Fingers;
With 5 You Sock Rightwingers.) 1928.

272. Fritz Heubner: Political poster for the
anti-Communist coalition *Bayrischer
Ordnungsblock.* 1920.

273. Anonymous photo of Chancellor Von Papen leaving a polling place.

Matejko, or even the fickle Engelhart or Schnackenberg, and on A.M.
Cay, a specialist in the genre who succeeded in making the posters for
six parties at once!

For the most part they were lacking in urgency, unlike the communists
Maslow, Frank, Griffel, Eickmeier, Stiller or the social democrats
Schwimmer, Kirchbach, Kraetke or Geiss. But the whole assemblage
remains mediocre, with the exception of Freddy Hormeyer's posters for
the socialists and the admirable montages of John Heartfield. With his
famous *Fünf Fingers hat die Hand* (The Hand Has Five Fingers), he was
the only one to find a trick to graphically indicate the number on the
voting list for which he was appealing.

Until the beginning of the Twenties, when American bank loans began
to ease the economy, misery reigned: with nothing to sell, there was no
need for advertising. Only the expanding cinema provided work for poster
artists. In most cases the result was mediocre, as they worked under the
thumb of distributors or owners of cinemas, but exceptions are numerous – enough to make this the golden age of the German cinema poster.
They were often designed by artists who at the same time made the décors
for films or for cinema houses. Joining Scheurich, already famous before
the war, was Kainer and especially Joseph Fenneker who designed for
the Marmorhaus and the Theater Am Moritzplatz. His designs, of a superb
dramatic intensity, make the figures stand out like apparitions from a
dark background, in a style between expressionism and Art Deco *(Blondes
Gift, Casanova, Totentanz,* and his poster for *Luna-Park).*

Less magical, though of high quality, are the posters of Kirchbach,
Victor Arnaud, Robert Leonard (for *V.T. Kurfürstendam Theater)* and of
Matejko (for the UFA Palast Theater). Lutz Ehrenberger specialized in
lascivious little women.

We are back on the trail of expressionism with Fritz Ahlers *(Die Mas-
kierte Tanzerin).* It triumphed in the posters of the Stahl-Arpke team
(Gespensterschiff, Whitechapel, and above all *Das Kabinett des Dr.
Caligari);* in *Der Golem* (no doubt by Poelzig who made the décors);
and in the very strange *Faust* by Michel.

These few masterpieces effectively make up all that expressionism has left, besides the art or political posters already mentioned, or posters for shows: *Schwartz-weiss Revue*, by Theodore Paul Etbaur, *Expressionistische Musik* by Fritz Lewy. The only exception we have found is Walter Kampmann's attempt to apply expressionism to advertising. The article that *Das Plakat* devoted to him in 1921 cites Richard Huelsenbeck in the 1920 *Dada-Almanach:* "Hatred of the masses, hatred of advertisement, hatred of sensation is that of people whose armchairs are more important to them than the noise of the street."

His posters for the perfumes of Doctor Morisse are stunning. In 1921, his poster for the *Kalender Fabrik Sam Lukas*, asymmetrical, made use of the circle and the rectangle. Let us finally mention the *Frankfurter Messe* of 1920 by Fuss, with its fumes of expressionism, and the designs of Mayer-Lukas *(Film Kunst, Phönix Stahl)*, which recall Fenneker.

As business took hold again in the Twenties, the poster was no longer what it was before the war. Doctor Sachs, who had interrupted the pub-

274. Josef Fenneker. *Tanja.* 1922.

275. Walter Kampmann. *Dr. Morisse.* 1920.

276. Karl Michel:
Murnau's film
Faust, 1926.

277. Joseph Fenneker:
Film, *Blondes Gift
(Blonde Poison)*. 1920.

278, 279. Ludwig Hohlwein: Two posters for the *Zeiss* optical firm, c. 1925.

280. Ludwig Hohlwein. *Italienischer Festball.* 1939

lication of his *Das Plakat,* went so far as to speak in *Gebrauchsgraphik* of a "Götterdämmerung" – the twilight of the German poster. Without going to that length, the publisher of the magazine, Professor Frenzel, had to recognize that "routine and technique dominate today." The style of the masters of the pre-war period had deteriorated. In Berlin, the great studios dominated, like those of Bernhard (directed after his departure for the United States by Hans Rosen), Arpke, Neumann and Matejko.

"Dresden, Leipzig, Cologne and Düsseldorf all have artists who provide good work of all kinds, but it is difficult to find among them a real personality."[1] Furthermore, posters remained in too small a format, the concessions made to advertisers strangled them, and poster making in general was behind that of other countries.

Munich, which had always vied with Berlin for artistic primacy, still sheltered a constellation of artists with their own special style: "It is because in Munich people are more concerned with problems of art than with problems of advertising. And strangely enough, this doesn't seem to harm advertising." (*Gebrauchsgrafik,* June 1929).

Ludwig Hohlwein, still unsurpassed, continued to produce poster after poster without any fundamental changes in his style: henceforward he used mainly watercolors which gave tenderer hues, more transparency, to his drawings. His masterpieces continued to follow upon one another: *Grathwohl Zigarette* – a man's shadow, showing only the glowing cigarette; *Pelikan Inks* – three stains of color in the form of hands on a black background; *Zeiss* – for which he created each time a new atmosphere. He demonstrated that his talent was not limited to animals, sportsmen and society people in his important series for the Maschinenfabrik Augsburg-Nürnberg (M.A.N.). He even received commissions from America, for Chesterfield cigarettes and Granger tobacco. In 1924, for his fiftieth birthday, he agreed to write a few lines; at the time he had more than three thousand creations behind him. "They have all re-

1. Klaus Popitz: *Plakate der zwanziger Jahre.* Berlin: Kunst-bibliothek, 1977.

281, 282, 283. Ludwig Hohlwein: Posters for the industrial combine *M.A.N.*, c. 1925.

284. Ludwig Hohlwein: *Pelikan* art supplies. c. 1925.

285. Ludwig Hohlwein:
Grathwohl cigarettes.
c. 1920.

286. Ludwig Hohlwein:
A 1935 Nazi propaganda
poster to be used in
France to publicize the
forthcoming Olympic Games
in Berlin in 1936.

287. Eugen Maria Cordier:
Schwabylon, a ball at the
Schwabing Brewery. c. 1925.

288. Valentin Zietara:
Carnival in Munich. 1929.

289. Franz Paul Glass: Exhibition of Bavarian handicraft in Munich. 1927.

291. Otto Ottler: Poster for a cigar importer. c. 1925.

290. Hermann Keimel: *Perutz* film. 1930.

mained pure Hohlwein," he said, while affirming he had neither recipe nor pupil nor assistant, that he did very well without them and that he hoped to long continue! The arrival of Nazism did not disturb him: he continued to produce without changing his style. The subjects changed: from then on they were splendid athletes in the manner of Arno Brecker, or impeccable soldiers. In 1944 his studio was destroyed—he retired to Berchtesgaden where he took up his youthful passion, watercolors of animals, until his death in 1949 at 75.

Hohlwein aside, the other Munich artists had their problems: a new Group of Six, formed by Max Eschle, Franz Paul Glass, Johann Baptist Maier, Tommy Parzinger, Otto Ottler and Valentin Zietara, offered their clients as before the war six designs at a fixed price, but without success: except for holidays, carnivals and exhibitions, the artistic poster had no more takers.

After the success of the great International Poster Exhibition that was held in Munich in 1928 at the same time as the World Advertising Congress in Berlin, the "Neue Vereinigung Münchner Plakatkünstler" was formed. Along with the Six, it brought together Cordier, Ehlers, Engelhardt, Heigenmoser, Hohlwein and Lindner. But it was helpless against the tide of the times and against Tschichold who had just been named head of the Münchner Schule für Grafische Gewerbe, a school for typographers and photographers.

Still, this group of artists which made the artistic poster its banner was unique in Germany. According to the statistics published in the excellent *Plakate in München 1840–1940*,[1] in 1930, 90% of the city's posters were concerned with culture, holidays, cinema, and sports! Schnackenberg, who makes many allusions to Lautrec, and Seche with his disquieting stylization, were the masters of the cabaret. Zietara, Ibe and the young Lindner had in common a love of the grotesque and of caricature which worked like a charm for carnivals. Although he could also be humorous (the frog of Perutz films), Keimel specialized in ample and stylized figures. For the *Münchner Plakat Kunst,* he attained a cubist rigor that we see again in the impeccable compositions of Franz Paul Glass. Cordier had a varied style, as did Ottler: they also could draw figures of fine dramatic intensity *(Andre Hofer* and *Reichs Reklame Messe* by Ottler, *Lehren J. Eibl's* and *München 1927* by Cordier). Max Eschle's work was of a pure geometric rigor *(München Sommer 1930).* Certainly the closest to the modern concept of the poster was Henry Ehlers who played with pure form in his series for the clothiers Bamberger & Hertz. For his other

1. *Plakate in München, 1840–1940.* Catalog of an exhibition in the Münchner Stadtmuseum, Munich, 1975.

292. Hermann Keimel: Poster exhibition at Munich. 1931.

293. Julius Engelhard: Munich cafe *Der Reichsadler.* c. 1925.

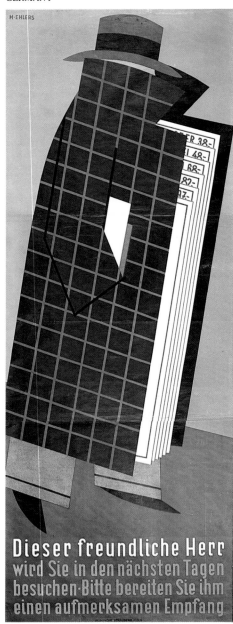

294. Henry Ehlers: Announcing the mailing of a clothing store catalogue. 1927.

295. Henry Ehlers: Another poster for the same firm, *Bamberger & Hertz*. 1927.

big client, B.M.W., he used modern typography and joined drawing with photography.

In an entirely different domain, Engelhardt, who was able to detach himself from Hohlwein's influence, was one of the rare German fashion illustrators whose drawing could, in its lightness, be likened to the French *(Deutches Theater, Agfa,* illustrations for the magazine *Die Elegante Welt).*

In Berlin, another artist, Jupp Wiertz, claimed attention with his lightness and the surprising facility of his drawing: awarded a prize in 1916 for a very rigorous *A.E.G.* poster, he quickly found his charming and

MODE- BALL

1 9 2 8

296. Julius Engelhard:
Fashion ball. 1928.

297. F. Neumann. *L.V.G.* ca 1918

298. Alfred Mahlau: Scandinavian festival at Lübeck. 1921.

delicate style which stands out from the Berlin heaviness and seriousness. Whether for show business *(Metropol Kabaret)*, beauty products *(Kaloderma* Soap), toiletries *(Odol)* or candies *(Riquet)*, Wiertz sold dreams and charm, with his elegant but never vulgar young women. He was also a remarkable landscape painter who left some of the most beautiful tourist posters made in Germany (his series for the *Deutsche Kraftposten, Allgau* etc.). In the same light tone, Zabel never quite detached himself from the influence of his teacher Klinger: he has the same elegance and humor *(Pelikan, Kaid Zigaretten, Im Reiche der Reklame)*.

But when the old masters had nothing left to say, a new generation with the passion for typography and rigorous composition moved forward. Herbert Bayer, who left the Bauhaus in 1928 to direct the opening of the Dorland agency in Berlin, found artists there whose work took the same direction as his own.

Since the beginning of the Twenties, new designers like Deffke, Korner or Schulpig had appeared.

F.H. Ehmcke, cofounder in 1900 of the Steglitz studio in Berlin, created typographic characters that he arranged magnificently in his posters *(Pressa Köln 1928, F.H. Ehmcke)*. Willy Petzold of Dresden took the same course: his stylized spider for the *Textil-Ausstellung* of Dresden in 1924, his reprise of the eye by Von Stück for the *Hygiene Ausstellung* of 1931, the *Radium Bad Oberschlema* – so many striking images with clear lettering which allied geometry to sensuality. His colleague Saxon Baus also used an ample and well-structured layout. In the North, Mahlau was quite austere in his creations in Lübeck and the Hanseatic cities, and his composition was dynamic and rigorous. We can also mention Marx Bittrof in Frankfurt who, though he had made few posters, made designs and photomontages of the highest order for Opel, as did Molzahn who worked especially on brochures, splendidly composed. In Berlin, we can further mention Hadang *(Cigarettes Oberstolz, Die Neue Rarität)*, and Trias, the pupil of Klinger *(Bulgaria Krone)*.

Although the automobile inspired few artistic talents, the steamship found its poet in Bernard Steiner. Aviation inspired Otto Fule, Theo Rockenfeller and Neumann Fred; then, in the Thirties, Werner Bencke.

The coming of fascism was a fatal blow to these efforts. The Bauhaus closed and Goebbels, who immediately created a ministry of propaganda, undertook to control all graphic expression. A good part of the avant-garde emigrated, other artists ran into trouble – like Cordier, whose poster for the *Kunstausstellung* of 1932 was called degenerate art! Hans Vitus Vierthaler in Munich in 1936 aped Lissitsky for the exhibition *Entartete Kunst (Decadent Art* – held in the White Room of the Police Headquarters). In a few months the poster had regressed fifty years into allegories, profiles of Minerva and reminiscences of the Bavarian renaissance style, or blonde Aryan athletes after the model of Arno Brecker. If one adds to this the most vulgar antisemite caricatures and photos of the Führer, one arrives at an exhaustive vision of National-Socialist non-creativity. It only continued to deteriorate with the escalation that led to the war.

299. Willy Petzold:
Textile show at Dresden.
1924.

300. Jupp Wiertz:
Kaloderma soap. 1927.

301. Fritz Helmuth Ehmcke:
Graphic arts exhibition at
Cologne. 1928.

302. Julius Klinger: Poster for an Austrian hydroelectric utility. 1922.

303. Hermann Kosel: *Kaspar & Co.* art supplies.

304. Cosl-Frey: Book publisher *Rikola*. 1920.

Austria

I n 1918, the empire was shattered into pieces, Austria was a ruin. Joseph Binder recalled: "Coming home from the war, I arrived in Vienna on November 10, 1918—there was no transportation and I had to make the journey on foot. I found Vienna under a blockade and there was absolutely no food."

Despite the dissolution of the Secession, Vienna remained a cultural capital, and from the point of view of graphic art, Austria was an important country.

Julius Klinger, "the moving spirit of Viennese design,"[1] returned from Berlin and opened a studio in Vienna. In a work published in Chicago in 1923[2] he made declarations of a shattering materialism: "Money is the true factor of power in the world. Money is the sole means of universal creation. . . .

"It is more or less indifferent to us whether the source of money is the state or a capitalist private enterprise."

In this rather delirious text he professes his faith in a modernism whose model was a mythic America with its skyscrapers and its cinema.

Klinger purified his style—less fanciful, fewer visual gags, more rigor in posters that were sometimes only typographical: his poster for *Völkerbund Anleihe* is punctuated only by an O treated as a blue sphere, the one for *Cigars No. 111* with majestic numerals. In his poster for *Tabu* cigarettes, he amused himself by knocking over the letters, and for the perfumer *Pessl*, he presented elegant, refined characters. He found his sense of humor again in the *Schwabe Druck* poster where little black, red and blue devils issue from the rotating presses; and in the poster for razor blades *Rasier-Klingen Mayer*.

Disciples gathered round him: Willrab, "a blond giant, celebrated goalie and ardent dancer," who surrounds the object for sale with a suitable décor (*Monso* ventilator, *Metalum, Thermos* bottles). He could also be rigorously and effectively graphic *(Gaz Gebe, Wiener Büro Ausstellung)*. The Cosl-Frey team tended to caricature (posters for *Elysium Klinge, Rikola Bücher)*.

But the key figure of the post-war period did not come from Klinger's circle. Joseph Binder, whom Klinger recognized as "the biggest talent and the greatest hope of Austrian graphic arts," worked alone, making his first posters in 1922. In 1924, he won the competition for the *Music*

305. Josef Binder: *Meinl* tea. 1925.

1. In *Gebrauchsgrafik*, 1926, No. 7
2. Julius Wisotski: *Poster Art in Vienna*. Chicago, 1923.

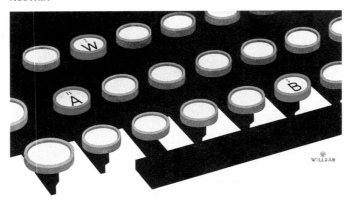

IV. WIENER BÜRO-AUSSTELLUNG
22-30. SEPTEMBER 1923 MESSEPALAST 9-6 UHR

306. Willrab: Office exposition in Vienna. 1923.

308. Klinger: *Tabu* cigarette paper. 1919.

307. Hans Wagula: Travel poster for *Dubrovnik*.

and Theater festival with two stylized heralds blowing trumpets, using only three colors: blue, red and black – Klinger's colors. From 1925 to 1929, he was entrusted with the designs for the Meinl tea and coffee importing firm. His exclamation-mark poster (made up of the coffee-drinker's fez and his cup) and other graphic tricks were an immediate success. He was also given the Persil detergent campaign – where he played with the white laundry.

Orders poured in, bringing successes, like the travel poster for *Raxbahn* where the B traces the route of a train around a mountain, or *Milch auf jedem Tisch,* a perfectly balanced still life promoting milk. Binder soon became a theoretician who taught in Austria and was frequently invited to America.

"We live in an epoch of modern spirit and life. Everything moves faster today. In conceiving the poster, we need the same speed to transmit the message effectively. Communication must be dramatic."[1]

He taught his students to start with the "Grund Formen" – basic forms like the sphere and the cube (in which he aligned himself with the Bauhaus, the U.A.M. in France and the avant-gardes).

He also interested himself in color, and published a book in 1934, *Color in Advertising* (Studio, London). In 1936 he settled in America where he continued to work.

Beside these two dominant figures, there were graphic artists of purely national importance, like Kosel with his well-constructed posters *(Wiener Messe,* 1931; *Wien und die Wiener);* Kurt Pebal *(Meinl Kaffee, Junghaus, Bally);* Andreas Karl Hemberger, working in the Art Deco vein *(Atlas Riemen);* and Slama, who made several posters for the Social Democrats. Georg Mayer-Marton made a beautiful, very well-constructed poster for the film *Danton's Death* in 1929. In Graz, Hans Wagula deserves mention.

Finally, let us mention Biro's posters; after the failed revolution in Hungary, he designed some remarkable film and commercial posters *(Meinl Kaffee)* in Vienna.

1. Carla Binder: *Joseph Binder*. Vienna: Anton Schroll & Co., 1976.

Milch

AUF JEDEM TISCH

309. Josef Binder: *Milk on Every Table*. 1928.

310. A. M. Cassandre:
Nord Express. 1927.

France Between the Wars

311. Georges Barbier. *Clotilde et Alexandre Sakharoff.* 1923

Unlike Germany, where the general level of advertising was high but where few personalities imposed their own graphic style, and unlike England, where clients like the London Underground or Shell-Mex exercised artistic control, France at this time was rich in strong personalities. Perhaps it was due to the spirit of Paris, capital of the arts, where instead of avant-garde movements there were individuals, working as their orders came in, who gave advertising its style. No doubt it is also due to a certain Roaring Twenties spirit – France emerging, unlike Germany, Austria, or Hungary, relatively carefree from the war.

Paris again became the capital of fashion and entertainment, and prominent painters gathered in Montparnasse to publicize dances, shows and exhibitions. Motoring and sports in general, the cinema and the music-hall, fast trains and voyages were the craze of the moment.

With Paul Poiret supreme, Parisian couturiers dressed the world. Lucien Vogel, who in 1912 created the *Gazette du bon ton* and then *Vogue*, called on illustrators who, in their precision drawings, resembled the artists of the late 18th century. These mannerists were occasional poster artists at the beginning of the Twenties, more for show business than for fashion.

Georges Barbier made a poster for the Sakharoffs and for *Le Bal des Petits Lits blancs*, Georges Lepape for *Spinelly* and *Le Bal de la Couture*, Andre Marty for *Toilettes d'Hiver, La Salle Marivaux* and a series for the *British Underground*. Guy Arnoux, in the style of late eighteenth century engravers, created posters for *Vins de Bourgogne*, for *Bal tricolore à l'Opéra* (1921), and several cinema posters (*La Kermesse Héroïque*, 1937). Robert Bonfils designed one of the posters for the Exposition of 1925, and Paul Iribe one for *Jeanne Lanvin*. Umberto Brunelleschi was more assiduous, and regularly announced the fashions for the *Palais de la Nouveauté* of the department store Dufayel, while the *Bon Marché* store called on René Vincent. Jean Dupas worked largely for the English: *Arnold Constable, Spring fashions*, 1928, 1929. Maggy Salzedo, A. Pecoud and Charles Garry were lesser lights who regularly worked for the major department stores.

The Ballets Russes and jazz revolutionized show business at this time, bringing into it modernism and rhythm. The Russian impressario Diaghilev, who engaged fine-art painters to make his scenery, also asked them for posters: Léon Bakst, of course (*Le Martyr de Saint Sebastien* and *Caryathis*, 1916), but also Jean Cocteau (1911) and Picasso (*Parade*, 1917). The Russian ballet performances at Monte-Carlo followed, with Derain (1932), and André Masson (1933), while the Swedish ballet, with Jean Borlin, called on Paul Colin and Gladky.

312. André-Edouard Marty: Winter clothing sale. 1923.

313. Georges
Lepape: Red
Cross charity
ball. 1924.

314. Léon Bakst: *Caryathis*. 1916.

315. Kees Van Dongen: A gala organized by the artist. c. 1925.

317. Jean Dupas: *Bordeaux* travel poster. 1937.

316. Robert Bonfils: Decorative arts exposition, Paris. 1925.

The music-hall, which had overthrown the café-concert, became a great consumer of posters. The stars all had their official poster artists. Mistinguett took on Charles Gesmar who, until his premature death in 1928, designed her costumes and a stunning series of posters which featured her in feathers and jewels. Zig, who also died young (1936), took over from him. Josephine Baker was linked for some time after her Paris debut in the Revue Nègre in 1925 with Paul Colin, then with Michel Gyarmathy and with Zig. Charles Kiffer, in broad flat tones, immortalized the protruding lips and straw hat of his friend Maurice Chevalier, as well as the silhouette of the young Edith Piaf (1938). In the Thirties, it was J.D. Van Caulaert who designed posters for a great many performers, from Marie Dubas to Cecile Sorel, and the inescapable Mistinguett. From the end of the Thirties, finally, Gaston Girbal, like Charles Levy at the turn of the century, made hundreds of portraits in a uniform realistic style, with a few masterpieces among them *(Alibert)*. There were decorators like José de Zamora, illustrators like Becan *(Rahna,* 1927) and J. Romains *(Knock),* who prepared an occasional poster. But there were also fashionable painters, attracted by the stage lights, who brought a considerable contribution to show business advertising: Van Dongen (for *Yvonne George, Arletty,* and *Vincent Escudero),* Don *(Rita Georg, Gaby Morlay)* and Jean-Gabriel Domergue *(Thérèse Dorny, Régine Flory, Parisys).* Let us finally mention André Girard's delicate posters for the stars of French Columbia records.

Aside from Paul Colin and occasional attempts by Jean Carlu (Pabst's *L'Altantide,* 1932), Boris Bilinsky (Fritz Lang's *Metropolis,* 1926), and Eric Aaes and Djo Bourgeois (Marcel L'Herbier's *L'Inhumaine,* 1924),

318. Charles Gesmar: *Mistinguett*. 1925.

319. Jean Gabriel Domergue: *Régine Flory*. 1923.

320. Charles Kiffer: *Maurice Chevalier*. 1936.

321. Gaston Girbal: *Alibert*. c. 1935.

322. Natalia Gontcharova:
Artists' ball. 1926.

323. Auguste Herbin:
Russian artists' ball. 1925.

191

324. Marie Laurencin:
Bal des Petits Lits Blanc. 1931.

325. Tsuguharu Fujita:
Ball of the *AAAA* artists' union. 1926.

326. André Lhote:
A Montparnasse costume ball. 1922.

the cinema did not employ the avant-garde and preferred a graphic mediocrity that was perhaps more effective and popular.

Only Jean-A. Mercier, who had been a successful commercial poster artist at the beginning of the Twenties (*Salon du Mobilier*, 1926; *Foires de Dijon et Marseille, Chaussures Unic* and his famous *Cointreau*), brought some distinction to film posters: *Jeanne d'Arc*, 1928; *A nous la liberté*, 1931; *14 juillet*, 1932; *Le Bossu*, 1934. Jean Dubout was one of those exceptional artists able to impose a style of his own, which is inextricably entwined with the films of Marcel Pagnol: *Marius*, 1931; *Fanny*, 1932; *César*, 1935; etc. Henri Cerutti enjoyed a similar symbiosis with Pagnol.

We have seen that painters, whether of the avant-garde or more prudently fashionable, did not disdain poster-making. Their Montparnasse existence, with its galas and its balls, led to some work: thus the *Bal de la Grande Ourse* of Herbin (1925) and the *Bal des Artistes Russes* by Gontcharova. For the *A.A.A.A.* (Aide Amicale aux Artistes), Othon Friesz (1923), Marie Vassiliev (1924), Maurice Utrillo (1925), Foujita (1926), Suzanne Valadon (1927) and Paul-Emile Pissaro (1930) worked in turns. The more worldly, like Raoul Dufy, presented events like the *Saison de Paris* (1933) and the *Journée mondaine de la Bicyclette* (1939); a dinner, *Un soir en mer à Cannes* (Picabia); or a less exclusive affair, like the *Bal des Petits Lits blancs* (Vertés, Marie Laurencin, J.-G. Domergue).

The surrealists left a superabundant production of tracts but few real posters. Those few toyed, of course, with the lettering.

Sports were fashionable for men and women: tennis, golf and motoring, as were cruises. Paid vacations permitted hiking and canoeing for the less affluent.

327. Djo-Bourgeois: Poster for the innovative film by Marcel L'Herbier, *L'Inhumaine*. 1924.

golf de Sarlabot
houlgate – cabourg

Les Imp.ies FILMS RÉUNIES - PARIS

328. René Vincent:
Tourist poster for
the Brittany resort
area. c. 1930.

329. Roger Broders: *Marseille*. 1935.

330. Sandy Hook: Travel poster for a steamship company.

While sport and tourism occasionally attracted even great creators like Cassandre, they also had their specialists, more concerned with elegance than with modernism. René Vincent, a fashion illustrator, was, even more, an automobile fanatic. His posters for *Salmson, Peugeot, Motobloc,* and *Bugatti* are masterpieces of refinement. At his death, Geo Ham (Geo Hamel) took his place *(Amilcar, BNC),* specializing like Falcucci in racing *(Rallye de Monaco,* etc.).

The shipping companies most often called on naval painters like Albert Sebille or Sandy Hook, recognizable by the anchor that followed their signatures. Their posters are true painted pictures—such as those designed by Geo Dorival, or those E. Paul Champseix made for the railroads, in post-impressionist style. Roger Broders distinguished himself with broad flat tones and a bold geometrism in his series of posters for the city of Marseille. The rich tones of his palette render the warmth of the South of France *(Cote d'Azur, Calvi, Sainte-Maxime,* etc.) as truly as they do the cold of the Alps *(Chamonix, Saint-Pierre-de-Chartreuse,* etc.), and he does not shy away from audacious compositions *(Tour du Mont-Blanc).* Eric de Coulon is often of comparable quality *(Allevard-les-Bains, Alpes & Jura).* So is Pierre Commarmond who, when he did not confine himself to landscape, could draw striking images *(Brighton,* and an admirable *Deauville).* For the fashionable resorts, posters were likewise prepared by fashionable artists, like Don *(La Baule, Biarritz).*

Beside this constellation of talents devoting themselves to fashion, show business and the elegant life in general, commercial advertising was also developing.

Advertising for products had been revolutionized by Cappiello as of 1905. After the war, his principles caught on, as did the scientific approaches to advertising that came from America. These precepts were

331. Eric de Coulon. *Alpes · Jura.* ca 1930

333. Leonetto Cappiello: The famous bull's eye poster for *Kub*. 1931.

332. Leonetto Cappiello: For *Lesieur* table oil. 1930.

presented in books like J. Aren's *La publicité lucrative* and *Sa Majesté la Publicité; Les affaires et l'affiche* by Paul Dermer and Eugène Gourmont; and *Traité pratique de publicité* by Louis Augé. These books were full of rules about legibility, compatibility of colors, how to develop a campaign, etc.

Cappiello's influence could also be seen in a whole generation of young graphic artists, including Cassandre and Carlu. While the best of them found a personality of their own, others, like Jean d'Ylen, a good poster artist in the long run (his campaigns for *Shell, Ripolin, Bally),* never detached themselves from the master's style. J. Stall, Henri Monnier and Paul Mohr were only lesser Cappiellos, while he himself continued his gigantic output (3000 posters!) until his death in 1942. Working for Devambez to whom he delivered his projects weekly, he was in turn elegant (*Poccardi*, 1922; *Mistinguett*, 1920; *Jane Raynouard*, 1921; *Studebaker*, 1925; *Golf de Font-Romeu*, 1929), flattering to beautiful women *(Asti Cinzano*, 1920; *Aix-les-Bains*, 1921), or flirting with geometrism (*O'Cap*, 1930; *Cinzano*, 1932), all the while retaining a unique intensity, as in the bull's eye of *Bouillon Kub* (1931), one of his masterpieces.

Achille Mauzan (1883-1952), although following an entirely different path, can nevertheless be compared with Cappiello in style. Leaving Italy in 1927, he launched the advertising poster in Argentina with some brilliant inventions *(Bilz Geniol)* which reflected the influence of the comic strip. He also produced the more classic *Agua Colonia Griet,* and *Crosley Radio,* more Art Déco. Returning to France in 1932, he produced only a few more posters *(Picon Cusenier, Brummell).*

At the beginning of the Twenties a new generation, fortified by Cappiello's principles and not hiding their debt to the master ("We all began by copying Cappiello", declared Carlu, Colin, Cassandre and Loupot in 1928), was ready to transpose them into a new style that emerged from

334. Achille Mauzan: A 3-sheet poster for an Argentine importer of *Crosley* radios. c. 1930.

335. Leonetto Cappiello:
Dubonnet. 1932.

336. Leonetto Cappiello:
Bally shoes. 1934.

337. A.M. Cassandre:
The newspaper
L'Intransigeant. 1925.

338. A.M. Cassandre: *Pivolo* liqueur. 1924.

the cubist and constructivist trends. Four great poster artists appeared, starting in 1925, each of whom in his own style revolutionized the poster by presenting radically new images. In 1923, Loupot brought out his *Voisin* posters, reminiscent of Cézanne; Cassandre came in with his geometric wood-cutter for *Bucheron;* then there was, in 1925, Paul Colin's *Revue nègre,* Carlu's *Monsavon,* Cassandre's *L'Intransigeant,* and the *Foire de Francfort* by Loupot. They were nicknamed The Three Musketeers (because they were four), and they were charter members of the Union des Artistes Modernes. For fifteen years they would dominate French advertising art and, in turn, serve as its example.

Born in Russia in 1901, of French parents, Cassandre (real name, Adolphe Marie-Mouron), the most spectacularly pure, was called by Blaise Cendrars "the stage director of the streets". Cassandre himself very clearly defined the principles that should guide the poster artist: "Painting is an end in itself, but the poster artist is only a medium of communication between the merchant and the public, something like the telegraphist: he doesn't emit messages, he transmits them; no one asks his opinion—he's only asked to make a clear, powerful, precise communication".

Through the application of this principle, as he set it down in a preface, "advertising art has hardly been born, but born it is". From 1925 on, with *L'Intransigeant* (the newspaper's name is shortened in his design), Cassandre retained the force and purity of his geometrism. It is necessary, however, in order to avoid facile or tortuous comparisons, to relate Cassandre to cubism, with which both he and the other Musketeers had been too readily associated.

339. A.M. Cassandre:
The Paris to
Amsterdam express,
Etoile du Nord. 1927.

340. A.M. Cassandre: *Triplex* auto glass. 1930.

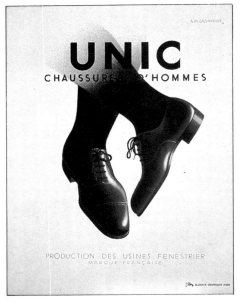

341. A.M. Cassandre: *Unic* shoes. 1932.

Cassandre never hid his sympathy with cubism: "As a reaction against individualism, cubism appeared to me as the capital event of the last twenty years." He was careful, however, to specify what he had taken from it: "Some people have called my posters cubist. They are so only in the sense that my method is essentially geometric and monumental". In fact, Cassandre felt himself closer to architecture, "the art I prefer to all the others".

Lettering, too often neglected, had an essential importance for him: "Too long misunderstood or underestimated by our predecessors, lettering in fact plays an essential role in the poster. It's the star of the wall stage because it alone is charged with telling the public the magic formula that sells. The poster artist should always begin with the text, and set it, as far as possible, in the center of the composition. The design should be based on the text and not inversely. . . . my architectural principles of the poster necessarily orient my preferences not towards a parody of the inscription, but towards a pure product of the ruler and the compass."

Cassandre was able to put these methods into practice when he left the employ of the publisher Hachard where he had met Maurice Moyrand, the sales representaive of the Danel printing firm of Lille. With him he formed the Alliance Graphique studio and began receiving commissions for railway posters. With Cassandre, the machine found its herald. First of all, the railways: there's a powerful inducement to travel in the rails fleeing into the horizon in the *Etoile du Nord* (1927); in the magnified image of the train at full speed in the *Chemins de Fer du Nord* (1927); and in the close-up of flaring headlights on the wheels in *LMS* (1928). His virtuosity with the airbrush, the rigor and geometrism of the composition, the layout of the lettering, whose details are relegated to the borders, all give these posters unrivaled beauty and effectiveness.

His steamships were also exemplary successes. After the variations on smokestacks and steamwhistles in *Statendam* (1928) and *Cote d'Azur* (1931), Cassandre scored again with the *Atlantique* (1931), using the *Normandie's* perfectly synthetic image by contrasting the outsized hull of the giant steamship on the page with a small tugboat and some gulls. The figure riveted to his steering-wheel in *Triplex* (1931) shows the same power.

But Cassandre was not limited to transport posters, or to any routine.

342. A.M. Cassandre: Britain's *L.M.S.*
Railroad. 1928.

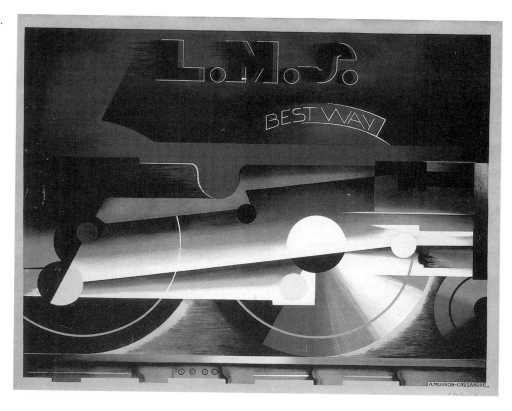

343. A.M. Cassandre:
Pathé records. 1932.

344. A.M. Cassandre:
Book poster. 1930.

345. A.M. Cassandre: *Normandie.* 1935.

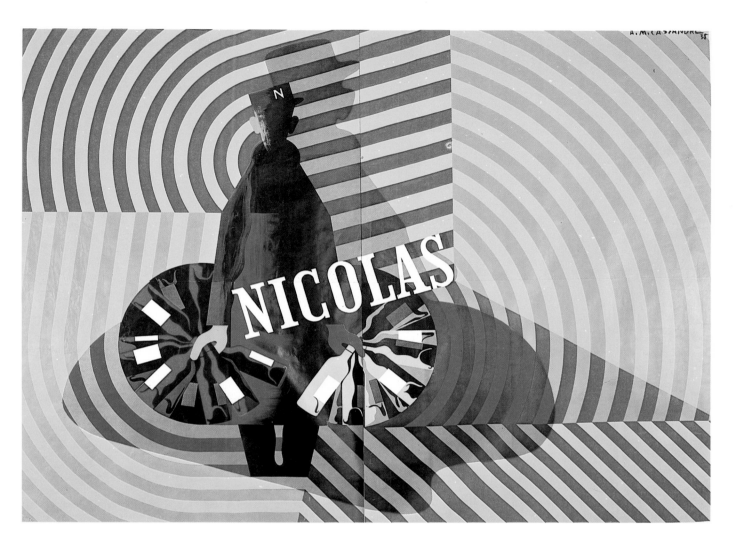

346. A.M. Cassandre: The wine merchant *Nicolas*. 1935.

347. A.M. Cassandre: Poster for *Prunier* restaurant's London branch. 1934.

348. A.M. Cassandre: Travel poster for Scotland. 1934.

349. Jean Carlu: *Monsavon* soap. 1925.

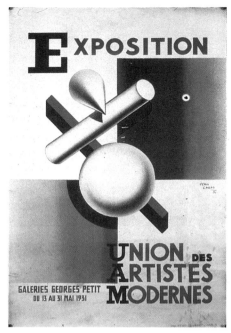

351. Jean Carlu: Art exposition. 1931.

350. Jean Carlu: A three-dimensional billboard for *Odéon* records. 1929.

In his designs for the *Unic* shoes (1932), the *Miniwatt Philips Radio* (1931) or the *Celtiques* cigarettes (1934), he made object posters where he simply represented the article for sale, thus following Lucian Bernhard and the new Swiss objectivity—with an additional warmth and panache. For the *Wagon-bar* (1932) and *Pernod* (1934) he played with photomontage. He could also use cinematic viewpoints, such as the extraordinary close-up of the tennis-ball he throws in the face of the passer-by *(Coupe Davis, 1932),* or the bird's eye view of the record for *Pathé* (1932). This cinematic vision is certainly in evidence in the series *Dubo-Dubon-Dubonnet,* where the figure adds color as it imbibes, while his version of *Nectar de Nicolas* (1935) foretells kinetic art. By 1934, Cassandre used supple lines and tender colors side by side with geometrism *(Angleterre, Ecosse, Fetes de Paris, Italie)* and after 1936, when he left for America, some of his designs had a touch of surrealism in them. In those years, Cassandre, little by little, abandoned the poster in favor of theatre decor and costumes, as well as painting.

Born in 1900, Jean Carlu gave up his architectural studies in 1918 after the loss of his right arm in an accident. After a reeducation spent in making posters for food products "à la Cappiello", he could at last apply the principles of cubism which he passionately studied (Gleizes and Juan Gris had a great influence on him), for *Monsavon* (1925), followed by the *Aquarium de Monaco, Dentifrice Gellé, Paris Soir,* and *Théâtre Pigalle.* He stated his theories in various articles and lectures: "The poster is a means of propaganda designed to associate a name with an image: it is necessary to reduce its role to that single ambition."

But to arrive at this, some rules must be respected. "To stay etched in the mind of the passer-by, the poster must be a closed composition, following the rhythm of a simple geometric system, which catches the eye more easily than a limited amorphous composition."

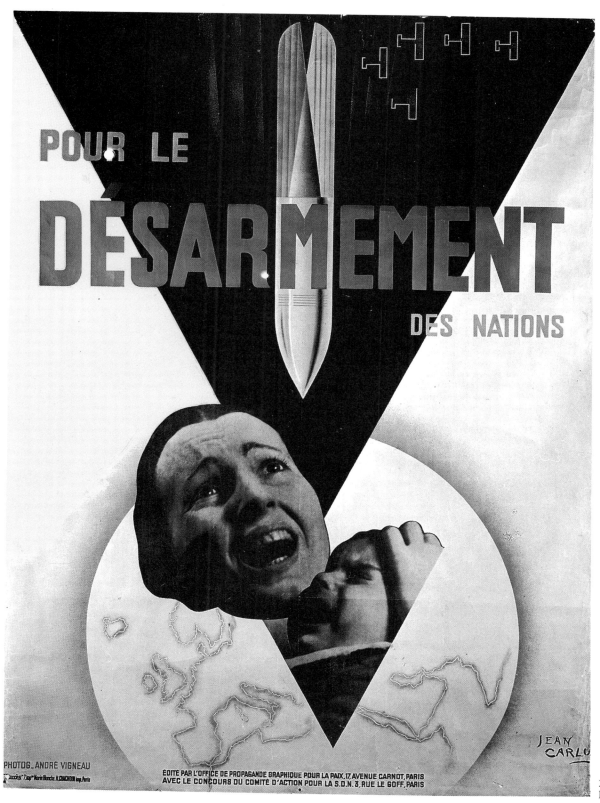

POUR LE **DÉSARMEMENT** DES NATIONS

PHOTOG_ ANDRÉ VIGNEAU

ÉDITÉ PAR L'OFFICE DE PROPAGANDE GRAPHIQUE POUR LA PAIX, 17, AVENUE CARNOT, PARIS
AVEC LE CONCOURS DU COMITÉ D'ACTION POUR LA S.D.N. 3, RUE LE GOFF, PARIS

JEAN CARLU

352. Jean Carlu:
For disarmament. 1932.

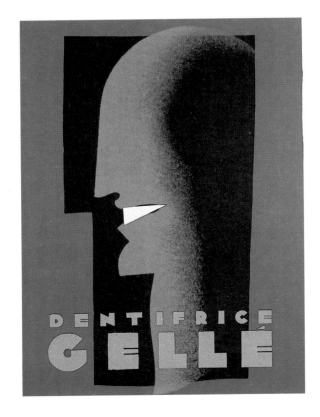

353. Jean Carlu:
Aquarium de Monaco. 1926.

354. Jean Carlu:
Gellé toothpaste. 1927.

355. Jean Carlu:
Larranaga cigars. 1929.

356. Jean Carlu:
Théâtre Pigalle. 1929.

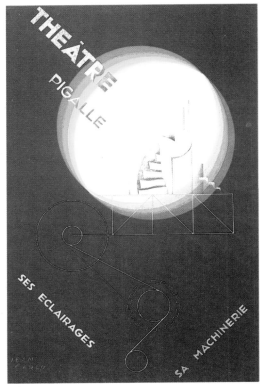

357. Charles Loupot: *Van Heusen* collars. 1928.

358. Charles Loupot: *Mira* blades. 1927.

We thus arrive at what Carlu calls "the graphic expression of the idea" which is the basic rule of the poster.

From 1932 on, Carlu became involved in various political causes: for the Agency of Graphic Propaganda for Peace, which he founded, he drew the poster *Désarmement* (1932); others in this vein include *L'Obole, Les Journées de la Paix,* etc. In these posters he made much use of photomontage, a technique he pioneered. He also made experiments, with the Martel brothers among others, in metal-relief posters (*Grande Maison de Blanc, Pavillion Ocel, Odeon*) and the luminous poster (*La Cuisinière électrique*). He abandoned geometrism little by little from 1934 on (*Grands fêtes de Paris*), turning to surrealism. He played an important role in the Paris Exposition of 1937 where he was given charge of the advertising section. In 1939, he went to the United States to take charge of the French pavilion at the World's Fair in New York, where he remained throughout World War II.

Charles Loupot began his work in Switzerland during the First World War, where he made his first posters, and rapidly became a master lithographer. His first works, most often for fashion (*Caillier, Grieder, Canton, P.K.Z.*), cigarettes (*Sato, Raga*) or automobiles (*Philipossian*), could be called "mannerist". Called to Paris by Devambez, he briefly collaborated on the *Gazette du Bon Ton.* In 1923 his two posters for *Voisin* "dropped like two stones into the frog-pond of the advertising imagination"

359. Charles Loupot: *Café Martin.* 1929.

360. Charles Loupot: *Valentine* paints. 1928.

361. Charles Loupot: Poster for a furniture store. c. 1928.

362. Charles Loupot: *St. Raphael* liqueur. 1937.

(R.L. Dupuy). After that, for Les Belles Affiches, an agency founded for him by the Damour brothers, he brought out a series of masterpieces in which his virtuosity as a lithographer appeared: he used shaded backgrounds, sometimes even leaving traces of sketches, to make his posters warmer; and he used successive printings with a slight displacement so that each patch of color blurred into the adjacent patches. Not loquacious, Loupot however left this declaration, the heart of his work: "The lazy eye must be continually surprised by a simple and perfect graphic art." There is the *Peugeot* automobile, set off at full speed, the *Austin* tractor, spectacularly surrounded by an immensity of dark earth, *Twining's* tea and *Martin's* coffee where a single cup manages to evoke their aromas. There are the *Mirus* posters, definitive images of a stove; the richly colored cubist designs (with gold and silver) for *Van Heusen, O'Cap,* and *Mira.* Faithful to Cappiello's principles, Loupot invented the *Valentine* paints' stylized painting figure, the wooden personalized carpenter for the furniture sale at *Galeries Barbès,* and a new version of the *Cointreau* clown.

After an unproductive spell at the Alliance Grahpique, Loupot revived his creative forces for the great industrialist Eugène Schueller. There are masterpieces of the airbrush: *Dop, Monsavon,* and especially *Coty* with its bewitching lips. In 1937, at Max Augier's request, Loupot redesigned the two *St. Raphael* men, whom he hung on the walls of the Exposition booth and all over Paris, beginning a work he would bring to an unequalled level of refinement after World War II. His qualities as a lithographer, his intransigence and his purity of style made Loupot an example for many disciples.

Born in Nancy in 1892, Paul Colin arrived in Paris in 1913. He vegetated there until 1925 when his poster for the *Revue Nègre* brought him overnight success. After that he became the poster artist, costumer and decorator of the hour. After his first, very geometric compositions (*Wiener et Doucet*, 1925; *Loie Fuller*, 1925; *Jean Borlin*, 1925; *Bal Nègre*, 1927; *Lisa Duncan*, 1928), he gradually switched to a very personal style made of superimposed planes (*L'Amour Magicien*, 1926; *Maya*, 1927; *La Rouille*, 1929; *Tabarin*, 1928; *Casino de Paris*, 1932), for the theater and music-hall. For many stars he also made posters which are portraits, where he gave free rein to his sketches (*Cora Madou*, 1929; *Damia*,

364. Paul Colin: Advertising Josephine Baker's recordings for French *Columbia*. 1930.

365. Paul Colin: Cabaret *Tabarin*. 1928.

363. Paul Colin: *Revue Nègre*, the American show which introduced Josephine Baker to Paris in 1925.

209

366. Paul Colin:
Lisa Duncan. 1927.

367. Paul Colin:
French *Columbia*'s recording
star *Damia*. 1930.

369. Paul Colin:
The clown *Grock*
recorded for
Odéon in 1930.

368. Paul Colin: *Wiener & Doucet* piano team. 1925.

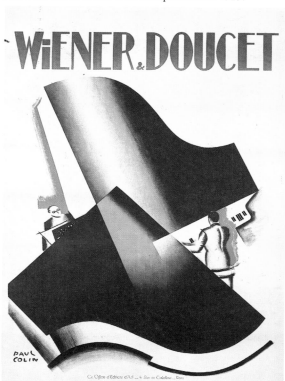

370. Francis Bernard: Poster for a gas utility promotion. 1928.

371. Francis Bernard: *Arts Ménagers* exhibition in Paris. 1933.

372. Francis Bernard: *Cunard Line*. c. 1930.

1930; *Pierre Meyer*, 1930; *Carlos Gardel* and *Grock* (1930). He also produced posters for the ballet *(Jean Weidt*, 1938; *Serge Lifar*, 1935; *Espanita Cortez*, 1938), for many balls, some good film posters *(A Nous la Liberté*, 1931) and the remarkable poster for the *Musée d'Ethnographie du Trocadero* (1935). Although he had little affinity for product advertising (the aperitif *R* is an exception), Paul Colin shared the opinions of Cassandre, Carlu and Loupot on the poster: "The poster should be a telegram addressed to the mind". Starting in 1926, he taught his theories in his own school, through which hundreds of aspiring poster artists passed.

Many other graphic artists emerged to carry on the principles of the modern poster based on the examples and teachings of these four giants.

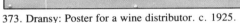

373. Dransy: Poster for a wine distributor. c. 1925.

374. Sepo (Severo Pozzati): *Anic* filter cigarettes. 1938.

376. Alexis Kow: Industry poster urging the French to buy domestic cars. 1939.

375. Munetsugu Satomi: *KLM* airline. 1933.

Sepo (Severo Pozzati) arrived in Paris in 1920. His style, imitative of Cappiello at first (*Maja*, 1923; *Stylo Dorland*, 1925), became geometric for the *Regie Franciase des Cigarettes* (1928) followed by *Cigarettes roulées* in 1931, by *Week-End* in 1936 (imitating Cassandre's *Route Bleue*), *Anic* in 1938, the *Palais de la Nouveauté* (1928), *Amieux* (1929), the *Chaussures Dressoir*, and above all, from 1928 on, by his work for *Chemises Noveltex*.

Satomi arrived in Paris from Japan in 1922, and worked for the *Six Jours*, *KLM* and Japanese companies.

Francis Bernard, a member of the Union des Artistes Modernes, like the four greats, is unjustly neglected: his cubist profiles for the *Bal des Petits Lits Blancs*, his experiments for *Black & Decker* (1931), his series for the *Arts Menagers* (1931, 1933), and likewise his tourist posters (*Maroc Cunard line*) are first-rate. His poster *Gaz* was the focus of the French exhibit at the Munich exposition in 1928.

Also to be mentioned are Leon Gishia, pioneer of photomontage and a good colorist (*Bleu du ciel, Vendre*, 1931; *Huilor et Oleo*, 1933; *Radio Gabriel Gaveau* and *Laines du Chat Botté*), and Alexis Brodovitch, who has been called the surrealist of the airbrush (*Bucheron*, 1929; *Vu*). De Valerio, very versatile in his production (he designed hundreds of sheet music covers, in a richly-colored palette), worked for *Air France, Chrysler, Stop Fire* and several aviation meets.

Roger Perot was also among those who produced powerful images for the *Arts Ménagers* (1934), *Laquolin* and for a coke company, but above all for the automobile (*Marchal*, 1927, *Peugeot*, 1931; *Delahaye*, 1932). Cassandre's perfect creations found an echo in his disciple Pierre Fix-Masseau, in *L'Exactitude, Chemins de Fer du Nord Starn*, the *Côte d'Azur* and the *Huiles Renault*. Maurus took up the motifs of the *Étoile du Nord* for the *United States Lines* and *Air Union*. Dil (Louis Malavielle) also took his inspiration from it in his poster for *Fiat*. Alexis Kow's designs for automobiles in *Cibie, Panhard* and *Hotchkiss*, and Solon's for airplanes in *Fairman*, also made good posters. Marton made a remarkable *Peugeot* motorcycle (1930), but so did Leroy (1931) and Fichet. Cassandre can also be glimpsed in J.-P. Junot's *Ducretet T.S.F.* (1936), his photomontage for the *Chemins de Fer du Nord*, the *BNCI* and *Peppermint*, and in the work of his assistant, the young Savignac (*Roquefort Maria Grimal, Grand Prix ACF*, 1937). Jacques Nathan, Jean Carlu's collaborator at the Exposition of 1937, began a considerable high-quality production in the Thirties: *Salon des Arts Ménagers* (1934), *Gebrauchsgrafik, Mumm* (1937), *Confitures Maître*.

Let us also mention Roger Bollinger (*Cook*), Roland Ansieau (*Marie Brizard*, 1932; *Axa*, 1931; *Nestlé*, 1932), René Ravo (*Le Beurre, Arts Ménagers*), Ponty (*Radiola, Paquet*), Pierre Zenobel (*Fêtes de Paris, Buvez du Vin*), Roland Hugon (*Autorails*), Dransy (*Nicolas*), Edgar Derouet (*Loterie Nationale*), Raymond Gid (*Vermouth Crucifix, Yoyo Duncan*) and the travel poster specialist Jean Picard Le Doux (*Syrie et Liban, Sicile*). And, finally, Claude Lemeunier's posters in relief.

Like the poster itself, poster-hanging made spectacular progress in France in the period between the wars. With the acceleration of life, it was necessary to catch the eye more quickly: the poster artist must land the strike, but the poster hanger aims it. The size of posters increased: surfaces measured up to 6½ square meters. The *Cadum* baby and *Saint-Raphael's* figures, gigantically enlarged, were spread out across the cities,

377. Roland Ansieau: *Eclipse* shoe polish. c. 1935.

378. Scene-shifters of the urban stage.

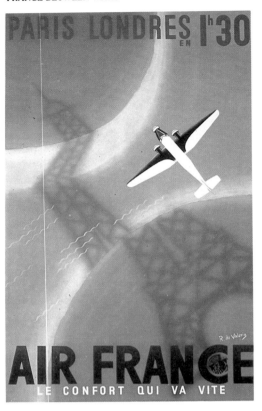

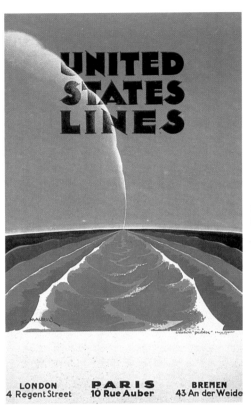

379. Raymond de Valerio:
Airline poster. c. 1930.

380. Edmond Maurus:
Steamship company. c. 1930.

381. Jacques Nathan-Garomond:
Arts Ménagers exhibitions. 1934.

colored by armadas of painters. The spaces for hanging evolved in the same way. At the turn of the century posters were rarely larger than 164 x 122 cm./64½x48 in. (the "quadruple colombier"), the most common size being the "double colombier" (120 x 80 cm./47¼ x 31½ in.). But now the format of 320 x 240 cm./126 x 94½ in. was frequently used. The new generation of poster artists, playing with bands of color, spread them on placards so enormous as to cover entire facades of buildings. As the automobile acceleratred everything, it also propelled the poster outside the cities and, along the first great highways like the Paris-Deauville route or the National 7, the first French billboards appeared. The automobile was not the only invention to revolutionize the poster: after 1923, airplanes were used by André Citroen to fly advertising banners. It was the same Citroen who, always shoulder to shoulder with progress and gigantism, from 1925 to 1936 lit up the Eiffel Tower with his name and trademark in a 250,000-watt display, with the help of the stage magician Jacopozzi. Neon, perfected by the engineer Claude, was also used for experimentation, notably by Jean Carlu for *Osram* bulbs. Three-dimensional posters in metal were perfected by Carlu for *Odeon* records and *Osram* bulbs, and used by Loupot for *Valentine* paints and *Nicolas* the wine merchant. Janko invented the talking poster (an arrangement with a hidden phonograph) for the newspaper *Paris Soir;* the giant letters of *Martini and Rossi* sailed on the Seine on a floating display called Mobilo. The dynamism, ingenuity and grandeur which marked this period were were served by the 1881 law, still in effect, which placed no limit to the imagination of advertisers.

382. Pierre Fix-Masseau: Promotion for the French State railways. 1932.

383. Léo Marfurt:
Belga cigarettes. 1925.

Belgium

384. Fernand Toussaint: Brussels Trade Fair. 1923.

The "Belgian energy", which had animated the country at the turn of the century, like the Art Nouveau that had inspired it, petered out after World War I. The country had not suffered more than the other European nations, but nothing dynamic emerged from its suffering. Absent from the large international graphic reviews, it was also absent from the Exposition of Decorative Arts in Paris in 1925. Nor was there an advertising creation that might have represented it.

The pre-war artists did continue producing, but Rassenfosse in Liège, who now managed the Benard printing house, had become banal; and Toussaint fell into a platitudinous historicism with his posters for the Brussels Fair. This medieval-realist style gained great popularity for fairs and expositions. Robert Hens and Médard Tytgat, who were its other exponents, are entirely without interest.

Francis Delamare, a true professional of the poster, is the only personality who stands out at the beginning of the Twenties: his figures constructed of match boxes and match sticks for *Union Match* are ingenious and effective.

The first attempt to revive Belgian poster art came from Marcel Baugniet, a member of the "7 Arts" group (avant-garde in the futurist-constructivist vein). In 1924, he designed for *Philips Argenta* the first Belgian post-cubist poster, much influenced by Delaunay. In a 1926 article[1] he declared: "I know that many ignorant minds still see in stylization a sort of outrage to morals, and become indignant at being tripped up in their short-sighted habits. That's why posters that enchant the eye with the unexpectedness of their rhythm are so rare here."

Help came from a Swiss artist, Léo Marfurt. Pupil of Jules de Praetere, he served for a time as director of the Schools of Applied Art at Basel and Zurich from 1905 to 1917, returned to Belgium in 1921, and settled in Antwerp in 1922. There he quickly found his first big client, Vander Elst, maker of *Belga* cigarettes. His Miss Belga, treated in colorful flat-tints, began a long career with many variations. In 1928 he publicized the *Flying Scotsman,* a crack train of the London and North Eastern Railway, where in fourteen colors and a play of oblique shadows, he painted a scene of a station platform. Pierre Baudson[2] rightly sees in it Jacques Villon's influence, specifically his painting *Soldats en Marche* of 1913. Also in 1928, Marfurt designed for *Chrysler* an automobile hood with the wings of the radiator-caps in outsized projected shadows. In

385. Marcel Baugniet: *Philips* lightbulbs. 1924.

1. Marcel Baugniet: "La Publicite Graphique," *La Newie,* Vol. 7, No. 3, 1926.
2. Pierre Baudson: Preface to catalog *Art de l'Affiche en Belgique,* Galerie CGER, Bruxelles, 1980.

FLYING SCOTSMAN

LEAVES KING'S CROSS (LONDON) 10.0 A.M. EVERY WEEK-DAY

PUBLISHED BY THE LONDON & NORTH EASTERN RAILWAY   PRINTED IN ENGLAND   HAYCOCK PRESS . LONDON

386. Léo Marfurt: Poster for an express of the LNER system. 1928.

1929, for *Remington* typewriters, he contrasted the somber and static mass of the machine with the moving keys and fingers. He had the same power and succinctness for *Minerva* automobiles, causing his friend Marc Severin, a post-cubist and occasional poster-maker, to remark: "The stylization, the symbol, condense and concentrate the thought and give it a power and graphic vigor that immediately capture and direct the attention, without dangerous anecdotal lingering, straight to the essentials."

For Belgian tourism, a quite different market, Marfurt could also find the symbol, the right image: In his 1938 poster for Belgian beaches *(Belgie-De Kust),* he gives us a simple still life with a balloon, a bucket, a shovel and a sandcastle, with the Belgian flag fluttering above them. The sand is yellow, the sea in the background green and blue, and the whole radiates in irresistible impression of heat and holiday. Marfurt also made several posters for fairs and expositions (*Anvers,* 1930; *Bruxelles,* 1935).

387. Auguste Mambour: For *Fabrique Nationale*, the Belgian auto and munitions monopoly. 1928.

388. Léo Marfurt: *Minerva* cars. c. 1930.

At the Munich International Poster Exhibition, Belgium was represented by 22 posters, 14 of them by Marfurt. At his side were Francis Delamare and other creators with geometric tendencies: Auguste Mambour and Milo Martinet, both from Liège, making felicitous use of the airbrush. Mambour also made an excellent poster for *Le Raid au Cap* and *Monsel* umbrellas. Let us also mention among the newcomers Lucien de Roeck, who made two superb images in purest Art Deco style for *Anvers* (1934) and *Ostende-Douvres* (1935).

Among good illustrators of the period, the very personal styles of Armand Massonet and Jacques Ochs *(Sabena)* are recognizable. In the tourism field, Herman Verbaere composed some highly colorful posters. Talented postermakers were numerous: Norbert Poulain gives a very complete list of them in *L'Affiche en Belgique*.[1] He also throws light on little-known movements, such as the revival of religious art that came with the mounting demands of Flemish Catholics: the posters of M. Derolez, Fritz Kieckens, Franz van Immerseel and others are powerfully mystical. Being a neighbor of Holland, the Flanders region of Belgium also felt the influence of de Stijl in the typographic posters of Karel Maes and Joseph Peeters.

1. Norbert Poulain: *L'Affiche en Belgique*. Catalog of an exhibition at Musée de l'Affiche, Paris, 1980. (Editions Lebeer-Hossmann, Brussels).

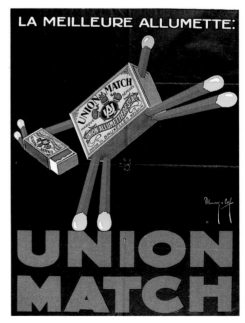

389. Francis Delamare & Cerf: *Union Match*. 1926.

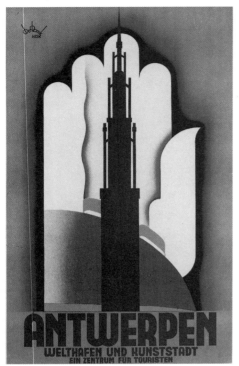

390. Lucien de Roeck: Tourist poster for Antwerp. 1934.

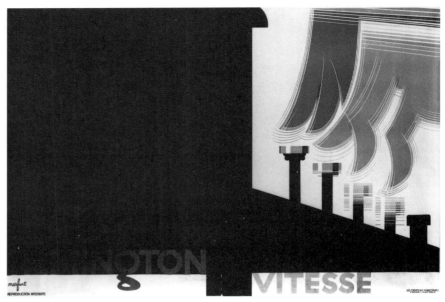

392. Léo Marfurt: *Remington* typewriters. 1929.

391. Karel Maes: Poster for an early demonstration of sound film. 1922.

Belgian advertising also profited from the contribution of its greatest surrealist painter, René Magritte. In 1914, he drew a poster for the *Pot au feu Derbaix*. His second poster, for *Primevère* in 1926, is in the style of the Art-Deco illustrations he used for music scores or for the couturier Norine. After a few more satisfying works (the catalogues of the furrier Samuel), Magritte and his brother founded the studio "Dongo" where, from 1930 to 1936, he produced several advertising creations. These are of little interest (aside from a few superb designs for *Belga),* and he did not hide the controversial side of his activities. He left, however, in a letter to his friend Nougé[1], evidence of his tribulations in the advertising world with which all poster artists can sympathize: "I designed the poster with the hands on a black background: the lettering was white. The effect was remarkable, as good as a successful painting. But the public absolutely must have mediocre things.

"At *Sunlight,* they refused the project for a different reason than might be expected: the poster had too strong an impact, and would work for a product that was just being launched. This house only wanted very discreet posters. For this to work, they wanted me to modify my first project: put in a camel with its shadow, a veiled woman etc. All this is not very encouraging.

"Decidedly, it's very rare that one can hope to get a remarkable idea through. At *Tabacofina,* my project, 'Message from the Orient,' was refused, as they've already used the idea of the Oriental prince who brings a pack of cigarettes to a European woman. The colorful design made use of a strong contrast between the two figures. I gave the man a mysterious quality. He seemed to come from a strange country. The color of his face made for a very different figure from that of the white woman who watched him coming."

1. Georges Roque: *Ceci N'est Pas un Magritte*. Paris: Flammarion, 1983.

FESTIVAL MONDIAL
DU FILM ET DES BEAUX-ARTS
BRUXELLES
DU 1 AU 30 JUIN 1947

393. René Magritte:
Film Festival
in Brussels. 1947.

MUSEUM OF
NATURAL
HISTORY
SOUTH KENSINGTON

394. McKnight Kauffer:
*Museum of Natural
History*. 1922.

England

While France shone between the wars thanks to a few first-quality artists who worked for many clients, the poster situation in Great Britain was characterized by a few large advertisers – the London Underground, the railway companies, Shell-Mex – who could maintain a high level in their campaigns. They provided work for a whole generation of artists, but the only true star to stand out from the lot was E. McKnight-Kauffer.

In 1908, Frank Pick took charge of the advertising for the London subways, which at that time covered a very extensive network, including the suburbs. With rare sureness of taste, he called on collaborators of the first order, such as the architect Charles Holden who redesigned the stations along unified modular standards, with the help of the decorator Harold Stabler. At Pick's request, MacDonald Gil designed his famous stylized map of the system. In 1913, Pick ordered a new alphabet from Edward Johnson: the sans serif characters were the first step toward a modern alphabet, quickly adopted all over the world (notably by the German avant-garde).

Once the structures were built, Pick turned the stations into veritable billboards by an absolutely new tactic of poster-hanging: at a rapid pace, he presented to the Londoners a kaleidoscope of events, the museums and monuments to visit and, especially in summer, picturesque sites outside the city served by the subways. It was a total success, and served equally well for commercial advertising.

Pick was inflexible as to the smallest details: "He realized that the poster, to effectively transmit its message, must be perfectly reproduced and attractively displayed" (*Art in Advertising*, Percy V. Bradshaw, 1925).

For thirty years this great advertising man gave work to dozens of artists, always leaving them great freedom of expression: Fred Taylor, Spencer Pryse, Frank Brangwyn, E.A. Cox, Joseph Pennel, Frank Newbould, F.C. Herrick, Austin Cooper (a museum specialist), Clifford and Rosemary Ellis (who designed extraordinary birds), Barnett Freedman, Graham Sutherland, Paul Nash, Richard Beck, as well as foreign talents, such as A.E. Marty and Jean Dupas from France and Severin from Belgium. He also often employed artists who were just visiting England, such as the German Hans Schleger (Zero), the Hungarian Moholy-Nagy, and the American Man Ray. Pick was the one who in 1915 gave his first order to McKnight-Kauffer, two posters for *Waterford* and *Oxney Woods,* the first gems of a collaboration studded with masterpieces: The *Winter Sales* of 1921, very bold in composition; the *London Museum* in 1922, centered around the flames of the Great Fire of London; the panels *Summertime* in 1925, decorative and richly colored. The poster *Power the Nerve of London's Underground* inaugurated the dynamic style of the

395. Fred Taylor: Travel poster. 1914.

396. Clifford & Rosemary Ellis: One of the posters of the London subway system. 1920.

397. Frank Newbould: Travel poster. 1925.

399. Barnett Freedman: London Subway Poster. 1930s.

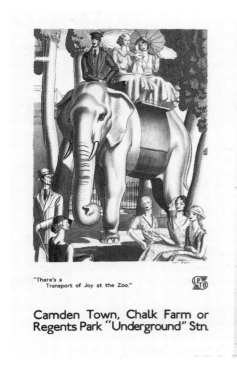

"There's a
Transport of Joy at the Zoo."

Camden Town, Chalk Farm or
Regents Park "Underground" Stn.

398. Jean Dupas: London Subway Poster. 1933.

Thirties, and then came a series for *The Seasons* where photos were combined with graphics.

Edward McKnight Kauffer was born in 1890 in Great Falls, Montana, of a family of German immigrants. After a short time at the Chicago Art Institute he left for Europe – Munich, then two years in Paris where he discovered Van Gogh; eventually he married and settled in London in 1914. At that time he was primarily a painter and a member of the Vorticist movement. His *Flight of Birds,* a stylization of a Japanese engraving, dates from this period. It was sold to the *Daily Herald* in 1919. "In 1919 I made the first and only English cubist poster," he said. After the London Group and the X Group which re-formed the ex-Vorticists without real success, he abandoned painting to devote himself to posters. A short trip to New York in 1921-22 having come to nothing, he made his career in England.

In 1925, a 10-year retrospective exhibition of his work already included 56 posters. They were highly colorful, slightly cubist, and rich in decorative motifs.

From 1927 to 1929 he worked for Crawford, a large agency whose artistic director was Ashley Havinden. His style followed the avant-gardes: symmetry, lettering in diagonals or grouped in blocks, soberer colors. He also discovered photomontage and the airbrush. His contacts with the surrealists (notably Man Ray, with whom he collaborated) led him before his departure for America in 1940, to lighter, more organic forms. During his stay in England he had worked for all the largest companies, and for special clients such as Eastman Cleaners.

OCTOBER 14TH TO 23RD

MOTOR SHOW

EARLS COURT

STATION ★ EARLS COURT
BUSES ★ 30·74

THE BAYNARD PRESS

400. McKnight Kauffer: *Motor Show*.
1937.

E.M.KNIGHT KAUFFER 1915

401. McKnight Kauffer: *Flight of Birds,* a 1913 design used in a *Daily Herald* poster in 1919.

402. McKnight Kauffer: A railway poster. 1932.

GREAT WESTERN TO DEVON'S MOORS

Following the Railway Act of 1921, only four railway companies remained: the London and North Eastern Railway (L.N.E.R.), the London-Midland Scottish (LMS), the Great Western and the Southern Railways. They gradually combined their advertising campaigns. Thanks to their joint efforts, they placed England in the foreground of the tourist poster.

The L.N.E.R., under Mr. Teasdale's direction, set the most brilliant example: people must be made to want to travel, to discover the northern ports and beaches the company served. Among the best artists employed were Fred Taylor, expert at the play of light and shade, delicate drawing and somber masses in his landscapes; Frank Newbould, working in flat tones; Brangwyn and Pryse, with their realistic and nervous drawing; Shep (Shepard) and Herrick, artistic directors of Baynard press, the largest printing-house, rigorous in their layouts and flirting with abstraction. Let us also mention Andrew Johnson who, like dozens of others, was an agreeable landscape painer expectly rendering the scenic views he was entrusted with.

A few improbable images stand out from the rest, such as the *Dining on the L.N.E.R.* and the *Night Scotsman,* two dream images by Alexandre

Nº 3 SAFE SANDS

EAST COAST JOYS
travel by L·N·E·R
TO THE DRIER SIDE OF BRITAIN

403. Tom Purvis: For the trains of the
LNER. 1935.

405. Alexandre Alexeieff:
Railway poster. 1932.

THE NIGHT SCOTSMAN
Leaves King's Cross nightly at 10.25.

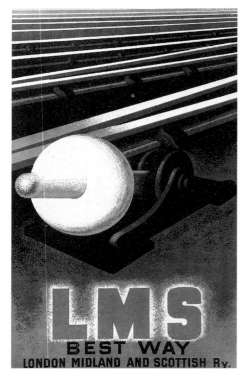

404. A.M. Cassandre: *LMS* Railway. 1928.

Alexeieff; Marfurt's *Flying Scotsman;* and Austin Cooper's series on the birthplaces of great German composers.

The most interesting of all these artists was Tom Purvis, whose railway designs were done exclusively for L.N.E.R. Following the Beggarstaffs and Hohlwein, he formed his figures solely from masses of color, without outline. The adroitness with which he composed his palette and laid out his figures often made little masterpieces of his posters: splashes around a diving board, a big red beach umbrella and children on the sand . . . his series for the clothier *Austin Reed* shows the same virtuosity, whether in images of moneyed elegance or in a bold close-up of *Interwoven Socks*.

The L.M.S., lagging behind the other railroads, called mainly upon artists of the Royal Academy who jotted down irreproachable but often boring landscapes. The masterpieces Cassandre made for them, with the piercing red headlights and the switch-box, remain brilliant accidents, as was the *Devon Moors* by McKnight-Kauffer for Great Western.

The Southern Railways, along with pictures for the ports and beaches of the south (such as *Portsmouth* by Kenneth Shoesmith, a great specialist in the genre), commissioned Austin Cooper to attract tourists to the continent.

Paris for the week-end is a marvelous pastiche of the cubist collage. Cooper, theoretician and pedagogue, principal of the Reimann School, defined the poster artist's philosophy as "a will to serve". In his geometrical style, often close to that of his French counterparts, he worked for all the big campaigns (*L.N.E.R., General Post Office,* etc.). He also designed regularly for *The Royal Mail Steam Packet* (R.M.S.P.), one of the Empire's principal shipping companies.

The R.M.S.P., to "remind the public that certain attractive and desirable destinations could be reached under agreeable conditions by modern means of transportation," called upon Shep, Horace Taylor and Herrick, who designed its best images. Waves were treated in a very personal manner, almost abstract, in the seashore poster. Then there were the usual designs by Shoesmith, Newbould, and Taylor, who also turn up for the *Orient*

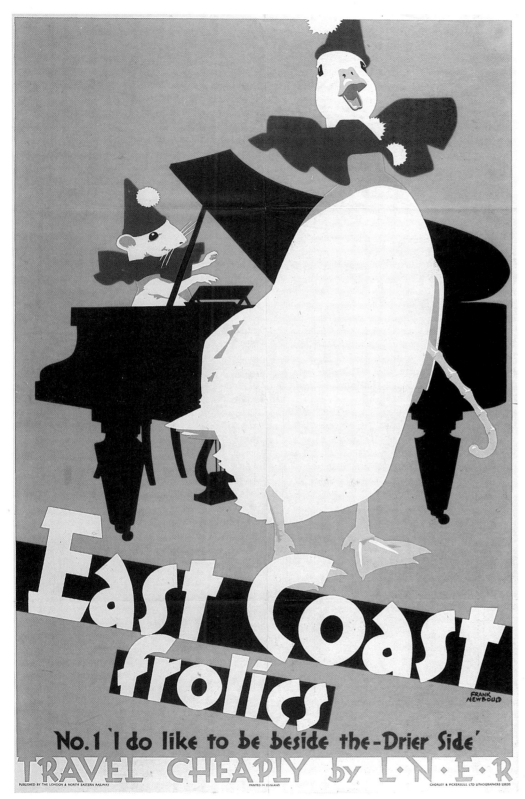

406. Frank Newbould: One of a series for the *London & North Eastern Railway*. 1933.

407. Tom Purvis: A London
clothier's poster. 1935.

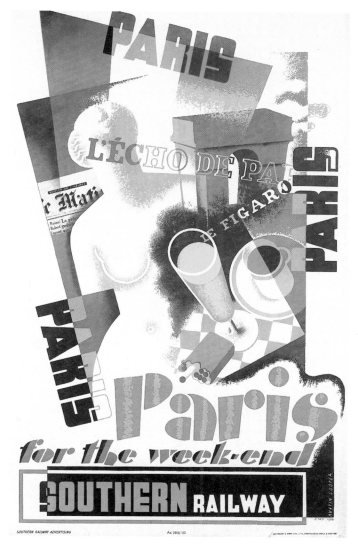

408. Austin Cooper: Travel poster for the *Southern Railway*. c. 1935.

409. Frederick Charles Herrick: *R.M.S.P.* steamship line. 1921.

Line, which continued to employ the old guard (Dudley Hardy, Hassal). Yet it turned towards the avant-garde in the person of McKnight-Kauffer, and at the end of the Thirties used the treated photos and photomontages of Richard Beck.

The Shell-Mex and B.P. oil companies merged in 1923, becoming, together with the London Underground, the most notable users of adveritsing art. Sir Kenneth Clark, head of the National Gallery, hailed them as "among the best patrons of modern art: they are all that patrons should be: they employ young or little known artists, they provide well defined subjects, and they make it possible for an artist's work to be enjoyed by a very large number of people."

The work of J.L. Beddington, director of publicity of Shell-Mex, was remarkable on all points. From the start he chose a policy, surprising in an oilman, of protecting the landscape and the environment. There are no posters in the *Shell* and *B.P.* campaigns to preserve natural beauty as

410. Alexandre Alexeieff: For the *LNER*.

411. Eckersley-Lombers: *Shell* Oil. c. 1935.

such, but he published a torrent of handbills to that end. Most of these were placed in the press and on his trucks which criss-crossed the country. In another remarkable concept, he called on young artists to whom he allowed, on a given theme, complete freedom of expression: McKnight Kauffer (who besides posters designed a little mannikin used throughout the whole campaign); Graham Sutherland and Paul Nash, who drew modernist landscapes; and Zero (Hans Schleger), fresh from Germany. Of course, the results of this huge campaign were unequal. McKnight-Kauffer designed some of his best posters for it: photomontages with asymmetrical lettering, or powerful landscapes like the startling *Stonehenge*. Some designs by Anderson, Tom Gentleman, and Eckersley-Lombers have become classics. Yet one also sees interesting landcsapes and works by painters having nothing in common with poster art.

Among other advertising clients who deserve mention is Imperial Air, whose publicity materials were often avant-gardist (McKnight-Kauffer, Ben Nicholson, James Gardner, Edgar Ainsworth and Lee Elliott). Sir John Tallent, who went from the Empire Marketing Board to the General Post Office, called on McKnight-Kauffer, and also young artists, such as Pat Keely. The series "Outposts of the Empire" is remarkable (John Vickery), as are those for the telegraph and telephone. To finish the list of exemplary clients, there is Eno's Fruit Salt which used as its trademark first a rooster designed by McKnight-Kauffer, but then radically changed its image with Ashley Havinden's stylized knight. Like Kauffer, Ashley was a modern graphic artist influenced by avant-garde movements, notably cubism: "Cubism, creating new realities parallel with life but not existing as imitations of life, was extremely valuable to advertising technique. The poster particularly has a similar task, namely to create visually an equivalent of a product or service when it cannot possibly be that product or service itself . . . For speed of visual communication in a hurrying world, the dramatic stylization suggested by cubism provided the stimulus towards a new kind of expression."

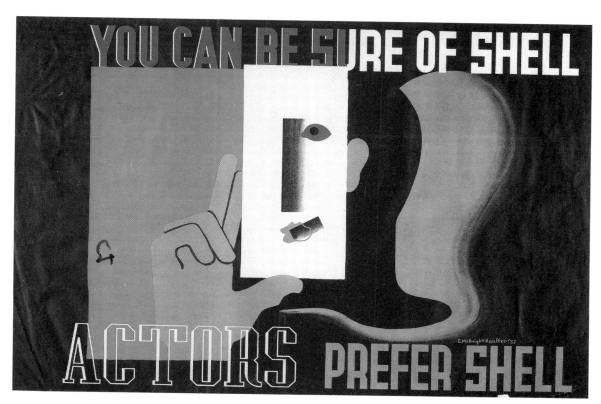

412. McKnight Kauffer:
Shell Oil. 1934.

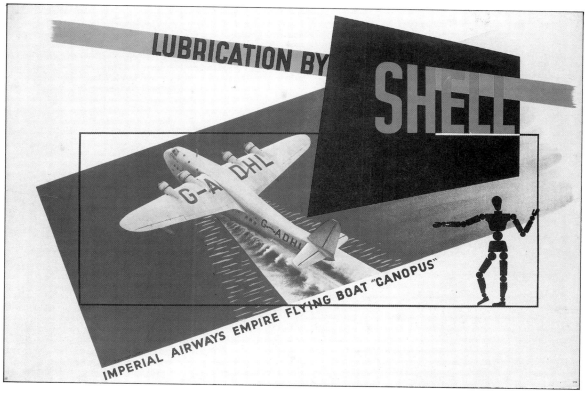

413. McKnight Kauffer:
Shell Oil. 1934.

414. McKnight Kauffer: *Shell* Oil. c. 1935.

415. Jack Miller: *Shell* Oil. c. 1935.

416. Graham Sutherland: *Shell* Oil. 1932.

417. Tom Gentleman:
Ethyl gasoline of the
BP company.

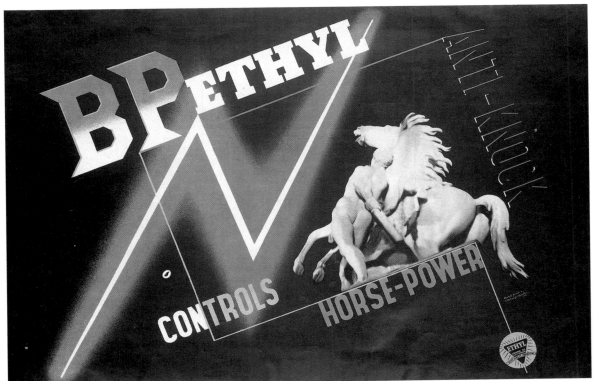

418. McKnight Kauffer:
BP Ethyl.

GRÜSSE

DEN NEUEN

PLYMOUTH

CHRYSLERS LETZTE SCHÖPFUNG !

PRENTIS

419. Ashley (Ashley Havinden): German version of his design for *Plymouth*. 1929.

Ashley put these principles in practice for Chrysler, for whom he stylized cars and figures for a world-wide campaign beginning in 1929. Like all the artists of his generation, Ashley broke from cubism at the end of the Thirties, but kept its power for communication – his poster *Milk*, in its economy of means, is of exemplary impact. Ashley was artistic director for Sir William Crawford, an eminent figure in British advertising, having connections with the Berlin Dorland agency (of which Herbert Bayer was artistic director) and instrumental in importing talents and their special style from the Continent. Crawford was responsible, for example, for Carlu's finding work across the Channel (*Larranaga Cigars*, among others). He was one of the first and most vehement defenders of modern advertising art: "The use of symbolism, in its special sense, and simplification were the progressive result of anticipating that poster design would become an independent branch of art."

420. Ashley (Ashley Havinden): *Eno's Fruit Salt*. 1927.

422. H. H. Harris: *Bovril*. c. 1925.

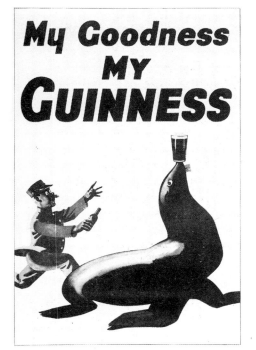

421. John Gilroy: One of many designs inspired by the *Guinness* slogan. c. 1935.

And finally, Guinness, thanks to John Gilroy's talent, came up with its humorous slogan *My goodness, My Guinness*. For the theatre, there was Aubrey Hammond. Aside from the larger companies, the production was mediocre.

Heavily advertised brands, such as Johnny Walker, the Cardinal Wolsey underwear, the charming ladies used by Lever and Kodak—these were designs without much interest.

However, it should be noted again that during this period, England demonstrated how a handful of powerful clients who understood the nature of publicity could keep a high artistic level in creating effective posters.

423. Eckersley-
Lombers:
The British
Post Office.
1938.

424. Otis Shepard: The *Wrigley Spearmint* leaf. c. 1935.

The United States

At the end of World War I, the United States was the greatest economic power in the world. Europe was in ruins. For ten years – until the great crash of 1929 – America was in a period of expansion and of euphoria unequaled in its history. Advertising – more precisely, advertising agencies – disposed of enormous budgets (1 billion dollars in 1925) to sell consumer goods and new products like the automobile to the four corners of the continent.

In 1926, addressing the International Advertising Association, president Coolidge declared: "The preeminence of American industry, which has constantly brought about a reduction in costs, is primarily the result of mass production. Mass production is not possible without mass demand. Mass demand has been entirely generated by the development of advertising."

In 1913, J.B. Watson published his theory of behaviorism. In 1920, he became president of the large Walter Thompson agency: he commissioned studies of buyer motivation, on the basis of which advertising stimuli were created to yield corresponding results. This scientific approach, unknown in Europe, was adapted by the leading American advertising executives such as Albert Lasker, O.B. Winters, Earle Ludgin and John H. Dunhain.

For each of their clients, they sought the message that would provoke the buying reflex. The slogan was the catchword of all American advertising, from Packard automobiles' *Ask the Man Who Owns One* to *Keep That Schoolgirl Complexion* of Palmolive Soap.

When George Washington Hill became president of American Tobacco in 1920, he charged Albert Lasker with the launching of Lucky Strike. By showing smoking women in many of the posters, Lasker multiplied sales by associating the product with women who had just acquired the right to vote and to participate in modern life.

The poster in America thought big. Percy Bradshaw in *Art and Advertising*[1] pointed out that, to carry out a poster campaign over the whole country, you needed $320,000 (in 1925) to cover 35,000 billboards.

American poster distribution at that time was remarkably well organized. The biggest companies were members of the General Outdoor Advertising Company, which standardized the outdoor poster format at 24 sheets—that is 25 x 11 feet—and the billboards were well maintained, cleaned and lighted.

All this and the sums of money invested in advertising budgets would naturally lead one to think that America in the twenties was a poster artist's paradise; but such was not the case.

The first reason is the small proportion of American advertising by

1. Percy Bradshaw: *Art in Advertising*. London: The Press Art School, 1925.

425. Clarence Underwood: Three posters in *Palmolive's* series, early 1920's.

426. A 1937 American street scene, with Cassandre's *Ford* poster prominently in view.

427. Josef Binder: The Trylon and the Hemisphere
were symbols of the 1939 *World's Fair*.

poster: the press was greatly preferred, and, when it appeared, the radio. Then, the quality of artistic invention to be found in Europe was cruelly lacking. "Their paralyzed gusto has limited their choice of pictorial subject and encouraged them unduly to glorify the commonplace" (Bradshaw). All the critics share this opinion; Professor Frenzel, writing in *Gebrauchsgraphik* in 1926, remarked that "in antithesis to the high development of advertising, the American poster, despite its enormous dimensions, is of no particular importance."

To please a public without cultural traditions, American advertising refused to go beyond mediocre realism, giving the public the same stereotypes in which they could easily see themselves reflected: cardboard dreams and tawdry romanticism.

J.C. Leyendecker covered the billboards with elegant young people for *Arrow Shirts,* who, becoming middle-class heros, turned up also in the *Chesterfield* series. Clarence Underwood pasted up pallid young girls for the *Palmolive* "Schoolgirl complexion." One also found them in the posters for *Ivory Soap.*

The poster was in the hands of illustrators whose images were enormously enlarged. The best known among these included Norman Rockwell,

William Meade Prince, Pruett Carter, Charles E. Chambers, Fred Cooper, Adolf Treidel and Burr Griffin, the specialist in children.

Among the realists, René Clark is the only one to stand out, notably in his work for *Wesson Oil*.

Only fashion, and only in the magazines, permitted flirtation with Art Deco, for artists such as Bobri (Vladimir Bobritsky), Helen Dryden and Gischia (who spent 3 years in New York).

Commenting on the American section of the great 1929 poster exhibition in Munich, Frenzel noted: "California seems to be the pioneer of American taste". To support this, he published in *Gebrauchsgraphik* very fine images in pure Art Deco style, created by J. Assanger (*Ganah Lumber Co., Parker Bros., Chesterfield*).

The depression of 1929 struck advertising very hard. Its slow recovery in the Thirties found the poster in evolution after the emigration of European artists.

The first, Lucian Bernhard, settled in New York in 1922. Once there he, too, observed that "Americans want 'an idea,' 'an image' — a purely visual idea isn't for them." He devoted himself to changing things, to creating posters, "in which the image treats the subject instead of illustrating it" (Ervine Metzl).

Also coming to America to change things were H.J. Bartschal, Brodovitch, Sascha Maurer, then in 1936 Josef Binder who settled there. Cassandre and Matter only passed through; in 1938 came Herbert Bayer, then Carlu and Allner in 1939, and finally Moholy-Nagy and Xanti Schawinsky.

Thanks to the magazines which gradually familiarized the American public with the European avant-garde, the poster evolved.

Otis Shepard created geometric designs for his *Wrigley's* campaigns. Other good campaigns were launched, such as Albert Staehle's "Starts like a Scared Rabbit" series for *Esso*. Photography arrived on the scene, thanks to Matter and Leo Lionni; Lester Beall and Eric Nitsche made their first posters. Cassandre's *Ford V8* was a success. Some progress evolved, but slowly. Prefacing the reflections on graphic art of Paul Rand (1947), McKnight-Kauffer, who himself returned to the United States in 1940, remained bitter: "When one thinks of the degree of standardization attained by advertising in the United States, and when one thinks that advertising and the sums devoted to it are always increasing, for sites as well as for production, it can be said that our advertising is generally of very poor quality. There are certain reasons for this, but they are no longer valid once we have excellent designers and slogan writers. At first glance, I would say that the main reason for the lack of distinction in our productions is the timidity of the over-organized advertising departments."

A plague that, after the war, would reach Europe!

428. Albert Staehle: *Essolene*. c. 1937.

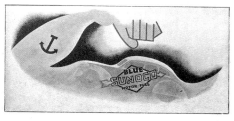

Three examples of avant-garde posters in the United States.
429a. Alexei Brodovitch: Traffic safety poster. 1938.

429b. Xanti Schawinsky: Poster for *Wanamaker's* department store. 1938.

429c. Eric Nitsche: *Sunoco* gasoline. 1938.

430. Peter Birkhauser:
For *PKZ*, the Zurich
men's clothier. 1934.

Switzerland

S pared by the war, Switzerland quietly and steadily nurtured the flowering of its advertising art: the designs were artistic, the printing remarkable, the poster-hanging impeccable. Otto Baumberger described those happy times: "From 1908 to about 1920, posters had, without any doubt, an artistic and national character. . . . Schupp, Cardinaux, Forestier, Mangold, Stiefel and Baumberger were the creators of the true Swiss poster. These artistic posters were introduced into the world of commerce, above all, thanks to the initiative and enthusiasm of the Zurich printer J.E. Wolfensberger. The artistic poster flourished, cultivated by a great many artists who lithographed their own designs and oversaw their printing. I have only to mention Stoecklin, Boscovits, Laubi, and others. Even well known artists like Hodler, Amiet, A. Giacometti made incursions into this new field."

It was at this time that the young Loupot, apprenticed to Wolfensberger, created his first, very decorative posters for *Canton, Grieder* and *Philipossian*.

Swiss graphic art evolved very quickly, and its high artistic level was maintained throughout the period between the Wars. Cuno Amiet made a tasteful placard for the buffet of the Basel train station (1921). Augusto Giacometti, with stains of vivid color close to abstraction and with an uncommon boldness of composition, designed a huge red parasol for the *Grisons Railways* (1924), and a great butterfly for the tourism poster *Die Schöne Schweiz* (1930). Pellegrini was the painter of the poor and oppressed for whom he brought support in his election posters. Maurice Barraud painted young girls in a style that certainly impressed Hans Falk.

Otto Morach was a singular artist. A member of Swiss avant-garde movements such as the expressionists (with Baumberger) and the radical artists in Zurich in 1919 (with Giacometti), the group "Neues Leben" with Arp, Janko and Picabia, in contact with the Bauhaus through the intermediary Schlemmer, he took an interest in several areas, from marionettes to stained-glass windows. He created a bizarre and enchanted universe in his few posters, abounding in viaducts, towering houses, angular patches of color evoking mountains or forests, all bathed in a blue, unreal atmosphere. On this background he may impose taxis (*Taxameter A. Welti-Furrer,* 1920), or show distant villages (*Davos,* 1921).

He was the first, in his poster for *Schweizer Werbung* in 1918, to make typography, that essential element of advertising graphics, the dominant part of his image.

It was in the Twenties that the Swiss poster developed in decisive fashion, to create a typically Swiss style. This style is doubtless due to

431. Charles Loupot: *PKZ.* 1921.

432. Augusto Giacometti:
Promoting travel
to Beautiful
Switzerland. 1930.

433. Otto Morach:
A. Welti-Furrer
taxicab company
of Zurich. 1923.

434. Niklaus Stoecklin: *PKZ*. 1934.

the assimilation of two opposing influences: France on one side, Germany on the other.

While Matter, Diggelmann, Lohse, Bühler, Erni, Leupin and Vivarelli traveled to Paris, Baumberger, Morach, Stöcklin and Gauchat passed through Munich, and Brun, Bill, Herdeg, Eidenbenz, Steiner and Willimann studied in Berlin. Many of these artists, in fact, were acquainted with both France and Germany. Zurich and Basel were the two centers of advertising art, and its two reigning artists were Otto Baumberger, who has been called the spiritual father of the Swiss poster, and Niklaus Stöcklin, head of the Basel school. By the volume, the quality, and the diversity of their work, they dominate the lot. Their common characteristic is that they are above all categories.

Baumberger was undeniably the originator of the new object identification, with *Baumann*'s top hat (1919), followed in 1923 by the overcoat for *P.K.Z.;* Stöcklin then came up in 1925 with the great red wheel for *Cluser Transmissionen,* and the *Valvo* bulb in 1931; he took the procedure to the limits of hyperrealism for the sunscreen *Bi-oro* (1941), *Binaca* (1943) and *Meta-Meta* (1941). Stöcklin was also one of the first to master the typographic poster *(Der Buchdruck* 1922, *Schweizerische Städtebau Aussstellung Zurich* (1928); Baumberger used it majestically for the B of *Brak Liqueur* (1937) and for the carpet firm *Forster* (1928-1930). They also made brilliant experiments in symbolism and simplification—*Gaba* by Stöcklin in 1927 and *Motor-Comptoir* by Baumberger in 1932. They remembered that they were painters in some of their freer designs, like Stöcklin's *P.K.Z.,* echoing Magritte, and the *Wählt freisinnig* poster by Baumberger (1933).

Besides these two giants, a third pioneer merits a place apart: Ernst Keller. From 1918, working for *Bliss Kleidung* clothiers, he arrived at a perfect simplification and harmonization of text and images. His influence as professor at the Zurich school of decorative arts, and the example that

436. A 1930 photo of a Swiss poster wall.

435. Max Bill: Typographical poster for the *Wulff* dance studio. 1931.

437. Otto Baumberger: *Brak Liqueur*. 1937.

438. Ernst Keller:
Tobacco industry
exhibition in Zurich.
1929.

439. Otto Baumberger: *PKZ*. 1923.

440. Niklaus Stoecklin: A 1925 poster for a machine company.

he gave, according equal expressivity to the text and to color in his images, often printed in linogravure *(Das Neue Heim, 1926; Tabak, 1929; Press Ball, 1932)* were considerable.

If the object poster (Sachplakat) can be traced to Lucian Bernhard's experiments in 1905, the Swiss, starting from the same principle, arrived at a singularly different result. The heaviness and flatness of the German images, replaced by volume and virtuosity of lithographic design, created a new current: the new objectivity. Baumberger was its father, and as we have seen, Stöcklin pushed it to its limits; after that, many artists folowed: Carl Boeckli *(Glasshütte Bülach)*, Birkhauser (the button for *PKZ, Globus)*, Diggelmann (the box of shirts for *P.K.Z.)*, Charles Kuhn *(Rigi, Omega)*, Pierre Gauchat *(Bally)*, Hermann Eidenbenz *(Bata)*, Leupin *(Savon Steinfels)*, Fritz Bühler *(Union)* . . . and even Loupot, whose style in France was quite different, drew a toothbrush for *Sérodent* toothpaste.

Typography, which had first seen the light in Germany, found its home in Switzerland. To the experiments and teachings of Keller and his disciples (Käch, Kumpel, Willimann) came to be added the work of Max Bill, back from the Bauhaus, who gathered around him the "Swiss construc-

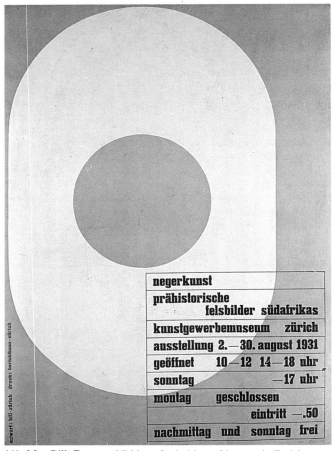

441. Max Bill: For an exhibition of primitive African art in Zurich. 1931.

443. Jan Tschichold: Constructivist Art Show in Basel. 1937.

tionists" Lohse, Neuburg, Vivarelli and Max Huber. And Jan Tschichold emigrated to Switzerland in 1933.

From these talents, all working in the same general direction, was born a series of posters, notably for the Kunstgewerbe Museum of Zurich, which have become classic models: *Negerkunst; Prähistorishe Felsbilder Südafrikas* (1931), *Zeitprobleme in der Schweizer Malerei und Plastick* (1936) by Max Bill who, for the *Tanz-studio Wulff* of Basel (1931), played more freely with the lettering and the color; *Form ohne Ornament* (1927) by Walter Käch, where the letters are made in the form of tools. Then there was *Konstruktivisten* (1937) by Tschichold, of absolute rigor; to this we should add the posters of Paul Renner, a German typographer and inventor of the Futura typeface (*Fachschulen Bayerns Ausstellung* of 1928), and *Abstrakte und surrealistiche Malerei und Plastik* (1929) by Hans Arp, with typography by Walter Cyliax. We can also mention, at Basel, Theo Ballmer's posters (*Bureau Bâle* and *Neues Bauen*, 1928). All these artists, many of whom also taught, contributed to the formation of a Swiss graphic art school which would impose itself even after the War.

Another field where the Swiss passed avant-garde techniques on to a wider public was photography. Its possibilities were revealed in Zurich

442. Hans Arp & Walter Cyliax: A Zurich Exhibition of Abstract and Surrealist Art. 1929.

by Lissitsky's poster for the Russian exhibition in 1929. Although Walter Cyliax was its pioneer *(Opticien Keech,* 1929; *Meubles Simmen,* 1930), it was Herbert Matter who, with his tourist posters, assured it a wide popularity.

After studying in Paris with Fernard Léger, whom he left for the studio Deberny and Peignot where he exercised his airbrush, Matter returned to Zurich where he made a name for himself with graphic posters *(P.K.Z.,* 1928). Between 1934 and 1936 he made his series of tourist posters, a veritable revolution in the genre which would be copied all over the world: *Pontresina* (closeup with sunglasses), *Engelberg* (a woman's face and gloved hand), *Winterluftwerk* (plane flying over the mountains). With their powerful composition and violently contrasting colors (only sky blue and snow white, with the text in red), they broke completely away from the usual rather faded landscapes. Interviewed by Remy Duval in *Arts et Metiers Graphiques* (No. 51, February 15, 1936) he declared: "The snap-shot is my preferred exposure. I carefully observe the progress of color

444. Helmut Kurtz: Household Design Exposition in Zurich. 1930.

445. Otto Baumberger: Advertising a sale at the *Forster* store. 1930.

446. Walter Kach: Exhibition "Form Without Ornament," Zurich. 1927.

447. Herbert Matter: To promote
auto travel in Switzerland. 1935.

448. Herbert Matter: Travel poster for *Engelberg*. 1935.

449. Walter Herdeg: *St. Moritz*. 1936.

450. Carlo Vivarelli: Travel poster for the resort of *Flums*. 1940.

photography, and amateur cinema is one of my passions. It's mainly for this reason that I am going to try my luck in America. I hope to find there more luxurious media at my disposition for a brand of cigarettes or of automobiles. Advertising in Europe is often lacking in boldness. Anyway I like to renew myself, to receive other influences."

These phrases say much for Matter's dynamism, and his illusions about American advertising!

Matter quickly attracted imitators: Emil Schulthess/Schocher and Steiner who took up, for *Pontresina*, the sunglasses motif of Matter's 1937 poster, and Walter Herdeg who, in his photos for *St. Moritz*, liked to introduce little graphic elements like a sun. For *Flums* (1940), Vivarelli also used photography but with a layout in the constructivist spirit. Photography also appeared in commercial advertising: the exhibition *Ausstellung Neue Hauswirtschaft* by Helmut Kurtz (1930), bouillon cubes *Le super bouillon de Liebig* by Haus Neuburg (1934), and the pair of *Bally* shoes, designed by Steiner from a photo by Heininger (1936).

The panorama of the Swiss poster at this period would be incomplete without mention of the exceptional series of posters made for a firm with

a highly refined sure taste: the men's clothing store P.K.Z. The complete
list of these posters would be interminable, but the principal ones tell a
great deal about the role of this store in the flowering of the Swiss poster:
after having called on Hohlwein, Cardinaux, and Mangold, they used
Baumberger (1917-1923, typographical posters and the famous overcoat),
Loupot (1921), Stöcklin (1923, 1934), Hugo Laubi (1923-1925), Hermann Blaser (1927), Arnhold (1927), Otto Morach (1928), Matter (1928),
Birkhauser (1934, the button), Diggelmann (1935, the box), H. Mahler
(1936), Charles Kuhn (1937) . . .

It is thanks to this sort of entrepreneur (Bally could also be cited) that
a country can have quality posters.

451. Niklaus Stoecklin: *PKZ*.

452. Otto Morach: *PKZ*. 1923.

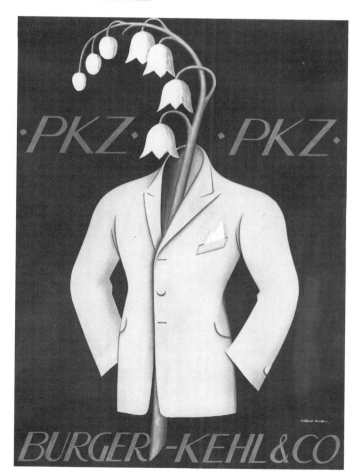

453. Hans Neuburg:
Liebig. 1934.

454. Arnhold: *PKZ*. 1927.

455. Marcel Vertes: Political poster deploring the executions ordered by Budapest military governor Lukacsics in an anti-Communist campaign. 1919.

Central Europe

The countries of Central Europe born—or reborn—from the new territorial divisions made by the peace treaties rapidly affirmed their identifies, notably in their graphic schools. Hungary, Czechoslovakia and Poland produced brilliant successes.

Hungary acquired its independence after the division of the old Empire, and was at first reconstituted as a republic. After a few months, power was seized by a Communist dictator, Bela Kun, who governed for a few months—March to August 1919—at the head of a socialist coalition before a military regime took power from them. These few months of revolution generated numerous posters. However, contrary to what took place in Russia, these images did not participate in the constructivist and futurist avant-garde but remained very traditional: poignant realism—to denounce crime and poverty, and monumental symbolism—an outsized worker or soldier crushing the capitalist.

Marcel Vertès specialized in the horrors of the war. His poster denouncing the crimes of *Lukacsics,* Budapest's military governor at the end of the war, was typical: a mother at the verge of collapse, surrounded by her children in tears, against a background of men falling before a firing squad. Printed all in gray with only the name of the executioner in blood-red letters, the image has terrible expressive force. The same theme is used in *Is this the way to pay the Czech bills?*

Michel Biro, who before the war was already the hope of Hungarian graphics, was the champion of allegories of the worker blown up to huge proportions. His most famous poster, for the paper *Nepszava,* represents a red-bodied giant, stylized and vividly outlined, brandishing a sledgehammer on the background of the newspaper's front page. For *Politika,* another newspaper, the same giant peers into parliament holding a lamp; on another poster, a worker paints the parliament red or a huge hand crushes the table around which capitalists are gathered.

Bereny, making the call to arms, found a lyricism that brings to mind the Soviet posters. His soldier with a red flag is of the highest quality, as are the marching soldiers of the expressionist painter Ujtz, the moving spirit behind the avant-garde publication *Ma.*

These posters proliferating everywhere were often printed in enormous formats (4 x 6 meters), and in the case of Biro's *Nepszava* attained a height of 12 meters!

With the conservative return to power, Vertès left for Vienna, then Paris and the United States; Biro and Bereny exiled themselves to Germany.

The country, where the landowners had again seized power, was in ruins, after five years of war and then revolution. Nothing really interesting

456. Michael Biro: Leftist newspaper *Nepszava.* 1918.

457. Michael Biro: Poster for a postwar lottery to help rebuild villages devastated in the conflict. c. 1919.

458. Robert Bereny: *Modiano* cigarettes.

happened until 1926 when Robert Bereny and Alexandre Bortnyik returned from Germany where their style had been shaped and solidified. In an article published in *Gebrauchsgrafik* and reprinted in *Arts et Métiers graphiques,* Karl Rosner views them thus: "Robert Bereny, painter *par excellence,* finds in the poster the problems of the picture; he resolves them as such. His posters have great suggestive force. Large well-lit surfaces contribute to putting the advertising aim in relief. The harmony and purity of the colors are another of the characteristics of Bereny's posters, as are the witty solution of a problem and an exact execution.

"Alexandre Bortnyik is the poster artist *par excellence . . .* he always puts the trademark in relief and subordinates all the poster's details. This sureness of composition, this expertness of design allow him to avoid everything that can be boring or forced in the poster."

These two paragraphs perfectly define each of the artists: Bereny was indeed a plasticist who knew how to organize forms and colors. His return was marked by a poster for *Cordatic* tires, whose lettering and little figure brought a gust of fresh air and modernity to Hungary. His series for Modiano cigarettes followed, where he stylized the smoker and his cigarette in a few circles, a few colored planes, and two or three undulating puffs.

For H.G. Wells' *Wonders of Life,* he superimposed three supple images in the manner of Paul Colin. Two containers for *Ambrosia* mustard and a stick of charcoal and lettering on the diagonal for *Kohinoor* charcoal are more directly graphic.

Bortnyik was above all a graphic artist. His series for *Modiano* cigarette papers was very different from Bereny's: the cigarette, the paper and the rolling hand—simple, pure and striking images, with nothing but the product's name. For the newspaper *Ujsag,* the poster was divided into horizontal planes where little figures mill around, attracting attention only by the white of the newspaper they all read. The only other white spot: the name of the newspaper—a clear and effective message. For *Dreber* biscuits, the name and the contours of a coffeecup in white against a background of biscuits suffice to create a mouthwatering atmosphere.

However different, Bereny and Bortnyik shared the same general conception of the poster: "At the beginning of the new advertising art, the slogan was: no more constructivity! Only logic! Only designs arrived at consciously! But today the pictorial art is reclaiming its due." (Bortnyik).

"The poster, too, should be painterly, for the simple reason that, psychologically speaking, the human being regards everything that is painted as painterly." (Bereny)

This pursuit of pictoriality clearly set off the Hungarian from the colder German poster. It can also be seen in the disciples of the two masters, among whom the following deserve special mention: Louis Csabai Ekes, Tihamer Csemicky, Andreas Farkas, Johann Repcze, Jules Kando, Stefan Israi, Lanyi (creator of a splendid series for the morning, afternoon and evening newspapers), and Victor Vasarely who, before turning to kinetic painting, made his debut in advertising art.

The Czech republic was founded by Thomas Masaryk in 1918. Mucha, who finally saw his country independent, designed its banknotes and a few posters, but they were already from another age: one can judge the distance covered in twenty years by looking at them. "As in other countries, the work of Czech artists indicates a desire on their part to express themselves in a modern and topical style" noted Professor Frenzel.

459. Lanyi: Poster for the newspaper *Pesti Naplo*. 1930.

460. Ladislav Sutnar: Business Exposition in Brno. 1929.

Ladislav Sutnar led the way of Czech graphic art: a personality of international scope, caught up in all the avant-gardes, he practiced the new typography, photography and photomontage with a skill comparable to Moholy-Nagy or Tschichold. A specialist in design and in three-dimensional advertising, he was in charge of the Czech pavilions at the major international expositions, among them the World's Fair of 1939 in New York where he eventually settled.

In the volume devoted to advertising in the series *L'Art International d'aujourd'hui,* Cassandre concentrates on other experiments: the post cubism of Jean Basch, Teige and Mrkvička, and Josef Čapek's expressionist-dadaist linogravures.

One of the most interesting Czech poster artists was František Zelenka: "Today no one will tolerate falsification and imitation . . . to reproduce the methods of painting in the poster is to falsify it. But the poster today is creating new means of action. First of all there is the photograph as an element independent of image . . . Typography is the second line of attack of the modern poster. It is the most effective arrangement of characters, the selection of appropriate sizes and fitting proportions. . . . The third line of attack is color. That is what makes everything a whole. It's the pulse, the consciousness, and the vital force of the poster."

He put his principles perfectly into application in his theater posters, playing with the lettering and the color contrasts in his very free designs.

A Parisian touch can be seen in the works of Willi Rötter who studied in Paris, working at Printemps and at Damour Studio. He specialized in elegance, fashions, and worked for *Škoda* automobiles. Emil Weiss was a fashionable caricaturist and poster artist while, on the contrary, Joseph Jäger announced the *Reichenberger Messe* fair in a very architectural style. Hannserich Köhler, who had studied in Dresden, Munich and Vienna, was also heavily influenced by German style.

As Janina Fijalkowska notes, "It wasn't until 1917 that acquisitions from European art of the prewar period could be noted in the forms of Polish Art, but they did not have an important influence on the ultimate development of the Polish poster."

It was not until the arrival of Bartomiejczyk and Zaminski at the Polytechnic School of Warsaw that a first advance could be noted: their drawing classes were the first to provide students with a training adapted to poster art. Bartomiejczyk, in 1925, adopted a geometric style in his posters. "The modern poster in Poland is the work of Tadeucz Gronowski; one need only back up ten years and remember the chaos of graphic art at the time to appreciate the value of the pioneering role Gronowski played in the area of the Polish poster," wrote the architect and theoretician Lech Niemojwski in 1927.

With a poster like *Radion* (1926) Gronowski placed the Polish poster at an international level: two cats, a black one and a white one, plunge into the laundry soap; a dynamic composition, vivid flat tones, simple lettering. Gronowski made several trips to France where he was influenced by post-cubism (asymmetrical compositions, geometric deformations) and by Cassandre, who led him to the airbrush. In 1930 he declared: "The art of the streets assimilates all the new conquests made by architecture and painting, and translates them into its own language, the language of advertising. What is a poster and what should it be? There are as many answers to this question as there are masters of poster art . . . Contemporary poster art tends to a simplification of form and a lapidary presentation of the subject, by concentrating attention on detail."

Besides Gronowski's works, Szcuka and Zarnowevowora made experiments in photomontage. Berlewi toyed with the lettering, in the dadaist, machine-oriented style, and together with Stanislav Brucz and Aleksander Wat founded the Reklame-Mechano advertising agency (1924).

Gronowski, by example and then by teaching, trained a new generation (Zaminski, Stryjenska, Skoczylas, John) and contributed to Poland's success at the Exposition of Decorative Arts in Paris in 1925 where 19 Polish artists were represented and Gronowski and Stryjenska won the grand prize. Bartomiejcyk, on his part, became titular professor of the chair of applied graphic arts at the Warsaw School of Fine Arts. His disciples were Piotrowski, Manteuffel, Hladki and Wajwod.

461. Henrik Berlewi: Design for advertising firm *Reklama Mechano*. 1924.

462. Bartomiejczyk: French language advertisement for a Polish Fair in Poznan. 1929.

Other young talents like Nowicki and Sandecka were able to detach themselves from Gronowski's influence. Let us also mention Berman and Surallo among the legion of young poster artists who made up what can be called the Polish School.

Lewitt and Him were the only ones with an entirely original approach, taking their inspiration from surrealist painting. They emigrated to England before the war, but their stamp can be seen in the posters of Trepkowski, highly symbolic, which triumphed at the 1937 World's Fair in Paris where, as in 1925, the Poles took numerous prizes (Kielkorski, Piatkowski, Bocianowski, Dodacki, Hryniewicz, Szomanski).

463. Nowicki & Sandecka: Poster for an international dance competition in Warsaw. 1933.

464. Osiecki: "Snow and Sun in Poland"—for the Polish State Railroads. 1938.

465. Tadeus Gronowski:
Poster celebrating
the Tenth Anniversary
of the Polish victory
over the Soviet
invasion of Poland
after World War I. 1930.

466. A.M. Cassandre:
Automobile and
Motor Show in
Amsterdam. 1929.

Holland and Scandinavia

Holland

Between 1915 and 1920, the most remarkable posters were still those for theaters and exhibitions by Roland-Holst *(Faust)*, Lebeau *(Hamlet)*, Molkenboer *(St. Franciscus)*, Lion-Cachet *(Utrecht Jaarbeurs)* and P. Alt Hofman *(Haagscher Kunst Ring)*. The artists were embroiled in heated debates over what the true role of the poster should be: a piece of information made as esthetic as possible (Roland-Holst), or, if it can be done, an outcry (Hahn). Advertising agents took advantage of these dissentions to increase their power by calling less and less often on fine artists. The rupture between the cultural sector (reserved for artists) and the commercial sector (the agencies' domain) was flagrant, with the agents becoming more powerful every day.

It was no doubt this situation that led Michael Wilmink in *Gebrauchsgrafik*[1] to write an article that began "There is no Dutch poster art." To support this, he describes the lamentable condition of the posters of the time: "Posters are hung aimlessly and tastelessly, following no definite rule . . . Most of these posters seem to have been imported from America or England, but they are all of the lowest order."

Yet, as Wilmink notes, there were some good artists. Jongert, in the special number of *Wendingen* devoted to the Dutch poster[2], divided them into three groups: the flamboyant (Van Sluijters, Van der Hem), the idealists (Roland-Holst, Toorop, Lion-Cachet, Van Diedenhoven) and the revolutionaries (Zwart, Schuitema, Huszar, Van Ravenstijn and Walter, Funk, Küpper and Hahn, Jr.). In the last group only the first four are revolutionary in their style.

While all these artists had difficulty finding work in advertising, no one being a prophet in his own country, it was Cassandre who, between 1928 and 1930, wrenched a series of contracts from the Dutch agencies: *Nederlandsche Nyverheidsten Toonstelling, Statendam and London via Vlissengen-Harwich* in 1928; *Automobiel & Motorrijwiel Tentoonstelling* and *Droste's Cocoa* in 1929; in 1930, *De Vries Robbe Stork-Hijsch;* and in 1931, *Pakjes Koffie Van Nelle*. These posters were enthusiastically received but changed nothing in the deadlock between artists and commerce. Cassandre did leave his mark, however, on Ten Broek's posters for the *Holland-Amerika Line* and on H. Nigh *(Heemaf)*.[3]

467. Bart Van der Leck: Art exhibition in Utrecht. 1919.

1. *Gebrauchsgrafik,* April 1927.
2. *Wendigen,* Vol. 5, No. 2, 1923.
3. See the Chapter "The Avant-gardes," p. 149 et seq.

468. E. Nerman: Theatrical poster. 1919.

469. Aage Rasmussen: The midnight train for *DSB*. 1937.

The artists connected to the de Stijl group still continued to plead the cause of the quality poster. Schuitema put the case brilliantly: "An architect should have a notion of the future use of his building. So should an advertising artist have an idea of the aim of his advertisement. Does this mean that artists cannot make good and even magnificent posters, if they are not conscious of their design? No, in practice the reverse is manifestly true, but such cases are always affairs of chance."

However, aside from exhibition and political posters to which they were too often limited, and where the imaginative typography of H.N. Werkman was resplendent, some orders arrived for Zwart and Schuitema from government agencies like the Post Office—thanks to Dr. Van Royen's intervention.

In these few works the new typography, photography and photomontage made their appearances.

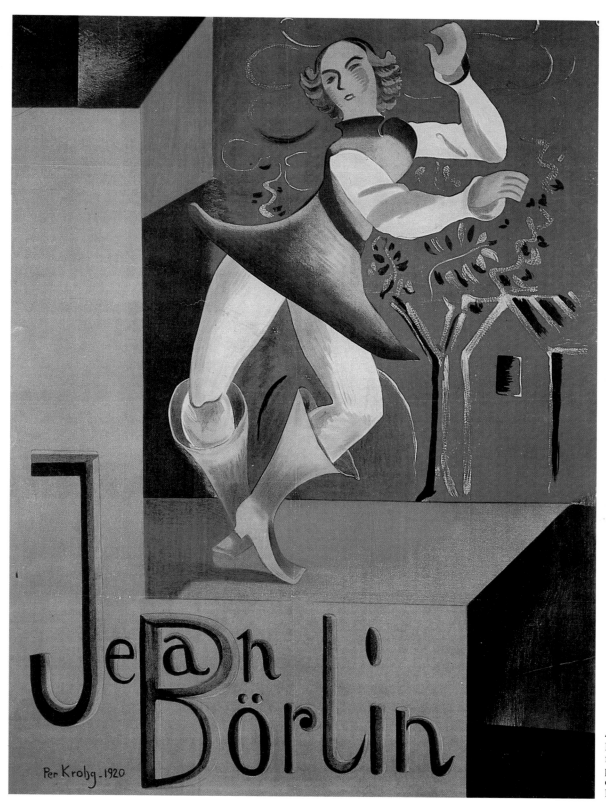

Per Krohg -1920

470. Per Lasson
Krohg: Poster
for *Jean Borlin*,
principal dancer
of the Royal Swedish
Ballet. 1920.

471. Thor Bogelund: Danish hunting exhibition. 1934.

472. N. G. Granath: Horse racing poster. 1934.

Sandberg, who went to work for the Stedelijk Museum, was another supporter of the quality poster: "A good poster should be audacious. Designers and clients are lacking in audacity."

And he gives us the word upon which to end this chapter, eclipsing problems of form: "The format of the Dutch poster is too small for it to be compared with the best international posters."

Scandinavia

Advertising art never attained full maturity in the Scandinavian countries. This was not the fault of the artists, but of the restrictions on poster-hanging. The poster, limited to small formats, parsimoniously displayed, could never obtain the spectacular results it enjoyed in more permissive countries. Esbjörn Hiort[1], speaking of Denmark, sums up the situation: "The fact is that the poster never found favorable conditions in Denmark. It has always been banned from fences and attractive large surfaces and has had to content itself with kiosks and authorized panels. For this reason the streets of Danish towns are not marked by posters. The format of the Danish poster is 62 by 85 cm., its size having been limited to the dimensions of the authorized hanging spaces. In the train stations, the spaces are however in the format of international tourist posters: 62 by 100 cm. Danish designers are thus deprived of the inspiration offered by very large formats." On the whole, these remarks apply to all the Scandinavian countries.

In Denmark, where no typographic tradition existed, lettering was considered an inevitable evil until the arrival of Thor Bögelund, the pioneer of the Danish poster. His clear-cut letters, his vivid colors, his innate sense of simplification make him the first true Danish poster artist and the one whose work is most important. His posters, mostly for publications or carnivals at Tivoli, are always well composed in a very Germanic spirit.

Next to him can be placed Sven Brasch with his severely stylized but repetitive style; Sikker Hansen, who with few colors printed in varying tones obtained rich results; Ib Andersen, strongly influenced by Cassandre; and Arne Ungermann, who gave very special attention to ideas.

Let us also mention Gunnar Biilmann Peterson, Erik Stockmar and Helge Refn, who at the end of the Thirties, after trips to Paris and London, designed posters in a very international style. Aage Rasmussen, infatuated with the airbrush, was a disciple of Cassandre. Let us finally mention Henry Thelander and Viggo Vagirby. Tom Purvis[2], immediately before the War, mentions the photographic posters of the Esselte Reklam agency.

Paul Lifschutz[3] states: "Swedish posters had their golden age in the Teens and Twenties."

The Swedes produced strong, well composed designs, in particular remarkable theatrical posters, which make up most of our documentation.

Eric Rohman (to whom *Das Plakat* devoted an article in June 1921) left a remarkable series of film posters: *Stambul Ros, Skandal, Sant Far Man Integöra, Klostret I Sendormir, Fröken Tingen Tangel,* etc., for the great American silent films. Nerman, working for the theater, using

1. Esbjörn Hiort: *L'Affiche Danoise*. Paris: La Société Danoise, 1952.
2. Tom Purvis: *Poster Progress*.
3. Paul Lifschutz: *Street Spectacle Sweden*. Stockholm: The Swedish Institute, 1982.

473. Helge Refn: Gardening show. 1935.

474. Hallman: Swedish Film Industry's production of *The Three Musketeers*. 1933.

flat-toned cutouts without outlines, is surprisingly modernistic. His poster for the *Folketeatern* (1919) is a masterpiece.

Käge, Forseth, Schwab, Hjortzberg and Janson were much influenced by the Germans, whose rigorous qualities they appropriated—and with them, their lack of lightness. When lightness does appear, it is a Viennese derivation, like Engströmer's *Carmen,* very much in Klinger's style. Magnusson worked dextrously in Art-Deco style *(Grand Hotel)*.

In Norway, again due to the draconian restrictions on poster-hanging, there is little to remark. Everything of note came through the Fabritius agency. The artists were Andreas Block, Olaf Krohn, Henrik Baker. The only one who became internationally known was Per Lasson Krogh, a painter who made a long stay in Paris and was known for his poster for the dancer *Jean Borlin* (1920). In his own country, he designed a curious poster for a beer, with very delicate lettering—and another for the newspaper *Dag Bladet*.

In Finland, nothing deserves mention, though a book has recently appeared on the subject.[1]

1. Helmirütta Honkauen: *Placatista Julisteeksi.* 1983.

475. Sven Brasch: *Casino*.

476. Federico Seneca: The green nun for *Buitoni*. 1928.

Italy

After the war, Italian advertising took its course again without major stylistic change: the prewar masters, Cappiello, Dudovich and Mauzan continued their work. Primo Sinopico, a newcomer, specialized in the automobile poster and worked for *Campari* with wild imagination and colors reduced to the necessary mininum. He was quickly able to publish a book of his 57 best works. The poster market was largely in the hands of Giuseppe Magagnoli, ex-director of the Paris printer Vercasson, who returned to Milan to open the "Maga" agency. He had Cappiello's Italian contract, also Mauzan's for a while, and other artists like Pupazzi, Nizzoli, Fabiano, Terzi, Amaldi, and the young Severo Pozzati, before he left for France and became Sepo (at that early period his style was perfectly Cappiellesque). Most of the posters brought out by the studio simply carried the signature "Maga". At the Milan Fair, Magagnoli exhibited his posters, attracting more industrialists and public administrators.

The movements in France and Germany that led to a new conception of the poster had few echoes in Italy in the Twenties. Only Federico Seneca, who entered the scene in 1922 with posters for the Perugina Company's *Buitoni* products, evolved a personal touch with modern overtones in Italian poster art, with his stylized, faceless figures. He continued to publicize Perugina products non-aggressively for the next six years; in 1928 he came up with the celebrated "green nun" for *Buitoni*, from whom there emanated a surprising tenderness. Questioned by *Gebrauchsgrafik* for his tenth anniversary, Seneca remarked: "No book, no newspaper, no review has ever given a few lines to the art of the poster. This fact shows very well the importance accorded to this art in this country."

The Roman artist Pupazzi, interviewed in the same issue, added: "We can say that advertising art has not yet chosen the path it should take in our country. Of course there are a few designers who have seized upon the most modern and the most audacious style, but there are many others who lack either the courage or the capacity necessary to renounce the old tricks of advertising or to abandon principles based on a totally outmoded point of view."

As the Thirties dawned, two conflicting tendencies began to create a stir: the official fascist art, tinged with the pompous memories of classical Rome, and avant-garde art, deriving its strength from Bauhaus and the French school, among others.

Not surprisingly, Fascism debased art. The countless portraits of Mussolini made by Buriko are entirely without interest, while those sketched by Xanti Schawinsky, paradoxically, a student of the German Bauhaus, are exceptionally sublime. The remainder turns upon reminiscences of

477. Fortunato Depero: Theater poster for a futuristic production. 1924.

Roman grandeur, with artists like Angelo Buratini, or Sironi, who lost the force he had in 1932 (the sword of *Mostra de la revoluzione fascista*) by falling into the flattest Romanisms (*Fiat 500,* adorned with the she-wolf, Romulus and Remus!).

In this hostile environment, the avant-garde laid foundations that would carry Italian design to the front rank. It was mainly the work of a few matchless personalities.

Edouardo Persico arrived in Milan in 1929 and became Giuseppe Pagano's co-director of *Casa Bella.* Fascinated with advertising, he became the mainstay of the new review *Campo Grafica,* which brought together Carlo Brari, Attilio Russi, Giorgio Muggiani and Luigi Veronesi. He brought to Italy the work of the Bauhaus (thanks to Guido Modiani, a publisher and typographer connected with Moholy-Nagy) and of the French post-cubist school. He served as spearhead for a whole generation of artists: Chiattone, Strada, Poli, Giani, Carboni, Munari, and the futurists Ricas and Depero.

Antonio Boggeri gave these talents a workshop when he opened his studio, where the European avant-garde gathered. Xanti Schawinsky joined up, fresh from the Bauhaus, as did Steiner and the Italians Nizzoli, Carboni, Ricas, Murani, Muratore and Grignani. Searching out any novelties, Boggeri used the Milan celebration of 1933-36 to integrate the typographical work of German artist Renner, just as he maintained relations with Deberny and Peignot in Paris. In 1940, Max Huber joined the studio, bringing with him the experience of the Swiss school. All daring and high-quality work came out of the Boggeri studio which, happily, found some exceptional clients.

478. Marcello Nizzoli: *Cordial Campari*.

479. Araca: Poster for the cotton industry. 1935.

480. Sepo (Severo Pozzati): *Lavol* soap. 1932.

481. Marcello Dudovich: Poster for a clothing sale at a department store. 1937.

Adriano Olivetti, visionary captain of industry, gave his enterprise, from the Thirties onward, the structure of the future: design and graphic excellence were from that time two essential elements. In 1931 he opened his advertising bureau with Zveteremich. With the Boggeri studio, he brought out the first works in a modern spirit, such as in 1933, for the 25th anniversary of the company, a spiral booklet with new typography, photos, and photomontages. Xanti Schawinsky made a first photographic poster in color for him. In 1936, Nivola and Pintori took over from him at Olivetti.

Campari, who from the turn of the century had called on the best artists of the moment, continued to give itself an avant-garde image: good examples include Nizzoli's post-cubist image of a siphon in 1931, the works of the futurist Depero, and the company advertising esthetics of 1931 prepared by Boggeri.

The Motta company, under Dino Villarri's direction, also called upon quality artists: Sepo, famous in France but forgotten in Italy, made a trenchant comeback in 1934: his sliced brioche with the Motta M in the background is still used today. Cassandre arrived in his footsteps, designing his dove in 1935 in the refined style he practiced at the time. E. Lionne also worked for Motta at this time.

Good posters had become commonplace. Depero worked for the *Società nationale gazometri* and for *Cirio* food products (1934). Nizzoli designed a poster for the Third Fair of Milan, using flags as the mane of a majestic horse (1931). Xanti Schawinsky designed for *Princeps* and *Illy* coffee,

482. Marcello Dudovich & Marcello Nizzoli: Travel poster for Venice. c. 1933.

483. Xanti Schawinsky: *Illy* coffee. 1934.

484. Erberto Carboni: *Shell* Oil's Italian poster. 1938.

as well as *Apestre* seltzer (1935); Carboni, much inspired by Cassandre, the *Mostra Nazionale d'Agrumicultura,* and *Shell Oil* (1938); Araca chimed in with the great P of the *Fiera di Padova* (1932) and the little cubist man of *Sniafiocco* (1935). Modiani was the pioneer of the photographic poster. The posters of Sepo *(Lavol* 1932) and Cassandre *(Italia* 1935, *Italia-Cosulich* 1936) were also decorating the walls.

In a more classic style, though flirting with geometrism, the old masters were still active for more traditional clients: Dudovich made elegant and ingenious images for *Rinascente;* he also produced posters for tourism *(Rimini, Venezia Lido)* and many other clients, among them Fiat, for their *Balilla* model.

Contrary to Germany, Italian graphic art thrived under fascism. Though this was only brought about by an elite, all the elements were united at the moment of the breakout of World War II for its triumphant development.

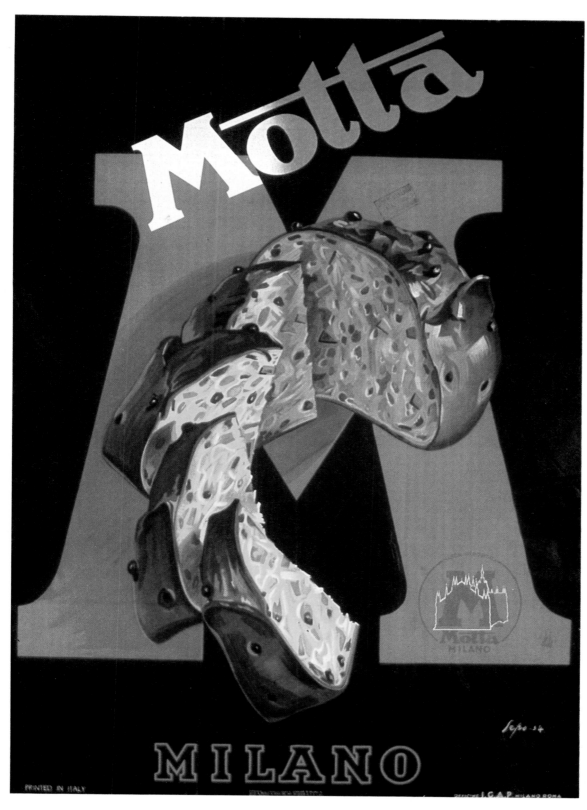

485. Sepo (Severo Pozzati): Poster for a Milan bakery. 1934.

486. Anonymous: Poster of the Spanish government condemning the bombings by the insurgents in the Spanish Civil War. c. 1937.

Spain

The Spanish artistic poster seemed, between the wars, to have purely and simply disappeared: The reviews of graphic art—French, English or German—as well as the international exhibitions, ignored it, even if a few samples found a corner for themselves in some cases.

Certainly no artist of international scope revealed himself during this period—though advertising continued to exist. Only Tom Purvis, in his excellent *Poster Progress,* gives us a few items of information together with this encouraging phrase: "Until their energies were largely diverted to war propaganda, Spanish designers were outstanding in poster publicity. Moliné, Ribera and Morell are three important men whose work lent itself particularly well to subjects of a spectacular kind."

José Morell and Paco Ribera both worked in a powerful Art Deco style, inspired by the French, with very stylized lettering and frequent use of the airbrush.

The layout is often bold, as in the great staircase that cuts a diagonal across the poster for *Gerone* (Morell), or the gigantic ear by Ribera for the *2nd Barcelona Radio Exposition* in 1932. All the works of these two artists are of high quality – it is doubtless only their lack of originality that has deprived them of an international audience. The same goes for Renau *(Arenas Balneario-Valencia)* and German Horacio *(L'Espagnolade).*

Far more unjust, it seems to us, is the oblivion into which the posters of the Catalan painter Antonio Clavé have fallen. At the beginning of the Thirties, he produced cinema posters thoroughly surprising in their sobriety, their symbolism, and the richness of their planes of color, in a very personal style – between Picasso and Cassandre. In a field where, at the time, a mediocre realism had spread throughout the world, it is surprising that the name of Clavé is not better known.

The civil war that broke out in 1936 shatterd commercial activities but gave rise to a mass of posters that are better known. The magazine *Arts et métiers graphiques,* which devoted an article to them, considered the production of the Catalonian republicans the most interesting—(which is not surprising from the political as well as the artistic point of view). At the beginning of the war, Marti Bas and Bofarull were the only professional graphic artists to lend their talents to their cause. The other artists were painters; but as poster production proliferated during the relatively short run of the war, many of them joined the bandwagon. After very simple beginnings (symbolic fists and slogans), and a pedestrian passage through Soviet and German influences, the republican poster achieved some real successes towards the end, especially with photomontage.

487. Marti Bas: Political poster dealing with the issue of industry for war or peace. c. 1936.

488. Paco Ribera: *Fiestas de la Republica.* c. 1932.

489. Antonio Clavé:
"And now what?"—
A Depression film
poster. c. 1930.

490. Renau: Tourist
poster for Valencia.

491. José Morell:
*The 6th Fair of
Barcelona.* 1933.

492. José Morell:
Exposition of
the *Primavera*
artist group. 1934.

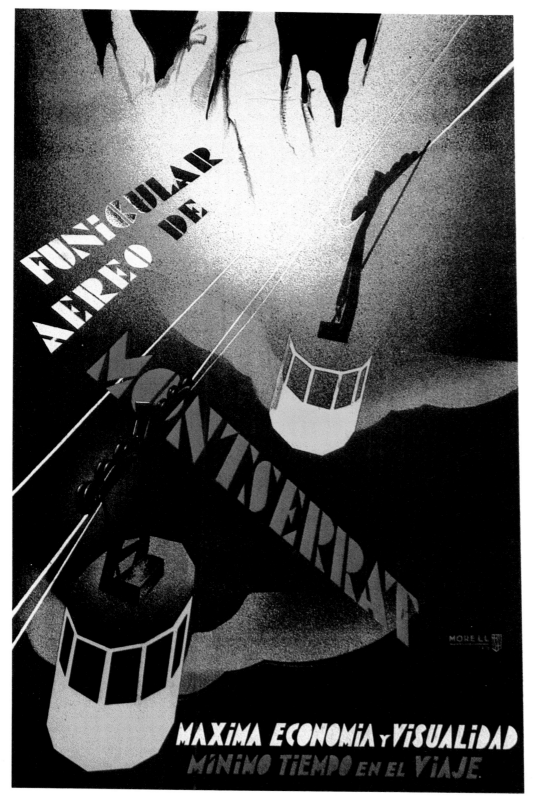

493. José Morell: *Montserrat*
tourist poster.

494. Mokuda Inoue:
Akadama port wine. 1932

495. Hokuu Tada:
Kirin lemonade. 1936.

496. Kinkichi Takahashi:
Poster for a sporting
goods store. 1939.

497. Hiromu Hara:
Poster for the *Nanking-
Shanghai News*. 1938.

Japan Between The Wars

At the end of the Taisho era, which lasted until 1926, posters of the chromo type representing a woman's face were all the rage. Ryuyo Machida drew them in vast quantities for the sale of beer, wines, medicines and also gas lamps and tires. This Nipponese Chéret, dabbling in coy portraits, was the most prolific poster artist. In 1922, for *Porto Akadama,* Mokuda Inoue represented a woman nude to the shoulders, causing quite a stir. Graphic art did, however, appear little by little: the Association of Advertising Artists, created in 1926, and the Group of 7 (Nananin-sha) led by Suguira played an important role in the evolution of styles.

The different movements that revolutionized Western art reached Japan little by little, and posters, abandoning their obsolete realism, adapted themselves to European models.

The cinema, which was developing in Japan as in the rest of the world, gave rise to posters more or less like those everywhere, featuring portraits of the actors. Many were produced by Shinkichi Yamada in the late 1920s, and by Hisamitsu Noguchi in the Thirties. With Takashi Kono, who also worked regularly for the cinema in the Thirties, it was quite another matter. His little figures, his stylized faces, his compositions and patches of color anticipated contemporary Japanese graphics, of which this versatile artist may be justly considered one of the pioneers.

During this period, commercial posters were designed by artists like Hokuu Tada whose posters for Kirin were among the first to find a language suitable to the medium. Gihachiro Okuyama drew his little grotesque figures in a style as personal as it was surprising. The influence of the Bauhaus and of the French and Swiss schools made itself felt at the end of the Thirties: Kinkichi Takahashi, whose drawing was very typically Art-Deco, also skillfully mixed photography and graphics. His poster for a sporting-goods store in 1939 was directly influenced by Matter. Hiromu Hara also used asymmetric typography and photography, and after World War II became one of the foremost exponents of the Japanese school. This was also true of Shichiro Imatake, who worked for the studios of the Daimaru department stores in Kobe, and later Takashimaya in Osaka; and of Ayao Yamana, the first to begin creating the Shiseido cosmetic firm's image.

498. Abram Games: British
Counterintelligence poster. 1942.

The Second World War

As in 1914, the poster again became one of the indispensable media of communication. It served primarily as government propaganda, and wherever it was placed, it called for patriotism, for guarding national security, for participating in production and being on guard against the invader.

On September 2, 1939, a general mobilization order was posted on French walls which resembled that of 1914: an official poster whose text was written in black was surmounted by two tricolor flags with crossed poles and with the date written in by hand. Germany had just invaded Poland, the conflict was worsening. The nations were on their way to a "total war" for which not only soldiers would be mobilized, but also civilians—women, children, old people. The images that issued from the Second World War were intended to reach the widest possible audience.

Their call to patriotism was made with graphic constants: symbol of the fatherland, the flag returned again and again like a leitmotif, and the hammer and sickle on the red star on Soviet posters, the German swastika, the French Cross of Lorraine.

At the beginning of the war one could still feel the remains of the humor which animated the posters of the school of Thomas and Bruce Bairnsfather during the First World War, as for instance, in the graphics of the English designer Bert Thomas *(Arf a Mo—National Service Needs You)*. But it soon became clear that the times had become graver and more urgent than any had ever been before, and it was time now to convince and not to smile.

For the first few years, starting with 1939, victorious Germany was in force. Posters, ordered mainly by Goebbels, accompanied images of resolute soldiers with texts of a frenzied optimism: *The New Europe is unbeatable; One battle, One victory!*

In a recruitment poster for the elite storm troopers, we find, against the background of a swastika, drawn by the official Nazi graphic artist Mjölnir in 1943, an Aryan soldier, bayonet in hand, exhorting German boys to join the Waffen-SS once their 17th birthday is passed.

On another poster, in the obligatory black-white-red color scheme, Zik, much influenced by Mjölnir's technique, showed a soldier characteristically illustrating the unequivocal assertion: *Victory will be ours.*

In counterpoint to this optimistic confidence, Henri Quignon's poster *Holding the Line,* apearing in the United States in 1942, showed the head of a determined Churchill on the body of a stalwart bulldog, with a flag in the background. A symbol of Britain since the Napoleonic wars, this dog with the jutting jaw and muscular body expressed the country's resolve to resist and to win.

More emphatic but no less effective, graphically simple, the Soviet

499. Paul Colin: French counterintelligence poster. 1940.

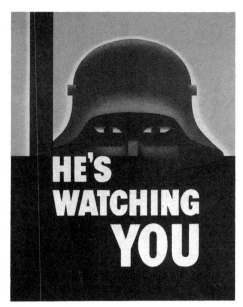

500. Glenn Grohe: British poster. 1942.

poster by Irakly Toidze, distributed in 1941, just after the German invasion, identified Russia with a woman draped in red, on a background of raised and menacing bayonnets.

The case of the French patriotic poster is rather special. In fact, before its actual entry into the conflict, France, as a half-involved nation, produced images of a country marked with a semblance of peace.

These posters, like the ones Maurice Toussaint specialized in in 1938 (*Enlist, re-enlist in the Metropolitan Forces; Englist, re-enlist in the Colonial Forces; For the Defense of the Empire, Enlist*) do not have the urgency that reigned elsewhere.

But already, in a convivial way certainly, Fix-Masseau encouraged schoolchildren to work for the soldiers on the front in a neatly square-ruled paper design.

After 1940, France was occupied, and a new generation of graphic artists appeared; the poster's tone changed, and very often, the propaganda message obscured the patriotic spirit. We can see this on the design by the German artist Matejko which advises the "abandoned population" to "trust the German soldier".

It was necessary to wait for the Liberation before the French poster could again express itself without external pressures. In 1945, Hansi, in naive images with a touch of the comic strip, celebrated the end of the war in his manner.

Corollary of patriotism, the national defense was the object of many posters. In time of war, everyone, soldier or not, is responsible for his neighbor's life, and the greatest rule is silence. The old adage *the walls have ears,* was illustrated several times. Bruce Bairnsfather did it with a touch of humor: *Even the walls; S'long Dad! We're shiftin' to . . . Blimey, I nearly said it.* But this had less of a visual impact than the photomontage – a much-used technique for this theme – made by Leonard. The task of these graphic artists was very complicated. There were no ready-made symbols for matters of security, no flags unfurled behind uniforms, no saving cross. It was necessary to transmit a delicate message containing a shade of paranoia, as Zbynek Zeman remarks in *Selling the War – Art and Propaganda in World War II*. Images that were too realistic (the parachutist by Herbert Morton who was killed before touching ground: *Careless talk got there first),* or too sentimental (on a shrouded dais, a cocker-spaniel mourns its master's death, *Because Somebody talked;* Yegley), while touching, lacked power.

The subject required inventiveness and subtlety. The force of a poster like *Award for Careless Talk* came from the clever exploitation by Stevan Dohanos of the attributes of the enemy. The message is troubling, and not immediately receivable: only the bottom line of text removes the ambiguity and addresses itself directly to the reader: *Don't discuss troop movements – ship sailings – war equipment.*

Graphic simplicity and an absence of emotion produced the best security posters: an enormous black chain wound around red lips in a Finnish poster; a hand that pulled a curtain across warships (*Keep it Dark* – in red obliquely on the black curtain – *Careless Talk Costs Lives* – below, like a verdict) in an American photomontage; two trusting Frenchmen spied on by a silhouette skulking in the shadows, in the famous, somewhat subtle, poster by Paul Colin, *Silence . . . the enemy is eavesdropping;* in the foreground, the face of listening soldier, and the plain slogan: *The Enemy is Listening, Be Silent,* in the Italian poster by Gino Bocasili.

501. Stevan Dohanos: Design using the German Iron Cross. 1943.

502. Anonymous: Russian artist's conception of Hitler. c. 1943.

503. S.P.K.: Churchill as octopus was the Nazi government's propaganda effort to rally Occupied France to its side. 1942.

On the other hand, certain illustrators chose the comic strip to silence the idle mouth: blustering graphics – the enemy creeping most likely in a serpent's skin – accompanied by an eagerly explicit text.

Finally, the most perfect joining of text and image was probably accomplished by the great English designer Abram Games. Named official war-poster artist in 1942, he brought out in the same year the famous *Your talk may kill your comrades,* where the waves issuing from a mouth form a spiral which unwinds into a sword piercing three identical figures who fall in unison.

The excellence of Abram Games' posters comes not only from the quality of the graphics, but also from the special care he gave to the lettering – the choice of characters and the layout – and to the striking, well-contrasted colors; not to mention that each design was supported by the artist's unshakable faith in the ideas he defended.

As images of an interior, weaponless war, preventive more than defensive, insidious, these national security posters had the effect of bringing civilians together in a common fight against the enemy.

Unlike the First World War, the Second had from its beginning drawn upon men as much as upon new techniques. Very soon, the generosity of civilians to support the war effort was called on.

They were solicited in two specific ways: they were asked on the one hand to subscribe to war bonds, and on the other to offer themselves to work in factories deserted by mobilized men. In this period of economic recession, where standard product advertising was suspended, the drive to subscribe to war bonds took the form of a true advertising campaign. After all, under the cover of patriotism – to come back to that – was it not a question of convincing in order to sell?

In France, in 1940, a whole series of posters appeared illustrating this theme. The tricolor is draped on a good many of them, such as Besniard's poster which shows a cannon pointed to the sky with the copy: *Every bond is a shot fired at the enemy*.

504. Ben Shahn: Poster asking the public to support the cause of the Free French. 1942.

505. Jean Carlu: A 1941 poster for the American war support effort.

506. Thomas Eckersley: British Post Office
poster of 1943.

The somber power of graphics was inherited from the style of the
Thirties. On another, less successful poster, we find the celebrated phrase
by Paul Reynaud: *We will win because we are the strongest,* laid out on
a planisphere. In the United States, where he had taken refuge, Jean
Carlu designed a striking symbolic poster: *America's Answer: Production*—a gloved hand with a wrench tightens a bolt, the first O of the
"production." He did it again in *Give them Both Barrels,* where he pointed
to the similarity of tools and weapons in an equally forceful way. The
United States holds the record for these images. To call upon Americans
to buy war bonds, graphic artists used every means available, with gratify-
ing results.

The poster *To Have and to Hold, War Bonds,* where a smiling soldier
unfurls a flag, clearly appeals to patriotic sentiment, while the face of
Roosevelt emerging from a quasi-mystical glow *(Victory Bonds)* attempts
to impose religious fervor upon the war.

85 MILLION AMERICANS *HOLD* WAR BONDS

507. Anonymous:
Poster for
World War II
bond drive. 1944.

508. Michel Jacquot:
A collaborationist
poster in Occupied
France: *Jews kill
in the dark—
Mark them to
recognize them!*
c. 1942

Finally, bordering on bad taste, a sinister poster assures us that war bonds are less expensive than grave markers.

Since money did not play the decisive role in the Soviet economy, that country's government concentrated its efforts on increasing production.

An effective 1941 poster, using a minimum of colors, succinctly shows airplanes and tanks springing from a pool of liquid steel and from a man's outstretched hand. Where the background shades off, we perceive clearly the hammer and sickle in bright red.

In Italy and England, women were being actively exhorted to work in the factories.

In Germany, it was the soldier himself who would urge the worker to be as brave as he in a different phase of the fight leading to the same victory.

Several American posters presumptuously suggested that the length of the war depended solely upon citizens' participation in universal production. Thus *When? It's up to you!* showed Hitler at bay, pursued by ever-growing squadrons of planes.

Vichy France, using the Marshall's slogan *Work, Family, Country,* urged the French to go work in Germany. *The hard times are over, Papa is earning money in Germany,* murmurs a radiant mama to her son.

During France's occupation, in fact, the struggle for the Liberation took place underground, and only the official artists, such as the team of Alain Fournier, Eric Castel and André Derain, among others, accepted the challenge.

With the accent on the close relation between the armed forces and universal production, wartime posters played a decisive role in the general mobilization. The obviousness of their message gave rise to simple, clear, immediately legible graphics.

Besides internal problems, the poster reflected the general war situation in its complexity, largely due to the friction among the Allies. It preached unity, expanding its theme of patriotism to the Allied nations, and becoming at times pure propaganda. Patriotically, it expressed forthrightly the trust the country placed on its allies.

The slogans, like the images, went straight to the point: *The victory of the United Nations is now Assured* is without ornament, solid, with the text occupying one fifth of the poster which shows three soldiers in the foreground—an Englishman, an American and a Frenchman—marching with a determined step in the same direction; behind them are planes, battleships, tanks. From London came posters to the glory of the French Forces of the Interior, encouraging the Resistance.

In 1942, American artists brought out a series of posters, glorifying the struggle of the minor allies. One of the most graphic is one that McKnight Kauffer designed for Greece: *Greece fights on:* a somber profile, helmeted and stylized, against the Greek flag.

Wherever they went, the Germans made use of the poster to show their power and to rally the invaded peoples to their cause. Phrases like *German Might Guarantees Victory* or *The German Soldier is the Guarantee of Victory* flourished on the walls, accompanied by the traditional allegories, seeking converts among the conquered, especially among the Danes and Poles, who met the criteria for racial purity, as potential recruits for the German military machine.

The Allies also used the poster as a propaganda tool. Although these posters were for the most part emphatic and conventional, some of them

509. O. Anton: A 1943 poster from Occupied Belgium gives a favorable view of the SS.

510. Matejko: German poster urges the French to trust the German soldier. 1940.

511. Anonymous: American
propaganda poster. 1943.

stand out. The best of them convey their message without copy, by sheer graphic impact. This is the case of the American poster of 1944 where the swastika is brushed over by three energetic, tricolored brushstrokes. Or another, more dynamic one, which shows the four branches of the swastika torn off by four hands identifiable by their cuffs as French, English, Soviet and American.

As a constant presence, coming from all directions, all the war posters were positive and bearers of hope from whichever side they arose. They sought to unite men around an ideal, calling upon moral values: courage and brotherhood.

But there is another category of images we must speak of here which appealed to man's vilest sentiments. They incited to xenophobia, to intolerance and antisemitism, opposing the Invader, Bolshevism or the Jews.

Many American posters presented the Japanese after Pearl Harbor as bloodthirsty beasts, such as the grinning Japanese who carries a white woman over his shoulder, having just apparently raped her. Behind him he leaves only desolation, ravages and houses in flames. *(This is the Enemy).*

Very often, the posters of the Second World War had recourse to this sort of soft-core pornography to increase the horror inspired by the enemy.

Between two calls for austerity (culinary and economic advice was posted on the walls such as the surprise omelette or herb broth), the Vichy government tried to incite the French populace against Great Britain: one design showed a bulldog devouring the world, while another had the tentacles of Churchill-the-Octopus methodically amputated.

The long-standing challenge to German power, Bolshevism, was the subject of many posters intended to inspire abhorrence, among them two sinister ones *(The Danger of Bolshevism* and *Never),* dissuasive and perfect in their ugliness. The message was almost always organized around the same symbols: blood, death, the gallows, crosses; and the colors ran to black and red.

In contrast, French posters intended to mobilize men for the struggle against Bolshevism are characterized by careful graphics, a structured layout, suggesting the order which must be re-established *(United Europe against Bolshevism; They give their blood, give your work to save Europe from Bolshevism; Enlist in the legion of French Volunteers against Bolshevism).*

But the Enemy with a capital E, the scapegoat of the Hitler regime, was the Jew. He was everywhere in German propaganda.

He was part of all opposition: some posters even make a synthesis of anti-sovietism and anti-semitism. A racist poster by Mjölnir, *Victory or Bolshevism,* shows on one side—light—a happy mother and child, and on the other—dark—the monstrous face of a Jew capped with a red star, overseeing the annihilation of the German people.

In German official rote, the Jew was the usurper of power: in 1944, two German propaganda posters assured the French that 97% of the press and 95% of the cinema in America were in the hands of Jews. The compliment had, of course, disastrous connotations for the Nazis.

In other Nazi propaganda, the Jew was seen as the power behind thrones. A poster from 1943, highly colored, shows an unsavory silhouette with a Star of David skulking behind a curtain of flags (British, American, Soviet). The message is delivered more expressly in a photomontage of high quality, ordered by the Germans from French studios in 1942 for

КРАСНАЯ АРМИЯ
НЕСЕТ ОСВОБОЖДЕНИЕ
ОТ ФАШИСТСКОГО ИГА!

512. Schmarinov: Soviet morale booster: *The Red Army Will Free You from the Fascistic Yoke.*

513. Anonymous: Clever German poster ridiculing the slow progress of Allied troops in Italy after the September, 1943 invasion.

the first issue of the antisemitic magazine *Le Cahier Jaune,* which addresses itself directly to the reader: *Who has stolen North Africa from us? Roosevelt. Who led him on? The Jews.* Haloed with the Jewish star, a malevolent counsellor bends toward the ear of the president of the United States.

514. Anonymous:
American
anti-Nazi
poster. 1944.

515. Raymond Savignac:
Monsavon soap. 1949.

Poster Trends — 1945-1970

After five years of cataclysms and difficult years of reconstruction, the world yet again returned to normal consumer economy. The two luminaries of the pre-World War II period practically abandoned the poster: Cassandre occupied himself with theater décors and his advertising creations no longer had their old force; McKnight-Kauffer, returning to the United States, could not recapture the inspiration of his British period. Like Paul Colin, whose style varied little, Loupot, in developing the campaign for St. Raphael, stayed closest to his pre-war experimentation. For the rest, the war seemed to have annihilated the erstwhile marked differences between countries, and the poster became European, international, its currents visible everywhere up to the end of the Sixties.

If we attempt to simplify the mass of available evidence, three principal directions may be discerned: the final years of the poster artists, discovering the visual gag or following the pictorial styles of the times; the consolidation of an international graphic art, born of the experiments of the Bauhaus and de Stijl; and the evolution of advertising itself, which, with the increasing importance of the agencies, changed the technique of producing commercial posters.

516. Charles Loupot: *St. Raphael* liqueur. c. 1950.

517. Charles Loupot: One of the many *St. Raphael* billboards he designed.

518. Raymond Savignac:
Bel Paese cheese. c. 1960.

519. Herbert Leupin: *Bata* shoes. 1954.

520. Herbert Leupin: Poster for a brand of liquor. 1955.

Cubism, which, to use Blaise Cendrar's expression, crumbled at the end of the Thirties, lost currency: one finds reminiscences of it in Ashley *(Liberty),* Allner or Nathan, but all the leading artists had abandoned it to flirt with surrealism: Lewitt-Him's poster for the *American Overseas Airlines* which borrows one of Dali's melting watches, and Carlu's centaur for *Cinzano* are the archetypes. After six years of suffering, it was however another direction that attracted advertisers and the public: the visual gag, whose star performer was undeniably Raymond Savignac.

Born in 1907, a pupil of Cassandre, whose influence shows through his first posters, Savignac (to use his expression), "was born at age 41 from the udders of the Monsavon cow." This project, refused before the war by Schueller, the head of L'Oreal, was rediscovered at the time of an exhibition and enthusiastically published in 1949. All the elements of the visual gag are in this poster: Monsavon was made with milk; Savignac showed us, in a brilliant ellipsis, a cow from whose udders a cake of soap emerges—simple, direct, effective. . . . you had only to think about it. The drawing was simple, stylized and powerful, the colors lively and gay. Dozens of images followed: the half-cow observing her own haunches being cooked for *Bouillon Maggi* (1960), the man whose head is a tunnel through which pass cars for *Aspro* (1964) and the half-passenger for half-price tickets for the French railway *(SNCF,* 1964). "If I express myself with gags, whims, pirouettes, if my posters are graphic clowning, it's first of all because the public is so bored in its daily routine that I think advertising should amuse them." The formula found a market immediately and orders poured in from all over France, of course, but also from the rest of the world: the *Laines d'Aoust* in Belgium, *Het Laaste Nieuws* in Holland, *Il Giorno* and *Bel Paese* in Italy, *Collie* and *Opel* in Germany, *Parisiennes* in Switzerland, the *New York Times* and *Blue Cheer* in the United States, and the *Times* of London. The graphic expres-

521. Hervé Morvan: *Gitanes* cigarettes. 1960.

522. Charles Rohonyi. *Bols.* ca 1955

523. Thomas Eckersley: *Gillette*. 1949.

sion of the idea, with humor as intermediary, spread everywhere: in France, Hervé Morvan devoted himself to it exclusively, with fine results *(Gitanes, Kelton, Gévéor),* but it appeared also in Jean Colin, Fix-Masseau, Charmoz and Villemot. In Belgium, there were Rohonyi and Capouillard, then Julian Key *(Café Chat Noir, La Libre Belgique* and, more recently, *Laurens Menthol).* In Italy there was Armando Testa

524. Armando Testa:
Design for *Scotch*
Tape. c. 1955.

525. Abram Games:
Guinness, c. 1950.

526. Julian Key:
Café Chat Noir. 1966

527. Thomas Eckersley: Poster for a London store.

528. Bernard Villemot: *Bally* shoes. 1974.

529. Helmut Jurgens: Poster for a concert *Musica Viva*. 1954.

530. Hans Hillmann: German release of the Alec Guinness comedy, *The Ladykillers*. 1955.

531. Hans Michel & Gunther Kieser: Advertising a season of classical music on German radio. 1959.

532. Celestino Piatti: *Blaser*. 1958.

(Pirelli, Scotch). In England, changing his style, Thomas Eckersley embraced it felicitously (his series for *Gillette),* as did, on occasion, Games and Henrion. In Switzerland, Herbert Leupin, abandoning objectivity, designed masterpieces of the visual gag for *Bata* shoes, *Agfa* film, *Eptinger* and *Coca-Cola*. His design for Coke showing an abandoned music stand became a minor classic.

533. Pierre Brenot: *Lido* cabaret. 1954.

534. Pierre Augsburger: *Bally* shoes. 1958.

535. Gruau (Renato de Zavagli): *Blizzand* raincoats. 1965.

The second direction the poster artists of the period followed was directly linked to the evolution of painting: the school of Paris. The vivid colors and thin outlines, the abstraction, the organic forms were all found under the most diverse signatures all over the world. Villemot employed them in his series for *Orangina* and *Bally:* "The feeling of painting is necessary, but of mural painting", he said. Georget used stylized forms, vivid colors and a violent outline for *Gitanes* cigarettes, while Excoffon *(Air France, Gaz de France)* pursued lyrical abstraction. In Belgium, Jacques Richez exemplified the style *Expo '58,* for which he designed its poster. In Germany, where the quality of the commercial poster had not fully recovered from Nazism and from the war, this same spirit however appeared in the organic forms of Hans Michel and Gunther Kieser for *Jazz at the Philharmonic,* Helmut Jürgens' play with the letter-

536. Jacques Richez: Brussels Exposition. 1958.

537. Hans Falk: Exhibition: *The Poster as the Mirror of Our Time*. Zurich, 1949.

538. George Tscherny: *Vat 69*. c. 1955.

539. Hans Erni: Circus *Knie*. 1965.

540. Dick Elffers: *Holland Festival*. 1961.

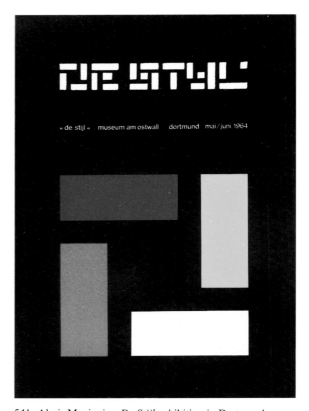

541. Almir Mavignier: *De Stijl* exhibition in Dortmund. 1964.

542. Pierre Monnerat: *Cinzano*. 1960.

ing for *Musica Viva,* Hans Hillmann's film posters or Vogenauer's creations. Hans Unger in England *(London Underground)*, Pla Narbona in Spain, Fabigan in Austria, Martti A. Mykkänen and Gideon Keich in Israel are other examples.

Fashion and the music-hall still had Paris as their capital, with their own poster artists such as the exceptional Gruau and Brenot. Elsewhere, only the Swiss Pierre Augsburger can be compared with them. Jean Denis Malclès brought a new type of image to show posters, as did the Dane Björn Wiinblad.

But it was Switzerland, whose graphic school was then at its zenith, that harbored the most astonishing painters of posters.

Celestino Piatti used stylization, vivid colors and a thick black outline. His output was enormous. Hans Erni was an eminent draftsman, constructing his image with fine lines which he accumulated in concentric order, standing out from somber backgrounds, in bold layouts; he was the specialist in exhibitions and works for great causes and made many posters for the leftist parties. He did not disdain photos in combination with graphics, as in his poster *No to Atomic War*. Hans Falk had an equally recognizable style: his posters, treated like paintings, nevertheless used masses of color and a composition that gives them a place entirely apart among graphic works. Like Erni, he did little work for commercial advertising, which called rather upon the veteran Stoecklin *(Bell)* and Donald Brun with their varied styles, and a constellation of other artists.

These fine art poster artists stood in contrast with the graphic constructivists, born of the between-the-wars avant-gardes, who used either graphics or photography, according to the problem posed them, and who attached primary importance to layout and typography. They were the ones who created a true international style in this period, giving the foundations to contemporary advertising style.

In this field, the Swiss also occupied a dominant position: besides Keller and Max Bill, still active, there was a whole school formed by them which was beginning to express itself. Müller-Brockmann employed irreproachable photographic images for great causes *(Protegez l'enfant, Weniger Lärm),* or played with the color, the graphic elements and the lettering starting in 1951 with his design for the *Tonhalle* in Zurich. His role as teacher and theoretician, especially in the area of typography, was essential: "The arbitrary and individual disposition of typographic elements is giving place to an objective layout responsive to the laws of typography itself.

"The principle which dominates over all others is typography without ornamental flourishes but whose form uniquely delivers the communication of the message.

"So conceived, typography becomes functional in so far as its technical

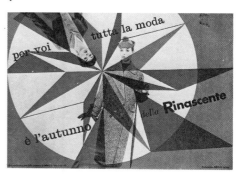

544. Max Huber: *Rinascente* store fashion poster. 1954.

543. Josef Müller-Brockmann: Poster against noise pollution. 1960.

545. Josef Müller-Brockmann: A *Musica Viva* concert in Zurich. 1958.

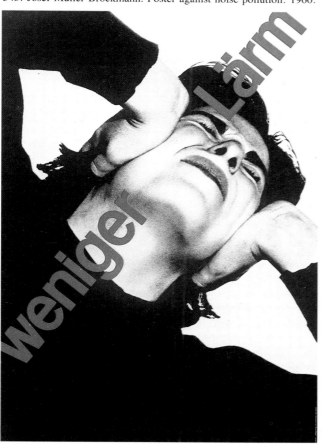

546. Giovanni Pintori: *Olivetti*. 1957.

548. Giovanni Pintori: *Olivetti*. 1957.

547. Armin Hofmann: *William Tell*. 1963.

conditions are respected, objective in view of the subordination of the lettering to the word and of the word to the sentences, of the disposition of sentences in function of their content, and finally thanks to a formal organization of the whole that responds to the internal relations of what is being said, of the content. And at the same time this typography is informative thanks to its easy legibility and the disposition of groups of sentences which results in our comprehending, easily and rapidly, what is being said."

Vivarelli, in his poster *For the aged,* and Armin Hofmann, in designs for the *Theater of Basel,* played with the same ease with lettering and photography, and so did Emil Ruder, Karl Gerstner or Richard Lohse. Rudi Külling applied the same principle to product advertising *(Bic, Maggi),* as did Pierre Monerat (his typography for *Cinzano).*

In Holland, in the footsteps of de Stijl and of Sandberg, there were Brattinga *(P.T.T.),* Dick Elffers, Otto Treumann, using photo-graphics and typography; and Wim Crouwel was one of the first to use computer graphics.

Germany, though it had been emptied of most of its talents, could however count on Mavignier, Kapitski and Hansjörg Mayer.

Italy, also, gathered the fruits of its pre-war efforts. Olivetti had Ettore Sottsas at the head of its design studio. Pintori designed a prestigious series of images, followed by those of Folon. Max Huber adapted his graphics and his constructivist photomontages to the exuberance of the times *(La Rinascente, Sirenella).* The Italians were as disciplined as the Swiss, but were not as rigid. Pino Tovaglia *(14th Triennale of Milan),* Franco Grignani *(Alfieri Lacroix, Mostra de Tessile);* Massimo Vignelli (notably for the *31st and 32nd biennale of Venice* and for *Pirelli)* and Bruno Munari *(Campari)* play in an exemplary manner with forms and colors.

549. Massimo Vignelli: Poster for an art festival. 1962.

550. Franco Grignani: Textile Show in Milan. 1957.

551. Carlo Vivarelli: Charity drive for the aged. 1949.

552. Pieter Brattinga: *PTT* Exhibition. 1950.

553. Herbert Bayer: Travel poster for *Aspen*.
1949.

554. Erik Nitsche: French *Atoms for Peace* ad
of *General Dynamics*. 1955.

England and France, where Hollenstein, Frutiger and Widmer came bearing the good word, remained in retreat.

America, on the contrary, which had been the refuge of the avant-gardes persecuted by Nazism, profited by this constellation of talents. Big companies hired top talent: the Container Corporation of America called upon Bayer, Man Ray and Matter; Reichhold Chemicals engaged Carlu. After the war, these artists, in addition to their teaching, continued to produce fine works: Bayer *(Aspen, Polio Research),* Matter *(Polio),* Binder *(The Most Important Wheels of America, U.S. Navy),* Lionni *(8 Automobiles).* A new generation trained on their principles soon followed: Paul Rand *(Interfaith Day, El Producto, No Way Out),* Saul Bass *(The Man With the Golden Arm, Edge of the City),* and Eric Nitsche, whose series for *General Dynamics* in 1958 is a lesson in graphic expression. Sustained by the larger magazines *(Esquire, Fortune, Harper's,* etc.), who vied with one another in the quality of their designs, the leading artists could express themselves and cause a new style to reach the public. Among these were Dorfman, Massey, de Harak, Lubalin, Tscherny, Danziger, Chermayeff and Gesmar. We should add to this list the artistic directors of advertising agencies who organized themselves in very powerful Art Directors' clubs and pushed for visual communication progress at top speed. Photo-advertisements like the Doyle-Dane-Berbach agency's series for *Volkswagen* were the outcome. New illustrators, following the examples of Ben Shahn and above all Saul Steinberg, also served the agencies, with Bob Blechman emerging as one of the trend setters.

555. Saul Bass:
For the film,
*The Man with the
Golden Arm*. 1955.

However, although graphics had made their definitive breakthrough, their effects on the poster remained problematic in this period in the United States. Restrictive legislation and, above all, television which took up the greater part of advertising budgets left a void in quality as well as in quantity. And added to this was photography, which at the time seemed the solution to everything and carried a final, almost fatal blow for the poster. "That the poster managed even to survive all these handicaps is something of a miracle," notes Ervine Metzl.

The United States was not the only country saddled with this situation, which gained upon Europe in the Sixties, as the big American agencies established their foothold there. They brought their working methods with them (motivation research and market studies), and above all their creative practices in which artistic directors, idea-men, writers and even businessmen participated in a collective effort.

Obviously this upset the old system, especially in England and in France where the poster had remained in the hands of poster artists who both conceived the design and executed the image, often directly selling the model to the client with the intermediary of an agent. Thus they were in direct competition with the agency and refused, of course, to submit to its humiliating terms: "Daughter of the streets, surely. But not a submissive daughter. The poster has not dogged the steps of the troops of Marketing since their invasion of Europe, has not enrolled under the starless banner of the 'ad'."[1]

For their part, the agencies were little inclined to call upon these rebels, especially since, as in the United States, they were under the spell of the sirens of photography. On the face of it, it semed the ideal response to advertising problems: docile, rapid, without surprises, it could also serve as well for a magazine advertisement as for a leaflet or a poster. The reality is quite otherwise, but it took ten years for agencies to realize it.

As for the poster artists, they gritted their teeth. Ashley launched an offensive in the London *Times* in 1964: "The creativity of the draftsman and of the poster artist have been sadly amputated. Photography is used in too many English advertisements today. Graphic design and the art of the poster as we know it seem to have entirely disappeared from billboards in favor of enlarged photos. Advertising these days does not appeal to

557. Josef Binder: Poster aimed at media buyers. c. 1950.

1. Andre Maisonneuve: "Interview with Raymond Savignac," in Eudes Delafon: *Ca C'est l'Affiche*. Paris: Les Presses du Temps Présent.

558. Henrion: *Murphy Television.*

the intuition of unconscious depths but to surface rationality tending to cupidity." Ervine Metzl added: "An artist can dream – a camera cannot." But this is belittling photography needlessly.

Certain French poster artists expressed themselves more calmly and reasonably, such as Jean Colin: "Why always oppose designers against photographers in poster art? Any procedure is valid if it arrests the view of the passerby, but the image and the idea must also distinguish it from other posters. It is in this that (the adherents of photography) are impoverished and lack effectiveness for selling. Many of us have been saying that it does not suffice to enlarge an Ektachrome to a 3x4 meter size to make it into a poster. Photography is materially founded on details, while the poster should be simplified and powerful.

"Photographic expression, then, must be adapted to the art of the poster, and up to now this has rarely happened."

Villemot went farther: "Any technique is valid if the results are good."

It is true that the photographic posters produced by the agencies in the Sixties were on the whole very bad, with a few exceptions (certain English creations like *Murphy Television* by Henrion or Arpad Elfer's series for *D.H. Evans*). But photography was a false problem, as advertisers quickly realized. Bernard Cathelat, director of the Eurocom communication center, explained: "No doubt it is an error to abandon the graphic techniques of traditional poster-making, and treat the poster like a magazine page crammed with details and nuances. It is equally wrong to reproduce catalogue photos whose realism is as sinister as the streets themselves. For the poster's function is to sublimate the product. Physically, it lifts it off the ground, makes it soar above the crowd, and puts it in a niche like the statues of saints in the facade of Notre-Dame."

So the commercial poster, conceived according to the norms of agencies which handled huge budgets, came thus to be, and it was good.

It was the poster artists of the Seventies who paid for its success. Conceived by teams of idea-men, a product image was consigned to a well-known photographer or to an illustrator who had only to produce the work required of him. A new era began.

But before studying this latest evolution, certain graphic schools whose originality marked the post-war period should be passed in review, without our detaching them from those we have already studied: the Poles, the Cubans, and the Chinese. We must also look at the evolution of the political poster and the reactions it provoked in an overly well-organized consumer society, and at the cultural poster, to which many good artists fled from the new constraints on advertising.

560. Anonymous. *Lux.* Soap. 1952

561. Henri Favre: *Gillette.* 1953.

562. Henryk Tomaszewski:
Poster for the 50th
Anniversary of the
International Puppeteers'
Organization. 1978.

The Post-War Polish Poster

Since 1925, the Polish poster had distinguished itself in international competitions, and its graphic and synthetic qualities were incontestably recognized. The new social and political conditions after the war led the poster to change its main thrust. Once purely commercial, it became a cultural agent. Its role was no longer limited to selling, but, using the same means that had made it justly famous, and the same graphic artists, it aimed at reforming society's esthetic and ideological standards.

At the end of the war, Poland, perhaps more than any other country, was a landscape of desolation. The purpose of the first non-commercial posters was to encourage reconstruction.

Tadeusz Trepkowski became the best-known artist in the genre, which he himself had created. Influenced by Cassandre, he designed posters with a pure line and great economy of means. He also made good use of the symbolism that had arisen out of the war.

In 1954, to celebrate the anniversary of the liberation of Warsaw, he used the silhouette of a woman, her hair streaming in the wind, brandishing a sword, standing out darkly from a light background. She wore a white scarf as a sling, the axis of the design.

In this time of restriction, lithography was the usual procedure and the format of posters was not very large. Their aim was to concentrate the viewer's attention on one or two essential points.

Besides Trepkowski, who vanished very early at the age of forty, two other poster artists belong to the first generation that appeared after 1945: Henryk Tomaszewski, professor at the Fine Arts Academy of Warsaw and the most painterly, and Eryck Lipinsky, whose very free cultural posters (cinematic and theatrical events) renewed the genre and lifted Polish poster art to the highest order, very sensitive to the different tendencies in painting. Both loved to shock: unusual associations, caricatures in Lipinsky, who made a number of great film posters in the Fifties (*Les Grandes Manoeuvres, Manneken Pis*, etc.), great graphic diversity in Tomaszewski who, as a culturally involved artist, spiritual son of the dadaists, demonstrated his absolute freedom of expression *(Boule de Suif, Citizen Kane, Henry Moore)*. His posters evoke a childlike atmosphere whose informality is often reinforced by gauche hand-lettering.

In focusing the viewer's interest with the synthetic thought behind the poster, these three graphic artists laid the foundation of the very essence of the Polish School, destined to influence the entire world.

They also contributed to demonstrating that realism, once considered the best means of artistically educating the people, reduced the evocative power of the poster, by imposing on it a unity of tone.

In the middle of the Fifties, the Fine Arts Academy of Warsaw, under its two directors Tomaszewski and Mroszczak, favored the development

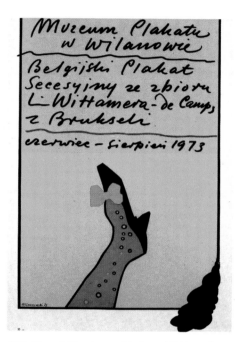

563. Henryk Tomaszewski: An exhibition of Belgian Art Nouveau posters in Poland. 1973.

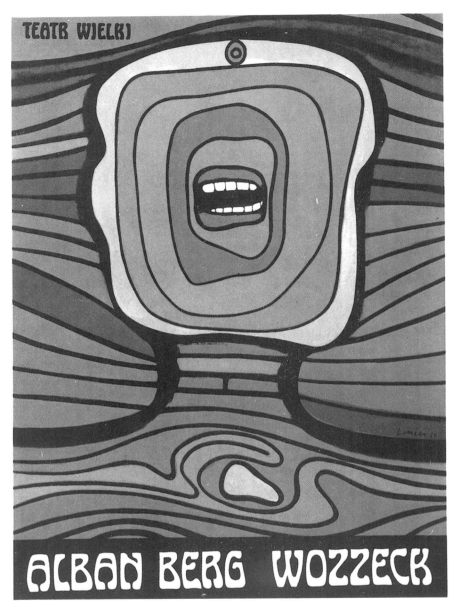

564. Julian Palka: Polish film *Pearl in the Crown*. 1971.

565. Jan Lenica: *Alban Berg—Wozzeck*.

of new techniques such as photography, and influenced a new generation of graphic artists, among them Roman Cieslewicz, Jan Lenica, Julian Palka, Franciszek Starowieski, Waldemar Swierzy and Maciej Urbaniec. Martin Mroszczak, himself also a designer, produced among others, two very beautiful opera posters: *Aida* and *Boris Godunov*.

Saturated with the symbolism which had arisen out of the last war, dissatisfied with the realism that had once seemed adequate, these young artists turned towards an expression stamped with poetry, and, moved by a constant wish to enlighten the people, they came to use a metaphoric imagery. In fact, the metaphor, a complex figure in communicative arts, does not yield an immediate receiveable message and demands active participation from the reader.

Jan Lenica, prodigiously inventive, could be by turns lyrical, dramatic, or surrealistic. At the start of the Sixties, with *Faust* and *Wozzeck,* he was one of the first to rediscover the swirls of Art Nouveau to which he, for a while, adapted his style, using a vigorous outline and vivid colors. His images are marvelous models of communication: the poster he designed in 1970 for an exhibition of surrealist painting is a perfect illustration of his art of concise statement. He gave play to his ironic touch in poster after poster, and sought an authenticity in which the man on the street could recognize his own states of mind.

Using the same vivid colors outlined with a thick stroke, and the same fluid forms, Jan Mlodozeniec made posters with the same tonic impact.

Palka, in his very personal style, made posters for the Italian New Wave cinema. He manipulated collages and montages with great virtuosity, and he is one of those who was best able to adapt the techniques of painting to the requirements of the poster.

In this respect, the one he conceived for Marcel Carné's *Les Enfants du Paradis* is a model in the genre: a portrait of Deburau with the paper showing through, bluish-white on a midnight-blue background. The mime holds a rose whose red color attracts the eye and warms the atmosphere.

Very versatile in his production, Urbaniec resembles Tomaszewski in the freedom of his means of expression: deceptive images, surprising montages, compositions structured around unusual objects which sometimes form some of the lettering.

A perfect draftsman, Swierzy, who can only be compared with artists of the stature of Milton Glaser, could manipulate every genre from symbolism to caricature. He was particularly at ease in his portraits of jazz or pop musicians. His drawings could become quite moving, notably in the homage that he paid to his colleague Mroszczak, who died in 1975.

567. Waldemar Swierzy: Circus poster. 1972.

568. Waldemar Swierzy: *Duke Ellington*. 1975.

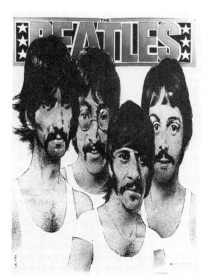

566. Waldemar Swierzy: *The Beatles*. 1977.

TEATR KLASYCZNY ■
H. IBSEN | **BUDOWNICZY SOLNESS**

569. Waldemar Swierzy:
Ibsen's play *The Master
Builder*. 1971.

322

570. Jan Lenica:
Exhibition of Polish
surrealists. 1970.

In film and theater posters, Franciszek Starowievski stands apart. In addition to designing posters, he presented adaptations of films and plays in his own theater, and contributed to *Projekt No. 5,* a Warsaw graphic-arts magazine edited by the government to encourage creativity. In his output, surrealism followed upon fantasy, the baroque upon the bizarre, dreams jostled with nightmares and chimeras with fantastic animals. Among his most representative posters were those for Pinter's *The Lover,* Jessua's *Jeu de Massacre,* and Godard's *Une femme est une femme.*

In the same vein, Czerniawski combined surrealism and poetry, humor and a sense of the absurd, with equal talent.

572. Franciszek Starowievski: Poster for a play, *With Three Crosses.* 1978.

571. Lech Majewski: Rumanian film *Beyond the Bridge.* 1976.

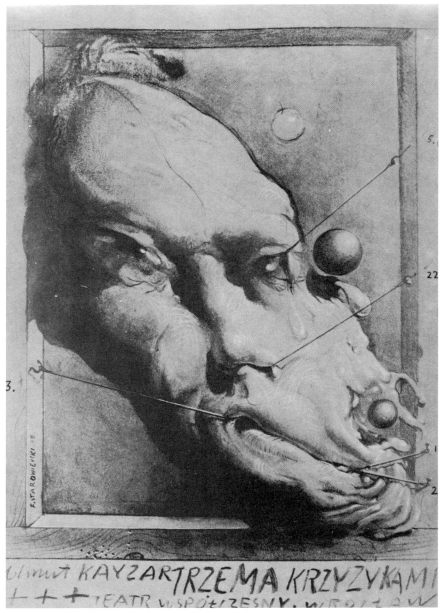

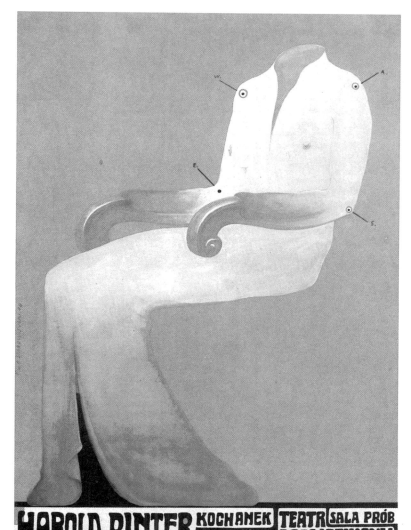

574. Roman Cielewicz.
Kafka. 1974

573. Franciszek Starowievski: Poster for the Harold Pinter play, *The Lover*. 1970.

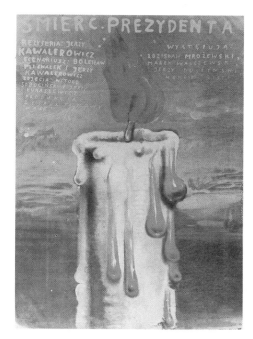

575. Jerzy Czerniawski: Poster for film *Death of the President*. 1977.

Among artists influenced by the Swiss school, Poland had Sliwka, whose political posters are especially effective because of their simplicity and synthetic power; Piskorski; and Holdanowicz, who liked to contrast the fluidity of the form and the color with structured, very graphic lettering. Other artists, such as Sawka and Gorka, preferred whimsical illustration (Sawka's jazz series, Gorka's *Cabaret* and *Sweet Charity*).

Serving as a bridge, the very beautiful poster by Krauze and Mroszczak for *Hamlet* synthesized these two tendencies.

As for Roman Cieslewicz, much influenced by informal painting, he abandoned traditional brush technique in the Sixties to concentrate his graphic experiments on photography. With Zamecznik and Majewski, he is one of the best representatives of the Polish photographic poster.

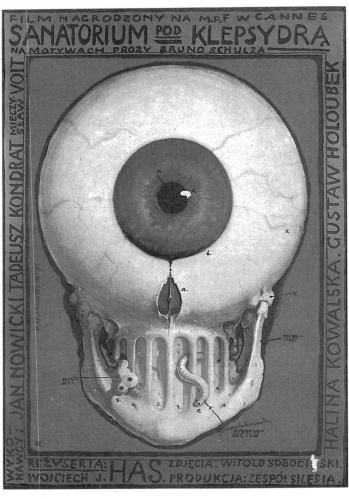

576. Franciszek Starowievski: Film, *The Sandglass*. 1973.

577. Roman Cieslewicz: Contemporary art exhibit in Paris. 1972.

All three worked directly on the film, painting photos with watercolors, scratching negatives and obtaining surprising effects with this new raw material. The illusion of movement and relief may be seen in the subtle play of light and shade in Kafka's *The Trial* by Cieslewicz and in *The Dwarf* by Zamecznick.

Cieslewicz, with his art of collage and of photography, and Zamecznik with his acute sense of construction and his dexterity in always expanding the plastic possibilities of new techniques, also both contributed greatly to the creation of a new language: modern, and founded upon experience.

In France, Cieslewicz pursued a brilliant career. His works for the Pompidou Center, notably the Paris-Moscow Exhibition, were exemplary.

Even though the Sixties were marked primarily by audio-visual developments, the Polish poster flourished, heavily supported by various govern-

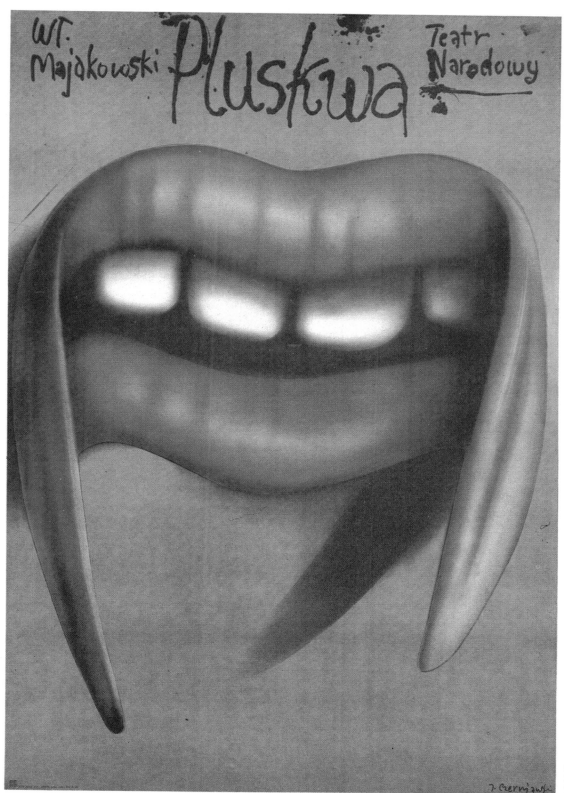

578. Jerzy Czerniawski:
Majakowski's drama
The Bedbug. 1975.

579. Jan Mlodozeniec: Polish release of French film *Le Conformiste*. 1974.

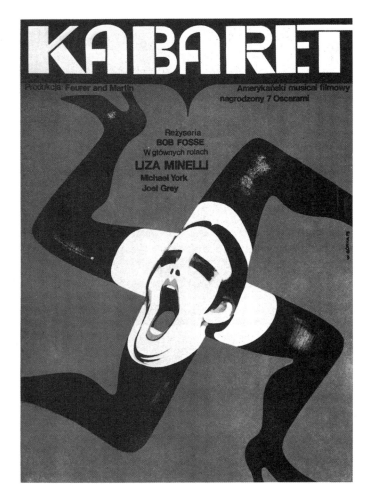

581. Wiktor Gorka: Polish release of *Cabaret*. 1973.

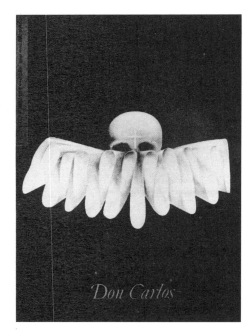

580. Maciej Urbaniec: Poster for Schiller's *Don Carlos*. 1971.

ment agencies such as WAG, which played the role of publisher and distributor, and which came to the aid of young artists and assured the sponsorship of their works. Apparently persuaded that a message was all the clearer the more esthetically it was treated, the number of institutions that called on professional poster makers kept growing: the theater, the opera, cinema, circus (especially remarkable), philharmonic orchestra, and with the expansion of tourism (Ruminski's series) and foreign trade, travel agencies and manufacturers.

The end of the Sixties was marked, here as elsewhere, by a debauchery of forms and colors which characterized the psychedelic style.

The Polish School played a determining role in the history of the socio-cultural poster after the war, stimulated by the organizing of an international biennial poster exhibition in Warsaw, established in 1966, which since then has greatly contributed to raising the poster to the rank of a work of art throughout the world. Polish graphic artists walked away with the prizes until the end of the Sixties, but competition is stiffer today, and must take into account Finnish and Japanese artists as well as the pupils of Polish masters, such as Grapus in France.

582. Andrzej Krauze & Martin Mroszczak: *Hamlet*. 1971.

583. Maciej Urbaniec: Political poster for disarmament. 1972.

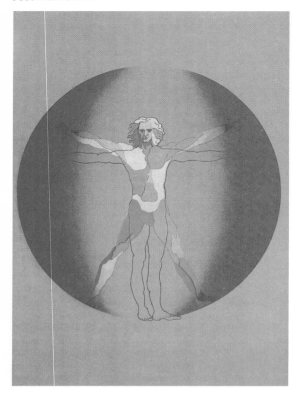

585. Maciej Urbaniec.
Jarmark Pultuski.
1976

584. Tomasz Ruminski:
Exhibition "Man and
Contemporary World."
1970.

587. Tadeusz Piskorski:
Pro Sinfonika. 1975.

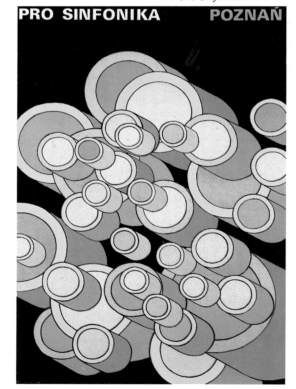

586. Jan Mlodozeniec:
Cepelia. 1972.

588. Maciej Urbaniec:
Poster for the National
Theater: *Wesele*. 1974.

589. Yusaku Kamekura
Poster for the 1964
Olympics.

The Post-War Poster
in Japan

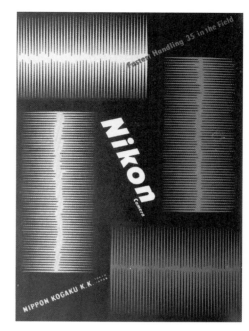

590. Yusaku Kamekura: *Nikon*.

After 1925, the Japanese poster tended to separate itself from traditional painting in order to find its own proper means of expression. And after the Second World War, a new generation of graphic artists revealed themselves, pioneers of an art that little by little would find a place of its own in international movements.

These new artists, for the most part born between 1900 and 1920, had not followed the classic road of painting, but having received professional instruction in design, sought to express themselves on another level. The problem was to find a harmony between the various Western styles and Japanese sensibilities.

One of the first to strike a happy medium were Takashi Kono and Shichiro Imatake, who strongly contributed to the transformation of the Japanese poster. Influenced by European pictorial movements (Bauhaus and De Stijl), they rescued it from its ancestral imagery of Fujiyama crowned with eternal snows and geishas in kimonos. They brought together uncluttered graphics with photography or painting. Kono's art is built upon an innate sense of measure: he arrived at a skillful synthesis between rigor of line and sensuality of color that was never lacking in humor.

Certain artists like Tadashi Ohoshi sought to surprise by associating traditional graphics with modern techniques, ideograms with Roman characters: a bird and sheaves of wheat or a lake scene worthy of the finest prints were woven into the campaign for the *Honda Civic,* the better to set off the new product that was discreetly, astutely placed in the design. Ohoshi's posters, which achieved this subtle alliance of tradition and progress, are like today's Japan, rich with a past it does not renounce but draws upon to construct the future.

Similarly, Ayao Yamana renewed the theme of woman, one of the constants of the old posters, by westernizing her; Hiromu Hara and Ikko Tanaka made stunning posters in which Japanese characters had an important part. Ryuichi Yamashiro managed to suggest a forest by using only artistically composed ideograms; Yoshio Hayakawa gave them an important part in his works, the only clean-cut figures in the midst of great splotches of color on the verge of the informal.

Yusaku Kamekura, an artist of international dimensions (who can forget his magnificent series, awarded the grand prize at the Warsaw Biennale of 1966, for the Tokyo Olympics of '64, where he manipulated photography, montage and drawing?), was the artist of this first generation who no doubt had the greatest influence on succeeding generations, because of the diversity of his talent: he could draw his inspiration from Op Art (posters for *Nikon,* for the *Osaka International Exposition,* and the *Eighth International Congress of the ICSID of Kyoto),* from the

591. Kenji Itoh: *Canon Camera*.

POSTER NIPPON 1955-'72
Japanese Posters by Screen Process

Circulated by
International Exhibitions Foundation
United States of America

592. Ikko Tanaka: An exhibition of Japanese silk-screened posters, *Poster Nippon 1955–1972*. 1972.

psychedelic style *(Edo Kyoko piano recital, Exhibition of the Yamagiwa Contest Entries)* from lettering *(Nikon 57)* or from photography *(Winter Sports* posters, the *Saporo Olympic Games).*

Encouraged by their elders, many of whom were professors, the second-generation artists, such as Shigeo Fukuda, Kazumasa Nagai and Ikko Tanaka, rapidly raised the Japanese poster to a very high level. And though solely commercial in its origins, the Japanese poster began to lend itself to cultural activities, enlarging the field for experiment and allowing graphic artists greater possibilities for expression. Kiyoshi Awazu distinguished himnself in this regard, making posters for the Bungakuza theater group which retain traces of the Edo period (1600-1867) modernized by flat tones of violent colors and by the role they give to the lettering, usually framed in a colored space.

Hayakawa's student, Tadaito Nadamoto shared his teacher's taste for broadly applied color. His works for the Osaka and Seibu theaters are particularly remarkable.

593. Shigeo Fukuda:
Self-defense. 1974.

596. Kazumasa Nagai:
Adonis. 1976.

594. Tadanori Yokoo:
Delica wine. 1978.

595. Yusaku Kamekura:
Poster for an
exhibition of
designers of light
fixtures. 1972.

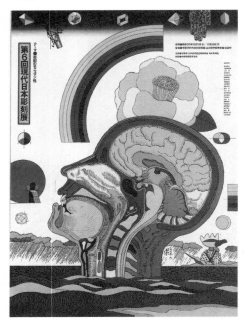

597. Kiyoshi Awazu: Exposition of modern sculpture. 1975.

598. Makato Nakamura: Poster for a nail polish: *Everything begins at the fingertips.* 1978.

But the great designer of Japanese cultural posters was Ikko Tanaka, the importance of whose work on lettering we have already mentioned: purely ideogrammatic posters like those for performances of Noh plays, playing with Roman characters for a *Recital by Teiichi Nakayama* in 1960, or mixing them with stylized drawings for Stravinsky's *Histoire du Soldat* or for *Hanae Mori*.

More unusual are the graphics of Makoto Wada and Akiro Uno. Wada brought a talent for caricature that combined humor and poetry to the production of both cultural posters *(Cinema Festival,* Chaplin's Comedies) and commercial projects *(Summer, Let's go back to nature, Merry Christmas)*. Uno took his inspiration from a fantastic and disquieting surrealism bordering on horror *(My Minitopia, My Minica; Pink Floyd, Wizards of Dreams and Magic)*.

Standing aloft like two shining beacons are Shigeo Fukuda and Tadanori Yokoo. Very graphic, with a natural tendency to paradox and grating humor, Fukuda's posters became well known in the middle of the Sixties. His very personal art plays upon symmetry, line, and black-and-white contrasts. In the poster for one of his own exhibitions, in 1975, he shows the top of a pair of masculine legs, in black, that become in the lower half feminine legs, in white. His simple and incisive graphics became at times the echo of a humanitarian message, such as in *Friendship,* where a hand of flesh has grasped a hand of barbed wire.

Tadanori Yokoo, who defies classification and has the mark of genius on him, has been rightfully regarded since the 1960s as one of the most innovative graphic artists, blending all styles with an innate sense of composition: photomontage, collage, traditional painting, whether Japanese or taken from the Italian Renaissance *(Greeting,* 1973), from Gustave Doré or from Ingres' *Turkish Bath*.

For *Dartimon* cognac in 1976 he made two radically different posters: one traditional—the bottle and glass photographed on a rock against a cliche landscape (pagoda, rising sun, misty sky and ancient cedar); the other modern—on a dark background, different illustrations in varied styles, haloed with light like so many constellations.

Makato Nakamura is famous for his (mainly photographic) posters for *Shiseido* cosmetics, and his participation in the Japan-Gioconda exhbition, where he presented *One Hundred Mona Lisa Smiles,* a pretext for the wildest graphic variations.

From this second generation of graphic artists, we must single out for praise the teacher of Yokoo, Kazumasa Nagai, who is one of the four or five most important Japanese artists, and probably one of the best in the world. His art is based on a sure graphic sense, optical effects, manipulated shapes and geometric figures, primary colors and photography. The body of posters Nagai has produced have a unity of tone that is very personal and striking *(Lili Color Wallpapers, Prince, Ga, New Music Media, Adonis)*.

Today's young artists, nourished with the experiments of two generations, continue to innovate, looking to America where they have sometimes done their studies.

In Takenobu Igarashi's work—concentrated on the lettering—can be seen the graphic preoccupations of Milton Glaser and his Push Pin Studio *(Zen Environmental Design; Graphics Designers of the West Coast; UCLA)*.

Throw your armour off, do not fear,
Bring that wine over here.
Baby, I want you tonight.

MANNS WINES

599. Harumi: *Manns Wines*.

音が氾濫している世の中だから、パイオニアは勉強しました。パイオニア・プロジェクト7000新登場。

600. Tokisa Hosokawa
& Iwao Hosoya:
Photomontage for a
stereo system. 1979.

601. Eiko Ishioka: Announcing
a design competition. 1973.

602. Teruhito Yumura: *Marinpic '83.* 1983.

Eiko Ishioka's photos and Harumi Yamaguchi's drawings, influenced by the vogue of hyperrealist painting, present a model of woman entirely freed of her oriental roots. Both have worked for Parco, a major Japanese department store chain.

Finally, Teruhito Yumura and Yunosuke Kawamura, born respectively in 1942 and 1944, have returned to the illustrated poster. Their graphics take their inspiration from the comic strip and purvey all the stereotypes of America of the Forties and Fifties, which they spoof in passing: Lucky Strike, a milk carton, plaid suit, the pick-up, the pin-up, palm trees and bikinis.

The colors are bright flat tones, the figures in caricature: their designs bring a breath of fresh air to the often rigorous graphic universe, and demonstrate the Japanese poster artists' will to continually renew themselves. In fact, Japan today, where schools of design proliferate, is one of the countries most preoccupied with the relation between advertising and graphic design, a relation in which every Japanese feels himself involved.

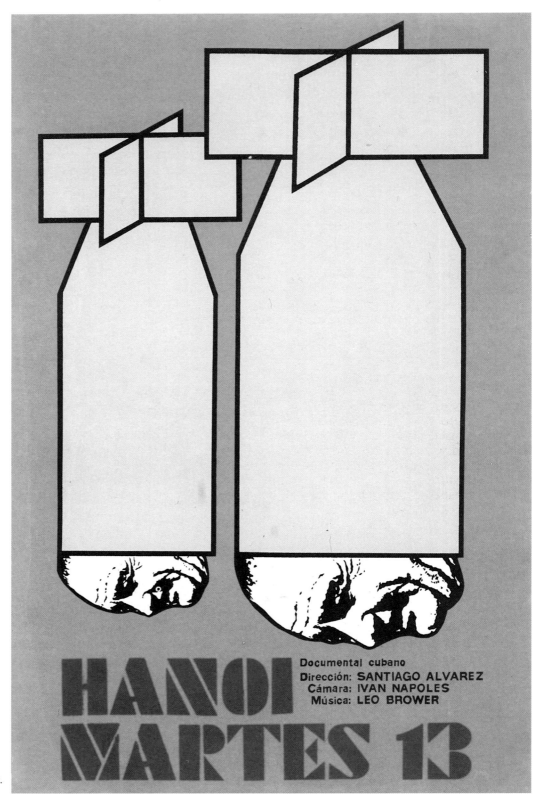

603. Alfredo Rostgaard: Poster
for the anti-American film
documentary on the Vietnam war.
1967.

Cuba and China

A tool for propaganda in times of war, the illustrated poster is also useful to further a revolution. With Cuba and with China, we are exploring two aspects of the collectivist poster.

The Cuban revolutionary poster was born from the wish to put art within the reach of the people. The theater, to whom the heavy task of educating the masses had been given, was still a minority interest, despite the considerable budget it commanded. But opposed in every particular to bourgeois art, which aspires to the singular, eternal and elitist, the poster, multiple and perishable, appeared as the means of expression best adapted to the revolution. It well served culture and politics.

The first graphic manifestations, which aimed at glorifying each person's work to incite them to participate in production, reproduced the cliches of the genre: virile workers bending over their machines, or the power of machines in action, in the tradition of Soviet socialist realism. Dissatisfied with this conventional form, the various Cuban cultural organizations, especially ICAIC (Instituto Cubano de Arte e Industria Cinematografica) cast an eye on the graphic artists of international reputation who used expressionistic drawing and wood-engraving as well as symbolism and collage.

It was the Cuban cinema poster that took the first steps toward simplification and effectiveness. Advertising *Muerte al Invasor* (Death to the Invader) in 1961, Morante made a poster based on a frieze of paper dolls in a newspaper at which a rifle hidden in the shadows is aimed.

The cultural poster tended more and more to use symbols. Reboiro's fine poster for *Hara-kiri* suggests ritual suicide by a single red slit that tears the image from top to bottom. These posters make the viewer transfer his attention away from the image to the name of the director or actors. Very colorful – sometimes using more than thirty colors – often silkscreened, the posters commissioned by ICAIC aim at conveying information while visually educating the people, familiarizing them with a symbolic language. The film industry allowed these designers to successfully create a visual art for the Cuban revolution.

Stuck in the stereotypes of academic graphics, the political poster also attempted to adapt itself to the work of the new generation of artists, from Saul Bass to Jan Lenica. But ideological guidelines made this a delicate task. In 1966, to escape from the dreariness of traditional political graphics, the International Commission of the Central Committee invited a group of highly respected designers and painters to work on the theme

604. Alfredo Rostgaard: Cuban film, *The Forgotten War*. 1967.

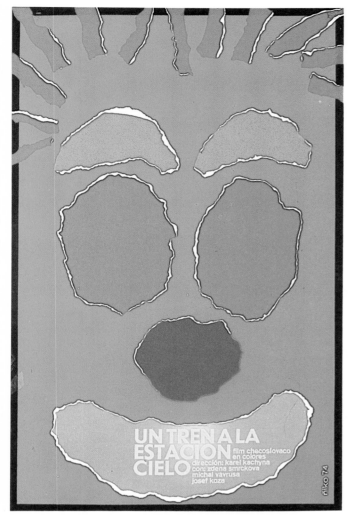

605. Niko: Poster for a Czech film, *The Train to Heaven*. 1974.

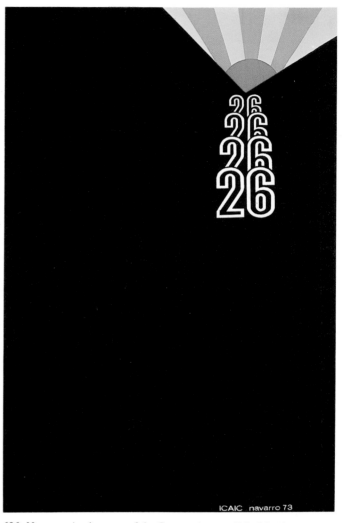

606. Navarro: Anniversary of the Castro takeover (July 26, 1953). 1973.

of "The Twenty-sixth of July", the day of Castro's seizure of the Cuban government in 1953. Three posters were selected.

Raúl Martinez and Alfredo Rostgaard made use of the patriotic value of the flag, while Fremez took the photograph of a cracked wall on which could be read the freshly-painted inscription: *Viva el 26.*

A new bridge had been crossed. The political poster had found a new language, based on synthesis. One of the models in the genre is the image that Rostgaard made in 1969, when he became the official graphic artist of the Cuban Communist Party—*Cristo Guerrillero,* which shows a Christ with a rifle over his shoulder, illustrating at once the religious and revolutionary romanticism inspiriting the Latin-American peoples.

The aim of the collectivist poster was essentially to codify Marxism, to alter consciousness, to educate the people. The means it used was a simplification of graphics compensated by an explosion of colors that brought them close to the psychedelic painters that were proliferating at that time on America's West Coast.

革命现代舞剧 红色娘子军 冲出虎狼窝

607. Anonymous: Dancer of the *Red Detachment of Women* ballet group. (Shanghai People's Publishing House.) 1971.

608. Chang Tong-ping: *Sun and Rain Nurtures New Buds*. 1973.

As a sample, we may point to the eight posters made by Olivio Martinez in 1970, encouraging the Cubans, step-by-step, to produce 10 million tons of sugar: no real image, but play with the numbers, the layout and color – *1 million – And That Makes 2 – The 3rd – Now 4 – Halfway There – Six – The 7th – 8 Now*. They never reached 10.

The portraits of leaders were also very popular, with Castro himself most frequently setting the pace. Because of the demand for production, the end-of-the-year holidays were deferred. The walls were soon covered with photos of Castro in a sugar-cane field, wearing a straw hat, a machete in hand, and the legend: *"Where will we be on January 2? In the cane-fields."*

Political posters did much to develop the cult of personality: the ones that showed Castro and Che Guevara run into astronomical figures. Some of them flirted with stark realism, like the unretouched photo Niko took to call the Cubans to a rally *(Todos a la plaza con Fidel);* some perpetuated a myth: stylized faces in flat tones – Fidel Castro *(Con Conciencia, Con Verguenza, 10 millions),* Lenin *(Centeniary),* Che Guevara *(Hasta la Victoria Siempre).*

Stern but joyful, the Cuban poster called its viewers to participation and international solidarity. It incited the people to action, under the guidance of their leaders and of their words with slogans drawn mainly from speeches.

The image of Che, with his long hair and the beret with the star on it, became the image of universal revolution, such as in the 10 posters made for the 10th anniversary of the triumph of the revolt (1959-1968) by Padron. Papiol and Faustino used the 10 letters of the word REVOLU-CION to form a graphic whole of rare quality to symbolize total revolution.

Though its goals were the same, the Chinese poster did not pose the same formal problems for itself that the Cuban poster succeeded in resolving. Whatever the message, the always colorful graphics are emphatic and demonstrative or naive and sentimental.

However, images of the leaders and their thoughts are also a standard Chinese formula: a poster in dominating red presents Mao surrounded by children or greeting a cheering crowd. Sometimes his portrait was also substituted for the little red book brandished by soldiers to commemorate the hundredth anniversary of the Paris Commune.

No particular attention is paid to the lettering, the legend being inscribed – in red, black or white – almost invariably below the illustration. Sometimes it is translated into three languages as on the poster which joins a soldier and two armed civilians in the same combat: *An indestructible wall—the combined defense of the People's Army of liberation and the people.*

A propaganda tool as in Cuba, the Chinese poster promotes internationalism: a poster titled *Revolutionary friendship is deeper than oceans* shows a young African woman in regional costume and a Chinese woman in blue work-clothes squatting at the foot of a tractor, smiling while their snapshot is taken.

A Korean, a Vietnamese, a Cambodian, an Arab, an Albanian, a Japanese and an African, all armed with rifles, are portrayed with the legend: *Long life to the world's united peoples.*

Another theme is woman. Entirely passed over in Cuba, she has a

609. Anonymous: *Harmonize a New Song.* (People's Fine Arts Publishing House.)

primary role in the People's Republic. She is represented in many posters that give her equal status with men, especially at work: she gladly dons a miner's clothing or seizes a doctor's bag.

In fact all of these posters, optimistic to a fault, with their scenes of peasant idylls, their figures seized with perpetual smiles, present a consistency of style, coloring and layout that seems to authenticate their communism.

"Proletarian literature and art are part of the total proletarian revolution," quoth Mao Tse-Tung.

Identical in their aims, the Cuban and the Chinese posters have used radically different means, even contrary ones. They rejoin one another however in their uniformity: standardization of originality on the one hand and of the conventional on the other.

610 Rick Griffin: Poster for an exhibition of five artists. 1967.

The Images of Revolt

he Sixties were marked by a wind of revolt which blew in the United States as in Europe, and which was arrestingly reflected in graphic production.

In America one saw a questioning of traditional values, especially among the young, in every area – music, painting, cinema, literature.

It was first of all on the West Coast, where in the Fifties the subversive ideas of the Beat Generation had emanated from San Francisco, that their new demands began to see the light. Soon there appeared a debauch of colors and forms fed by drugs, for which so many of the posters were apologies (Rick Griffin: *A puff of kif in the morning makes a man as strong as a hundred camels,* 1967), and graphic representations of the beat of rock music.

In the middle of the Sixties, the Bay area was a magnet for every type of dissident. Family Dog at the Avalon Ballroom and Bill Graham at the Fillmore Auditorium produced rock concerts to which the "new" American youth flocked, long haired and strung out on pot. To design the posters announcing these concerts, the producers called on Rick Griffin, who was at the time known as one of the five greats of psychedelic painting, together with Wes Wilson, Stanley Mouse, Alton Kelly and Victor Moscoso.

As a teenager at the end of the Fifties, Rick Griffin divided his time between his somewhat reluctantly undertaken studies and his real passions: surfing and music. The poster he made in 1965 for the Jook Savages, his own group, was a bombshell, and it started him on his career. His graphics ignored the asceticism dictated by the Bauhaus, humorously took their inspiration from Wild West posters, and reinvented the wild arabesques of Art Nouveau.

Most of these posters announcing the Grateful Dead, the Jefferson Airplane, or Captain Beefheart were printed in lithography. All of them — and especially Wes Wilson's – put into question the functionality of lettering, to the point of defying legibility, and suggesting the visual disturbances brought on by hallucinogens so vividly they may have contributed to popularizing them.

Mouse and Kelly did not hesitate to copy (and to distort with the text and with the fluorescent treatment of colors) Mucha's posters, as in *Zig Zag man* and *Girl with Green Hair,* 1967.

The impact of these posters which all, in some fashion, focused the trends and ideas of the times, was particularly strong in the use of color of which Victor Moscoso, who had studied at Yale with Josef Albers, was the consummate master. Another element was the rediscovery of the graphic fluidity of Art Nouveau, but the languor of its line was replaced by an explosion of energy meant to be consumed in the street and on the spot. The same phenomenon soon appeared in the East, illustrated notably by Peter Max. Whether he campaigned for New York's mayoral candidate Lindsay or against smoking, one quickly understood that the esthetic forms took precedence over the ideas that first sustained them. In fact

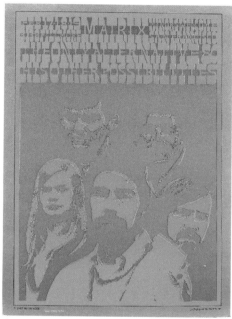

611. Victor Moscoso:
Matrix—The Only Alternative. 1967.

612. Tomi Ungerer: *Black Power/White Power* political poster. 1967.

613. Paul Davis: Poster for the magazine *Evergreen Review*. 1968.

they do not have either the funky lyricism or the spontaneity that throve in the Bay area and had by then also reached London.

In New York, psychedelic art became organized, tamed, and normalized. It gave birth to one of the most important graphics workshops of the Sixties: the Push Pin Studio founded by Milton Glaser and Seymour Chwast. Serving as the outlet for the newest in popular culture, Push Pin's posters, with heightened colors and full of swirls, advertised music, whether it be *Dylan* or *Bach* by Glaser, and cinema, especially the productions of *Elektra* and *Peridot* film companies, whose posters were prepared by Chwast.

After graduation from Cooper Union, Milton Glaser and Seymour Chwast decided to unite their talents to further their graphic experiments. They began by publishing a little collection, the Push Pin Almanack, to publicize their work. It was composed with so much freshness and ingenuity that their style was soon acknowledged and imitated. They put their brushes in the service of advertising and were immediately in the current of the hippie movement which flourished on the East Coast. Thus the review *Eye,* which attempted to combine the hippie philosophy with establishment advertising, showed its readers a *Portrait of Aretha Franklin* by Milton Glaser whose forms were taken from Art Deco and whose clashing colors arranged in flat tones recalled the delirious West Coast posters.

Echoes of this first manifestation of psychedelic American graphics reached Europe, where in London Michael English made a few art objects that were commercialized on Carnaby Street, such as the sunglasses with the British flag on the glass distributed by Gear. In December, 1966, English met Nigel Waymouth, owner of the most avant-garde London boutique, Granny Takes a Trip, on King's Road, and painted the giant face of an American Indian on its facade. Together they established a publishing house for posters, The Hapshash and the Coloured Coat. Their first posters were for rock concerts and were in the line of the psychedelic West Coast posters.

One of the most representative images of this underground movement that was spreading in London was the poster with fluorescent (and silk-screened) lips glamorously announcing the *Love Festival.*

Push Pin's purpose was not to express profound convictions in its designs, but to promote a product. It was not in revolt against The American Way of Life – even if in a certain fashion, by sweeping aside the old criteria of advertising, it disavowed them; its battle, for it fought one, was elsewhere. For the sixteen years of its existence the Push Pin studio fought against banality of ideas and affectation of style. To do this, it used the different forms of psychedelic art and ingeniously adapted them to whatever ends its medium called for: Milton Glaser, for example, did not hesitate to illustrate for *New York Magazine* an article on the abuse of amphetamines, creating a morbid atmosphere (reptiles and skulls) and using strong colors. The same graphic solutions were also favored — for quite different reasons – by Rick Griffin, in his posters for *Jimi Hendrix* and the *Grateful Dead.*

The Push Pin Studio produced images that jarred with the advertising language then in force. Its twenty-odd members, which included Paul Davis, Isadore Seltzer, Loring Eutemey, Barry Zaid, Tim Lewis and John Alcorn, permanently maintained an experimental attitude which gave rise

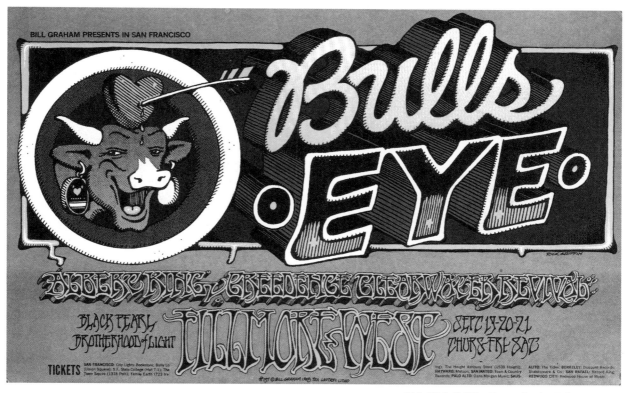

614. Rick Griffin: Poster for the *Fillmore West*. 1968.

to a diverse, imaginative and, even today, modern production. With its important work and innovative use of color, form and typography, the Push Pin Studio would influence all the graphic art of the next ten years.

But in the second half of the Sixties, political events forced artists' hands. In the United States, the Vietnam War was causing an outrage, and in Europe workers and students united to denounce a decrepit social system. Born in peace, love and understanding, Flower Power wilted. "The Times They Are A-changin'," sang Dylan; dissidence hardened, and the poster was suddenly the mirror of a bitter revolt.

It was at the University of California at Berkeley that the premises for this more hardened revolt were established. Forbidden by university authorities to distribute tracts, the students began the Free Speech Movement that eventually shut down the university and resulted in students' expulsion. 1965 was also the year of the Watts riots in Los Angeles, with its bitter racial overtones.

In this tense climate, Tomi Ungerer made two posters whose extreme simplicity, cruelly laconic text and sober colors painfully expressed the disaffection of a whole generation of Americans – *Black Power-White Power* and *Eat*.

Political groups had images of their own: the Black Panthers called for "Power to the People" and the White Panthers denounced the CIA. Artist's collectives like RAPE and the Berkeley Student Workshop drew posters with all sorts of messages, from *Recycle Nixon* to *Unite Against the War*, using all sorts of materials, even computer software.

A poster titled *SP4 Vietnam* was made of torn-out newspaper articles surrounding a tortured face that cried for freedom. The Art Workers

615. Milton Glaser: For the *Dylan* record album. 1966.

616. Peter Max: *Toulouse-Lautrec*. 1967.

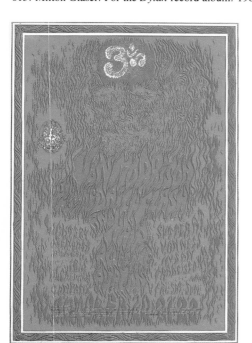

617. Wes Wilson: Rock concert with *Van Morrison and the Daily Flash* at the Avalon. 1967.

Coalition turned to realism in a photo by Haeberle showing a road strewn with children's corpses *(Q. And babies? A. And babies.)*. A whole series of anonymous posters came out of the Berkeley Student Workshop, silk-screened in simple and striking designs: *Napalm* written like the famous *Coca-Cola* trademark; *Home, Sweet Home* with gravestones.

The dissidents, called unpatriotic by the authorities, often incorporated the American flag unflatteringly in their posters: *USA Surpasses All the Genocide Records!* by George Machiunas; *Give a Damn, Mend America* by Michael Lynne. Certainly with the use he made of it in 1969, the painter Jasper Johns brought the graphic expression of revolt to its final word with *Moratorium*.

In Europe, the Dutch movement *Provo* was launched in 1965. It united all sorts of dissident factions: workers, artists, mods, rockers, pacifists, students, anarchists—rallying around the ideas of Niewenhuis, one of the founders of the Activists' International. This movement aimed at a new right to create, no longer reserved for an elite but open to all, because "to live means to be creative, that is, to transform everything that exists," as was explained in the fourth issue of the newspaper *Provo*.

The Provos tried to demystify art by street actions. Their *Hi-ha-happenings* were meant to unite artist and spectator, the active and the passive.

Shaken by these playful and unarmed agitators, the Dutch authorities responded with extreme—and disproportionate—violence to the inoffensive manifestations of the Provos, demonstrating to the larger public the conditioning to which society submits.

The posters of Willem (Bernard Holtrop) and of the group "Ontbijt op bed" (Breakfast in Bed) traced the phases of the Provo struggle. On March 10, 1966 Princess Beatrice married a German suspected of having uncommendable sympathies during the war. Provo chose this day as Anarchy Day. Willem spread the word by putting up a giant letter A, mimeographed upside down, beneath which he unambiguously set the text: *March 10, Anarchy Day.*

When it stood for municipal elections, where it finally obtained a seat, Provo's poster presented a tiny figure in outline brandishing an ax against the imposing black-booted legs of authority and the simple words *Vote Provo, Line 12.* Willem's satiric comic strips with eminently direct messages often caused Provo publications to be seized by the police. "Ontbijt op Bed" was charged with disseminating the movement's cultural ideas. It used serigraphy and text more often than pictures. But it put youth on its guard against the alientation of the educational system then in force and announced that, according to Provo theory, "From now on, art will be a non-object".

It can be said that the Dutch Provo movement opened the way to European dissidence. Many West European countries were won over to its philosophy, and even after its dissolution in 1967, very many graphic artists continued to express themselves in that mode.

A wave of dissidence, dormant for years, from the various liberation movements and from the growing desire for a pacifist world, exploded, suddenly, everywhere, and crystallized in France in the events of May 1968. An essential arm of this battle, the May poster was composed not in the bourgeois way by one person, but following on a collective decision it was printed in the Ateliers Populaires; it resuscitated, of necessity, some outmoded techniques: lithography, stenciling and lineoleum intended for the printing of larger posters, and above all silk-screening, which required a minimum of equipment while permitting adequately large production—about sixty posters per hour. Offset lithography, most costly because it had to be done outside the Atelier, was reserved for the posters with the greatest impact: *La Chienlit, c'est lui* (He's dogshit); *Le Point de non-retour* (The Point of No Return); *Ensemble Étudiants Travailleurs* (Students and Workers Together). They were to be distributed by the thousands. All the May posters were printed on recycled paper, bundles of newsprint brought from the printing houses of the daily papers or butcher's paper bought in reams.

The first of these Ateliers Populaires was set up in the Paris Ecole des Beaux-Arts which, like most of the other faculties, was on strike and its buildings occupied. At the entrance to the Atelier was written: "To work in the Atelier Populaire is to concretely support the great movement of striking workers who are occupying their factories against the antiworker Gaullist government. In putting all his capacities in the service of the worker's struggle, everyone in this studio also works for himself, for he opens himself through practice to the educating power of the masses."

To the artists working there, the goal was to attain the most direct means to the end. "Imagination holds the power." What was necessary was an equal impact by the image, preferably synthetic, and by the resonance of the slogan.

From technical constraints, from the poverty of means and from the will to overcome, images of great richness arose: in only two colors, a

MORATORIUM

618. Jasper Johns: *Moratorium.* 1969.

619. Willem (Bernard Holtrop): *Provo.* 1967.

620. Atelier Populaire des Beaux-Arts: *He's Dog Shit!* 1968.

621. Atelier Populaire des Beaux-Arts: Lesson in political science. 1968.

622. Atelier Populaire des Beaux-Arts: A yes vote for the new *Université Populaire*. 1968.

menacing fist emerged from a factory smokestack. The famous poster *CRS-SS* shows a helmeted member of the CRS anti-riot police brandishing a bludgeon, wearing a shield with the intials SS. On the poster printed by refugees from the Atelier Populaire at the School of Medicine when the Beaux-Arts was raided by the police on June 27, we see a CRS policeman biting down ferociously on a paintbrush, with the text: "The police posts itself at the Beaux-Arts—the Beaux-Arts posters the streets."

Along with the atelier Populaire, other movements expressed themselves with the images appropriate to their ideas. The Activists' International often had recourse to comic strips, the popular genre par excellence, to illustrate its most virulent critiques. The greatest artists of this group include Gérard Joannès, Raoul Vaneigem, Guy Debord, and others.

Well known artists living in Paris in this troubled period also supported the students' rebellion, selling pictures whose profits would go to the various strike committees: *It Takes Black to Make the Red Stand Out* and *Yes, Create Continuous Revolution"*, proclaimed Degottex.

Others of interest include Alechinsky *(Anyone who Studies Himself is for the Students);* Karel Appel, one of the founders of the COBRA movement *(In Action, They Have Shown the Source of their Beauty);* Asger Jorn, a member of COBRA and of the Activists' International *(Break the Frame that Strangles the Picture);* and the writer Michel Butor *(Dawn, Time Awakes,* with Bernard Dufour). Appel and Jorn were fine-art painters who put the forceful colors that characterize their paintings in the service of the students' cause.

Some of these posters were published by galleries, such as the Galerie du Dragon, others were printed by the artists in their own studios.

Finally, "dailies," informing the populace of the day's scandals, were hung on the walls, illustrated or not, more or less comic, largely anonymous; they were especially common in Toulouse up until 1972.

Together with a shared enthusiasm, there was the will to affirm solidarity and unity in struggle. This tendency of the poster, upholding revolution, spread throughout all Europe.

In Denmark, Rode Mor produced linogravures in favor of various liberation movements, with graphics and composition that recalled the psychedelic style. Slumsttormerne's striking serigraphs incited the Danes to *occupy livable spaces* and violently opposed the repression of squatters: *Full Prisons, Empty Houses.*

The English collectives Poster Workshop, Paddington Printshop (which is still active, and following its principles of improving working conditions) and Red Dragon used serigraphy to sensitize the public to questions of the right of prisoners and to denounce government policy on housing.

Unsigned posters presented a new ideal with portraits of *Che Guevara* and the *Beatles,* while John Lennon and Yoko Ono, during their 1969 stay in Amsterdam, had themselves photographed in bed to proclaim *Stay in Bed – Hair Peace – Bed Peace.* For Christmas, they financed a very widely distributed serigraphed poster that affirmed in very large letters *The war is over* and beneath, in much smaller ones, *if you want it.*

Despite Provo's disappearance, the Dutch poster remained very active as an expression of revolt. When it was not calling for peace, it was opposing the census or the demolition of the Nieuwmarket quarter. It was even used to censor posters that the artists group De Vrije Zeefdrukker judged uninteresting – *This poster is pasted over a really dull one.*

In West Germany, the Roter Rache collective printed posters on wallpaper and in serigraphy to denounce the eviction of squatters. Klaus Staeck and Ernst Volland used photomontage, printed in offset or seriraphed, to denounce the anti-democratic tendencies of German politics. In 1970, three German artists, Beuys, Hafner and Stüttgen, wrote a manifesto calling for a boycott of the 1971 elections.

In Italy, Machno-Marghera and Scarabeo put out posters defending anarchism against neo-fascism.

The Finns Peter Lindholm and Tapio Tyni exploited the nudity of black-and-white photography to show the climate of aggression that had invaded the world.

In Japan, where ancestral tradition led to stagnation, psychedelic swirls burst out in Kiyoshi Awazu, effective and involved graphic art was perfected by Fukuda, and a new form of communication appeared in the delirious designs of Tadanori Yokoo *(The Fourth World)*.

Spain, Sweden, Greece, Belgium, Poland, the Soviet Union (which prosecuted young people with long hair), and even Switzerland were touched by this phenomenon of rejection of the established order, leaving behind the printed traces of their revolt.

In England and in the United States, finally, after 1975, when most of the collective workshops in the West had disappeared, women's collectives took up a virulent and colorful campaign to defend women's rights. The Women's Graphic Collective of Boston called on women to strike — sexually, domestically, etc. – their design using little pieces of fabric sewn like quilts.

The thousands of posters that were made in optimism or rage between 1965 and 1975 expressed a whole generation's frustrations. They may seem naive to us today, but they visibly changed minds and, above all, brought a formidable creative energy to light.

623. British group design: A Stratford presentation.

125 — WOMEN'S POSTERS BRIGHTON
Work buy consume die
(Travaillez, achetez, consommez, mourrez)
Grande-Bretagne, ç 1973
Sérigraphie, 51 × 38
Coll. Steef Davidson
• A peine un dessin, mais comme le texte est bien vu ! • (compliments
142 d'un collectif d'artistes de Bristol).

624. Women's Posters Brighton: Poster for the Women's Movement. 1973.

625. Pablo Picasso:
Exposition Vallauris. 1952.

Painting, Culture and
The Consumer Society

Parisian art galleries immediately after the war were at their zenith, and the School of Paris dominated the art world. This good fortune and a new aura of prestige brought a new type of poster: the gallery poster, till then almost nonexistent.

Jacques Jaujard, then assistant director of the French national museums, had been reviving posters to announce exhibitions at the Louvre, the Petit Palais and the Orangerie since 1927. A few salons followed, notably the *Salon des Independents* whose poster was designed by Matisse in 1937. But it was not until after the war that the movement really developed.

In 1946, for one of his own exhibitions, Georges Braque made a full-sized model, with the collage of a drawing on a piece of cardboard. Two hundred copies of the poster were lithographed. Since 1942, Braque had been working in lithography, at the Mourlot printing shop, and he did not hesitate to work directly on stone when necessary.

In 1948-49, the international review *Poster Annual* gave, for the first time, two pages to gallery posters. They were *Mirobolus Macadam* by Dubuffet and sculptures by Maria at the Drouin gallery, *I like this drawing* by Matisse, *Black is a color* by André Marchand and two posters by Miro, one of them the *Surrealist Exhibition* of 1947 at the Maeght gallery.

Launched by Aimé Maeght, for whom all the current artists tried their hands, usually successfully, at lithographs and posters – almost always at Mourlot's – this type of advertising enjoyed a prodigious success. It was not a question of the artists reproducing one of their paintings, but rather of conceiving a new image to fulfill the special requirements of the poster: format, composition, color, printing techniques.

Besides Aimé Maeght (Braque, Chagall, Miro), there were Berggruen (Braque, Miro, Matisse), Louis Carré (Léger), Pierre Bérès (Matisse), Louise Leiris (Picasso) and La Maison de la Pensée Française (Léger, Picasso, Matisse). Almost all these posters were lithographed. Only Picasso, working with the printer Arnera in Vallauris, regularly employed linogravure.

Too beautiful to be merely placed in the windows of cafés, tobacco shops and drycleaners, these posters were also printed in limited editions on Arches or other heavier and special paper, and sometimes numbered and signed by the artist. Their total printing amounting to less than 1000 copies, they remained reserved for an elite in the little world of art lovers.

It was the English and the Americans who made the poster market explode in the Sixties. At that time the fading School of Paris was giving way to pop art and other American currents. After that, the wind blew from New York with Rauschenberg, Oldenburg, Jasper Johns, Lichtenstein, Stella and Warhol. Their youth and their conception of the role of

626. Henri Matisse: Tourist poster for *Nice*. 1948.

Bank by Andy Warhol. Gaudy savings by RCA Color Scanner. Pretty as a pigture, huh?

627. Andy Warhol: Poster for an electronic color-separating machine for printers. 1968.

628. Joan Miro: Poster for his own exhibition. 1950.

the artist in society made them far readier than the French artists were to lend their talents to their country's cultural adventures. The List Art Posters publishing firm brought out posters in large printings by many pop artists. It had many successors.

In the United States, it was the Lincoln Center, heralded in 1964 by a poster ordered from Push Pin Studios, that commissioned some of the most successful graphic works. In 1967, it called on Andy Warhol, who made a stunning serigraphed poster – his famous large admission ticket — for a festival he had organized.

This graphic effervescence led certain galleries to act as publishers. In New York it was Leo Castelli, whose gallery brought together the major American pop painters, who best illustrated this tendency, though André Emmerich, Sidney Janis, and the Pace Gallery were also important poster publishers. These posters, which had lost their function as a communication medium, were given vast printings and sold at moderate prices. And a generation anxious to possess its own images bought them. They pasted their walls with Roy Lichtenstein's comic strips, Rauschenberg's collages, Andy Warhol's repetitive serigraphs, Helen Frankenthaler's and Morris Louis' vibrant colors, Frank Stella's playful geometry, Tom Wessel-

629. Alexander Calder: Poster for
a dance performance. 1976.

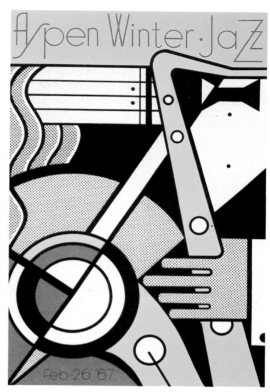

631. Alechinsky: Experimental
Film Festival in Belgium. 1974.

630. Roy Lichtenstein:
Jazz festival in Aspen.
1967.

632. Frank Stella:
*Lincoln Center
Festival*. 1967.

PARIS
l'Opéra
le plafond de Chagall (détail)

633. Marc Chagall: French Government tourist poster featuring Chagall's ceiling design at the Paris Opera. 1965.

634. Richard Lindner: Alban Berg's opera *Lulu* at the Spoleto Festival. 1974.

mann's and Milton Glaser's flat hues, and David Hockney's elegant sketches.

Once unleashed, the poster movement rapidly spread, and international museums helped to create an atmosphere for the real art poster movement, by lavishing the greatest care on the posters they published and distributed – such as the Moderna Museet of Stockholm, the Basel Kunsthalle, the Musée d'Art Moderne de la Ville de Paris, the Guggenheim and the Museum of Modern Art in New York, and many others.

The gallery poster, which had faded away with the School of Paris, revived with new vigor and gained new ground in many European countries.

In Paris, besides Maeght, which carried on with Lindner, Steinberg, and others, there were the excellent posters from Alexander Iola's gallery, featuring such artists as Reynaud, Raysse, Tinguely, Magritte, Ernst, Niki de Saint Phalle and Man Ray. In Basel, the Galerie Beyeler's posters (Rothko, Dubuffet, Calder, etc.) merit special mention. In London, in the delirious atmosphere of King's Road and Carnaby Street, where it was soon plain that culture and commerce are not necessarily mutually exclusive, the poster market, led by Michael English and Nigel Waymouth, expanded considerably.

The poster had won the day. It answered a new generation's need for images, ushering in a new style of life and a new style of decorating. Entering houses and offices, the poster entered the modern way of life.

Though Pop Art passed away, the poster market organized itself in serious fashion. Besides the large galleries, posters were now produced by companies that specialized in the distribution and sale of posters.

Quite early on, Evelyn and Leo Farland, who were themselves collectors, realized the advantage of opening a space solely to sell (and later, to publish) art posters. POL (Poster Originals Limited) presented a large selection of European and American art posters; among them, together with those already mentioned, the posters of Seymour Chwast and Milton Glaser, as well as several series, such as one from 1972, where 26 international artists celebrated the Munich Olympics, and another made for *Amnesty International;* Polish posters, and other series grouped by a single theme or subject.

These posters were printed on quality paper, in lithography or in serigraphy, or, if the artist wished, on foil paper.

In addition, POL, like most of its offshoots, offered its clients a framing service, for the time had passed when teenagers simply stuck posters on their walls. In England, Marlborough Graphics offered works ranging from Henry Moore to Joe Tilson.

And in France, Nouvelles Images defined its name as meaning posters chosen from all of twentieth century art: not exclusively the masters, not exclusively the avant-garde, but a free selection from among the best works. That meant Calder, Braque and Magritte, as well as Folon, Warhol, Topor and Lichtenstein.

The market dictated the message. It had to answer the demands of the young, who wanted to recognize themselves in the images they bought. Folon, with his little man lost in the crowd, fulfilled this demand from the Marquet gallery. A rose growing out of the cement, a tightrope walker, a sphinx imposing in its silence, for the cinema, architecture, the Spoleto

636. Georges Mathieu: Airline poster. 1968.

635. Michael English: *Coke*. 1970.

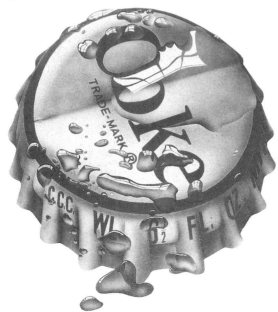

637. Antes: The 1972 *Olympic Games*.

638. Folon: *Foultitude* Exhibition at Musée des Arts Décoratifs, Paris. 1969.

639. Patrick Nagel: *Just Looking* Home Furnishing Store, Encino, Californa. 1978.

640. David Lance Goines: Poster for an exhibit of the Pacific Film Archive. 1975.

Festival, the League of French Teachers, or the Musée de l'Affiche, in serigraphy or in offset – Folon's designs had produced the spark they had been waiting for.

Posters became decorative objects, almost luxury goods, chosen for their esthetic value. And even though some samples of poor taste came on the market (wild horses galloping in the sunset, a doe in the moonlight), galleries specializing in posters almost all shared a demand for quality.

In 1973, in San Francisco, an exhibition organized around the work of David Lance Goines gave the new poster its patent of nobility: a beautifully designed catalogue encompassed posters produced between 1968 and 1973 and did much to strengthen this market.

But above all the market would find new impact with, on the one hand, the renewed interest in Art Deco which Patrick Nagel's posters aroused in America and the reprinting of Cassandre in France, and on the other, the new taste for artistic photography which gave rise to some very fine posters (*Tulips* by Mapplethorpe).

Today, it would seem that the golden age is over. Publishers, with few exceptions, vie with each other in banality, and have imprisoned graphic art in the ruinous conformity of hyperrealism and in a pseudo-Art-Deco. Instead of seeking to further the evolution of graphic art, merchants seek only to satisfy the tastes of the middle class.

As this market for the cultural poster developed, there was a parallel diminishing of the commercial image, which had reigned supreme in Europe of the Thirties. In fact, since the beginning of the Fifties, when

641. Grapus: Theatrical
poster. 1981.

642. Lienemayer, Ranbow & Van de Sand:
Political design: *The First Day of Peace.*

the consumer society had begun to boom and the password was to sell
at all cost, the emergence of the audio-visual world no longer made the
poster the best way of reaching that goal. Professional poster artists were
little by little replaced by idea men attached to advertising agencies,
whose sole occupation was to insert posters into ad campaigns. These
policies led to a suppression of creativity, and what had been the art of
creating a poster was often reduced to the simple technique of enlarging
an advertising photo that had appeared in the press.

But then again, well known painters have been called on to distinguish
an ad campaign: Air France used Mathieu and the French railways (SNCF)
entrusted itself to Salvador Dali. Thus, the situation is at best fragmented.

And so a whole generation of young designers found itself unemployed.
Rejected by the public, these professional graphic artists depended upon
the cultural and political sectors. Since 1966, they have found a refuge
at the Warsaw Biennale, whose prizes have served to unveil the latest
great poster makers: Lienemayer, Ranbow, Van de Sand, Matthies and
Edelman in Germany, Topor and Grapus – the socially involved artists'
collective – in France, Wasilewski and Swierzy in Poland, and the
Japanese.

From these examples was born a socio-cultural poster of high quality
in France, with artists like Michel Quarez and Alain le Quernec. But for
political reasons and because of their refusal to make concessions, these
talents do not profit from advertising or from the poster market – for their
posters are not conceived as decorations, but as a medium to transmit
communication effectively.

643. Alain le Quernec: A political anti-pollution
poster. 1978.

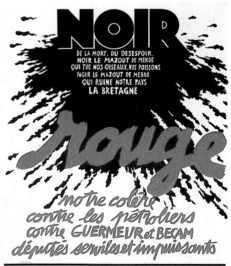

CINZANO.
LE TEMPS NE PEUT RIEN CONTRE NOUS.

644. TBWA Agency: *Cinzano.*
("Time Can't Harm Us.") 1974.

CINZANO BITTER

The Poster Today

Through all its transformation the poster, in spite of attacks by its detrators and lamentations by nostalgia buffs, is very much alive today. Certainly there is a seemingly unbreachable gap between the commercial and the cultural poster. But the advertising poster is no worse off than before.

Once the crucial turning point of the Sixties was past, the poster gained new vigor, and today is of a high quality. The graphics vs. photography debate is over, and throughout the world the Seventies have seen the development of an effective visual communication. Most of the time the conception is no longer an artist's; it is the result of teamwork, and it is an agency that signs the poster. But many advertisers have recovered their enthusiasm for this most spectacular of media, and as a result, every country has developed again a national style. It depends upon the designers, of course, but also on regulations on posters that considerably vary their possibilities for expression. And in the same way, the relative importance of posters to other media – radio, press, TV – makes the creative richness vary.

For example, the Scandinavian poster remains limited, as in the past, by its display posts – mainly railway and public transport stations – which limit the image to the railway format. Switzerland, too, the cradle of modern graphics, suffers by being limited to its "world format." Furthermore, the creation of new display posts is forbidden except on certain construction sites. These provide the only opportunities for Swiss poster makers to break out of the usual format which elsewhere limits them to enlarged announcements.

In the United States the reverse is true: there are no limits on format. A billboard is a veritable monument, with concrete abutments for support, a ladder and platform for maintenance and lighting. But exterior advertising occupies a tiny part of budgets devoured by the press and television. It largely serves products prohibited on television, such as cigarettes and hard liquor. The results are, on the whole, disastrous: "European posters seem to me more oriented to the public than, as in the United States, to the product. The result is that American posters are more constricted and generally ugly," recently declared Harvey Baron, creative director of TBWA/USA.[1]

The American billboards confirm it with their poor layouts of cigarette packets and whiskey glasses. Campaign strategies seem no longer to exist. The exceptions – such as the current NIKE campaign – are that much more remarkable.

1. In *Affichage*, No. 15, Oct. 1977.

645. ECOM Agency: One of a series for the Paris Rapid Transit System. 1982.

646. André François: The newspaper *Observateur*. 1973.

In England, billboards are large and elongated, and relatively scarce. The slogan – concise, pointed, and often very funny – serves well designed images – notably remarkable photographs. Germany seems to have at last returned to posters worthy of its tradition. Although they tend to overuse pedagogic texts, the prize winners of the 1980 Triennial organized by the Deutsches Plakat Museum in Essen confirmed the high standard of posters produced between 1977 and 1980. The series *IBM* and *Westdeutsche Zeitung* by the GGK Düsseldorf agency are on the highest international level. The ABC Bank has not hesitated to call on Tomi Ungerer, Salamander on Klaus Held, in a very surrealist spirit, and the publisher Fischer on Lienemayer, Ranbow and Van de Sand who produced a series for him that is among their best creations.

Belgium suffers from its small size (which leads to simply importing campaigns from abroad), and its bilingualism (which encumbers the poster). Spain has a redundancy of posters, in large formats (up to 8 x 3 meters), but without exceptional creativity. Italy produces nothing remarkable.

But France deserves attention. Unlike other countries, 15% of advertising budgets are still allotted to posters – and the percentage is increasing. The rest of the world limits itself to 2 or 3%! This situation is due, of course, to very limited access to television advertising in France.

The high quality of the French poster also comes from the enthusiasm of a new generation of advertisers who, at the beginning of the Seventies, felt an upsurge of interest in the medium. Feldman, Seguela, Brochant and Philippe Michel who dominate the profession today, have put the French poster again in the forefront of world production. This creative effort has been sustained by poster companies which have created new display areas (the urban mobile of Jean-Jaques Decaux) but also by ever more sophisticated distribution allowing advertisers more elaborate and better aimed campaigns. Today they make great use of teaser campaigns, which reveal only part of the message to excite curiosity; the campaign by Avenir Publicité: *September 2 I'll take off the top, September 4 I'll take off the bottom* was the most sensational recent example. There are also campaigns of multiple simultaneous visuals *(Darty,* the *Club Méditerannée* and radio company campaigns). The prize-winners of the Grand Prix de l'Affiche, set up in 1973 by the Union de la Publicité Extérieure (Outdoor Advertising Society), whose jury consists of the

647. FCA Agency: *Woolmark.* ("Wool is Real"). 1978.

schreIBMaschinen

648. GGK Agency, Dusseldorf: *IBM Typewriters*. 1978.

649. An English roadside scene. 1977.

650. Lienemayer,
Ranbow & Van de Sand:
Poster for a publisher.

651. US Poster.
Chiat & Day Nike.
1984

652. Alice Agency. *La mer a un pays, la Grèce.* 1978

Dormir.

Club Méditerranée. 296.10.00

653. Synergie Agency: *Club Méditerranée*. ("Sleep"). 1979.

leaders of the profession, form an excellent resume of the past decade's evolution.

What first strikes one is that the ten prize winners are all photographic posters, with the exception of *Darty* which reduces graphics to its simplest expression, and of *Renault*. The triumph of the French poster is thus the triumph of photography. And, looking closer, it is even more the triumph of photomontage or of an excellent concept upheld by a quality image.

The sheep of *Woolmark* (1973), the little *Cinzano* cafe (1975), inaugurated a new use of photography, which was no longer a dull picture but a structured, enhanced, modern application of the first experiments of Lissitsky and Moholy-Nagy. *Urgo* (1974), *Carrefour* (1976), *Les Aeroports de Paris* (1977), *La Grèce* (1979) and *Club Méditerrannée* (1983) signaled a decisive step in the contemporary French poster: the association of a strong slogan with an equally strong image. The evocative power of the poster, *The sea has a country: Greece;* or the *Club Méditerranée* campaigns make them models of the most inviting travel posters. The series of *His Master's Voice* dog for Pathé-Marconi showed that humor is not out of place. The model Miriam's striptease for Avenir

654. Dassas-Gabelin Agency. *Pathe Marconi.* 1980

655. RSCG Agency: *Orly, Le Bouget, Roissy:* "The Most Beautiful Avenue in the World."

Publicité (1982) was a real event that proved the impact of posters.

In most cases it was not a single poster that was awarded the prize, but a series of posters out of a whole campaign.

Illustrators also had their just deserts. The example given by Delpire at the beginning of the 70's with André Francois (*Le Nouvel Observateur, Citroën*) has not been followed up. Of course, Villemot has kept his clients *(Orangina, Bally),* and Savignac has made a spectacular comeback for Jacques Seguela with *En Avant Citroën,* but on the whole drawing is little used, and used less well than photography. Hyperrealism serves as a sort of ersatz photography. Castiglioni had at one time a surrealist dimension; in the wake of Peyrolle, Coulon, and Broutin, "hyper" illustrators are legion; but they are directed so closely as to thwart all creativity. Their realistic images take graphics many years backwards – but the fault

656. Havas-Conseil Agency: For the chain of Darty stores: "Against the Stress of Prices." 1982.

657. Publicis Agency: *Renault* car advertisement. 1982.

658. Pierre Peyrolle:
Original design for
Crédit Agricole bank.

659. Bélier Agency:
Europe 1 radio channel.

"A Paris..." de Boisrond et Di Rosa
Exposition réalisée par la Fondation Bélier et les magasins Félix Potin

La Fondation Bélier et Félix Potin ont souhaité présenter au public l'œuvre commune de deux jeunes peintres français, François Boisrond et Hervé di Rosa dont le talent commence à être reconnu par les musées et les critiques, aussi bien à Paris qu'à New York.

À travers cette exposition, nous avons cherche à faire connaître le groupe Figuration Libre qui oppose à l'art austère des années précédentes une peinture colorée et expressionniste, utilisant tous les supports. Il se réfère à Picasso et aux peintres anonymes populaires, en passant par le cinéma et la bande dessinée.

La Fondation Bélier, créée par la troisième agence de publicité en France, a pour vocation de promouvoir de jeunes talents français et d'attirer des créatifs vers les métiers de la communication. Félix Potin, présent avec ses magasins dans chaque quartier de Paris, a voulu faire découvrir aux Parisiens la vision de ces jeunes artistes et rapprocher ainsi l'art contemporain du grand public.

660. Bélier Agency: A poster for an exhibition of the works of François Boisrond and Hervé di Rosa sponsored by the Bélier Foundation and the chain of Félix Potin stores, in Paris.

belongs to the art directors. Fortunately, thanks to the renaissance of painting, the post-modern images of the Bande Dessinée (Comic Artists) have begun to appear. Artists like Ever Meulen, Kiki Picasso, Gilles Bogaerts are opening new paths. The *Europe 1* campaign of 1982, carried out by Agraph Studios for the Bélier Agency is a phenomenon we hope is indicative of the future.

Things seem, in fact, to be looking up. Wall painting has come back into use at the initiative of the O.T.A. Dauphin outdoor advertising firm. Japan, now in fashion, is exporting its graphic artists. This "Figuration libre" art may be seen in Parisian metro stations thanks to the Bélier Foundation. Nonconformist painters' work appears on billboards. All this activity is the surest indication and a positive proof that the poster continues to evolve and, above all, to fascinate artists as much as advertisers.

661. CLMBBDO Agency: A three-part billboard self-promotion for Avenir, the French outdoor advertising firm. *On Sep. 2 I'll take off the top* (Upper left); *On Sep. 4 I'll take off the bottom* (Upper right); *Avenir: The Agency that Keeps its Promises.* (Bottom). 1981.

Biographical Notes

ALDIN, Cecil (1901–1935)

English painter and poster artist. Studied at Eastbourne College and Solihull Grammar School. Further studies in anatomy at South Kensington and animal painting with Frank W. Calderon. Published his first design in 1891 in the journal *The Graphic* and, between 1894–1895, illustrated *The Jungle Book* by Rudyard Kipling for the *Pall Mall Gazette.* Made many advertising posters, among them the first for *Colman Blue.* Specialist in drawing of dogs.

ALEXEIEFF, Alexander (1901–1982)

Russian decorator, graphic artist, designer and poster artist. Studied at the Institute of Oriental Languages in Paris. Drawn to the theater by Serge Sudeikin, he designed sets and costumes between 1922 and 1925, and made show posters. But he is best known for his work in film animation. With his wife Claire Parker he invented an animation technique for drawings using luminous pins on a screen. He used the technique for his first film, *A Night on Bald Mountain,* then applied it to the illustration of books.

ANQUETIN, Louis (Etrépagny, Eure, 1861–Paris 1932)

French painter and graphic artist. Studied in the ateliers of Bonnat and Cormon. In 1887 he exhibited with E. Bernard, Van Gogh and Toulouse-Lautrec, and in 1889 at the Café Volpini for "Groupe Impressioniste et Synthétique." Landscapes, Parisian Street scenes and the Bohemian life are his principal themes. As a painter, he was influenced by Rubens, Jordaens, and Delacroix (a monumental painting, *Le Combat,* presented to the Salon de la Societé des Beaux-Arts is a witness to these influences), while as a draftsman, he tended to lean to Daumier. Worked for the journals *L'Escarmouche* and *Courrier Français.* Theater sets for *The Merchant of Venice* (1917), designs for the products of the Gobelins and Beauvais manufacturers (1920).

ASHLEY (Havinden Ashley) (1903–1973)

English graphic artist, textile designer, and abstract painter. Studied drawing and design at the Central School of Arts and Crafts, 1922; joined the W.S. Crawford advertising agency in 1929. He was named its artistic director and vice-president in 1960. Worked for the Milk Marketing Board, The General Post Office, the Brewer's Society and Simpson. 1933: designs for carpets and fabrics for J. Duncan Miller, Edinburgh Weavers, Campell Fabrics and the Wilton Royal Carpet Factory. Advertising for Morton Sundour Fabrics; many exhibitions in Europe and the United States. 1953: President of the Society of Industrial Artists.

AUGSBURGER, Pierre (Basel, 1933)

Swiss graphic artist. Many advertising posters (*Bally*). Currently living in Territet-Veytaux.

AWAZU, Kiyoshi (Tokyo, 1929)

Japanese graphic and poster artist. Grand prize of the Japanese Association of Advertising Art (AJAP); member since 1956. Designed the amusement park for the Osaka International Exposition (1967). Film decor for *Shinju Ten no Amijima* (1969).

BARBIER, Georges (Nantes 1882–Paris 1932)

French graphic artist, watercolorist, illustrator, theater decorator. As a pupil of J.P. Laurens in Paris, he was much influenced by Persian miniatures and the art of Beardsley. Worked on many newspapers, principally fashion journals, *Gazette de Bon Ton* and *Jardin des Dames.* Illustrated literary works, among them: *Danses de Nijinski* by F. Miomandre, 1912; *Chansons de Bilitis* by Pierre Louys, 1922; *Roman de la Momie* by Théophile Gautier, 1929. Many costumes for the theater, including Maurice Rostand's for the role of Casanova. Decor of R. Valentino's film *Monsieur Beaucaire.*

BARRERE, Adrien (Paris, 1877–1931)

French painter, lithographer, poster artist and caricaturist. Studied Law and Medicine. Posters for the theater, *Grand Guignol,* (notably for *Dranem*), and for advertising; his series of six color lithographs of the professors at the School of Medicine and the Law School was printed in 420,000 copies and made him famous. Many posters for the earliest films of Pathé Frères.

BASCH, Arpad (1860–?)

Hungarian designer and poster artist. Studied in Vienna and Paris. At the age of 23, his poster for the millenium of the foundation of the Kingdom of Hungary attracted attention, and he quickly became one of the best known poster artists of the time. The English magazine *The Poster* devoted an article to him. Worked for the Kühne E agricultural machinery works in Budapest, and for several bicycle firms.

BASS, Saul (1921–)

American graphic and poster artist. Worked as designer and artistic advisor for industry and advertising agencies. Created many corporate design images, including that of the Celanese Corporation. Well known for distinctive cinema posters (*The Man with the Golden Arm*).

BAUGNIET, Marcel-Louis (Liege, 1896–)
Belgian painter, designer, and decorator. Studied with Jean Delville at the Brussels Academy where he befriended Magritte, Delvaux and Flouquet. Member of the "7 Arts" group from 1922 to 1929. Worked on several art journals as art critic, and wrote an essay on the psychology of forms. Worked in woodcuts, lithography; made tapestry designs and furniture. Co-founded the movement "Coll'Art" with Jules Milo in 1971.

BAUMBERGER, Otto (Zurich 1889–Weiningen, 1961)
Swiss designer, lithographer and poster artist. Learned lithography while attending Eduard Stiefel's course at the Applied Arts School in Zurich. 1908: studies at the Munich Academy. 1911: employed as a lithographer at J.E. Wolfensberger, whose partner he became in 1914. 1916–1918: many theater posters. 1920: decoration and illustrations in Berlin. 1920–1932: professor of lithography and drawing at the Applied Arts School of Zurich. 1932–1959: faculty chairman and professor at ETH (Federal Polytechnic School in Zurich).

BAYER, Herbert (Haag, 1900–)
Austrian architect, painter, photographer and poster artist. Studied architecture with Schmidthammer in 1919; became Emmanuel Margold's assistant in 1920. From 1921 to 1923, student at the Bauhaus in Weimar. Drawn for a while to typography, he joined Kandinsky's studio. From 1925 to 1928, he was studio head for graphic art and typography at the Bauhaus. Worked on *Vogue* (Berlin 1928–1930), and left for the United States in 1938. From 1946 to 1956, artistic advisor to the Container Corporation of America, and also architect and adviser at the Aspen Institute of Colorado. Since 1966, artistic advisor to the Atlantic Richfield Company. Author of several works on the Bauhaus and on graphic art.

BEAUCE, Vivant (Nolay, 1818–Paris, 1876)
French painter, lithographer, engraver and illustrator. Known for his book illustrations, his posters for booksellers, and his frontispieces for *Les Contes du Temps passé* by Perrault and *Les Trois Mousquetaires* by Dumas. From 1858 to 1868, he was employed as a designer at the Royal Porcelain Manufacturers in St. Petersburg, Russia.

BEARDSLEY, Aubrey Vincent (Brighton, 1872–Menton, 1898)
English designer, engraver, poster artist, painter and writer. His encounter with Burne-Jones in 1892 was a turning point in his career. Inspired by turns by the Old Masters, the Pre-Raphaelites, the Japanese print, Greek antiques and eighteenth-century French art. Illustrated Malory's *Morte d'Arthur* (1892), Oscar Wilde's *Salomé* (1894) and *Lysistrata* (1896). He was artistic director of *The Yellow Book* (1894–97), a symbolist review of Art Nouveau, and co-founder of the *Savoy* (1897–98). He was a decisive influence on modern graphic art in general, in particular on Bradley in the United States and on Lechter in Germany.

BEGGARSTAFF BROTHERS. Pseudonym of James Pryde and William Nicholson from 1894 to 1898.

Pryde, James (Edinburgh, 1869–London, 1941)
Poster artist, portraitist, graphic artist, wood-engraver. Studied at the Royal Scottish Academy of Edinburgh and at the Académie Julian in Paris, in Bouguereau's studio. Member of the International Society of Sculptors, Painters and Graphic Artists. Contributed to the development of the modern English poster, and the poster in general. With his brother-in-law William Nicholson (see next), he defined the specific style of the English poster.

Nicholson, William (Newark-on-Trent, 1872–Blewbury, Berkshire, 1949)
Poster artist, painter, graphic artist, wood-engraver, illustrator and theater decorator. Studied a short time at the Academie Julian in Paris, otherwise self-taught. Celebrated as a painter for his pictures of London society, his landscapes and his still lifes, he played an important part in the renaissance of English engraving. Together with James Pryde, as Beggarstaff Brothers, became the father of the modern English poster.
   Hamlet for the W.S. Hardy's Company and *"Kassama Corn Flour"* (1894) made the Beggarstaff's reputation as poster artists. Their popularity was further affirmed in 1895 with the publication of *Beefeater*.

BEHRENS, Peter (Hamburg, 1886–Berlin, 1940)
German architect and designer. Starting out as a painter and engraver, he turned to applied arts, was strongly influenced by the Jugendstil, then, from 1898, by his involvement in industrial esthetics—he became a designer for the AEG conglomerate in 1907. In 1889, became a member of the Darmstadt "Group of Seven." From 1903 to 1907, director of the School of Arts and Crafts in Düsseldorf. Pioneer of modern architecture in Germany, he advocated a strict functionalism: machine factory of the AEG in Berlin (1909); German Embassy in St. Petersburg (1911–1912); offices of I.G. Farben at Hoechst, near Frankfurt (1920–1925).

BERCHMANS, Emile (Lüttich, 1867–1947)
Walloon painter, decorator, poster artist and illustrator. Studied at he Lüttich Academy. Newspaper illustrations for *La Plume*, and for *Caprice Revue*, which he himself founded with Donnay, Rassenfosse and Maurice Siville, and for books *(Contes pour l'aimée)*. He was one of the very first Belgian artists to take an interest in the art of the poster, whose development he abetted. Exhibits at L'Art Indépendent and La Libre Esthétique in 1896 and 1899.

BERNARD, Francis (Marseille, 1900–)

French designer and poster artist. Member of the Union des Artistes Modernes, like Colin, Carlu, Loupot and Cassandre. Made posters for *Le Bal des Petits Lits Blancs, Black and Decker,* 1931, and series for tourism *(Morocco).* Art director of the Salon des Arts Mènagers for over 300 years.

BERNHARD, Lucian (Emil Kahn) (Vienna, 1883–New York, 1972)

Austrian poster artist, graphic artist and decorative architect. Studied at the Munich Academy. Initiated into the art of the poster by Growald in Berlin. The creator of the Roman, Gothic and Italic characters that bear his name, he quickly became a well-known poster maker. In the field of poster art, he was considered by Julius Klinger as the father of advertisement. During the first World War, he made many designs for National Defense loan posters. Emigrated to the United States in the 1920s.

BERTHON, Paul (Villefranche, 1972–Paris, 1909)

French painter, lithographer and poster artist. Pupil of Grasset and of Luc-Olivier Merson whose influence he shows. 1895: first poster for the Salon des Cent. Many posters for the *Chemins de Fer de l'Ouest.*

BILL, Max (Winterthur, 1908–)

Swiss architect, painter, sculptor and essayist. Studied in Zurich and at the Bauhaus (1927–1929). Settled in Zurich as an architect; practiced sculpture and painting as well as industrial arts and advertising graphics. From 1951 to 1956, he directed the Hochschule für Gestalltung of Ulm, which he also designed. From 1932 to 1936, participated in the *Abstraction et Création* movement in Paris. 1936: Grand Prize of the Milan Triennale. 1949: Prix Kandinsky in Paris.

BINDER, Joseph (Vienna, 1898–1972)

Austrian graphic artist, designer, painter and poster artist. From 1933, worked as a graphic artist and taught in the United States. Had a considerable influence on the art of his time. Many exhibitions (Vienna Museum of Applied Arts, the Neuberger Museum at New York University, etc.)

BIRD, Elisha Brown (Boston, 1867–1943)

American illustrator and posterist. Contributed to magazines, including *Massachusetts Institute of Technology, The Inland Printer, The Chap Book, The Red Letter.* Influenced by Beardsley.

BIRKHAUSER, Peter (Basel, 1911–)

Swiss graphic artist, poster artist and painter. Studied at the School of Arts and Crafts from 1928 to 1934. From 1931 to 1934, advanced studies in the studio of Niklaus Stoecklin. Travels and studies in Italy and France. Many advertising posters (*P.K.Z., S.B.B., Feba, Globus . . .*)

BIRO, Michael

Hungarian poster artist. During and after the First World War, made graphically effective posters.

BONFILS, Robert (1886–1972)

French designer and poster artist. In the mannerist tradition of the eighteenth century, he made, among others, a poster for the Exposition of 1925.

BONNARD, Pierre (Fontenay-aux-roses, 1867–Le Cannet, 1947)

French painter, watercolorist, designer, engraver. Son of a civil servant, he studied law, and in 1888 entered the Académie Julian where he met Denis, Rawson, Roussel and Vuillard. Member of the Nabis group; fascinated by Japanese prints. 1889: the poster *France—Champagne,* a great success. 1894: *La Revue Blanche.* While pursuing his career as a painter (1896: exhibition of paintings, posters and lithographs at the Galerie Durant-Ruel; starting in 1906, regular exhibitions at Bernheim Jeune), he also created models for furniture, sets for the Theatre de l'Oeuvre, black-and-white and color lithographs, book illustrations (*Parallèlement* by Verlaine, 1900; *Daphnis et Chloé,* 1902; *Grand Almanach du Père Ubu* by Alfred Jarry, 1901). Many travels (Belgium, Holland, Spain, Tunisia, Algeria). Produced a series *Nudes at Their Dressing Tables* that is particularly remarkable. In 1909, in association with Manguin, he developed his skills as a colorist. 1918: honorary co-president (with Renoir) of the group "Jeune Peinture Française". Twice received the Carnegie Prize (1923 and 1936).

BOUISSET, Etienne Maurice Firmin (Moissac, 1859–Paris, 1925)

French painter, engraver, lithographer, book illustrators and poster artist. Pupil of Cabanel at the Ecole des Beaux-Arts. Famous for his portraits of children, he illustrated *Les bébés d'Alsace et de Lorraine.* In 1886, he made decorative panels for children's rooms; in 1912, menus and calendars. He also used his favorite subjects in advertising posters: *Le chocolat Meunier,* printed in the tens of thousands, assured his fame.

BRADLEY, William (Boston, 1868–La Mesa, California, 1962)

Poster artist, illustrator, graphic artist, printer, editor. Learned drawing from his father, the caricaturist Aron Bradley; began his career as a printer. 1894–1895: covers for *The Inland Printer* and advertisements for inks of *The Ault and Wiborg Co.* At the end of 1895, opened his own printing-house, Wayside Press, in Springfield, Massachusetts, and brought out a monthly, *Bradley—His Book,* himself filling all the roles, from writer to printer. When the periodical folded and the printing house closed down, he was for a while artistic director of the Cambridge University Press, later worked for the

American Type Founder's Company, illustrated children's books and was an editor at *Collier's*. Between 1915 and 1917, Bradley was chosen by William R. Hearst as artistic director for a series of films; in 1918–1919, he wrote scenarios, and directed in 1920; acted as artistic and typographical advisor for the journals, newspapers, and films of the Hearst Corporation. In Europe as in America, Bradley reshaped typography and the art book. With Rhead and Penfield, he was one of the most famous American poster artists of his time.

BRATTINGA, Pieter (Hilversum, 1931–)

Dutch graphic and poster artist. Studied in Leyden, London and Paris. Taught for a time at the Pratt Institute of New York (Department of Visual Communication). Artistic director of Steendrukkereij De Jong & Company from 1951 to 1974. Commissioner of Exhibitions for the Dutch government. Editor of *Quadrat Print*. Honorary member of Form Mediation International. Co-author with Dick Dooijes of *The History of the Dutch Poster*.

BRODERS, Roger (1883–1953)

French designer and poster artist, specialist in tourism. Series of railway posters for Marseille, the Spa towns, the Midi, and the mountains, all of high graphic quality.

BRODOVICH, Alexei (St. Petersburg, 1900–Le Thor, Vaucluse, 1971)

Russian theater decorator, poster and graphic artist. 1917: fled to France with his family. From 1920, engaged by Diaghilev as a painter for the sets of the *Ballets Russes*. In 1924, began his career as a graphic artist (posters for *Martini Vermouth, Le Printemps, Le Bon Marché*). 1928: worked as artistic director for Trois Quartiers and for Madelios (fabric design). In 1930, taught advertising at the Philadelphia Museum's School of Industrial Art. From 1934 to 1958, artistic director of *Harper's Bazaar*, while still making posters. In 1948, director of the prestigious magazine *Portfolio*, founded by Frank Zachary. In 1957, interned in a psychiatric clinic upon his wife's death; died miserably, sick and forgotten, on April 15, 1971.

BURCHARTZ, Max (1887–1961)

German designer and graphic artist. 1906–1908: studied in Düsseldorf, Munich, and Berlin, After the war, he allied himself with Kurt Schwitters, El Lissitsky, Theo van Doesburg, and Wassily Kandinsky. During the Twenties, founded the Werbebau Agency at Bochum, where he devoted himself to commercial graphic art. 1926: joined the faculty of the Folkswangschule in Essen, which he left in 1933, to return in 1949. Later, worked as an industrial designer.

BURTIN, Will (Cologne, 1903–New York, 1972)

German graphic artist and illustrator. Studied

typography. 1927–1938: graphic activity in Germany; then emigrated to the United States. 1939–1943: taught graphic communication at Pratt Institute. Artistic director of the Upjohn Company and of their magazine *Scope;* also worked for IBM. Winner of several prizes, including the Medal of the American Institute of Graphic Arts. Member of the New York Art Directors' Club.

CAPPIELLO, Leonetto (Livorno, 1875–Nice, 1942)

French painter, designer, caricaturist and poster artist of Italian origin. Settled in Paris in 1898. Two of his eighteen caricatures of Parisian actresses from the series "Nos actrices" were published in *Rire* and assured his success. Drawings for *Le journal, L'assiette au beurre, Cri de Paris, Le Figaro, Le Gaulois*. His poster for the newspaper *Frou-Frou* (1899) created a sensation and made him an overnight celebrity. The poster *Chocolat Klaus* in 1903 definitively established his style and made him the most popular poster artist of his time. Besides his vast poster output, he made comic statuettes and portraits in oils.

CARBONI, Erberto (Parma, 1899–)

Italian architect, graphic artist, scenarist, illustrator and painter. Studied architecture at the Parma Academy of Fine Arts; 1921: entered advertising. Participated in numerous exhibitions (Rome 1936; 7th Triennale di Milano, 1940; Paris, 1937, Biennale di Venezia, 1972). Gold Medal of Advertising for his Berolli campaign. Member of the International Graphic Alliance (AGI).

CARDINAUX, Emile (Berne, 1877–1936)

Swiss painter and poster artist. Studied law, then a pupil of the painter Franz Stück. In Paris, he won a gold medal for a project intended to export the image of Switzerland abroad (stations, hotels, steamboats . . .). Recruited by Kaiser, who ordered his first two posters for *Villars* chocolate (1905). He is best known for his tourist posters.

CARLU, Jean (Bonnière-sur-Seine 1900–)

French designer and poster artist. Began by studying architecture, which he was forced to abandon in 1918 following the accidental loss of his right arm. Inspired by cubist painting, his graphics were influenced by Gleize and Juan Gris. He clearly defined the basic rule of the poster as "the graphic expression of the idea." From 1932, began to involve himself in political causes, making posters for the likes of the Agency of Graphic Propaganda for Peace: *Disarmament, L'Obole, Days of Peace*. He sought to revivify the art of the poster with photomontage, the use of metal in relief, and lighting. From 1934, abandoned realism for surrealism. In 1937, he had charge of the advertising section at the International Exposition in Paris.

CASAS, Ramón (Barcelona, 1866–1932)

Spanish publisher and poster artist. Art editor of the Catalan weekly *Pel et Ploma*. His graphic work is deeply marked by the influence of the French masters Jules Chéret and Henri de Toulouse-Lautrec.

CASPEL, Johan G. van (Amsterdam, 1870–)

Dutch painter and poster artist. Studied at the Rijks Academy Van Beeldende Kunsten of Amsterdam. Portraitist and furniture designer. One of the most important poster artists of the emerging Dutch poster.

CASSANDRE (Adolphe Mouron) (Kharkov, 1901–Paris, 1968)

French painter, poster artist, theater decorator and typographer. Studied at the Académie Julian in the studio of Lucien Simon. To earn his living, he worked at the Hachard printing house at the Place de la Madeleine in Paris and, from 1922, signed his posters with the pseudonym A.M. Cassandre. From 1923 to 1928, there were already a few masterpieces among his works: *Au Bucheron, Pivolo, L'Intransigeant, L'Etoile du Nord* and *Nord Express*. In 1927, he obtained major orders from French railways and also English and Dutch companies. 1929: creation of the typographical alphabet *Le Bifur*, then another character, *L'Acier*. Finally, Cassandre designed the *Peignot* (from the name of the typefounder he worked with), which is still in use today. Also created several characters for Olivetti typewriters. Co-founder, in 1930, of the Alliance Graphique with Loupot and a young printer from Northern France, Maurice Moyrand. From this graphic studio emerged most of the best posters of the period. In 1934, when Moyrand died, the studio closed its doors.

Designed brochures and catalogues for *Nicolas* and *Dubonnet*, while directing a little school of graphic art from 1934 to 1935 (attended by André Francois, Raymond Savignac and Bernard Villemot). From 1933, theater decor and costumes. Travels in the United States. In 1936, the Museum of Modern Art in New York organized an exhibition of his posters. Contributed to *Harper's Bazaar,* and for Ford made his most famous American poster, *Watch the Fords Go By.* Returning to France in 1939, he almost completely abandoned the poster in favor of theater decorating and painting, much influenced by his friend Balthus. Up to the mid-Fifties, he worked a great deal for the theater and made a few more posters. In 1963, he designed the famous logo YSL for Yves Saint-Laurent. The last years of his life were marred by poverty and psychological decline; he committed suicide in June, 1968.

CASSIERS, Henri (Antwerp, 1858–Brussels, 1944)

Belgian painter, watercolorist, engraver and poster artist. Began as a designer in an architect's office. Member of the Académie Libre of Brussels. While traveling in England, he encountered the painter C.W. Bartlett who greatly influenced him. He made most of his posters for shipping companies such as the *Red Star Line* (today the Holland American Line). Illustrations for books by Camille Mauclair *(Trois Femmes de Flandre)* and by Cyril Buysse *(Contes des Pays-Bas).* Postcards for the Brussels publisher Dietrich, calendars and other small graphic works.

CAZALS, Frédéric Auguste (Paris, 1865–Paris, 1941)

French poet, designer and lithographer. Contributed to various publications, including *La Plume* and *La Vie Franco-Russe.* 1903: showed a portrait of Verlaine at the Société Nationale des Beaux-Arts that brought him notice. Produced many posters, including one for the first *Salon des Cent,* and many portraits of writers and artists, as well as book and newspaper illustrations.

CHERET, Jules (Paris, 1836–Nice, 1932)

French painter, lithographer and poster artist. From the age of 13, he studied lithography; three years later he worked in a studio and took evening classes with Lecoq de Boisbaudran at the Ecole Nationale de Dessin. He made his debut in 1855 with three posters in black-and-white; then in 1858, in three colors, he made a poster for Offenbach's *Orphée aux Enfers.* Between 1859 and 1866, he studied the industrial processes of color lithography in London and, helped by the perfumer Rimmel (for whom he had worked), he set up his own printing house in Paris (which he would later turn over to Chaix, while continuing as its director). His experiments with color showed their effects in the Eighties and Nineties. Known as "the king of posters," Jules Chéret contributed to the development of poster printing techniques and was an innovator in the field of advertising. He designed about one thousand posters.

CHWAST, Seymour (1931–)

American graphic artist, designer and poster artist. Studied at the Cooper Union in New York. Co-founder, with Milton Glaser, of the Push Pin Studio. Illustrations for record jackets, prospectuses, packaging, advertisements. Founder of the Push Pin Press. Awarded many prizes, among them the Cooper Union's St. Gauden Medal. He has also been elected to the honor roll of New York Art Directors.

CIESLEWICZ, Roman (Lwow, 1930–)

Polish illustrator, graphic and poster artist. Graduate of the Cracow Academy of Fine Arts. Member of the AGI. Has been awarded more than 35 grand prizes. Since 1963, living in Paris; contributes to various French publications and to the Center National d'Art Contemporain. Since 1973, teacher at the Ecole Superieure des Arts Décoratifs, and director of a graphic arts studio.

CISSARZ, Vincenz (Danzig, 1873–Frankfurt, 1942)

German painter, graphic artist, architect, decorator and poster artist. Studied at the Academy of Dresden. Professor at the Frankfurt School of Decorative Arts, 1916. Used the applied arts in many fields.

COLIN, Paul (Nancy, 1892–)

French poster artist, decorator and costumer. Arrived in Paris in 1913. In 1925, sudden success with his poster for the *Revue Nègre*. Much work for theaters and music halls (*Loie Fuller*, 1925; *Bal Nègre*, 1927; *Tabarin*, 1928; *Damia*, 1930; *Carlos Gardel*, 1930; *Casino de Paris*, 1932). He also produced many posters for the ballet (*Jean Weidt*, 1938; *Serge Lifar*, 1935), for balls and for the cinema (*A nous la liberté*, 1931) and for the *Musée d'Ethnographie du Trocadero* in 1935. In 1926, he opened a school where he taught graphic art.

COMBAZ, Gisbert (Antwerp, 1869–Brussels, 1941)

Belgian painter and graphic artist. Starting as a lawyer, he later turned towards art and was influenced between 1897 and 1914 by Japanese painting. He took active part in the exhibitions by *La Libre Esthétique* in Brussels and made many posters for them. He then devoted himself to Asian art (architecture and painting), and Khmer art. His last work, *Masks and Dragons*, appeared posthumously in Asia in 1945. He was professor of decorative composition at the Académie Royale des Beaux Arts of Brussels, professor at the Institute Belge des Hautes Etudes Chinoises, and president of the Societé Belge des Etudes Orientales.

COOPER, Austin (1890–1964)

English painter and poster artist. Studied at the Cardiff School of Art and, from 1906 to 1910, at the Allan Frazer College of Art. He resided at first in Canada where he made a solid reputation as an advertising artist. Going to England during the First World War, he settled in London in 1922 and worked for the *London and North Eastern Railway*, the *Underground Electric Railway Co.*, the *Royal Mail Line*, *Cadbury*, *Yardley*, and others. From 1936 to 1940, principal of the Reimann School of Industrial Art. In 1943, turned to painting. His first one-man exhibition took place in 1948 at the London Gallery.

CORDIER, Eugène Maria (Strasbourg, 1903–Munich, 1974)

German painter and graphic artist. Studied at the Munich Academy under Diez. Contributed to *Jugend*; member of the Munich Artists Association. As a painter, made decorative murals and worked for the Transatlantique Co. Also designed stamps. Produced a large body of graphic work.

COULON, Eric de (Neuenbourg, 1888–Thielle-Wavre, 1956)

Swiss designer and poster artist. Studied architecture in Zurich. 1913: lived and worked in Paris while continuing to fill orders from Switzerland. 1918: founded an advertising agency on Rue Jacob in Paris which he dissolved in 1921. 1939: settled in Bellevue-sur-Cressier. Known especially for tourist posters.

CRESPIN, Adolphe Louis Charles (Anderlecht, 1859–Saint-Josse, 1944)

Belgian painter and artist. Pupil of Janlet, Blanc-Garin, Henri Baes and, in Paris, of Bonnat. Attracted to art and architecture, he designed facades for many buildings: private houses, bakeries, others. In 1887, his collaboration with Edouard Duyck led him to make costumes and posters for the revues at the Alcazar and the Palais d'Eté. His work has an important place in Belgium and abroad, both for the development of the poster and for the development of Art Nouveau. Awarded a prize for his poster *La Kermesse de Bruxelles*. Sport was one of his favorite themes. At first, he engraved the stone himself, then gave the task to his friend, the lithographer Paul Verdussen. Contributed to many newspapers, Belgian (*Le Petit Bleu*) and French.

CZERNIAWSKI, Jerzy (Kwiatowo, 1947–)

Polish graphic artist and illustrator. Graduated from the Wroclaw School of Fine Arts. Awarded many prizes.

DAVIS, Paul (Centrahoma, Oklahoma 1938–)

American painter, graphic and poster artist. Studied at the School of Visual Arts. Contributed illustrations to many journals in the United States and abroad. 1969: one-man show at Delpire's in Paris. Member of the Push Pin Studio. Professor at the School of Visual Arts and the University of Colorado.

DELAMARE, Francis

Belgian advertising artist. Created his first posters before the end of the First World War. In the Twenties, founded an advertising agency with Cerf that bears their names and has produced many posters: *Union Match*, *Electrolux*, *Saint Michel* cigarettes, and others.

DETHOMAS, Maxime (Garches, 1867–Paris, 1929)

French painter and designer. Much influenced by his friend, Toulouse-Lautrec, he mainly drew street scenes in the tradition of Steinlen and Forain. From 1911, he worked mainly for the Théâtre des Arts directed by Jacques Rouché (sets and costumes for *The Brothers Karamazov* and *Le Carnaval des Enfants*).

DEUTSCH, Ernst (a.k.a. **Ernst Dryden**) (Vienna, 1883–Los Angeles, 1938)

German fashion designer, graphic and poster artist, set designer. He moved to Berlin in 1911 and gained fame in poster design. In 1919, he changed his domicile back to native Vienna, opening a fashion studio. Moving on to Paris in 1926, he produced designs for magazines and for various advertisers. Arriving in Hollywood, in 1933, he changed his name to Dryden and became a set designer for the movies.

DEXEL, Walter (Munich, 1890–1973)

German painter and poster artist. Studied history of art in Munich. He soon devoted himself to commercial art and typography. He designed advertisements and posters, and worked on the development of lighted advertising billboards. Collaborated closely with the Bauhaus (1919–1925) and especially with Theo Van Doesburg (1921–1923). 1927: organized the first exhibition of commercial art: *New Advertising.* 1928–1935: professor at Magdeburg; and from 1936 to 1942, at the Berlin-Schöneberg National School of Art.

DONNAY, Auguste (Lüttich, 1862–Lüttich, 1921)

Belgian landscape painter and graphic artist. 1878: pupil of Emile Berchmans, then at the Atelier Julian in Paris. Much influenced by Gustave Moreau, Puvis de Chavannes and Henri Rivière. 1901–1905: professor of decorative art at the Lüttich Academy. Between 1887 and 1900, contributed to many publications: *La Wallonie, L'Almanach des poètes,* and illustrated books (the works of Maurice Maeterlink and the *Contes pour les enfants d'hiver* by A. Mockel). Many of his mural paintings have been lost. His major work is the tryptich he painted for the Church of Hastière-par-delà, which relates the story of Saint Wallère (1914–1919). 1908: participated in exhibition of modern art in the Berlin Secession.

DUDOVICH, Marcello (Trieste, 1878–Milan, 1962)

Italian lithographer, poster artist and painter. 1895: lithographic drawing at Ricordi; he worked with his teachers and friends Hohenstein and Metlicovitz. Left to work for Chapuis in Bologna in 1899. Considered one of the greatest of Italian poster artists. Gold Medal for his poster for the *1900 Paris World's Fair.* Illustrations for many magazines: *Novissima, Rapidista, Ars et Labor* and, in 1911, *Simplicissimus.* Participated as a painter in the Venice Biennales of 1923 and 1925. Designed numerous posters for La Rinascente department store of Milan and continued to produce travel posters until the end of his life.

DUPAS, Jean (Bordeaux, 1882–1964)

French decorator and poster artist. Pupil of Carolus Duran and Albert Besnard. Made a poster for *Bordeaux,,* his native town, in 1937, and worked for the English store *Arnold Constable.*

ECKERSLEY, Tom (1914–)

English graphic artist. Studied at the Salford Art School where he met Eric Lombers, with whom he collaborated from 1934 to 1940. Together they worked for *The London Transport Board, Shell-Mex, B.P. Ltd., The B.B.C., Architectural Review, News Chronicle, Austin Reed . . .* From 1937 to 1939, taught graphic art at the Westminster Art School. Map-making and posters for the R.A.F. during the war. 1950: Member of the International Graphic Alliance. 1976: designed the walls of the new Heathrow Airport in London.

EDEL, Edmund (Stolp, 1863–Berlin, 1933)

German painter, graphic artist, advertiser and writer. Studied in Munich and in Paris, Worked in Berlin from 1892. After 1897, became one of the best-known poster artists. He devoted himself to writing after the first World War.

EHLERS, Henry (Aix-la-Chapelle, 1897–)

German graphic artist and illustrator. Studied at the Munich School of Fine Arts under Wirnhier and Ehmcke. Member of the New Munich Association of Poster Artists. 1928–1938: in charge of all advertising campaigns of the Munich textile enterprise *Bamberger and Hertz.* Produced a large body of graphic work.

EHMCKE, Fritz Hellmuth (Hohensalza, 1878–Munich, 1965)

German advertising artist, decorator, architect and illustrator. A professional lithographer, he returned to school to study at the Berlin Museum of Decorative Arts, directed by E. Doepler Jr. and L. Menzel. Co-founder in 1900 of the Steglitzer Werkstatt fur Künstlerische Drucksachen (Steglitz Studio for Artistic Printing). From 1903 to 1913, he taught at the National School of Applied Arts. Created several type characters which bear his name and was equally well known as a typographer.

ELFFERS, Dick (Rotterdam, 1910–)

Dutch graphic artist and painter. Pupil of Jongert, Schuitema and Piet Zwart. Professor at the Rotterdam Academy, then interior architect of the Rijksmuseum, and theater decorator for the ballet.

ELLIS, Clifford and Rosemary

English poster artists. Created a dozen posters for the *London Transport,* and some others for *Shell.*

ENGELHARDT, Julius Ussy (Bindjay, Sumatra, 1883–Munich, 1964)

German painter, poster artist and illustrator. Studied at the Munich Academy under Stück. Contributed to many German sporting papers and fashion journals, and to the journal *Simplicissimus.* Member of the New Munich Association of Poster Artists. One of the best-known poster artists before and after the first World War. Very large graphic production, internationally renowned.

ENGLISH, Michael (London, 1939–)

English painter, designer and, poster artist. 1962–1965: studied at the Ealing Art School in London. Co-founder, with Nigel Waymouth, of the avant gardist movement "The Underground" and of a small poster publishing house *The Hashash and The Coloured Coat* which produced a considerable number of posters for Osiris Visions between 1966 and 1968. At present, Michael English pursues a career as a painter, while still occasionally working in advertising *(ICI* and *Philip Morris).*

ERDT, Hans Rudi (Benediktbeuren, 1883–Berlin 1918)

German graphic artist, advertiser and lithographer. Pupil of Dasios at the Munich School of Decorative Arts. One of the best known Berlin poster artists after 1908.

ERNI, Hans (Lucerne, 1909–)

Swiss painter and graphic artist. Studied in Lucerne, at the Académie Julian in Paris and at the State Academy in Berlin. Pupil of Derain and Braque. Considered one of the best of the Abstraction-Creation group which includes Arp, Baumeister and Calder. Internationally known for his book illustrations as well as his pictorial works. Living at present at Meggen.

FALK, Hans (Zurich, 1918–)

Swiss painter and poster artist. Many posters for the circus and for social causes. Lives in New York and Urdorf.

FENNEKER, Josef (Bocholt, 1895–Frankfurt, 1956)

German painter, theater decorator and poster artist. Large production of cinema posters at the beginning of the century.

FEURE, George de (Georges Van Sluijters) (Paris, 1868–Paris, 1943)

French painter, illustrator, and decorator. Son of a Dutch architect. Bookseller at The Hague, then dramatic author and stage decorator in Amsterdam. In 1891, he went to Paris where he designed decor for the *Chat Noir* cabaret and illustrations for the *Courrier Français* and *Le Boulevard.* 1892: Exposition of watercolors at the Galerie le Barc de Boutteville. Before he found his own style, his posters were very much in the style of Chéret. For S. Bing's gallery L'Art Nouveau, opened in 1896, he made decorative panels and fine furniture, fabrics, embroideries and carpets, windows, vases and other furnishings. He illustrated editions of Shakespeare and Byron's works and *La Porte des Rêves* by Marcel Schwab. Interior and exterior decorations for Bing's Art Nouveau Pavilion at the 1900 Paris World's Fair. 1902: his porcelains for Gérard Dufraisse of Limoges at the Turin World's Fair created a sensation. With the architect Bruno Möhring, he was charged with fitting out the Kongs restaurant in Paris; with the architect Cossman, he founded the Atelier de Feure for furniture-making. After fifteen years in England where he chiefly worked at theater decors, he returned to France in 1928 and did the furnishings for Madeleine Vionnet's fashion house.

FISCHER, Otto (Leipzig, 1870–Dresden, 1947)

German painter, lithographer, engraver and decorator. Studied at the Dresden Academy under Dehme F. Preller and K. Starke. One of the pioneers of the art poster in Germany.

FOLON, Jean-Michel (Brussels, 1934–)

Belgian watercolorist, engraver, graphic artists, cartoonist, and poster artist. Studied architecture, then contributed to several French and foreign magazines: *Time, Fortune, Graphis, The New Yorker, L'Express, Le Nouvel Observateur.* Began as a cartoonist, then moved into advertising (poster for *Larousse).* Worked for *Olivetti* with Georgio Soavi, and illustrated various literary works of Prévert, Boris Vian, Ray Bradbury, Kafka and Lewis Carroll. Made a fresco for the Brussels metro and another for the Waterloo Station in London. Series of engravings, animated film, advertising and cultural posters *(Spoleto Festival),* opera decors, designs for Aubusson tapestries. Finally, Folon is the star of several feature films directed by M. Polac, M. Dugowson, and Y. Bellon.

FOUJITA (Tsuguharu Fujita) (Tokyo, 1886–Paris, 1953)

Japanese painter of the School of Paris. Famous for his paintings of women and of cats. Converted to Christianity towards the end of his life, he adopted the first name Leonard and painted religious scenes.

FRANÇOIS, André (1915–)

French painter, sculptor, engraver, designer, theater decorator and poster artist of Rumanian origin. Contributed to many magazines: *Punch, The New Yorker,* cover illustrations for Penguin Books. Illustrations for literary works: *Ubu Roi* by Jarry, *Brave New World* by Huxley, *Jaques le Fataliste* by Diderot, and children's books. Made posters for *Citroen, Kodak,* the *Printemps* department stores, *Esso, Le Nouvel Observateur,* films . . . Theater decors: ballets of Roland Petit, *Le Pas de Dieu* of Gene Kelly.

FREEDMAN, Barnett (1901–1958)

English painter and lithographer. From 1917 to 1922, he worked in an office during the day and took night classes. From 1922 to 1925, studies at the Royal College of Art. Illustrations for *Memoirs of an Infantry Officer* by Siegfried Sassoon. Bookcovers for Faber and Faber, Cassell, John, Murray, Batsford . . . For the London

Transport Board, he made a fine series of lithographed posters. In 1935 his project was chosen for the stamps for the jubilee of King George V. From 1941 to 1945, he was named official war artist for the Admiralty.

FUCHS, Heinz (Berlin, 1886–Berlin, 1961)

German painter and graphic artist. Taught in Berlin and Weimar. Member of the group "November." 1947: professor at the Berlin College of Art. Political posters.

FUKUDA, Shigeo (Tokyo, 1932–　)

Japanese painter and graphic artist. Gold medalist at the fourth international Warsaw Biennale (1972). First prize in the international competition for silver commemorative coins for the Montreal Olympics. Ministry of Education's prize (1976). Bugei-Shunju prize for cartoon drawing (1977).

GAMES, Abram (London, 1914–　)

English designer and poster artist. Studied at the St. Martin School for Art. Worked for *Shell*, the *General Post-Office* and the *London Transport*. 1941: commissioned by the Public Relations Department to design posters for the army during the Second World War; the results were often controversial.

GAUDY, Georges (Saint-Josse-ven-Noode, 1872–　)

Belgian painter, illustrator and poster artist. Contributed to many sporting and other papers such as *Le Cycliste Belge Illustré, Véloce, Foyer, Flirt;* most of his posters are for sporting events. His first poster in 1893 treated *Le Vélodrome de Bruxelles.* Gaudy was also one of the best Belgian cyclists of his time.

GAVARNI (Sulpice-Guillaume Chevalier) (Paris, 1804–Paris, 1866)

French designer, lithographer, watercolorist and painter. Architect's clerk, then employed at a framer's in Tarbes before devoting himself to engravings (he made more than 8000 of them), of which some appeared in *La Mode, Caricature, Charivari.* He sketched, without flattery, The Students (1838–1840), the Actresses, the Men and Women of Letters.

GENTLEMAN, Tom (1930–　)

English designer and poster artist. Book illustrations and cover designs. Made many posters, notably for the London Transport.

GESMAR, Charles (1900–1928)

French designer and poster artist. Mistinguett's chosen poster artist, for whom he designed costumes and a very fine series of posters.

GIACOMETTI, Augusto (Stampa, 1877–Zurich, 1947)

Swiss painter and poster artist. Famous for his tourist

posters (*Grisons Railways*, 1924, *Beautiful Switzerland*, 1930). Experimental work tending to abstraction.

GILROY, John (1898–　)

English poster artist. Created the *My Goodness, My Guinness* campaign. Representative of the English humorous poster.

GIPKENS, Julius (Hanover, 1883–　)

German graphic artist, advertiser and decorator. One of the best-known self-taught poster artists before and after the First World War. Many other activities: Window displays, lighting, furniture and interior design.

GLASER, Milton (New York, 1930–　)

American graphic artist, designer and poster artist. Studied at the High School of Music and Art and at the Cooper Union. Studied engraving in Bologna with Giorgio Morandi. Founding member of the Push Pin Studio, advisor to Art Horizon Books, director of design at the School of Visual Arts, and member of the International Graphic Alliance. Co-author of the book *The Underground Gourmet*, a very popular guide to New York restaurants. Many international exhibitions; book illustrations.

GLASS, Franz Paul (Munich, 1886–1964)

German graphic artist. Studied in Munich with Diez. 1909–1910: studies in Italy. Member of the "Group of 6" and of the New Association of Munich Poster Artists. Large graphic production.

GORKA, Wiktor (Bielsko-Biale, 1922–　)

Polish graphic and poster artist. 1952: graduated from the Cracow Academy of Fine Arts. 1969–1970: taught classes at the University of San Carlo in Mexico to spread the art of the poster, and in 1970 taught Cuban students.

GOULD, J.J.

One of the most famous American poster artists of his time. Like Carqueville, he worked almost exclusively for the Philadelphia monthly *Lippincott's.* Sometimes signed J.J. Gould, sometimes J.J. Gould Junior. Influenced by Penfield, Carqueville and Bradley.

GRANDVILLE, Gérard (Jean Ignace Isidore) (Nancy, 1803–Vanves, 1947)

French designer, watercolorist, lithographer and illustrator. In 1829 he had a resounding success with his *Changing Times of Day,* where he introduced his half-man-half-animal figures. In 1830, he was a widely appreciated political caricaturist. Together with Daumier, he contributed to the magazines *Les caricatures* and *Charivari.* Illustrations for numerous books (*Fables de la Fontaine, Scènes de la vie des animaux* by

Balzac . . .). He could be considered one of the precursors of surrealism.

GRAPUS (Creative collective founded in 1970)

Today composed of: Jean-Paul Bacholett, Pierre Bernard, Alexander Jordan, Gerard Paris-Clavel. Many political posters representing diverse tendencies of communism, and cultural posters. Gold and silver medals at the Warsaw and Brno biennales. First prize at the fourth biennale of Lahti (Finland). Many exhibitions in France and abroad starting in 1975.

GRASSET, Eugéne-Samuel (Lausanne, 1845–Sceaux, 1917)

French painter, graphic artist, architect and theorist of art. Son of a Swiss cabinet maker. Naturalized as a French citizen in 1891. In Paris, he began by designing fabrics and carpets. Between 1881 and 1883, illustrations for *L' histoire des 4 fils d' Aymon,* inspired by medieval paintings. Contributed to various magazines: *Le Courrier Français, Paris Illustré, La Revue Illustrée . . .* Made designs for furniture, tapestry, embroidery, faience, mosaics, stained-glass windows; furniture for Charles Gillot; fireplace and lantern of the Chat Noir cabaret, 1879–1881; mosaics for the church of Saint-Etienne de Briare 1893–1897; windows for the cathedral of Orleans, representing the life of Joan of Arc, 1893; the windows of the Paris Chamber of Commerce, 1900. Very prolific, Grasset made posters, decorative panels, and calendars, as well as playing cards and designs for postage stamps. Taught a class in Decorative Arts drawing at the Ecole Guérin in Paris. 1898–1899: his book *The plant and its Ornamental Applications* appeared, followed in 1905 by *The Method of Ornamental Composition.* Grasset's work has a fundamental place in the pantheon of Art Nouveau, and his conception of art contributed to a certain democratization of it.

GRIFFIN, Rick

American designer, illustrator, painter and poster artist. Contributed to the review *Surfer* and was a member of the Jook Savages band. 1965: First poster for the Jook Savages Art Show at the Psychedelic Shop in San Francisco. Worked for Family Dog and for promoter Bill Graham. Co-founder of a publishing house with Bob Siedmann and Louis Rappaport.

GRIGNANI, Franco (1908–   )

Italian graphic and poster artist. Worthy successor to Cappiello. One of the best Italian representatives in typographical experiments.

GRONOWSKI, Tadeusz (1894–   )

Polish poster artist. 1918–1925: studied at the School of Architecture at the Polytechnical School of Warsaw, then at the Ecole des Beaux-Arts in Paris. The first professional Polish poster artist. Also illustrations for book and magazine covers, typographic compositions, designs for labels, pamphlets and postage stamps, theater decor, mural paintings, furniture designs. Co-editor of the bi-monthly *Grafika.* Very often awarded prizes in international competition (1925, Paris; 1939, New York).

GRUN, Jules Alexandre (Paris, 1886–1934)

French painter, illustrator and poster artist. Pupil of Lavastre, the decorator of the Paris Opera, and of the landscape painter Antoine Guillemet. Still life, portraits and scenes of Parisian life were his favorite subjects. 1890: illustrations for the *Chansons Sans Gêne* of Xanrof made him the poet of the bohemian element and the Montmartre atmosphere. With Faivre, Léandre, Steinlen and Willette, he took part in decorating the Taverne de Paris, and worked as an illustrator on several periodicals *(La Caricature, Fin de Siècle, Le Courrier Français).* The most famous Montmartre cabaret singers are shown on his posters. He illustrated, with many of his friends (Bofa, Brunelleschi, Cappiello, Faivre, and Sem), an *Album de Luxe* published in 1912 by the Society of Cartoon Artists.

GUILLAUME, Albert André (Paris, 1874–Fontaine-les-Chablis, 1942)

French caricaturist, poster artist, painter and watercolorist. Pupil of Gérôme at the Ecole des Beaux Arts. Designed many posters in the style of Chéret, chiefly for the theater and industry. His illustrations for different periodicals *(Gil Blas Illustré, Le Gaulois, Le Rire)* made him one of the most popular caricaturists of his time.

GULBRANSSON, Olaf (Oslo, 1873–Tegernsee, 1958)

Norwegian designer, painter and poster artist. Studied in Oslo and Paris. From 1902, worked on *Simplicissimus* in Munich. International fame for his political caricatures. Taught at the Munich Academy.

GYSIS, Nikolaus (Sklavahory, island of Tenos, Greece, 1842–Munich 1901)

Greek painter. Studied art in Athens, then at the Munich Academy. From 1874, taught at the Munich Academy.

HANSEN, Knut (Copenhangen, 1876–1926)

Danish painter, illustrator and poster artist. Studied in Copenhagen and Berlin. Contributed to several German satiric publications and made a series of cabaret posters.

HARA, HIROMU (Nagano, 1900–   )

Japanese graphic and poster artist. Graduated from the Tokyo School of Technical Art in 1921, where he taught until 1946. He took a special interest in photography and made the first photographic mural for the Japanese pavilion at the Paris World's Fair of 1937. Co-founder of the Advertising Artist's Club in 1951. Professor at the

Murashino University of Art from 1952 to 1970. Many prizes (Mainichi, Leipzig Book Fair, etc.)

HARDMEYER, Robert (Zurich 1876–Wallisellen, 1919)

Swiss painter, illustrator and poster artist. To earn his living, he made posters, notably for the Zurich wine merchant J. Diener, which made him one of the pioneers of the art of the poster. However, he preferred to illustrate schoolbooks and children's books, and even to write them.

HARDY, Dudley (Sheffield, 1867–London, 1922)

English painter, illustrator, graphic and poster artist. Son and pupil of the painter Thomas B. Hardy. Studied at the Düsseldorf Academy, then in 1884 in Antwerp in the class of Verlat. Finally, in 1888–89, in Paris with Raphael Collin and Dagnan-Bouveret. From 1886, he was sought after as an illustrator by the London magazines *(The Pictorial World, The Lady's Pictorial)*, and humor magazines *(The Sketch, Pick-me-up* and *Black and White)*. In 1890, his picture "Dock Strike," shown at the London Academy, was a lively success. After that, he participated in many exhibitions (Royal Academy, Society of British Artists, Munich Palace of Glass, Parisian Salons . . .). After 1893–94 his posters, notably for the *Prince of Wales Theater, Drury Lane Theatre* and for the weekly *To-Day*, brought him great popularity. He became widely known in 1894 through his posters for the musical comedy *A Gaiety Girl*. Eventually he was acknowledged by his contemporaries, Beardsley, Greiffenhagen and the Beggarstaff Brothers, as one of the most important designers of the modern poster.

HASSAL, John (1868–1948)

English designer and poster artist. Studied at Worthing, then at Newton Abbot College, and finally at Neuenheim College in Heidelberg. Hoped for a military career but failed the exams: returned to the family farm and applied himself to sketching. In 1890, his first sketches appeared in the *Daily Graphic*. Contributed to *Punch*. Took up his studies again in Paris at the Académie Julian, in the classes of Bouguereau and Ferrier. In London, he met the printers David Allen and Sons who were seeking artists for advertising. Their association lasted for seven years, during which Allen published hundreds of Hassal's posters. Founder of a school for poster artists. His most famous disciples were Will Owen and Cecil Aldin.

HEARTFIELD, John (Berlin, 1891–)

German graphic artist. Studied at the Munich School of Decorative Arts where he was the pupil of Diez, Dasio and Engels; then at the Berlin School of Arts and Crafts. Collaborated with Gross on several satirical and political reviews for the German Communist Party. Studied political photomontage. Taught in 1933. Active in East Germany since 1950. Winner of the National Prize and member of the (East) German Academy of Fine Arts.

HEINE, Thomas Thédor (Leipzig, 1867–Stockholm, 1948)

German designer, illustrator, painter, poster artist and writer. Studied at Düsseldorf. Drawings in many satirical periodicals, among them *Simplicissimus*. Known for his political caricatures. Emigrated in 1933. One of the best known German poster artists of his time.

HENRION, Frederick Henry Kay (1914–)

Designer, poster and graphic artist of English origin. In charge of Exhibition planning for the Ministry of Agriculture, the Ministry of Education, the War Office, etc. between 1940 and 1945, and artistic advisor to the American Embassy and American War Office during the war. After the war, posters for the GPO, BOAC, LPTB, COID. One-man show in 1960: Designing Things and Symbols.

HERDEG, Walter (Zurich, 1908–)

Swiss graphic artist and publisher. Author of a unified advertising campaign for St. Moritz (from letterheads to posters), in collaboration with Walter Amstutz, then-director of the Tourist Office. Publisher of *Graphis* magazine.

HERRICK, Frederick Charles (Mountsovrel, Leicestershire 1887–1970)

English poster artist. Studied at Leicester College of Arts and Crafts and at the Royal College of Art. From 1919 to 1926, made posters for Baynard Press. In 1925, he was the only British artist at the Exposition of Decorative Arts in Paris, and his poster won the grand prize. Later, he taught at the Royal College of Art and at the Brighton College of Art. His style is similar to that of McKnight-Kauffer.

HEUBNER, Friedrich (Fritz) (Dresden, 1886–Munich, 1974)

German painter, graphic artist, illustrator and watercolorist. Pupil of Diez in Munich in 1908, then student in Paris in 1913. From 1932 to 1940, professor at Nuremberg, and after that, at the Munich Academy. Contributed to *Jugend* and to *Simplicissimus;* member of the Group of 6. Large graphic production.

HILLMANN, Hans (Nieder-Mois, 1925–)

German graphic and poster artist. 1948–1953: studied in Kassel as a pupil of Hans Leitsikow. 1959: founding member of the Novum Gesellschaft für Neue Graphik. From 1961, professor of graphic art in Kassel and since 1958, member of the artistic advisory council for German postage stamps. Made many graphic works for the cinema and pharmaceutical products.

HOFMANN, Armin (Winterthur, 1920–)

Swiss graphic artist and teacher. Cultural posters, often based on photographs.

HOHENSTEIN, Adolfo (St. Petersburg, 1854–)

Italian poster artist and designer of German origin. His first poster was published in 1889 by Ricordi in Milan, where he directed the art department. Contributed drawings to the magazine *Emporium*. He was the most important poster artist in Italy at the turn of the century.

HOHLWEIN, Ludwig (Wiesbaden, 1874–Berchtesgaden, 1949)

German poster artist, decorator and architect. Studied at the Munich Technical College; then assistant to Wallot in Dresden. Devoted himself to poster making from 1906; his very large production won international fame. He is the most prolific and brilliant German posterist of the 20th century.

HUBER, Max (Baar, 1919–)

Swiss painter and graphic artist. Advertising posters and magazine covers in Switzerland and Italy. Living at present in Sagno.

IBELS, Henri Gabriel (Paris, 1867–Paris, 1936)

French painter, graphic artist and writer of Dutch origin. Attended the Académie Julian in Paris, where he joined the Nabi group. Participated in various salons and exhibitions (Salon des indépendants, Galerie le Barc de Boutteville with Toulouse-Lautrec). Theater decor and program designs for the Théâtre Libre and the Théâtre de l'Art, and posters for various painters. 1893: publication of the collection of lithographs *Le café concert,* made in collaboration with Toulouse-Lautrec. 1894: one-man show at the gallery of the *Théâtre d'Application, La Bodinière.* Contributed satiric drawings to several periodicals, including *L'Escarmouche, Le Cri de Paris, Le Rire, La Baionnette, L'Echo de Paris,* and *L'Assiette au Beurre.* In his own journal, *Le Siflet,* he took a stand on the Dreyfus affair opposing the nationalist newspaper *Psst!* founded by Forain and Caran d'Ache. He drew political and social caricatures, and illustrations of literary works *(La Terre* by Zola). 1895: took part with 8 other artists, among them Bonnard, Toulouse-Lautrec and Vallotton, in a project to design windows for Tiffany which overlooked the entrance to the gallery *L'Art Nouveau.* Starting in 1900, he devoted himself almost exclusively to the theater. Worked with André Antoine, Gaston Caillavet and Robert de Flers. Taught at the Ecole d'Art Appliqué of the city of Paris. He was responsible for the introduction of the copyright system for artists.

IMATAKE, Shichiro (Kobe, 1905–)

Japanese illustrator, graphic and poster artist. Considered the father of the Osaka style of graphics. Artistic advisor to the Osaka Bureau of Railways, then to the Osaka Industrial Bureau, in 1931. Member of the Mainichi Committee. Still working in his own studio.

ISHIOKA, Eiko (Tokyo, 1938–)

Japanese poster artist and designer. Director of the design studio Eiko Shioka. AJAP prize (1965); ADC Tokyo prize (1975); Mainichi prize for industrial design (1976); Kodansha prize for publication (1977). Medalist at the Warsaw International Poster Biennale.

ITOH, Kenji (Tokyo, 1915–)

Japanese poster and graphic artist. Participated in many exhibitions and was awarded several prizes: Mainichi, ACD, Dentsu.

JOSSOT, Gustave-Henri (Dijon, 1886–Tunis, 1951)

French painter, graphic artist, illustrator and caricaturist. Illustrations for various reviews: *L'Epreuve, L'Estampe Originale, La Plume, Le Rire.* Caricatures were his strength. His most famous poster was for the fifth *Salon des Cent.* 1894: publication of his album *Artistes et Bourgeois.* Between 1895 and 1911, he showed at many salons. In 1913, he retired to Tunis where he converted to the Moslem faith and under the name Abdul Karim painted oriental motifs (wash drawings).

KÄCH, Walter (Ottenbach, 1901–Männerdorf, 1970)

Swiss graphic artist and teacher. Author of many posters and magazines covers.

KAMEKURA, Yusaku (1915–)

Japanese designer and poster artist. Director of the Kamekura Design Institute. Best designer of the year, 1975. Two Mainichi prizes for industrial design, three Dentsu prizes, two AJAP prizes, 4 Gold medals from the Tokyo ADC. In 1966 and in 1968, awarded prizes at the Warsaw biennale; he also received a silver medal at the Brno Biennale of Graphic Arts.

KEIMEL, Hermann (Munich, 1948–)

German painter and graphic artist. Studied at the Munich Academy with Diez and Jank. Professor at the School of German Painting in Munich. Member of the Munich artistic group The Twelve, and of the New Munich Association of Poster Artists. Large graphic production.

KELLER, Ernst (Viligen, 1891–Zurich, 1968)

Swiss graphic and poster artist. Learned lithography, then in 1911 worked in a typographical studio in Leipzig. 1918: professor at the Zurich School of Applied Art. 1920–1956: professor of applied graphics. Had great influence on the younger generation of Swiss graphic artists.

KEY, JULIAN (Julian Keymolen) (Aventen, 1930–)

Belgian graphic artist. Pupil of the painter Tuyaerts; then employed at the age of 18 by the Vanypeco agency, of which he became artistic director in 1960. Made many posters and participated in several shows (Helsinki, Warsaw and Brno biennales). In 1974, became an independent graphic artist and taught at the Saint-Luc School in Brussels.

KIESER, Gunther (1930–   )

German graphic and poster artist. One of the most original of contemporary poster artists, he is known especially for his innovative use of photography for jazz and theatrical posters.

KIFFER, Charles (1902–   )

French illustrator and poster artist. Worked for the music-hall. Many posters for his friend Maurice Chevalier and for Edith Piaf (1938).

KLIMT, Gustav (Vienna, 1862–Vienna, 1918)

Austrian painter, designer and decorator. His work was influenced by the graphics of Toorop and by Japanese prints. 1897: founded and directed the Vienna Secession, which propagated Art Nouveau in Austria. Worked in Hoffman's Studio of Applied Art and executed the two ceramic figures of the Hotel Stoclet *(The Kiss, 1906–1909)*. Also painted landscapes, many portraits, symbolic figures and several posters for the Vienna Secession.

KLINGER, Julius (Vienna, 1876–1950)

Austrian painter, graphic and poster artist. Studied at the Arts and Crafts Conservatory in Vienna. From 1897, drawings in several Berlin satirical papers and many posters. Back in Vienna, he opened his own studio in 1918. With Bernhard, he is one of the most important Berlin posterists.

KLUTSIS, Gustav (Latvia, 1895–Siberia, 1944)

Soviet artist. Studied at the Riga Art Institute, then in St. Petersburg and finally with the art group Vkhutemas, with Malevich and Pevsner. In 1923, involved in the Soviet revolution, Klutsis was one of the founding members of the group October, intended to educate the masses and serve the needs of the proletariat (architecture, photography, films, posters and other media). The group was dissolved in 1932 by decree of the Communist Party; Klutsis was arrested in 1938 and died in a work-camp in 1944.

KOKOSCHKA, Oscar (Pöchlarn, 1886–1980)

Austrian painter, graphic and poster artist, and poet. Contributed to *Sturm* from 1915. 1920–1924: professor at Dresden. 1934–1938: taught at the Prague Academy, then emigrated to England. 1954: returned to Austria.

KOLLWITZ, Käthe (Königsberg, 1867–Moritzburg, 1945)

German graphic artist, painter and sculptor. She lived and worked in the working-class section of Berlin, and her work is allied with the German labor movement. Taught at the Berlin Academy, but was dismissed in 1933 when the Nazis came to power.

KONO, Takashi (Tokyo, 1906–   )

Japanese graphic and poster artist. 1929: graduated from the Tokyo National University of Fine Arts and Music. In 1961, he was named Japanese representative to the International Graphic Alliance. In charge of decoration of the Japanese pavilions at the 1964 Tokyo World's Fair. Member of the design committee for the Olympic games.

KOSEL, Hermann (1896–   )

Austrian designer and graphic artist. Studied at the Vienna Academy. Member of the Association of Viennese Artists. Honorary member of the Austrian Association of Advertising Graphic Artists, and from 1950 to 1955, vice-president of the Federation of Austrian Graphic Artists. Contributed to periodicals, including *Graphis, Commercial Art, Vendre;* awarded several prizes (Vienna, Rimini, Bibione, Venice). International exhibitions (Vienna, Paris, Warsaw, Toronto).

KOW, Alexis (Moscow, 1901–France, 1978)

French graphic artist and advertising designer of Russian origin. After the obliteration of the family fortune by the Bolshevist revolution, Kow studied at the Technical College of Arts and Crafts in Geneva. At the age of 19, he became a designer in a small car body shop of Levallois-Perret. When the firm closed he turned to advertising design for other car makes, including Panhard, Hotchkiss, Peugeot, Marchal and Delahaye.

KOZLINSKY, Vladimir (1899–1967)

Soviet graphic artist and stage designer. One of the founders of the Studio for Propaganda Posters, the Petrograd branch of the ROSTA in 1920. Illustrations for texts by Mayakovsky (1919). Contributed to many newspapers. Professor at the Moscow Institute of Industrial Art and Design.

KRAUZE, Andrzej (Dawidy Dankowe, 1947–   )

Polish graphic artist, satiric sketcher and poster artist. 1973: graduated from the Warsaw Academy of Fine Arts. Made designs for posters with M. Mrosczak. Won a first prize for a poster when still a student.

KURTZ, Helmuth (Zurich, 1877–Uerikon, 1959)

Swiss graphic artist. Many advertising posters (*Shell Mex,* 1932).

LANGE, Otto (Dresden 1879–1944)

German painter and graphic artist. A professional decorator, he later attended the School of Decorative Arts in Dresden. From 1925, taught at the National School of Textile Arts and Industries in Plauen.

LASKOFF, Franz (Bromberg, Poland, 1869–)

Painter and graphic artist. Worked for Ricordi in Milan, where he made notable posters *(Suchard)*. Later worked in Strasbourg and Paris. Nothing is known of him after 1921.

LAURENCIN, Marie (Paris 1885–1956)

French painter, engraver, sketcher and poet. While pursuing her career as a painter, made a few posters *(Bal des Petits Lits Blancs)*, worked on stage decorations *(Ballet Les Biches* by F. Poulenc), and illustrations for literary works (Gide, Lewis Carroll).

LAVINSKY, Anton (1893–1968)

Soviet graphic and poster artist. 1920: professor and director of the sculpture department of Vkhutemas. Member of Inkhuk, a group of artists concerned with the theory and definition of constructivism. Made many posters, including some ROSTA windows and a poster for the film *The Battleship Potemkin*.

LEBEDEV, Vladimir (1891–1964)

Soviet illustrator and decorator. His first drawings were published in newspapers. With Kozlinsky, he directed the Petrograd branch of the ROSTA (1920–1922). He originated a new concept of children's books.

LEFLER, Heinrich (Vienna 1863–1919)

Austrian painter and illustrator. Pupil of Griepenkerl at the Vienna Academy. From 1891, a member of the Künstlerhaus; in 1900, co-founder of the Hagenbund.

LENICA, Jan (Poznan, 1928–)

Polish graphic artist, illustrator, architect, theater decorator and poster artist. Received a degree in architecture in 1952; satiric sketcher, poster artist since 1952; worked in cinema from 1957. Member of the AGI, author of several works on poster art. Has worked in France and Germany for some years.

LEPAPE, Georges (1887–1971)

French illustrator and poster artist. Contributed in the early Twenties to the *Gazette du Bon Ton*, then to *Vogue*, and made some mannerist posters for fashion sales.

LE QUERNEC, Alain (Le Faouet, Morbihan, 1944–)

French illustrator and poster artist. Certified professor of plastic arts. Made posters for the Galeries Réunies of Metz in 1969, and a series of jazz for The 4 Cat Club. 1971: studied graphic art with Tomaszewski in Warsaw. Organized many exhibitions since 1974 (Roman Cieslewicz, Hans Hillmann, Jan Lenica...) and, up to the present, has created more than five hundred posters *(Amoclo Cadiz, Amnesty International,* the *French Socialist Party)*.

LEUPIN, Herbert (Basel, 1916–)

Swiss poster artist. Studied in Basel at the Eidenbez Studio and at Paul Colin's school in Paris. 1936: awarded 3 prizes and the silver medal at the Paris Fair. After the war, worked in collaboration with the Donald Brun Studio in Basel, then went independent. Made many posters, illustrated nine books of *Grimm's Fairy Tales*.

LHOTE, André (Bordeaux, 1885–Paris, 1962)

French painter, illustrator and art critic. Studied decorative sculpture in Bordeaux, then settled in Paris where he took an interest in African art. 1912: exhibited at the Section d'Or. Founded an academy on the Rue d'Odessa in 1922, where he played an important role as pedagogue and critic.

LICHTENSTEIN, Roy (New York, 1923–)

American painter, illustrator and poster artist. Studied at the Art Student League with Reginald Marsh (1939). 1940–1943: attended the University of Ohio; later taught there between 1949 and 1951. Between 1957 and 1960, he taught at New York University, and from 1960–1963 at Rutgers. Works and lives in New York.

LIENEMAYER, Gerhard (1936–)

German graphic and poster artists. The collaboration between Ranbow and Lienemayer began when both were students at Kassel. 1960: creation of the Ranbow and Lienemayer Studio. Michael Van de Sand joined them in 1973.

LISSITSKY, Lazar Markovich (El Lissitsky) (Potchinok, 1890–Moscow, 1941)

Soviet painter, designer and graphic artist. 1909–1914: studied architecture at the Polytechnic College of Darmstadt in Germany. 1915–1918: worked and lived in Moscow. 1925: founder, with Ehrenburg, of the periodical *Veshtch (Subject)*. Professor at the Vkhutemas and Vkhutin art schools. Designed pavilions for international expositions and created many constructivist posters. Noted for posters for Pelikan inks and carbon paper.

LIVEMONT, Privat (Schaerbeek, Belgium 1861–1936)

Belgian decorator, poster artist and illustrator. As a pupil and assistant of Lamaire, took part in the decoration of the City Hall. Collaborated for two years with J.B. Lavastre, decorator of the Paris Opera. In 1885, the two designed innovative decor for the Théâtre Français. Then worked with Duvigneaud at the Comédie Française. In Paris, he worked for several firms and decorated private houses. 1890: he opened his own shop and worked for the firm of the engineer Mors in Passy, and for Hèle and for the Maison du Blanc in Brussels. From 1895, he turned to the poster. He drew most of them on the stone himself (for exhibition of the Artistic Circle of Schaerbeek, various firms and official events).

LOUPOT, Charles (Lyon, 1892–Paris, 1962)

French illustrator and poster artist. Made his first posters in Switzerland during World War I and quickly became a master lithographer. His first works for fashion *(Canton, Grieder, PKZ)*, cigarettes *(Soto, Raga)* and automobiles *(Philopóssian)*, could be called mannerist. Called to Paris by Devambez, he contributed for a while to the *Gazette du Bon Ton*. But in 1923, the two posters he made for *Voisin* marked a turning point in his style. He brought out a series of lithographic masterpieces for the agency Les Belles Affiches which the Damour brothers founded for him: *Peugeot, Austin Tractors, Twining's Tea, Martin's coffee, Mirus stoves* . . . He invented trademark characters that made him famous: the Valentine man, the new Cointreau man and worked on Nectar, the figure of Nicolas. 1930: co-founder, with Cassandre and Maurice Moyrand, a young printer from the north, of the Alliance Graphique studio. Worked with the industrialist Eugène Schueller, using the airbrush *(Dop, Monsavon, Coty* . . .*).* In 1937, redesigned the two St. Raphael men, which were revealed that year at the Paris Exposition. Loupot's work is distinguished by its lithographic qualities and its purity of style.

McKNIGHT-KAUFFER, E. (Edward Kauffer) (Great Falls, 1891–New York 1951)

Poster artist, illustrator and theater decorator of American origin. Studied painting in the United States. Settled in England in 1914 and made a name for himself with a 1915 poster for the *Underground Railway Co.* In 1921, he gave up painting and devoted himself to advertising *(London Transport Board, Shell-Mex, B.P. Ltd., Great Western Railway, The Orient Line* . . . .*).* Also illustrated several books: *Don Quixote* (1930); *Triumphal March* by T.S. Eliot (1931); and *Venus Rising from the Sea* by E.A. Bennett (1931). Member of the Council for Art and Industry. Considered the best poster designer in England between the two World Wars. Returned to U.S. in 1939.

MAMBOUR, Auguste (Liège, 1896–1968)

Belgian painter and lithographer. Studied at the Liège Fine Arts Academy, where he taught in 1931. 1923: Rome prize for painting. From 1929 to 1931, he contributed to the review of Fabrique Nationale and designed posters and models for Renaud and Tisserand. In 1938, he made a mural for the Léonie de Waha School in Liège.

MANGOLD, Burkhard (Basel, 1878–1936)

Swiss painter, glass etcher and posterist. Pupil of Böcklin, Hans Sandreuter, he produced some beautiful posters *(Winter in Davos).* As an artist of major stature, he is regarded as one of the pioneers of the Swiss poster.

MARFURT, Léo (Aarau, 1894–Antwerp, 1977)

Designer and poster artist of Swiss origin. Studied at the Aarau School of Arts and Crafts; printing apprenticeship from 1910 to 1914. In Basel he became an assistant to he Belgian artist Jules de Praetere at the advertising workshop he had founded. During that time, he also atended classes in graphics and painting at the Geneva School of Fine Arts. In 1921, he followed De Praetere to Belgium, where from 1923 he was sought by various firms: *Vander Elst Tobaccos, Chrysler, Minerva* . . . From 1927 to 1957, he directed his own Brussels agency Les Creation Publicitaires. From 1953, he taught at the Plantin Institute of Typographic Studies in Antwerp.

MARTY, André Edouard (Paris, 1882–)

French engraver, illustrator and theater decorator. Studied in Cormon's class at the Paris Ecole des Beaux Arts. Contributor to various magazines: *La Gazette du Bon Ton, Le Sourire, Vogue.* Illustrated Alphonse Daudet's *Lettres de Mon Moulin*, M. Maeterlinck's *L'Oiseau Bleu*, and an anthology of A. de Musset. Posters for the *Ballets Russes* at the Paris Opera in 1910, and for the *Grand Nom* by N. Léon and Léo Feld, a play for which he also designed the costumes and sets.

MATALONI, Giovanni

Italian lithographer and poster artist. Lithographer at Ricordi from 1890, he attained prominence with his *Brevetto Auer* poster of 1895, and became the first Italian poster specialist.

MATTER, Herbert (Engelberg, 1907–Springs, N.Y., 1984)

Swiss graphic artist, designer and poster artist. 1923–1925: studied at the Ecole des Beaux-Arts in Paris with Léger and Ozenfant. Was interested in photography and influenced by Cassandre. Worked at the Deberny and Peignot agencies. Contributed to *Vogue.* 1930: returned to Switzerland, producing many posters. Since 1935 has had his own studio in New York where he worked for *Harper's Bazaar, Ladies Home Journal, Life*, Knoll Associates. Professor at Yale University.

MAUZAN, Achille Lucien (Gap, 1883–1952)

French poster artist. At 22, left for Italy where he had immense success *(Moretti* raincoats, *La Borsa*, series for *Isota Fraschini* and *Ciprie* perfumes). Founder of *Clamor* agency. Well known, also, for a series of posters for French and Italian silent films. Later his career took him to Buenos Aires, where he made posters for *Firestone* and *Agua Colonia Giret.* In 1933, he returned to Paris *(Brummel, Cusenier* . . .*)*

MAVIGNIER, Almir (1925–)

Brazilian graphic and poster artist. His graphically

avant-garde posters have contributed as much to the new face of Brasilia as its works of sculpture and architecture. Invited to hold important posts in the graphic field in Ulm and Hamburg.

MAY, Philipp (Wortley, 1964–London, 1903)

Self-made caricaturist and poster artist. 1885: poster for *The Private Secretary;* 1885–86: drawings for the *Sydney Bulletin* in Australia. Famous for his caricatures, he contributed to various satiric magazines such as *Punch.* 1896: published *Sketchbook* and *Guttersnipes.* 1897: *Alphabet.* 1898: *Green ou Rougemont* and *The Little Minister Souvenir.* Posthumously, *Sketches from Punch, A Phil May Picture Book* and *A Phil May Medley.*

MAYAKOVSKY, Vladimir (Bagdadi, 1893–Moscow, 1930)

Russian and Soviet poet and graphic artist. Studied at the Moscow Academy of Fine Arts. 1912: with Bulyuk, Krutchonik and Khlebnikov, publication of a manifesto on Russian futurism: "A Slap to the Public Taste." Much involved in the revolution, he became a poet of propaganda, author of political posters (ROSTA) and slogans, and an early Soviet film maker. Disappointed by the slow progress of the Russian revolution, exhausted by personal difficulties and the hostility of certain literary and political circles, he committed suicide in 1930.

METLICOVITZ, Leopoldo (Trieste, 1868–Pontelambro, 1944)

Italian painter and poster artist. Having worked at Ricordi since 1892, he became a full-fledged posterist in 1896 with designs such as *Distillerie Italiane.* Awarded prizes at many competitions, notably at the Milan International Exposition of 1906 for his poster for the inauguration of the Simplon tunnel.

MEUNIER, Georges (Paris, 1869–Saint-Cloud, 1934)

French painter, illustrator and poster artist. Pupil of Bouguereau and of J. Robert Fleury at the Ecole Nationale des Beaux-Arts. Also studied at the School of Decorative Arts. Took part in the exhibition of the Salon of the Society of French Artists, and from 1909 to 1913 showed his works at the Salon des Humoristes. Much influenced by Chéret, he worked for the Chaix printing house: *Almanach du Parisien pour 1895; Paris Almanach 1896; C'est ça l'amour* by Richard O. Monroy, 1901; and *Les Fêtards de Paris* by P. Decourcelles, 1902.

MEUNIER, Henri (Brussels, 1873–1922)

Belgian engraver, lithographer, posterist and painter. Debut in 1890 with engravings at the Salon de Mons. From 1897, participated in the Sillon exhibitions. Considered one of the best Belgian poster artists. His best posters were those for orchestral concerts, concerts of the Eugène Ysayes quartet, as well as *Rajah* coffee and *Cartes Postales Dietrich.* Designed postcards and Ex-libris; contributed to the magazine *Le Petit Bleu.*

MICHEL, Hans (1920–   )

German poster and graphic artist.

MIGNOT, Victor (Brussels, 1872–Paris, 1944)

Belgian painter, engraver, illustrator and poster artist. After contributing drawings to the sport journal *Le Cyclist Belge,* he made a poster for the shadow play theater *Le Cénacle* in 1895, and a year later was awarded a prize.

MLODOZENIEC, Jan (Warsaw, 1929–   )

Polish illustrator, graphic artist, satiric illustrator and poster artist. Graduated from the Warsaw Fine Arts Academy. Member of the International Graphic Alliance.

MOLKENBOER, Theodorus (Leeuwarden, 1871–Lugano, 1920)

Dutch painter and decorator. Studied at the Rijksnormaal-School Voor Tekenonderwijs and at Rijks Académie van Beeldende Kunsten in Amsterdam. Worked with the architect H.P.J. Cuypers and the painters G.W. Dijsselhof and A.J. Derkinderen. Illustrator of books and director of the Henrick de Keyser School in Amsterdam.

MONNERAT, Pierre (Paris, 1917–   )

Graphic artist of French origin. Worked chiefly in Switzerland. Best known for advertising posters *(Cinzano)* whose major element is the lettering.

MOOR, Dimitri (Novocherkask, 1883–Moscow, 1946)

Soviet poster artist and illustrator. 1910–1917: studied at the P. Keline Studio and contributed to the magazine *Boudilnik.* He was one of the creators of the political poster. Made ROSTA "windows." Specialized in political satire and illustrated newspapers *(Izvestia, Pravda,* the journal *Krasnoarmeyets).* One of the founders of the humor magazine *Krokodil.* 1928: artistic director of the magazine *Bezbojnik.* Participated in various exhibitions: Decorative Arts in Paris; Revolutionary Posters in Berlin; Graphic Arts, Posters and Books in Danzig. Member of the group October. 1922–30: professor at the Vukhutemas in Moscow.

MORACH, Otto (Solothurn, 1887–Zurich, 1973)

Swiss painter, decorator, and poster artist. Studied mathematics at first at the University of Bern. 1909–1914: studied painting in Paris, Munich, Dresden and Berlin. 1914–1918: taught and painted at Solothurn. 1919–1953: professor of painting at the School of Applied Arts in Zurich. From 1953, independent painter in Zurich, working in different fields of applied art (stained glass, mosaics, panels, murals, etc. . . . .). 1918–1922: member of the group New Life in Basel with Arp, Janko and Picabia . . . Worked with Oskar Schlemmer in his studio at the Bauhaus. Pioneer of the Swiss marionette theatre, together with Sophie Tauber-Arp.

MORVAN, Hervé (1917–1980)

French poster artist. After having chiefly devoted himself to cinema posters, Morvan turned to advertising and made many posters for *Gitanes* cigarettes, *Kelton* watches, *Alsacienne* biscuits, *Gévéor* wine, the exhibitions *Salon de l'Auto* and *Salon de l'Enfance*, and the fairs of Paris and Lyon.

MOSCOSO, Victor (1936–)

American painter, graphic and poster artist. Studied at Cooper Union, then at Yale and, in the early Sixties, at the San Francisco Institute. Worked for a while in advertising graphics, then joined the psychedelic movement and made posters for the *Family Dog*.

MOSER, Koloman (Vienna, 1868–1918)

Austrian decorator, painter and poster artist. Studied in Vienna. From 1896, member of the Kunstlerhaus. In 1897, founding member of the Secession. 1899–1900: taught at the Vienna School of Art. 1903: co-founder of the Viennese Studio. Member of Klimt's group in 1905.

MROSZCZAK, Martin (Nowy Targ, 1910–Warsaw, 1975)

Polish graphic and poster artist. Studied in Cracow from 1930 to 1933 and in Vienna from 1934 to 1936. Since 1950, professor at the Warsaw School of Fine Arts. Member of AGI and president of the International Poster Biennale from 1906 to 1975.

MUCHA, Alphonse (Ivančice, Moravia, 1860–Prague, 1939)

Czech painter, designer, lithographer, and posterist. From 1885 to 1887, studied at the Munich Fine Arts Academy under Ludwig von Löfftz and Johan Caspar Herterich, then until 1889 at the Académie Julian in Paris with Jules Lefebvre, Jean Paul Laurens and Gustave Boulanger. His encounter with Sarah Bernhardt determined his career. From 1894 (*Gismonda*) to 1903, he designed all the great actress' posters, the decor and costumes for her plays. He signed an exclusive contract with the Champenois printing house (posters, calendars, menu-cards, newspaper heads, decorative panels, among them the famous *Seasons* in 1896 and *Flowers* in 1897). 1898: opened a painting school, Académie Carmen, together with James Whistler. He quickly became one of the chief exponents of Art Nouveau and attained wide renown, exercising his talent in many fields: stained glass (for Champigneulle in Paris), tapestries, jewels, (for Sarah Bernhardt, executed by the jeweler Fouquet) and

many posters (*Job, Nestlé, Lefevre-Utile, Bénédictine.*). In 1904, he made the first of his six trips to the US where he worked as a decorator (such as for the Deutsches Theater in New York in 1908), poster artist (*The Maid of Orleans*) and portrait painter. In 1912, he returned to his native country to devote himself to what he hoped to be his life's work. "The Slav Epic", a cycle of vast paintings of his country's history. After 1918, he designed stamps, banknotes and police uniforms for the Czechoslovakian Republic. Many exhibitions, in France, England, America, Japan and Czechoslovakia, have attested to the value of his works.

MÜLLER-BROCKMANN, Josef (Rapperswil, 1914–)

Swiss graphic artist. Professor at the Kunstgewerbeschule of Zurich since 1957. Founder and co-editor (in 1954) of *Neue Graphik*, a journal in three languages. One of the most important and influential graphic artists.

NAGAI, Kazumasa (Osaka, 1929–)

Japanese poster and graphic artist. Director of the Japanese Design Center. Awarded the silver medal and four bronze medals at the Tokyo A.D.C.; gold and silver medals at the International Poster Biennale in Warsaw; and the AJAP and Mainichi prizes for industrial design.

NAKAMURA, Makato (Marioka, 1926–)

Head of advertising for the Shiseido company. AJAP price (1953 and 1964); gold medal of the Tokyo ADC (1964); Members Prize of the Tokyo ADC (1973); gold medal (advertising section) at the Warsaw Poster Biennale.

NATHAN-GARAMOND, Jacques (Paris, 1910–)

French graphic artist, decorator and poster artist. Studied at the School of Industrial Applied Arts and at the School of Decorative Arts. Assistant to Paul Brandt (interior decoration and jewelry). From 1931 to 1933, contributed to *Architecture d'Aujourd'hui*, then made posters for the Salon des Arts Ménagers and the Home Design Exposition (1934). Participated in the decoration of the advertising pavilion at the Paris International Exposition in 1937. Since 1945, active in advertising (*Mazda* Lightbulbs, *SNCF*).

NEUBURG, Hans (Grulich, 1904–Zurich, 1983)

Swiss painter, graphic artist and publicist. Many posters, among them *Telefon Rundspruch, Super Bouillon Liebig*.

NEUMANN, Ernst (Kassel, 1871–Düren, 1954)

German painter and illustrator. Studied in Kassel, Paris and Munich. Contributed to various journals such as *Jugend* and *Simplicissimus*. 1901–1902: artistic director for the cabaret The 11 Henchmen, using the name of the hangman Caspar Beil. 1912: member of the Werkbund.

NEWBOULD, Frank (Bradford, 1887–1950)
English poster artist. Studied at the Bradford Art School while working for a printer. In 1919, settled in London and worked as a poster artist for the *Empire Marketing Board*, the *Great Western Railway*, and the *Orient Line*, among others.

NITSCHE, Erik (Lausanne, 1908–   )
Swiss graphic artist. Known for his series of 12 posters, published in 9 languages, for two international conferences "Atoms for Peace" held in Geneva in 1955 and 1958. In 1958 and 1960, he designed the Exploration of the Universe series for the same American client, General Dynamics.

O'GALOP (Marius Rossillon) (Lyon, 1867–Carnac, 1946)
French illustrator and watercolorist. Contributed to *Rire* and to *L'Assiette au Beurre.* Creator of the famous Michelin tire man. Poster for the comic opera *La Tortue.* O'Galop was one of the most important personalities of Montmartre before 1914.

OGE, Eugène (Born in Paris, dates unknown)
French designer and lithographer. Designer-in-chief of the Charles Verneau printing house, he attained renown with his first signed poster *L'Exposition du Livre.* Also made decorative panels. Exhibited at the Salon of the Society of French Artists.

ORAZI, Emmanuel Joseph Raphaël (Rome, 1860–Paris, 1934)
Painter and illustrator. Specialist in exotic themes. Contributed to various magazines: *Paris Noël* (1892), *Figaro Illustré* (1896 and 1900), *L'Assiette au Beurre* (1903). Produced some illustrations for books and many posters, including one for Sarah Bernhardt in *Theodora,* and one for *Loie Fuller.* Designed jewelry for La Maison Moderne, the renowned Paris Art Nouveau jeweler.

PAL (Jean de Paléologue) (Bucharest, 1860–Miami, 1942)
Rumanian painter and poster artist. After serving in the Rumanian army, he settled in London where he created drawings for *The New York Herald, Strand Magazine* and *Vanity Fair.* In 1893, he moved to Paris, and contributed to such magazines as *La Plume, Le Rire, Cocorico, Frou-Frou, Sans Gene* and *La Vie en Rose;* he illustrated

PALKA, Julian (Poznan, 1923–   )
Polish graphic and poster artist. 1951: graduated from the Warsaw Academy of Art. From 1950, worked in the field of poster design and organized graphic exhibitions. Member of AGI. At present, vice-chancellor of the Warsaw Academy of Arts.

Les Petits Poemes Russes. He produced a number of fine posters, invariably featuring luscious females, such as those for *Cabourg* (1893), *Rayon d'Or* (1895) or *Clément* bicycles. In 1900 he moved to the United States.

PARRISH, Maxfield (Philadelphia, 1870–Plainfield, New Hampshire, 1966)
American portraitist, landscape artist, illustrator and poster artist. Son of the painter and engraver Stephen Parrish, Maxfield Parrish studied drawing at the Pennsylvania Academy in Philadelphia and at the Drexel Institute in Howard Pyle's Studio. Illustrations for *Scribner's* magazine and for children's books. Member of the National Academy of Design from 1908. Participated in the Pan American Exposition in Buffalo in 1901.

PAUL, Bruno (Seifhennersdorf, 1874–Berlin, 1968)
German architect, decorator, painter and designer. One of the most influential representatives of the Jugendstil in Munich, and one of the founders of the United Studios for Arts and Crafts in 1897 in Munich. Directed the School of the Museum of Decorative Arts in Berlin in 1907, then the National School of Liberal and Applied Arts from 1924 to 1932.

PENFIELD, Edward (Brooklyn, N.Y., 1866–Beacon, N.Y., 1925)
American poster artist, illustrator, lithographer, decorative painter. Pupil of G. du Forest Brush. From 1891 to 1901, artistic director of the publishing firm Harper and Brothers in New York. From 1893 to 1899, he devoted himself exclusively to *Harper's,* for which he made posters announcing each monthly issue, as well as posters for other Harper books, including *Three gringos in Central America and Venezuela* by Richard Harding Davis and *On Snow Shoes to the Barren Grounds* by Caspar Whitney. In 1901, worked for *Collier's* magazine, illustrated many articles and decorated Randolph Hall at the Rochester Country Club. Together with Louis Rhead and Will Bradley, Penfield is one of the most famous American poster artists.

PESKE, Jean Miscelas (Yalta, 1880–Le Mans, 1949)
Naturalized French painter, engraver and lithographer. Studied at the Académie Julian. Participated in various exhibitions, such as Salon de la Société Nationale des Beaux-Arts, Salon d'Automne, Salon des Indépendants, Salon des Tuileries and Salon des Peintres-Graveurs. His painting was influenced by Pissaro. 1950: retrospective exhibition at the Salon des Indépendants.

PETZOLD, Willy (Mainz, 1885–   )
German graphic artist, poster artist and painter on glass. Lived in Dresden. His most important posters were published between 1920 and 1930.

PIATTI, Celestino (Wangen, 1922–)

Swiss painter and graphic artist. Prolific Swiss arist; created over one hundred posters since he opened his studio in Basel in 1948, and illustrated many children's books. Also a printmaker. Best known to Germans and Swiss for the hundreds of book covers he has designed for DTV, the paperback publishing firm of Munich.

PINTORI, Giovanni (Sardinia, 1912–)

Italian graphic and poster artist. Studied in Monza in 1930. In 1936, he joined the advertising department at Olivetti, which he directed until 1950. His series of calendars by different artists is justly famous. He left Olivetti in 1968 to open his own studio in Milan. An exhibition was devoted to his works in Milan in 1981.

PRUSAKOV, Boris (1900–1952)

Soviet painter and poster artist. 1911–1918: studied at the Stroganov School in Moscow, then at the Vkhutemas. Participated in the exhibitions of Obmekhu (young constructivist artists), and between 1925 and 1935 made many posters.

PURVIS, Tom (Bristol, 1888–1959)

English poster artist. Studied at the Camberwell School of Art, then worked at an advertising agency for 6 years before striking out on his own with *Dewar's Whiskey.* Regularly commissioned by *Bovril, London and North Eastern Railways, Shell-Mex, B.P., Austin Reed . . .* Vice president of the Royal Society of Art. Official poster artist during the Second World War.

RAMINSKI, Tomasz (Zwierzyniec Lubelski, 1930–)

Polish graphic artist and theater decorator. 1956: graduated from the Poznan College of Art.

RANBOW, Günther

German graphic designer. Co-founder of an advertising studio with Gerhard Lienemayer (q.v.). Since 1974, Ranbow has taught graphic arts and photography at the University of Kassel.

RAND, Paul (New York, 1914–)

American graphic artist and designer. At 23, artistic director of *Esquire.* At 32, he published his famous book *Thoughts on Design,* a veritable bible for the graphic artist. From 1956, he was much in demand as a designer by *IBM, Westinghouse* and *Cummins Engine Co.* Created logos for *IBM, UPS* and *ABC Television.* Professor at Cooper Union, Pratt Institute and Yale University.

REED, Ethel (Newburyport, Mass., 1876–)

American painter, illustrator, designer, caricaturist, poster artist. From the age of 18, she was known for her book illustrations, and soon after, for her posters. She drew groups of children in the Kate Greenaway tradition, illustrated the stories of Louise Chandler-Moulton,

published a series of clowns influenced by Willette, and contributed to the English magazine *Punch.* In 1895, one of her most interesting posters appeared, for Gertrude Smith's book *The Arabella and Aramina Stories,* which she had also illustrated. She then worked for the publisher Lawson, Wolffe and Company.

RHEAD, Louis John (Staffordshire, England, 1857–Amityville, N.Y., 1926)

Illustrator and poster artist of English origin. Studied at the South Kensington School, and in Paris with Boulanger. Made his first posters in England, for *Cassell's Magazine, The Weekly Dispatch* and *Phitesi* boots. In 1883, he moved to the United States where he contributed to various publications: *The New York Sun, The Journal, Scribner's, The Century* and *The Boston Transcript.* He also produced illustrations for the Appleton Company, and posters for *Century, Harper's* and *St. Nicholas* magazines. Between 1891 and 1894 he continued his studies in London and Paris, where Grasset's style strongly influenced him. After 1900, he devoted himself to illustrating literary works and wrote several books on fishing.

RICHEZ, Jacques (Dieppe, 1913–)

Belgian graphic artist. Studied at the Royal Academy of Fine Arts in Mons. Free-lance graphic artist since 1944. Author of many posters, notably for the Théâtre de Poche and, in 1958, for the Brussels Exposition. In 1969, he designed the graphics for the International Fair of Kinshasa, Zaire. In charge of seminars at the Technical School of Advertising in Brussels.

RIQUER, Alexandre de (Calaf, Spain, 1856–Mallorca, 1920)

Spanish landscape painter, writer, illustrator and poster artist. Much influenced by the works of Mucha and Grasset. A talented dilettante, he traveled in France, England and Italy, published his childhood memories which he illustrated himself, and worked with stained glass and frescos for the monastery of Montserrat. His posters for *Granja Avicola de San Luis* and for an exhibition of the *Circol de Sant Lluch* in Barcelona assured his reputation as a poster artist.

ROBBE, Manuel (Paris, 1872–Paris, 1936)

French painter and graphic artist. A specialist in Parisian scenes of the Belle Epoque; his first works were published by Sagot, then by Pierrefort. After the First World War, he devoted himself entirely to print-making, and signed his work with the name Lafitte.

RODCHENKO, Alexander (St. Petersburg, 1891–Moscow, 1956)

Soviet artist. 1907–1914: studied at the Kazan Art School with N. Fechine, then at the Moscow Stroganov Institute.

In 1920, he organized and participated in the exhibition at the 3rd Congress of the Komintern. In 1925, he participated in the International Exposition of Art and Industry in Paris. *The Workers' Club*, designed by him and exhibited in Paris, was given to the French Communist Party. He produced some of the "ROSTA Windows" and worked for the Soviet cinema as posterist.

ROECK, Lucien de (Termonde, 1915–   )

Belgian graphic artist and watercolorist. Graduated from the National College of Architecture and Decorative Arts (La Cambre) in 1935. Worked on various publications after 1945, doing layout and illustrations: *La Lanterne, Phare Dimanche, La Cité.* In 1954, he designed the star which served as the emblem of the Brussels Exposition of 1958. From 1958, taught typography and book arts.

ROHONYI, Charles (Budapest, 1906–   )

Graphic artist of Hungarian origin. Begun as an assistant in the Hungarian film studios, then as photographer and reporter before turning to the poster in 1936. He designed at first political posters, then book covers, display decor, prospectuses, mural paintings, etc. In 1948, he settled in Belgium. In 1950, his poster for *Remy Macaroni* made his reputation. Co-founder of the Belgian Chamber of Graphic artists in 1963, in charge of seminars at the Brussels School of Advertising, and contributor to the German periodical *Novum*.

ROLAND-HOLST, Richard (Amsterdam, 1868–Bloemendaal, 1938)

Dutch painter, graphic artist and author. Exponent of Art Nouveau, organizer of the first Van Gogh exhibition in Holland, in Amsterdam in 1892. Later, made many lithographic posters, mural paintings and stained-glass windows. Professor and director at the Royal Academy in Amsterdam.

ROUBILLE, Auguste Jean Baptiste (Paris, 1872–1955)

French painter, designer, and comic illustrator. From 1897, contributed to various periodicals: *Le Courrier Français, Le Rire, Le Sourire, La Vie Parisienne, Cocorico.* Illustrated the works of Claude Farrère, Pierre Loti and Colette. With Sem, he created decorative panels, made dioramas and posters, and took part in many exhibitions *(Salon des Humoristes, Salon des Indépendants,* and *Union de l'Affiche Française).*

SANDECKA, Stanislava (1910–   )

Polish graphic and poster artist. Studied architecture in Warsaw. Co-founder, with Nowicki, of a studio of art graphics. Awarded an honorary diploma at the International Exposition of Art and Technology in Paris in 1937. After the War, active in architecture in the United States.

SATOMI, Munetsugu (1902–   )

Japanese poster artist. Arrived in Paris in 1922 and worked for *Les 6 Jours, K.L.M.,* and Japanese companies.

SAVIGNAC, Raymond (Paris, 1907–   )

French designer of posters, stage decorations and costumes. Studied at the Lavoisier School until 1945, then worked as a designer at the Compagnie des Transports Parisiens, while taking night classes in industrial design. His first poster, *Maria Grimal,* was published by Alliance Graphique. Collaborated with Cassandre until 1938. In 1940, met advertising agent Robert Guerin and worked under his guidance. Gave a boost to his career by exhibiting with Villemot in 1949. Traveled to the United States, then opened a studio in Paris. Made many posters *(Monsavon, Dunlap, Teafl, Cinzano . . .).* Worked on theater decorations and costumes for the Comédie Française in 1969.

SCHAWINSKY, Xanti (Basel, 1904–   )

Italian painter and graphic artist. Studied painting and architecture in Zurich, Cologne, Berlin; in 1929, worked at the Bauhaus in Weimar. During 1928, he traveled in France and Italy with Bayer and Breuer. Worked for the Boggeri studio, Olivetti, Motta, Italia Cosulich, for the journal *Natura, San Pellegrino.* In 1936, he left for the U.S. at Albers' invitation, and taught at Black Mountain College in North Carolina. Continued his collaboration with Gropius and Breuer. Between 1939 and 1944, taught design at the City College of New York. From 1960, devoted himself to painting. 1974: one-artist show at the Gallery of Modern Art in Bologna.

SCHEURICH, Paul (New York, 1883–Brandenburg, East Germany, 1945)

German painter, sculptor, graphic artist, illustrator, decorator and poster artist. Studied at the Berlin Academy. One of the best-known Berlin poster artists before 1914. Later, created models for porcelain figures for various manufacturers, including Meissen. Also did book illustrations.

SCHLEIFER, Fritz

German designer and architect. Studied at the Bauhaus in Weimar. Made a touchstone poster for a Bauhaus exhibition in 1923.

SCHLEMMER, Oskar (Stuttgart, 1888–Baden-Baden, 1943)

German painter and sculptor. Studied in Stuttgart; then taught sculpture and stage design at the Bauhaus. His poster for his *Triadic Ballet* is an illustration of his very personal approach to design. He left the Bauhaus in 1929. Persecuted by the Nazis, he nevertheless remained in Germany and died in poverty and isolation.

SCHMIDT, Joost (1893–1948)

German graphic and poster artist. Studied at the Weimar Academy. In 1925, director of the sculpture department and professor of typography at the Bauhaus in Dessau, then succeeded Herbert Bayer as the head of commercial typography. Under his direction, and with Bayer and Moholy-Nagy, the Bauhaus typography, influenced by the Jugendstil and expressionism, moved toward a functional esthetic.

SCHNACKENBERG, Walter (Lauterberg, 1880–Degendorf, 1961)

German painter designer, illustrator and theater decorator. Studied at Knorr's School of Painting in Munich (1889–1904). 1907: studied with Stuck at the Munich Academy. 1908–1909: residence in Paris. 1911: member of the Luitpold group in Munich. Contributed to the *Jugend* magazine and made many fine posters.

SCHUITEMA, G. Paul H. (Groningen, 1897–)

Dutch graphic artist, photographer and builder. Studies at the Beeldende Kunsten Academy in Amsterdam. One of the champions of pure typography in the Thirties. Also active in interior architecture, furniture design, as well as photomontage and publicity films.

SCHWABE, Carlos (Altona, 1866–Davon, 1926)

Painter, designer and illustrator. Childhood and adolescence in Switzerland where he was the pupil of the painter Joseph Mittey. From 1884, he worked as a painter and decorator in Paris. In 1892, he designed a poster for an exhibition *Salon Rosecroix* at the Galerie Durand Ruel. Best known for his many book illustrations, Baudelaire's *Fleurs du Mal, L'Evangile de l'Enfance de N.S. Jesus Christ, Selon Saint Pierre, Hesperus* by Catulle Mendes, *La Vie des Abeilles* by M. Maeterlink, and others.

SCHWITTERS, Kurt (Hanover, 1887–Ambleside, England, 1948)

German painter, sculptor, poster artist and poet. Studied at the Dresden and Berlin Academies and at the Technical College of Hanover. In 1918, he produced a series of posters for the journal *Merz*, collages in the Dadaist spirit, which became very widely known. At his own agency, he made posters and advertisements for many clients, such as the City of Hanover. In 1929, he worked under Gropius as a typographer for the Dammerstock exhibition at Karlsruhe. In 1937, he left Nazi Germany for Oslo, then when Norway was invaded, he fled to Scotland. Spent his last years in England.

SECHE (Joseph Sechehaye) (Cologne, 1880–Seefeld, 1948)

German painter and graphic artist. Studied architecture in Stuttgart and at the Munich Academy with Habermann and Stuck. Professor at the Reimann School in Berlin. Very large graphic production.

SEPO (Severo Pozzati) (Comacchio, 1895–)

Poster artist of Italian origin. Studied at the Bologna Academy of Fine Arts. Began painting in 1914, befriended Baccheli, De Pisis, and Govoni. In 1917, worked in advertising, notably for the Maga agency in Bologna. Arrived in Paris in 1920, and from 1923 used the pseudonym Sepo. He designed many advertising posters and his style, at first reminiscent of Cappiello, later tended towards geometrism. In 1957, he returned to Bologna and recommenced painting.

SHAHN, Ben (Lithuania, 1898–New York, 1969)

American painter and graphic artist. Emigrated to the United States in 1906, and learned lithography by 1911. Studied biology at New York University, which he abandoned to study at the Art Students design League; in 1925, studied in Paris at La Grande Chaumière studio. Returning to the U.S. in 1929, he discovered photography with Walter Evans, and, a little later, the silk screen process. Magazine illustrations and advertisements followed. Professor at the Universities of Colorado and Wisconsin. Named one of the 10 best American painters by *Look* magazine in 1948.

STAROWIEVSKI, Franciszek (Cracow, 1930–)

Polish painter, designer, graphic artist, theater decorator and poster artist. Graduated from the Warsaw Fine Arts Academy in 1955.

STEINLEN, Theophile Alexandre (Lausanne, 1859–Paris, 1923)

French designer, graphic artist and painter of Swiss origin. His philosophic and literary studies at the College of Lausanne incontestably influenced his graphic production: note for example his designs for Emile Zola's book *L'Assommoir*. From 1879 to 1881, he designed for the textile industry and painted porcelains based on his grandfather's watercolors (Mulhouse). Since 1901, he has been recognized as the chronicler of Montmartre. At the Chat Noir he met Verlaine, Toulouse-Lautrec, Vallotton and Forain, and from 1883 to 1895 he was an illustrator for the *Chat Noir* publication. In 1885, he painted the large mural "The Apotheosis of Cats" for the entrance to the cabaret. He made another similar mural in 1905 for the Taverne de Paris. He also worked for the Mirliton, Aristide Bruant's cabaret and newspaper, where he drew under the pseudonym Caillou. Much concerned with social problems of his day, he used another pseudonym,

Petit Pierre, under which he contributed to the socialist newspaper *Le Chambard*. His dissident drawings also appeared in *Gil Blas Illustré, L'Echo de Paris,* and *L'Assiette au Beurre,* and made him as famous as did his drawings of cats. He also illustrated Maupassant's *The Vagabond* and Richepin's *Chanson des Gueux* with original lithographs. Together with Albert Langen, he founded the journal *Simplicissimus* in Munich in 1894. During the First World War, he made propaganda posters at the request of the French government. In 1918, he published a book, *La Guerre*. Near the end of his life he worked with Diaghilev on the *Ballets Russes* and with Jean Börlin on the *Swedish Ballet.* With Toulouse-Lautrec, Steinlen is one of those artists whose poster production passed far beyond the French frontiers.

STEINBERG, Saul (Rumania, 1914–)

American painter and graphic artist. Studied philosophy and literature at the University of Bucharest, then studied architecture in Milan (graduated in 1940). 1942: enlisted in the American Marines; 1943: became an American citizen. War correspondent for *The New Yorker,* for which he made many covers and illustrations. Executed mural paintings for the Plaza Hotel in 1967, and for the American pavilion at the Brussels Exposition in 1958; also worked on opera decors and many cultural posters.

STENBERG BROTHERS: Vladimir Stenberg (Moscow, 1899–1982); Georgij Stenberg (Moscow, 1900–1933)

Soviet decorators and poster artists. 1912–1917: studied at the Stroganov School in Moscow, then at Svomas. 1922–1931: decors for the Kamenny Theater, then completion of the ornamentation of the Red Square, which they began in 1928. Numerous set designs, notably for *St. Joan* by Bernard Shaw, *The Hairy Ape* and *Desire Under the Elms* by Eugene O'Neill, and *The Threepenny Opera* by Brecht, as well as some 300 cinema posters. In 1925, they organized the first exhibition of film posters at the Kamenny.

STOECKLIN, Niklaus (Basel, 1896–)

Swiss graphic and poster artist. Pupil of Burkhard Mangold and of Heinrich Müller. He is the representative artist of Swiss New Objectivity. As a graphic artist, he is the major personality of the Basel School. 1958: artistic prize of the City of Basel. Between 1920 and 1960, made around 110 large-sized posters.

STUCK, Franz von (Teltenweiss, 1863–Tetshen, 1928)

German painter, graphic artist, architect and sculptor. Studied at the School of Decorative Arts and at the Munich Academy. Pupil of Lindenschmidt. Contributor to the art magazine *Jugend,* co-founder of the Munich Secession in 1893. Later, professor at the Munich Academy.

SUTTERLIN, Ludwig (Lahr, Baden, 1865–Berlin, 1917)

German painter, artisan and designer. Artistic studies in Berlin. He created various posters and was also active in leatherwork.

SWIERZY, Waldemar (Katowice, 1931–)

Polish graphic artist, illustrator, theater decorator and poster artist. 1952: graduated from the Katowice Academy of Art. Devoted himself to posters after 1950. Member of the AGI. Head of faculty at the College of Plastic Arts of Poznan. Best known for striking cinema, circus and concert posters.

TANAKA, Ikko (Nara, 1930–)

Japanese poster and graphic artist. Projects for the International Exposition of 1970 and for the Oceanographic Exposition in Okinawa in 1975. Awarded many prizes: AJAP prize, prize of the Warsaw Biennale, ADC, Mainichi prize for industrial design.

TAYLOR, Fred (London, 1875–Camberley, 1963)

English poster artist and illustrator. Member of the Royal Institute of Watercolorists. Posters for the *London and North Eastern Railway Company,* decorative panels for *Lloyds.* Illustrations for Arthur Ransow's *Bohemia in London* in 1907.

TERZI, Aleardo (Palermo, 1870–Castelletto, Ticino, 1943)

Italian designer, illustrator, poster artist and painter. Worked successively in Rome, Milan and London, as magazine illustrator: *La Lettura, Rapidista, Ars et Labor,* and *Novissima;* and as a poster artist for Chapuis and Ricordi. As a painter, he belongs to the Rumanian Secession (1913–1916). From 1925 to 1930, he directed the Institute del Libro in Urbino.

TESTA, Armando (1917–)

Italian graphic and poster artist. Notable for his advertisements for the *Pirelli* tire company.

THIRIET, Henri

French posterist. His life is not known to us, but he created several memorable posters, including *Cycles Omega (1895), Absinthe Berthelot (1895), Le Blanc à la Place Clichy (1898).*

THORN-PRIKKER, Johan (The Hague, 1868–Cologne, 1932)

Dutch painter and decorator. Studied at the Academic Van Beeldende Kunsten in The Hague. Designed and made stained-glass windows, mosaics, and mural panels. All his work is very representative of Dutch Art Nouveau. Dean of studies at various schools in Krefeld, Essen, Munich, Düsseldorf and Cologne.

TOMASZEWSKI, Henrik (Warsaw, 1914–)

Polish decorator, graphic and poster artist. 1934–1939: studied in Warsaw at the School of Industrial Graphics and at the Academy of Art. Satiric drawings, theater decors, and, after 1936, his first posters. Professor at the Warsaw Academy of Art. Member of A.G.I. Often honored in international competitions.

TOOROP, Jan (Poerworedjo, Java, 1885–The Hague, 1928)

Dutch painter and graphic artist. Studied at the Technische Hogeschool of Delft and at the Brussels and Amsterdam Academies. Monumental paintings and book illustrations. One of the pioneers of the Dutch poster.

TOULOUSE-LAUTREC, Henri (Albi, 1864–Malromé, 1901)

French illustrator, painter, lithographer and poster artist. Descendent of an old aristocratic family, he was left a dwarf and hunchback as a consequence of two falls from horses. Very gifted at drawing. He was encouraged by the animal painter René Princeteau. From 1882, studied in Paris at Bonnat's studio, then at Cormon's, where he met Van Gogh. He began to paint equestrian and military scenes and settled in Montmartre. Starting in 1891, he produced a series of 31 posters and more than 500 prints, which depict the life of balls, music-halls, cabarets and dives which he frequented: *Moulin Rouge, Bruant, Divan Japonais . . .* A great painter, his realist art opened the way to expressionism.

TOUSSAINT, Fernand (Brussels 1873–1956)

Belgian painter and poster artist. Studied at the Brussels Academy in Portaels' studio. Exhibited with the Sillon group, at the Salon des Artistes Français in 1901, and at the Libre Esthétique in 1910. His poster for the Brussels Commerce Fair has been re-used for a considerable number of these events up to the present.

TSCHERNY, George (1924–)

American poster and graphic artist. His work leans to symbolism. Uses photomontage and gives an important role to typography.

TSCHICHOLD, Jan (Leipzig 1902–1974)

German graphic artist, typographer and poster artist. Studied typography and graphic art from 1922 to 1925, then made film posters. He published a manual, *Die Neue Typographie,* codifying the rules of the new trends of his era. In 1933, he moved to Switzerland and lived in Basel, In 1947, he obtained work from Penguin Books. In 1954, he was elected director of the Munich Graphic Academy, but turned down the post. Wrote for many magazines and received many honors, including the gold medal of the AGI and the Gutenberg prize of the city of Leipzig.

UNDERWOOD, Clarence (Jamestown, N.Y., 1871–)

American poster artist. Famous in the Twenties for his sentimentally realist posters, notably for *Palmolive* soap.

URBANIEC, Maciej (Zwierzyniec Lubelski, 1925–)

Polish graphic and poster artist. 1952–1958: studied in Wroclow and at the Warsaw Fine Arts Academy. Member of AGI. Professor at the Warsaw Academy of Fine Arts.

UTRILLO, Miguel (1862–1934)

Spanish painter and poster artist. Also active as a critic.

VAVASSEUR, Eugène Charles Paul (Paris, 1863–)

French artist and lithographer. Pupil of Cabanel at the Ecole des Beaux Arts. Contributed to various periodicals: *La Caricature, La Silhouette* and (under the pseudonym of Ripp) *L'Eclipse, La Gaudriole, La Revue Illustrée.*

VELDE, Henri Clemens van de (Antwerp, 1863–Zurich, 1957)

Belgian painter, graphic artist, theoretician of art and architect. Studied painting at the Academy of Antwerp and with Carolus-Duran in Paris. Influenced by Millet, Seurat and Van Gogh. 1889: member of the Group of Twenty, he took an interest in all the arts (furniture, books, carpets, ceramics) and ceased to paint in 1893. Contributed to the avant-garde journal *Van Nu en Straks* then turned to advertising for which he made very graphic posters *(Tropon).* 1905–1908: construction of the School of Applied Arts, which he directed until 1914, and which would give birth, in 1919, under Gropius, to the Bauhaus.

VERTES, Marcel (1882–1958)

Hungarian painter and illustrator. After political poster activity in Budapest following World War I, he settled in Paris, where he painted scenes of the Roaring Twenties in the city, and made some posters for social events. He then moved to the United States.

VIGNELLI, Massimo (1931–)

Italian architect and graphic artist. Studied architecture in Milan and in Venice. He settled in New York where he worked for both America and European clients: graphic program for *Knoll International; Bloomingdale's; American Airlines* (1983). He earned the gold medal of the American Institute of Graphic Arts. Professor at the principal universities in America and elsewhere.

VILLEMOT, Bernard (Honfleur, 1911–)

French poster artist. Pupil of Paul Colin, made many advertising posters for *Orangina, Bally,* and *Perrier,* and also for *L'Electricité, SNCF,* and banks. He lives and works in Paris.

VILLON, Jacques (Gaston Duchamps)
(Deauville, 1875–Puteaux, 1963)

French painter, designer and engraver. Brother of Raymond Duchamp-Villon, of Marcel and Suzanne Duchamp. Notary's clerk in Rouen; then, in 1894, student at the Beaux-Arts in Paris in Cormon's studio. Worked at first in engravings, posters and drawings, making Parisian scenes in the style of Steinlen and Toulouse-Lautrec. Comic drawings for *Le Rire, L'Assiette au Beurre, Gil Blas Illustré, Chat Noir;* various posters for cabarets. He was influenced by the fauves, then, along with his brother, by cubism; he founded his own studio in Bordeaux. Belonged to the circle of friends of Apollinaire and Cocteau, and to the group of French cubists trying to define and discover the so-called golden number. In 1912, he was one of the principal organizers of the Exhibition of the Golden Section at the Galerie La Boétie. After the First World War he turned toward abstraction, and until 1930 he engraved reproductions (Manet, Picasso, Matisse, and Dufy) for his living. Exhibiting in the U.S. after 1940, he returned to his favorite themes—airplanes and horses. 1950: Carnegie prize; 1957: the first Venice prize assured his fame.

VINCENT, René (1879–1936)

French painter, illustrator and poster artist. Known for his fashion posters and especially for automobile posters (*Salmson, Peugeot, Motobloc, Bugatti . . .*).

VIVARELLI, Carlo (Zurich, 1919–)

Swiss painter and sculptor. Known for his use of photography in posters.

WALKER, Fred

Architect and poster artist. Best known for *The Woman in White* poster of 1871, he also produced works for *Fuller's Nougat, Fuller's Ices,* and *Coffee.* Much influenced by Japanese prints; all his works for Fuller are wood-engravings.

WEISGERBER, Albert (St. Ingbert, Saarbrücken, 1878–Fromelles, Ypenn, 1915)

German painter, graphic artist and illustrator. Studied at the Karlsruhe School (1897), and in 1898 at the Munich Academy with Stuck and Häckl. Co-founder of the

"Munich Secession". From 1904, contributed to *Jugend* and made his debut as a poster artist. Very large graphic production.

WIERTZ, Jupp (Aix-la-Chapelle, 1881–Berlin, 1939)

German graphic and poster artist. Studied at the School of Decorative Arts in Berlin. Pupil of Klinkenberg and later of Ernst Neumann. One of the best known German poster artists of his times, especially those promoting tourism.

WILLETTE, Adolphe Léon (Chalons-sur-Marne, 1857–Paris, 1926)

French painter, graphic artist and caricaturist. Between 1878 and 1979, pupil of Alexandre Cabanel at the Ecole des Beaux Arts. At first academic in style, he found a style of his own in 1886 with *La Veuve du Pierrot.* He belonged to a circle of Montmartre painters and decorated several cabarets (La Chat Noir, La Taverne de Paris, L'Auberge du Clou). Illustrations for the *Courrier Français,* the *Echo de Paris,* the *Figaro* and the *Assiette au Beurre,* and for his own periodicals *Pierrot, Le Pied de Nez* and *La Vache Enragée.* Like Chéret, Willette was fascinated by eighteenth-century painting. The figure of Pierrot is at the center of his work. 1919: publication of his autobiography *Feu Pierrot (The Late Pierrot).*

WILSON, Wes (1937–)

American painter, graphic and poster artist. Famous psychedelic posters for the Fillmore and Avalon Ballrooms in San Francisco.

YAMAGUCHI, Harumi (Shimane province, 1940–)

Japanese painter and poster artist. Diploma in oil painting from the Tokyo University of Graphic Arts. Worked for the Japanese department store Parco and for the Manns wine company.

YENDIS, Mosnar (Sidney Ransom)

Caricaturst and poster artist. His posters for *Cinderella, The Dandy Fifth* and *The Poster* magazine are representative of his art of caricature.

YOKOO, Tadanori (Hyogo, 1936–)

Japanese poster and graphic artist. Grand prize of the Biennale of Young Artists in Paris (1969). Unesco prize at the Warsaw Biennale (1972). Jury prize at the exhibition of Japanese engraving (1973). Grand Prize (poster section) at the International Doll Festival (1974). Gold medal at another Warsaw Biennale, silver medal at the Graphic Arts Biennale.

YUMURA, Teruhito (Tokyo, 1942–)

Japanese designer and poster artist. Graduated from the

University of Graphic Arts at Tama, design section, and worked for a record company. From 1976, participated in many exhibitions, such as "Identity 1976" and "Print Media".

ZIETARA, Walenty (Valentin) (Friedrichau, 1883–Munich, 1935)

German graphic artist. Apprentice chimneysweep, then studies in decorative painting in Breslau. 1908: left for Munich with his friend M. Schwarzer. Member of the "Group of 6"; very large graphic production.

ZWART, Piet (Zandijk, 1885–Leidschendam, 1977)

Dutch interior designer, graphic and poster artist. 1902–1907: studied at the School of Decorative Arts of Amsterdam. From 1911, made his first models for furniture and his first interior decorations. His own experiments enriched his later contacts with van Doesburg, Wols, Mondrian, Schwitters, and Lissitsky, whose outcome in 1937–38 was a new concept, the Bruynzeel kitchen, which would have great influence on the modernization of domestic space. In the field of graphics, his major work was the *NFK* catalogue (Dutch cable factory); he also taught, worked for the Dutch post office, organized exhibitions (Film und Foto, Stuttgart . . .). His typographic compositions have been acquired by various Dutch Museums and by the Museum of Modern Art in New York. In 1964, he received the David Roëll prize for his work.

Bibliography

While not claiming to have a complete listing, we have tried to compile
the chief reference works in the poster field, and subdivided them by
geographical and temporal factors as in the text.

HISTORY AND OVERVIEW

Books

Alexandre, Arsène et al.: *The Modern Poster*. New York: Scribner's, 1895.

Barnicoat, John: *A Concise History of Posters*. London: Thames & Hudson, 1972.

Bauwens, M. et al.: *Les Affiches Etrangères Illustrées*. Paris: G. Boudet, 1897.

Booth-Clibborn, Edward & Baroni, Danièle: *The Language of Graphics*. New York: Harry Abrams, 1980.

Constantine, Mildred & Fern, A.M.: *Word and Image*. New York: Museum of Modern Art, 1968.

Datz, P.: *Histoire de la Publicité*. Paris: J. Rothschild, 1894.

Depreaux, Albert: *Les Affiches de Recruitement du XVIII siècle à nos Jours*. Paris: J. Leroy & Cie, 1911.

Gallo, Max: *The Poster in History*. New York: American Heritage Publishing Co., 1974.

Hillier, Bevis: *Posters*. New York: Stein & Day, 1969.

Holme, Bryan: *Advertising: Reflections of a Century*. London: Heineman, 1982.

Hutchinson, Harold F.: *The Poster: An Illustrated History from 1860*. New York: Viking Press, 1968.

Maindron, Ernest: *Les Affiches Illustrées, 1886-1895*. Paris: G. Boudet, 1896.

Malhotra, Ruth et al.: *Das Frühe Plakat in Europa und den USA*. Vol. 1. *British and American Posters*. 1973. Vol. 2. *French and Belgian Posters*. 1977. Vol. 3. *German Posters*. 1980. Berlin: Mann Verlag.

Metzl, Ervine: *The Poster, Its History and Its Art*. New York: Watson-Guptill, 1963.

Müller-Brockmann, Josef & Shizuko: *History of the Poster*. Zurich: ABC Editions, 1971.

Presbery, Frank: *The History and Development of Advertising*. New York: Doubleday & Doran, 1929.

Rossi, Attilio: *Posters*. London: Paul Hamlyn, 1966.

Schindler, Herbert: *Monografie des Plakats*. Munich: Süddeutscher Verlag, 1972.

Sponsel, Jean Louis: *Das Moderne Plakat*. Dresden: Gerhard Kühtmann, 1897.

Wember, Paul: *Die Jugend der Plakate*. Krefeld: Scherpe, 1961.

Westen, Walter von zur: *Reklamekunst*. Bielefeld & Leipzig, 1914.

Exhibition and Auction Catalogs

Reims, 1896: *Exposition d'affiches artistiques* by Alexandre Henriot.

Munich, 1971: *Internationale Plakate 1871-1971*. Haus der Kunst, Munich, 1971.

Rutgers University, 1978: *The Color Revolution: Color Lithography in France 1890-1900* by P.D. Cate & S.H. Hitchings. Santa Barbara, Calif.: Peregrine Smith, 1978.

New York, 1979: *A Century of Posters 1870-1970* by Jack Rennert. Phillips New York, 1979. Auction.

New York, 1980: *Poster Classics* by Jack Rennert. Phillips New York, May 1980. Auction.

New York, 1980: *The World of Posters* by Jack Rennert. Phillips New York, November 1980. Auction.

New York, 1981: *Poster Pleasures* by Jack Rennert. Phillips New York, April 1981. Auction.

New York, 1981: *100 Poster Masterpieces* by Jack Rennert. Phillips New York, May 1981. Auction.

New York, 1981: *19th and 20th Century Posters*. Phillips New York, November 1981. Auction.

Paris, 1983: *Rouchon—Un Pionnier de l'Affiche Illustrée*. Musée de la Publicité.

New York, 1983: *Rare Posters* by Jack Rennert. Phillips New York, November 1983. Auction.

Japan, 1984-85: *Timeless Images* by Jack Rennert. Posters Please, 1984.

New York, 1985: *Premier Posters* by Jack Rennert. Poster Auctions International, March 1985. Auction.

THE GOLDEN AGE OF THE POSTER

Books, general

Abdy, Jane: *The French Poster*. New York: Clarkson N. Potter, 1969.

Arwas, Victor: *Belle Epoque: Posters and Graphics*. London: Academy Editions, 1978.

Bolton, Charles Knowles: *The Reign of the Poster*. Boston: Winthrop B. Jones, 1895.

Marx, Roger; Rennert, Jack; & Weill, Alain: *Masters of the Poster 1896-1900*. New York: Images Graphiques, Inc., 1977.

Rickards, Maurice: *Posters at the End of the Century*. New York: Walker & Co., 1968.

Schardt, Hermann: *Paris 1900*. New York: G.P. Putnam's Sons, 1970.

Thon, Christina: *Französische Plakate des 19. Jahrhunderts*. Berlin: Mann, 1977.

Weill, Alain: *L'Affiche Française*. Paris: P.U.F., 1982.

Books, individual artists

Bonnard

Bouvet, Francis: *Bonnard: L'Oeuvre Gravée*. Paris: Flammarion, 1982.

Chéret

Broido, Lucy: *The Posters of Jules Chéret*. New York: Dover, 1982.

Mauclair, Camille: *Jules Chéret*. Paris: Maurice Le Garrec, 1930.

Grasset

Arwas, Victor: *Berthon & Grasset*. Paris: Denoël, 1978.

Mucha

Bridges, Ann, ed.: *Alphonse Mucha: The Complete Graphic Works*. New York: Harmony Books, 1980.

Henderson, Marina & Mucha, Jiří: *The Graphic Works of Alphonse Mucha*. New York: St. Martin's Press, 1973.

Reade, Brian: *Art Nouveau and Alphonse Mucha*. London: Her Majesty's Stationery Office, 1963.

Rennert, Jack & Weill, Alain: *Alphonse Mucha: The Complete Posters and Panels*. Boston: G.K. Hall, 1984.

Scharf, Aaron; Henderson, Marina; & Mucha, Jiří: *Mucha*. New York: St. Martin's Press, 1974.

Steinlen

Cate, Phillip & Gill, Susan: *Théophile-Alexandre Steinlen*. Salt Lake City: Gibbs Smith, 1982.

Crauzat, E. de: *L'Oeuvre Gravée et Lithographique de Steinlen*. Paris: Société de Propagation des Livres d'Art, 1913.

Toulouse-Lautrec

Adhemar, Jean: *Toulouse-Lautrec: His Complete Lithographs and Drypoints*. New York: Harry N. Abrams, 1965.

Adriani, Gotz & Wittrock, Wolfgang: *Toulouse-Lautrec: Das Gesamte Grafische Werk*. Cologne: Dumont, 1976.

Delteil, Lois: *Le Peintre-Graveur Illustré*, Vols X and XI. Paris, 1920. Reprinted by Da Capo Press, New York, 1969.

Huisman, Philippe & Dortu, M.G.: *Lautrec par Lautrec*. Lausanne: Edita, 1964.

Joyant, Maurice: *Lautrec*. Paris: H. Floury, 1927.

Jullien: *Les Affiches de Toulouse-Lautrec*. Monte Carlo: Sauret, 1967.

Wittrock, Wolfgang: *Toulouse-Lautrec: The Complete Prints*. London: Philip Wilson, 1985.

Catalogs of exhibitions

Paris, 1980: *L'Affichomanie* by Alain Weill. Musée de l'Affiche.

Brno, 1979: *Alfons Mucha—Plakáty* by Jana Šmejkalová. Moravská Galerie.

Paris, 1980: *Mucha*. Dossiers d'Orsay. Musée du XIX Siècle.

Berlin, 1978: *Théophile-Alexandre Steinlen (1859-1923)*. Staatliche Kunsthalle.

Periodicals

La Plume, Paris
The Poster, London
The Poster, New York
Cocorico, Paris
L'Estampe et l'Affiche, Paris
Le Rire, Paris

FRANCE 1900-1945

Delhaye, Jean: *Art Deco Posters and Graphics*. London: Academy Editions, 1977.

Karcher (ed.): *25 Ans d'Affiches d'une Imprimerie 1912-1937*. Paris: Galerie du Luxembourg, 1979.

Moles, Abraham: *L'Affiche dans la Société Urbaine*. Paris: Dunod, 1970.

Individual artists

Cappiello

Vienot, Jacques: *Cappiello*. Paris: Editions de Clermont, 1964.

Cappiello 1875-1942. Catalog of an exhibition, Paris, 1982.

Carlu

Jean Carlu. Catalog of an exhibition, Paris, 1980.

Cassandre

Brown, Robert K. & Reinhold, Susan: *The Poster Art of A.M. Cassandre*. New York: E.P. Dutton, 1979.

Vox, Maximilien: *A.M. Cassandre: Posters*. St. Gall, Switzerland: Zollikofer & Co., 1948.

Colin

Rennert, Jack: *100 Posters of Paul Colin*. New York: Images Graphiques, 1979.

Periodicals

Arts et Metiers Graphiques, Paris, 1925-1939
Vendre, Paris, 1925-1930

BELGIUM

Books

Beaumont, Alexandre Demeure de: *L'Affiche Belge*. Toulouse: published by author, 1897.

Oostens-Wittamer, Yolande: *De Belgische Affiche 1900*. Brussels: Koningklijke Bibliotheek, 1975.

Catalogs of exhibitions

Brussels, 1962: *Le Groupe de XX et Son Temps*. Musées Royaux des Beaux-Arts de Belgique.

New York, 1971: *La Belle Epoque—Belgian Posters—Wittamer—De Camps Collection*. New York: Grossman.

Liège, 1980: *Affiches de l'Imprimerie Besnard*. Musée de la Vie Wallone.

Brussels, 1980: *L'Art de l'Affiche en Belgique 1900-1980*. Galerie CGER.

Paris, 1980: *L'Affiche en Belgique 1880-1980*. Musée de l'Affiche.

Antwerp, 1979: *Affiches Belle-Epoque*. Museum Vleeshuis.

Brussels, 1981: *Affiches Sportives en Belgique*. Passage 44, Brussels.

L'affiche en Wallonie. Catalog of the Musée de la Vie Wallone, Liège, 1980.

ENGLAND

Books

Bradshaw, Percy V.. *Art in Advertising*. London: Press Art School, 1925.

Cooper, Austin: *Making a Poster*. London: The Studio, 1938.

Hiatt, Charles: *Picture Posters*. London: George Bell & Sons, 1896.

Jones, Sydney R.: *Posters and Their Designers*. London: The Studio, 1924.

McKnight-Kauffer, E.: *The Art of the Poster*. London: Cecil Palmer, 1924.

Purvis, Tom: *Poster Progress*. London: Studio, 1938.

Rogers, W.S.: *A Book of the Poster*. London: Greening & Co., 1901.

Sparrow, Walter Shaw: *Advertising and British Art*. London: John Lane, 1974.

Periodicals

Commercial Art, London
Posters and Publicity, London
The Studio (International Studio), London

Catalog of an exhibition

Paris, 1972: *L'Affiche Anglaise: Les Années 90.* Musée des Arts Décoratifs.

UNITED STATES

Books

Black, Mary: *American Advertising Posters of the Nineteenth Century.* New York: Dover, 1976.
Higbee, William Tryon: *Some Posters.* Cleveland: Imperial Press, 1895.
Keay, Carolyn: *American Posters of the Turn of the Century.* New York: St. Martin's Press, 1975.
Margolin, Victor: *American Poster Renaissance.* New York: Watson-Guptill, 1975.
Pollard, Percival: *Posters in Miniature.* New York: R. H. Russell, 1897.
Price, Charles Matlack: *Posters.* New York: George W. Bricka, 1913.

Catalogs of exhibitions

New York, 1967: *The American Poster* by Edgar Breitenbach & Margaret Cogswell.

Individual artists

Leyendecker
Schau, Michael: *J.C. Leyendecker.* New York: Watson-Guptill, 1974.

Parrish
Ludwig, Coy: *Maxfield Parrish.* New York: Watson-Guptill, 1973.

Penfield
Yonkers, N.Y.; 1984: *Designed to Persuade* by David Gibson. Hudson River Museum.

Shahn
Prescott, Kenneth W.: *The Complete Graphic Works of Ben Shahn.* New York: Quadrangle, 1973.

ITALY

Bortolotti, Nadine: *Gli Annitrenta: Arte et Cultura in Italia.* Milan: Gabriele Mazzotta, 1982.
Carluccio, L. & Postiglione, F.: *L'Arte Grafica in Italia.* Turin: La Ilte, 1959.
Menegazzi, Luigi: *Il Manifesto Italiano.* Milan: Electa, 1975.

Individual artists

Dudovich
Cuci, Roberto: *Marcello Dudovich.* Trieste: Edizioni Lint, 1976.

Mauzan
Lancelotti, A.: *Mauzan: Affiches, Oeuvres Diverses.* Milan: Bestettie Tumminelli.
Mauzan, A.: *Cartellonista deggli Anni Ruggenti.* Treviso: Canova, 1983.

Sepo
Sepo. Universite de Parme, 1979.

GERMANY

Popitz, Klaus: *Plakate der Zwnziger Jahre.* Berlin: Kunst Bibliothek, 1977.
Rademacher, Hellmut: *Das Deutsche Plakat von den Anfangen bis zur Gegenwart.* Dresden: VEB Verlag der Kunst, 1965.

Individual artists

Hohlwein
Frenzel, H.K.: *Ludwig Hohlwein.* Berlin: Phönix Illustration, 1926.

Schnackenberg
Bie, Oskar: *Schnackenberg: Kostume, Plakate und Dekorationen.* Munich: Musarion, 1922.

Exhibition catalogs
Munich, 1975: *Plakate in München 1840-1940.* Münchner Stadtmuseum.
Bremen, 1977: *Kunst in Alltag.* Kunsthalle.

Periodicals

Das Plakat 1909-1921
Gebrauchsgrafik 1924-1939

AUSTRIA

Koschatzky, Walter & Kossatz, Horst-Herbert: *Ornamental Posters of the Vienna Secession.* New York: St. Martin's Press, 1974.
Wisotski, Julius: *Poster Art in Vienna.* Chicago: 1923.

Individual artists

Binder
Binder, Carla: *Joseph Binder.* Vienna: Anton Schroll, 1976.

Exhibition catalogs
Vienna, 1957: *Oesterreichische Plakate 1890-1957.* Vienna: Anton Schroll, 1957.
Vienna, 1981: *Wiener Plakate: Das Tagebuch der Strasse.* Wiener Rathaus.

THE NETHERLANDS

Dooijes, Dick & Brattinga, Pieter: *A History of the Dutch Poster.* Amsterdam: Scheltema & Holkema, 1968.

SPAIN

Jardi, Enric & Manent, Ramon: *El Cartellisme a Catalunya.* Barcelona: Edicions Destino, 1983.

SCANDINAVIA

Honkauen, Helmirütta: *Placatista Julisteeksi*. Helsinki: 1983.
Lifschutz, Paul: *Swenska Affischer 1895-1979*. Stockholm: Kulturhuset, 1979.
Street Spectacle Sweden. Catalog of the Paul Lifschutz Poster Collection. Stockholm: The Swedish Institute, 1982.
Exposition d'Affiches Danoises. Catalog of an exhibition. Copenhagen: Det Danske Selskab, 1952.

SWITZERLAND

Luthy, Wolfgang: *Swiss Poster Art*. Zurich: Verlag der Visualis, 1968.
Margadant, Bruno: *The Swiss Poster, 1900-1983*. Basel: Birkhaus, 1983.
Wobmann, Karl: *Tourism Posters of Switzerland*. Aarau: AT Verlag, 1980.
Wobmann, Karl & Triet, Max: *Swiss Sport Posters*. Zurich: ABC Editions, 1983.

Individual artists

Leupin

Hohl, Reinhold: *Herbert Leupin: Plakate 1939-1969*. Basel: Gewerbemuseum, 1970.

Müller-Brockmann

Müller-Brockmann, J.: *Les Problèmes d'un Artiste Graphique*. Teufen: Arthur Niggli, 1961.

Stoecklin

His, H.P. & Hernandez, A.: *Niklaus Stoecklin: Plakate*. Basel: Gewerbemuseum, 1966.

Exhibition catalogs
Zurich, 1981: *Werbestil 1930-1940: Kunstgewerbe der Stadt*. Züricher Museum für Gestaltung.
Paris, 1982: *Affiches Suisses, 1905-1950*. Bibliothèque Forney.

THE SOVIET UNION

Bosko, Szymon: *New Graphic Design in Revolutionary Russia*. New York: Praeger, 1972.
Constantin, Mildred & Fern, Alan: *Revolutionary Film Posters*. Baltimore: Johns Hopkins University Press, 1974.
Waschik, Klaud: *Seht her, Genossen!* Dortmund: Haremberg, 1978.

Catalogs of exhibitions
Paris, 1980: *Paris—Moscou*. Musée National d'Art Moderne. Paris: Centre Georges Pompidou, 1980.
Paris, 1982: *Affiches et Imageries Russes 1914-1921*. Musée des Deux Guerres Mondiales.

POLAND

Amman, Dieter: *Polnische Plakatkunst*. Dortmund: Haremberg, 1980.
Bosko, Szymon: *Polski Plakat Wspoleczny*. Warsaw: Agencja Autorska, 1972.
Kowalski, Tadeusz: *The Polish Film Poster*. Warsaw: Filmowa Agencja Wydawnicza, 1976.

Schubert, Zdislau: *Plakat Polski 1970-1978*. Warsaw: Kreakowa Agencja Wydawnicza, 1979.

Catalogs of exhibitions

Berlin, 1980: *Das Polnische Plakat von 1892 bis heute*. Hochschule der Kunst.
Paris, 1980: *Affiches Polonaises*. Paris: Bibliothèque Forney.

JAPAN

L'Affiche Japonaise des Origins à nos Jours. Catalog of the Musée de l'Affiche. Paris, 1979.
Tanikawa, Koichi: *100 Posters of Tadanori Yokoo*. New York: Images Graphiques, 1978.

CHINA

Fraser, Stewart E.: *100 Great Chinese Posters*. New York: Images Graphiques, 1977.

THE AVANT-GARDES

Ades, Dawn: *The 20th Century Poster—Design of the Avant-Garde*. New York: Abbeville Press, 1984.
Belleguie, Andre: *Le Mouvement de l'Espace Typographique: Années 1920-1930*. Paris: Jacques Damase, 1984.
Lusk, Irene Charlotte: *Montages ins Blauen: Moholy-Nagy 1922-1943*. Berlin: Anabas, 1980.
Moholy-Nagy, Laszlo: *Vision in Motion*. Chicago: Paul Theobald, 1969.
Wingler, H.: *Das Bauhaus, 1919-1933*. Cologne: Dumont.

POSTER TRENDS 1945-1970

Books

Gerstner, Karl & Kutter, Markus: *Le Nouvel Art Graphique*. Teufen, Switzerland: Arthur Niggli, 1959.
Johnson, J. Stewart: *The Modern American Poster*. Boston: Little, Brown, 1983.
Weill, Alain: *Les Reclames des Années 50*. Paris: Le Dernier Terrain Vague, 1983.

Individual artists

Savignac
Savignac, Raymond: *Savignac Affichiste*. Paris: Robert Laffont, 1975.

Ungerer
Rennert, Jack: *The Poster Art of Tomi Ungerer*. New York: Darien House, 1971.

Exhibition catalogs

Washington, D.C., 1975: *Images of an Era—The American Poster 1945-1975*. The Smithsonian Institute.
Munich, 1982: *Deutsche und Europäische Plakate 1945-1959*. Münchner Stadtmuseum.

Periodicals

Graphis
Modern Publicity

ART AND CULTURE

Czwilitzer, Christopher: *Posters by Pablo Picasso, 1923-1973*. New York: Random House, 1981.

Jouffroy, Jean-Pierre & Ruiz, Edouard: *Picasso de l'Image à la Lettre*. Paris: Temps Actuels, 1981

Mellinghoff, Frieder: *Kunst-Ereignisse*. Dortmund: Haremberg, 1978.

Mourlot, Fernand: *Les Affiches Originales des Maîtres de l'Ecole de Paris*. Monte Carlo: A. Sauret, 1959.

THE POSTER TODAY

Ades, Dawn: *Posters*. New York: Abbeville Press, 1984.

Delafon, Eudes: *Ca c'est l'Affiche!* Paris: Temps Present, 1979.

Enel, Francoise: *L'Affiche: Fonctions, Language, Rhétorique*. Paris: Mame, 1971.

SPECIAL SUBJECTS

Bicycles

La Petite Reine. Catalog of an exhibition at the Musée de l'Affiche, Paris, 1979.

Rennert, Jack: *100 Years of Bicycle Posters*. New York: Darien House, 1973.

Circus

Haenlein, Carl A. & Till, Wolfgang: *Zirkusplakate 1880-1930*. Hanover: Kestner, 1978.

Fox, Charles Philip: *American Circus Posters in Full Color*. New York: Dover, 1978.

Malhotra, Ruth: *Manege Frei*. Dortmund: Haremberg, 1978.

Rennert, Jack: *100 Years of Circus Posters*. New York: Avon, 1974.

Rennert, Jack: *100 Posters of Buffalo Bill's Wild West*. New York: Darien House, 1976.

Trix, J. Markschiess van & Nowak, Bernhardt: *Artisten- und Zirkus-plakate*. Zurich: Atlantis.

Wild, Nicole & Remy, Tristan: *La Cirque Iconographie*. Catalog. Paris: Bibliothèque Nationale, 1969.

Dance

Rennert, Jack & Terry, Walter: *100 Years of Dance Posters*. New York: Darien House, 1975.

Film

Borga, J.M. & Martinand, B.: *Affiches du Cinéma Française*. Paris: Delville, 1977.

Capitaine, Jean Louis & Charton, Balthazar J.M.: *L'Affiche de Cinéma*. Paris: Fréderic Birr, 1983.

Kobal, John: *Fifty Years of Movie Posters*. London: Hamlyn, 1973.

Lenica, Jan: *Plakat a Film*. Warsaw: F&K.

Morella, Joe; Epstein, Edward Z.; & Clark, Eleanor: *Those Great Movie Ads*. New Rochelle, N.Y.: Arlington House, 1972.

Schapiro, Steve & Chierichetti, David: *The Movie Poster Book*. New York: E.P. Dutton, 1979.

Performing Arts

Broido, Lucy: *French Opera Posters 1868-1930*. New York: Dover, 1976.

Caradec, Francois & Weill, Alain: *Le Café Concert*. Paris: Atelier Hachette-Massin, 1980.

Haill, Catherine: *Theatre Posters*. London: Victoria and Albert Museum, 1983.

List, Vera & Kupferberg, Herbert: *Lincoln Center Posters*. New York: Harry N. Abrams, 1980.

Reynolds, Charles & Regina: *100 Years of Magic Posters*. New York: Darien House, 1975.

Weill, Alain: *Le Café-Concert 1870-1914*. Catalog of an exhibition at the Musée des Arts Decoratifs, Paris, 1977.

Weill, Alain: *100 Years of Posters of the Foliés-Bergère and Music-Halls of Paris*. New York: Images Graphiques, 1977.

Wild, Nicole: *Les Arts du Spectacle en France: Affiches Illustrées 1850-1960*. Paris: Bibliothèque Nationale, 1976.

Propaganda and Protest

Gasquet, Vasco: *Les 500 Affiches de Mai 68*. Paris: Balland, 1968.

Malhotra, Ruth: *Horror Galerie*. Dortmund: Haremberg, 1980.

Medeiros, Walter: *San Francisco Rock Poster Art*. San Francisco Museum of Modern Art, 1976.

Poitou, J.C.: *Affiches et Luttes Syndicales de la CGT*. Paris: La Chêne, 1978.

Rickards, Maurice: *Banned Posters*. London: Evelyn Adams & Mackay, 1969.

Walker, Cummings G.: *The Great Poster Trip: Art Eureka*. Palo Alto, California: Coyne and Blanchard, 1968.

Yanker, Gary: *Prop Art*. New York: Darien House, 1972.

Catalogs of exhibitions

Haarlem, Holland, 1981: *The Art of Protest: Posters 1965-1975*. In de Knipscheer.

Paris, 1982: *L'Apartheid: Le Dos au Mur*. Musée de la Publicité.

Paris, 1982: *Images de la Revolte: 1965-1975*. Musée de la Publicité.

Paris, 1979: *Sur les Murs de France: Deux Siècles d'Affiches Politiques*. Editions du Sorbier.

Paris, 1984: *La Memoire Murale Politique des Français de la Renaissance à nos Jours,* by Alain Gesgon.

Individual artists

Davis

Davis, Paul: *Paul Davis—Posters and Paintings*. New York: E.P. Dutton, 1977.

English

Michael English 1966-1979. Paris: AMP Editeur, 1980.

Glaser

Glaser, Milton: *Milton Glaser—Graphic Design*. New York: Overlook, 1973.

Griffin

Gordon, McClelland: *Rick Griffin*. Paris: AMP Editeur, 1980.

Mouse and Kelley

Martyn, Dean: *Mouse et Kelley*. Paris: AMP Editeur, 1979.

Travel

Belves, Pierre: *100 Ans d'Affiches des Chemins de Fer*. Paris: La Vie du Rail, 1980.
Hillier, Bevis: *Travel Posters*. New York: E.P. Dutton, 1976.
Hutchinson, F. Harold: *London Transport Posters*. London: London Transport Board, 1963.

Shackleton, J. T.: *The Golden Age of the Railway Poster*. Paris: New English Library, 1976.
Wedel, Peter Graf von: *Die Reise ins Bad*. Dortmund: Haremberg, 1980.

World Wars

Darracott, Joseph: *The First World War in Posters*. New York: Dover, 1974.
Marchetti, Stephane: *Image d'une certaine France: Affiches 1939-1945*. Lausanne: Edita, 1982.
Rickards, Maurice: *Posters of the First World War*. London: Evelyn Adams & Mackay, 1968.
Theofiles, George: *American Posters of World War I*. New York: Dafran House, 1973.
Zeman, Zbyněk: *Art and Propaganda in World War II*. London: Orbis, 1978.

List of Illustrations

Index of Names

Page numbers in boldface correspond to illustrations of cited artists.

Printed in Spain by
Printer Industria Gráfica S.A.
Provenza, 388
08025-Barcelona
D.L.B. 22358-1985